Denkart Europa | Mindset Europe

Denkart Europa|Mindset Europe presents international academic analyses and contributions on a broad range of Europe-related subjects. The book series addresses the general public worldwide and contributes to the reflection on political and societal developments in Europe. With Denkart Europa|Mindset Europe, the foundation ASKO EUROPA-STIFTUNG and Europäische Akademie Otzenhausen present the outcomes of their versatile activities. Its monographies, anthologies, essays and handbooks invite to a continuous interdisciplinary discourse on Europe.

edited by ASKO EUROPA-STIFTUNG, Saarbrücken and Europäische Akademie Otzenhausen.

Europäische
Akademie
Otzenhausen

Sophie Schram

Constructing Trade

The Negotiation of the Comprehensive Economic
and Trade Agreement (CETA) in Quebec

 **Nomos**

With the support of the German Research Foundation and ASKO-Europa-Stiftung.

The Deutsche Nationalbibliothek lists this publication in the
Deutsche Nationalbibliografie; detailed bibliographic data
are available on the Internet at http://dnb.d-nb.de

a.t.: Trier, Univ., Diss., 2017

ISBN   978-3-8487-4954-6 (Print)
         978-3-8452-9166-6 (ePDF)

British Library Cataloguing-in-Publication Data
A catalogue record for this book is available from the British Library.

ISBN   978-3-8487-4954-6 (Print)
         978-3-8452-9166-6 (ePDF)

Library of Congress Cataloging-in-Publication Data
Schram, Sophie
Constructing Trade
The Negotiation of the Comprehensive Economic and Trade Agreement (CETA) in
Quebec
Sophie Schram
348 pp.
Includes bibliographic references and index.

ISBN   978-3-8487-4954-6 (Print)
         978-3-8452-9166-6 (ePDF)

1st Edition 2019
© Nomos Verlagsgesellschaft, Baden-Baden, Germany 2019. Printed and bound in
Germany.

Preface

When I started the research for this doctoral thesis in late 2013, the negotiation of the *Comprehensive Economic and Trade Agreement* between the EU and Canada was moving forward quickly. On both sides of the Atlantic, CETA was depicted as a prototype or a blueprint for a series of so-called new-generation trade agreements, which were more comprehensive in nature than previous agreements and included, for example, chapters on foreign direct investment protection, government procurement, regulatory standards and geographical indications on food labels. The EU had already concluded a similar agreement with South Korea and negotiations were underway, among others, with Singapore and the US.

When travelling to Canada and especially to Quebec for field research in late 2013, I found that international trade and economic integration were central political topics in Canada and in Quebec. In the EU, international trade was not among the most salient political topics then, at the time when I first travelled to Canada. Although there had been moments of strong political contestation and opposition to further trade liberalisation – especially in France – trade policy seldom reached a similar level of political relevance as it did in Canada and the Canadian provinces. In the 1980s, Canadian federal elections were fought over North American economic integration. Political parties in Quebec made trade and economic integration a key topic of their political programmes and closely connected them to their provincial development policies.

In the EU, trade policy was considered to a large extent an a-political topic, left mostly to the expertise of the bureaucrats of the European Commission. Even though the member states need to implement trade agreements in accordance with their respective internal procedures, national parliaments' involvement in the negotiation processes has mostly been fairly limited. This was to a large extent because of a general consensus on the benefits of free trade. Furthermore, governmental levels below the member states were rarely involved in trade discussions. In Canada, to the contrary, the different provinces and even the larger cities have firm positions on Canada's international trade relations, considering them to have profound implications on their local development. Even though the federal government has sole jurisdiction over Canada's international trade agreements, the provinces develop their own positions and try to influence federal policy-making my various means, about which I will say more in the course of this book.

By now, the picture in the EU and worldwide has become an entirely different one: international trade has moved center-stage of the political agendas in several European states and civil society involvement has increased. A trigger of the politicisation of trade in the European Union was the negotiation of the Transatlantic Trade and Investment Partnership (TTIP) with the US. Since mid-2014, civil society opposition to this agreement has been growing across European member states – including in Germany, where internal trade is a backbone of the (export-oriented) economy. At the same time, sub-federal actors in the EU have become more vocal. They actively monitor the impacts of international trade agreements on the economic development of their region and, sometimes, even threaten national governments to withdraw their support. On an international scale, especially with the election of US president Donald Trump, the long-standing consensus among Western political elites, that more openness to trade eventually leads to more wealth, has lost ground. The benefits and drawbacks of new trade deals are now more explicitly measured against the yardstick of expected impacts on the respective national economic spaces. For example, especially the US has recently instrumentalized tariffs to protect domestic industrial sectors or retaliate unilaterally against perceived unfair public policies. International trade has become one of the most salient topics of international relations by now, and an almost-forgotten vocabulary in trade comprising terms such as protectionism, national economic development, and unilateral retaliation has quickly re-gained ground in the international political discourse.

By looking at the Quebec and Canadian cases where political debates on trade and nationalism are closely inter-twined, I better understood recent developments in the EU and on the international scene. The analysis of the discourse on the *Comprehensive Economic and Trade Agreement* (CETA) and the historical discourses underpinning it helped me – and I trust the readers of this book – to find answers to why and how the long-standing consensus on the benefits of free trade slowly began to crumble in the EU as well.

This research would not have been possible without generous support.

I first wish to thank the *International Research Training Group Diversity* and the *Deutsche Forschungsgemeinschaft* for generous support -financial and intellectual- without which extended research stays in Canada and the EU would not have been imaginable. Apart from a generous scholarship, the Training Group's members – especially Ursula Lehmkuhl and Lutz

Schowalter – also provided invaluable support in mastering the intricacies and administrative hurdles associated with crossing national borders. I also thank my colleagues in the Training Group who made doctoral research not only stimulating intellectually, but also very enjoyable. Especially, I thank Sarah Pröwrock, Xymena Wieczorek, Jeri Rahab, Dave Poitras, Kaisa Vuoristo and Ahmed Hamila for friendship and controversial discussions.

I also thank the *Europäische Akademie* in Otzenhausen and the *Asko-Europa-Stiftung* for many conferencing and teaching opportunities. I thank the editors for generous financial and marketing support for this book. I hope that my contribution to their series *Denkart Europa* triggers a new perspective on the EU's international trade relations.

I am deeply indebted to my interview partners for their time and insights. My interviewees let me glimpse behind the (too often) closed doors of trade policy-making. Especially, I wish to thank Pierre-Marc Johnson, Quebec's chief negotiator, and Jean Charest, Prime minister in Quebec for most of the time when CETA was negotiated, for sharing their insights and establishing contact with several members of Quebec's government. At the same time, I am deeply grateful to the many researchers who helped me understand Quebec and Canadian politics, especially Frédéric Mérand at the Université de Montréal's Cérium, and Jörg Broschek and Patricia Goff at Wilfrid Laurier University.

Foremost, I thank my supervisor Prof. Joachim Schild for accepting to supervise, in a political science department, a topic so heavily inspired by cultural studies and sociology. In this vein, I thank him for bringing my floating ideas into a more organised form and shape, as well as for his high availability and professionalism.

This piece of research would not have been possible without the open doors and spirit at Jane Jenson's chair at the Université de Montréal. Her generosity and intellectual curiosity allowed me to learn and grow. She continues to be a true role model and thought leader for many young women including myself.

I give love and thanks to my family for 'being there', for their liberal thinking, for letting me grow up without boundaries and for providing the so-much needed home-base for someone moving their home so often. Especially, I am deeply grateful to my spouse Dominik Groß, my best friend, for his love.

Table of Contents

List of Figures

List of Tables

List of Abbreviations

AGP	Canada–United States Agreement on Government Procurement
ARRA	American Recovery and Reinvestment Act
CAD	Canadian Dollar
CAQ	Coalition Avenir Québec
CETA	Comprehensive Economic and Trade Agreement
CORIM	Conseil des Relations Internationales de Montréal
CUPE/ SCFP	Canadian Union of Public Employees/ Syndicat Canadien de la Fonction Publique
CUSFTA	Canada-US Free Trade Agreement
GATT	General Agreement on Tariffs and Trade
GDP	Gross Domestic Product
GPA	Agreement on Government Procurement (WTO)
NAFTA	North American Free Trade Agreement
OECD	Organisation for Economic Co-operation and Development
PLQ	Parti Libéral du Québec
PQ	Parti Québécois
RQIC	Réseau Québécois d'Intégration Continentale
SFPQ	Syndicat de la Fonction Publique et Parapublique du Québec
WTO	World Trade Organization

List of Abbreviations

Introduction

On 28 October 2016, the European Commission, the European Council and the Canadian government were scheduled to sign the Comprehensive Economic and Trade Agreement (CETA), a trade and investment agreement officially negotiated between 2009 and 2014. However, shortly before they could do so, the Belgian Government was compelled to hold back its signature: three sub-federal legislative bodies declined to support the agreement and urged their respective executives to prevent the Belgian federal government from giving its approval to CETA in the European Council. Subsequently, the Belgian sub-federal entities, under Wallonia's aegis, refused to endorse their federal government's commitment to CETA. As a consequence, Belgium was unable to sign. Daylong intense negotiations in Brussels ensued. They included representatives from various levels of government, ranging from the European to the national and sub-federal level. Yet, the Belgian sub-federal opponents' objections to provisions on social, health and environmental standards, agriculture as well as the investment protection and dispute settlement clauses, made a compromise impossible. Thus, opponents did not only challenge CETA because they feared negative consequences for certain sectors, but also because of cross-cutting societal issues. Hence, this missing signature from Belgium precluded the European Union (EU) from signing CETA at the scheduled EU-Canada summit.

As surprised as many commentators were by the institutional strength of Belgian sub-federal actors, European negotiators and political leaders should have been familiar with the institutional and political relevance of sub-federal actors and their representations of economic development in the CETA negotiations. In fact, even before CETA negotiations were officially launched in May 2009, European Trade Commissioner Peter Mandelson ensured that Canadian sub-federal actors, mainly the ten provinces, were involved in the negotiation process.[1] In fact, the Trade Commissioner was well aware of the provinces' ability to refuse implementing Canada's

---

1 In the following, the focus will be on the Canadian provinces, not the three decentralised territories. Unlike the territories, the provinces are considered to be sovereign in their areas of jurisdiction as spelled out in the Constitution Act. The territories, to the contrary, have power delegated to them by the Canadian parliament.

international commitments in their areas of jurisdiction. Furthermore, the Commission was conscious that CETA provisions might interfere with provincial economic interests regarding some issues among which were public procurement, agriculture or foreign direct investment; in the past, the provinces were reluctant to conform to some of Canada's international commitments in this regard. Fearing that trade agreements would erode their constitutional powers (Robinson, 2003), the provinces mainly did so because they wanted to retain leverage over their economies without federal interference. Ironically, however, the European Commission neglected to assure the very same support from sub-federal entities in the EU.

Given the importance and high degree of involvement of sub-federal actors in CETA negotiations on both sides of the Atlantic, and the relevance of collective understandings of economic development, the following analysis aims at documenting the way sub-federal political actors developed their positions on trade policy in a complex issue and institutional environment. In doing so, I will focus on the Canadian provinces, and more specifically on Quebec. Canada's provinces have been involved in the CETA negotiations since the very beginning, including during the agenda-setting stage. In addition, Quebec played an active role in bringing CETA to policy agendas on both sides of the Atlantic. Furthermore, the heterogeneity of provinces' respective economic development paths, combined with the necessity to find a common Canadian position, renders developing a negotiation position a complex process. For instance, some provinces have more resource-based economies, while others focus on manufacturing or services. In addition, they attribute different roles to their provincial state's capacity in provincial economic development. Some provinces, including Quebec, have wished to retain control over their public spending as fiscal and social instruments without oversight from Ottawa. Given the centrality of questions related to state activity in CETA, such as the protection of foreign investments, labour rights or regulatory convergence, the provinces are a good starting point to understand if and how these representations, values and interpretations were expressed, or not, in negotiation positions. Finally, unlike in Belgium, the involvement of Canadian provinces in the negotiation process did not block, but considerably advanced trade negotiations. It was key to successfully concluding negotiations and making substantial progress in areas so far exempted to a large extent from

---

In addition, their governments played a limited role during the CETA negotiations.

Canada's international trade commitments. Quebec's contribution to this process was significant.

From an analytical perspective, there are three main reasons why the Canadian provinces are important actors in Canada's trade policy-making. Canadian political scientist Grace Skogstad highlighted two of them (Skogstad, 2007). First, trade contributes to provincial economic welfare and, for some provinces, it is essential for their economic development. Hence, provinces required a say in Canada's trade-policy. They did so according to collectively shared representations of economic and social development. Second, there is a constitutional imperative: according to article 91 of the Canadian constitution, foreign trade relations are under exclusive federal jurisdiction. However, the Canadian provinces, and to some extent the territories, have to implement trade provisions falling under their jurisdiction. According to the Labour Conventions Decision by the Privy Council (1937), the federal government cannot force the provinces to implement these provisions, unlike in many other federal systems. In Canada, the federal government only retains exclusive jurisdiction over tariffs, intellectual property, rules of origin, trade facilitation, dispute settlement, competition policy and temporary entry, while key issues on the global trade agenda, such as services, investment, public procurement, environment, labour, state companies, sanitary and phyto-sanitary measures, and agriculture, are under provincial jurisdiction. In addition, Quebec claims the right to participate in the ratification process of all agreements that significantly involve issues under its jurisdiction. In Canada, the provinces and to some extent also the territories have exclusive jurisdiction for many of the issues included in CETA. Their procurement markets, including procurement by public entities under provincial authority, have been at the core of many trade negotiations, albeit with little success. Also, several investment-related issues such as property rights, certain tax and subsidy issues, energy, the environment and natural resources are under their jurisdiction. Furthermore, they legislate in the health and education sectors, which impact upon the implementation of provisions on labour mobility. They also continue to play an important role in the production and distribution dynamics in the agricultural sector, where every province has jealously guarded its own set of historically grown and collectively supported public policies. As a consequence, Canada's internal market remains highly heterogeneous, complicating the federal government's task to establish a coherent Canadian position in trade negotiations. Hence, if Canada wants to appear as a credible partner in international negotiations, its federal government needs to assure provincial commitment. In fact, a number of international agreements concluded by Canada have been limited in scope or remained void in some parts because of provincial resistance to undertake the necessary legislative, regulatory and administrative changes. Prominent examples where the provinces inhibited Canada's international activity are public procurement (Collins, 2008, 2011a) and agriculture (Skogstad, 1998).

In addition to Skogstad's remarks, many commentators recently highlighted that provincial participation increased as the nature of trade agreements evolved. During the Canada-US Free Trade Agreement negotiations (CUSFTA, 1989) and the North American Free Trade Agreement negotiations (NAFTA, 1994), the provinces had a mere consultative role. Federal officials were in charge of all aspects of the negotiations, while the provinces could only communicate their position in meetings with the federal level. These meetings were the First Ministers' Conference, the newly created Committee on Trade Negotiations (for CUSFTA negotiations), the federal-provincial Committee for North American Free Trade Negotiations (for NAFTA negotiations), as well as individual meetings between executives and officials on both levels. During the CETA negotiations, this role was altered considerably and they became active negotiation partners in their areas of jurisdiction; indeed, each province appointed a chief negotiator (Atkey, 1971; Brown, 1993; Campbell, 1995; De Boer, 2002; Delagran, 1992; Dupras, 1993; Fafard and Leblond, 2013; Johnson, Muzzi et al., 2013; Kukucha, 2003, 2004, 2008, 2011a, b, 2013, 2016; McIllroy, 1997; Paquin, 2013; Thakur, 2012; VanDuzer, 2013).

This involvement can be partially explained by the evolving nature of trade agreements. From an initial focus on tariffs and quota, trade policy negotiations have gradually shifted to non-tariff trade issues involving domestic policy-making and cutting across traditional production sectors, which is why they have often been qualified as "behind-the-border issues" (Bodeur and Van Assche, 2014; Gandolfo, 2014; Morgenstern, Tamayo et al., 2007; Orefice, 2016; Saksena and Anderson, 2008; van Assche, 2016; van Overmeire and Nychay, 2016; Young, 2007, 2016). Even though non-tariff issues figured on the agenda of several negotiation rounds of the General Agreement on Tariffs and Trade (GATT), they are now put centre stage. To give but a few examples, non-tariff barriers touch upon investor rights and protection, market access rights, regulatory standards, intellectual property, labour mobility and services. With the increasing importance of non-tariff issues, trade policy increasingly penetrates domestic policy spaces; in fact, measures considered obstacles to trade are often part of a specific public policy mix. Therefore, and contrary to tariffs, non-tariff trade issues are not overtly protecting any particular industry, but represent country-specific ways of production, transformation, distribution and consumption. They have evolved in a specific historic, social, political and economic context, and contribute to domestic economic policy-making. Thus, trade agreements have shifted from a focus on negative measures—i.e. the reduction of tariff barriers—to measures encouraging positive market integration. In this vein, CETA strongly focusses on behind-the-border issues, given that most tariff lines between the two economies were already very low.

Given that CETA affects all ten provinces, why focus on Quebec in particular? First, as explained earlier, Quebec played a crucial role in launching CETA. Its government approached the European Commission with the idea to launch a new economic agreement between Canada and the EU in early 2007. Subsequently, Quebec became one of the main promoters of the agreement at the Canadian domestic level and in the EU during its agenda-setting stage. Second, some of Quebec's negotiation positions were empirically puzzling and thus require further attention. For example, Quebec acquiesced to including provincial public procurement in the negotiations, thereby considerably altering its previous position. Furthermore, the province altered its position on agriculture during the negotiation process. While it first threatened not to ratify CETA if its agricultural production was included in the agreement, its representatives later argued that they would not jeopardise the overall agreement for the sake of one sector. Third, documenting the negotiation processes in Quebec also has methodological value. Since my preliminary remarks drew attention to the importance of certain themes and collective representations, restricting the analysis to one polity will allow me to examine how exactly these themes and representations mattered in different policy fields in the same context. Fourth, and since the debate on the role of discourses in trade policy is still in its infancy (De Bièvre and Poletti, 2014), it was important to choose a system where the influence of sectoral groups was likely to be high: Quebec is a corporatist economic system, hence the influence of sectoral groups might be high (Montpetit, 1999). Indeed, there are numerous potential access points for interest groups, including small electoral districts and a the-winner-takes-it-all electoral system. It was therefore not very likely that national representatives pursued their own strategy independently from interest groups' influence. Quebec would thus prove a strong case in support of the relevance of collectively shared themes and representations in trade policy-making should the analysis reveal that these mattered even in such a setting.

Building upon these analytical observations and empirical puzzles, the aim of my analysis is to understand how Quebec's provincial representatives, including its government, deputies and negotiators, developed their province's trade policy position during CETA negotiations. My research question is the following:

Through which processes did Quebec's provincial representatives develop their positions on and acquire support for trade policy during the agenda-setting phase (2006-2009), and in the fields of public procurement, foreign direct investment, and agriculture during the negotiation phases of the Comprehensive Economic and Trade Agreement (2009-2014)?

This piece of research aims to contribute to two bodies of literature. The first contribution is to the literature on trade policy. Contemporary trade policy literature mostly focusses on domestic societal interests, institutional factors and negotiation dynamics when explaining trade policy outcomes. However, as already noted, contemporary trade agreements often have diffuse and cross-sectoral effects in addition to traditional sectoral effects, which renders explanatory frameworks that focus on specific sectors partially inadequate. Furthermore, international trade seems to have become an increasingly complex policy field that penetrates domestic, including sub-federal, policy spaces. In this process, place-specific sets of political representations about the effects of trade on domestic economies mattered. Therefore, we need to account for the possibility that the structural position of a sector in the domestic or international economy cannot sufficiently explain trade policy choices. My analysis aims to attract attention to the importance of discourses in trade policy.

A second contribution is made to the emerging literature on trade policy and federalism. The evolving nature of trade negotiations and a shift towards positive market integration make sub-federal actors increasingly relevant. However, they not only matter institutionally with regard to their specific role in the federal setting. They also may become active at different moments in time regardless of their constitutional prerogatives; while Quebec sought involvement in the CETA negotiations from the incipit, Belgian Wallonia waited until the very end. There seems thus to be a strategic use of federalism which requires further attention.

Chapter 1: Theoretical, Conceptual and Methodological Considerations

The policy positions of Quebec's government during CETA negotiations are difficult to account for if following conventional theories of trade, which highlight the structural condition of sectors in the domestic and international economies, which change relatively slowly and which Quebec cannot affect or change. Conventional models have usually deduced the determinants of international trade agreements from countries' structural conditions, be they of economic nature—such as technological differences or differences in factor endowments—or of institutional nature—such as electoral systems or access points for lobby groups. They have often followed the assumptions of economic models (mainly the classical, neo-classical and Heckscher-Ohlin theories). Even though more recent theories have relaxed the assumptions of perfect competition and perfectly homogeneous goods assumed in these models (see for an overview Gandolfo, 2014), they have usually distinguished between the representatives of sectors seeking export opportunities, one the one hand, and those competing with new importers and fearing international competition on domestic markets, on the other hand.

Yet, during the negotiation of CETA, Quebec supported the liberalisation of its provincial procurement markets, albeit with some exceptions, as well as the liberalisation of a considerable part of its agricultural sector even though structural conditions did not undergo major changes in comparison to previous trade negotiation settings, as the following empirical analyses will show. During previous trade negotiations, Quebec and other provinces aimed at shielding public procurement and agriculture from international competition in order to support domestic producers and strengthen the provincial economic base. Hence, by sticking to conventional theories, we do not understand, first, what led Quebec to reaching the conclusion that many formerly protected sectors should be exposed to international competition and, second, how the province's government was able to overcome domestic opposition to doing so.

In the face of the complexity and unevenness of global economic integration, and the dynamics of Canadian federalism, I will turn to another body of literature, recently labeled actor-centred constructivism (Saurugger, 2013). Aiming to shed light on complex processes of economic integration and institutional change in multi-level systems, this body of literature combined economic rationality and interest with constructivist accounts of economic policy-making. Actor-centred constructivism has not played an important role in the analysis of trade policy yet. Nevertheless, it seems particularly interesting for the analysis of international trade negotiations since it aims to bring together ideational and interest-based accounts in explaining economic policy to shed light on processes of uneven (economic) integration that we encounter in trade policy. It assumes that actors have unclear and sometimes contradictory interests that stem from their embeddedness in several different interpretative systems of the world, which trigger varying and sometimes conflicting definitions of their interests.

At the end of this chapter, the reader will be familiar with the way I construct discursive strategies on trade policy as my object of research as well as with my main concepts of analysis. As will become clear, the aim of my analysis is to trace complex discursive processes and show the discursive possibilities for political action. Hence, the intention is not to establish any causal claims linking interests to specific factors in a more or less deterministic way. Rather, I will show how discourses underpinned political choices and how political actors mobilised these discourses to evaluate their interests, define their positions and build coalitions.

Section 1: Changing Perspectives on Theorising Trade Policy: From the Attribution to the Subjective Development of Interests

Quebec's trade policy position during the CETA negotiations is puzzling with regard to existing trade policy theory. First, Quebec considerably repositioned itself in comparison with the interests it advocated in previous trade negotiations, while the external conditions in which its economy was embedded had not fundamentally changed. Furthermore, Quebec's government also encountered strong opposition from domestic groups, ranging from business representatives to trade unions and civil society groups. Given that societal group interests have been crucial variables identified in trade policy literature to account for a country's interests in trade policy, Quebec's sudden shift of position requires further scrutiny.

The following section reviews existing explanations on trade policy-making and then suggests to turn to public policy theories to find better tools to understand the ambiguities and complexities of the CETA negotiation in Quebec.

1. Trade as a Function of Attributed Interests and Ideas

The following literature review will necessarily be selective, given the diversity and number of analyses of trade policy. Its aim is not to give a comprehensive review on all the literature on trade policy, nor on specific aspects of it. Rather, my intention is to show that most approaches predominantly attributed interests and ideas to different units of analysis, be they states, nations,[2] classes or sectors of production at different levels of analysis (individual-, domestic- and international-level approaches). In fact, interests have mostly been derived deductively from analyses of the positioning of states or sectors in the domestic and international economy and have hence been exogeneous to the negotiation process and internal domestic processes. Whether groups acted in export-oriented sectors; whether they faced a risk of unemployment due to higher competition; whether they belonged to the class of capital-owners or labour; whether they have been exposed to a specific set of economic ideas, etc. determined their interests in trade policy outcomes. Trade interests were therefore mostly conceptualised as exogeneous to states, sectors or classes, stable, and simple. In fact, they existed before trade negotiations began and were not affected by internal negotiation processes.

During the first wave of modern trade theory[3] in the late 1960s and early 1970s, many analyses focused on nations and states as units of analysis. Research questions concerned states' openness to or closure from international exchange and the emergence of interdependencies between political systems.[4] Most significantly, interests were observed or deduced from states' relative positioning in the international system of states, such as the decisions taken by other states such as in the influential interdependency theory developed by Keohane and Nye (1977); a country's international market orientation and degree of international political activity (Lake, 1988); strategic interaction with other states in a model developed by Lake

---

2   In most theories of trade policy, nations and states are represented as nation-states. In many cases, or for the sake of analytical simplicity, they are associated, yet need to be disentangled for two reasons. First, disaggregating the nation-state is necessary to shed light on the dynamics between state and nation. Second, the province Quebec is not a nation-state, but a nation and partially sovereign polity embedded in a federal system.

3   In large parts, this review follows the classification of trade policy theories suggested by David A. Lake (2009) and Eugenia da Conceição-Heldt (2013).

4   David A. Lake (2009) gives a comprehensive overview of the development of the field in a critical assessment of Open Economy Politics.

and Powell (1999) linked to trade theory by Jeffry Frieden (1999); the relation between (poor) periphery and (rich) core (Frank, 1966); or, in hege-
monic stability theory, that state interests were a function of the relation
between the hegemon and other states. Charles P. Kindleberger (1973) attributed the economic instability between the two World Wars to the lack
of a hegemon in the international state system. Also focussing on the role
of economic powers, Gilpin (1975) and Krasner (1976, 1978) posited that
large dominant states had an interest in open international markets and
therefore coerced, induced or persuaded other states to open their economies to international exchange. Countries might also use trade policy to
form alliances on the international scene (Gowa, 1994).

In contrast to the vast literature that focused on large states and their trade policy, Peter Katzenstein (2003) developed a model to study small states
and their behaviour in international trade. He started his investigation of
small European states with the observation that they were able to combine
economic flexibility and openness to trade with high degrees of political
stability. According to him, small states depended upon world markets for
their resource supply *and* had a strong ideology of social partnership, conducive to developing a model of corporate capitalism. Given Quebec's
small size, this theory is useful to evaluate its trade policy position.[5]

Alongside this body of literature anchored in International Relations, a
smaller set of trade policy analyses focused on the relation between trade
and various forms of nationalism (Nakano, 2004). Studies in this line of
thought were sometimes labelled economic nationalism. Often misrepre-
sented, economic nationalism did not refer to 17th century mercantilism—a period when modern nationalism did not exist—nor necessarily to
protectionism or reactionary policies. Rather, it referred to the relation between nationalism and economic development (Harlen, 1999). These authors explained trade policy as a function of a nation-wide cost-benefit analysis; according to them, nations utilised trade policy as a means to increase their power, wealth or unity. More recently, Bandelj argued that nationality affiliations and categorisations influenced preferences related to future global economic transactions as well as the interpretation of actual
global economic transactions (Bandelj, 2011). Unsurprisingly, theories based on nationalism and trade also engaged with a more general literature
on norms, worldviews and beliefs. One set of approaches worked with the
concept of national identity to explain foreign policy choices, including

---

5 See section 2 of this chapter.

trade policy (Alons, 2013; Harnisch and Stahl, 2009; Hecht, 2009; Miller, 1995; Rankin, 2004; Stahl, 2006).

Looking at the state or national level, as these two bodies of literature did, has three main weaknesses, as Conceição-Heldt highlighted (2013). First, state-centred approaches cannot account for variation across policy fields within states. Second, trade policy inevitably and visibly creates winners and losers at the domestic level, and perhaps more so than other fields investigated in International Relations. It therefore necessarily produces conflict at the domestic level, as it did in Quebec. Third, these approaches depict trade policy-making as an apolitical process, where governing coalitions do not matter and executives are unified by shared preferences (Gourevitch, 1978, also made this argument). Yet, during the Canada-EU negotiations, political parties in Quebec many times disagreed about what Quebec's interests were. They also reinterpreted these interests in the course of the CETA negotiations. Hence, economic interests cannot simply be *attributed* to Quebec on a provincial scale.[6]

Hence, a focus on the state or national level would miss an important part of the overall picture and trade policy analysis has therefore recently turned predominantly towards domestic factors. Apart from specific studies on the international bargaining processes—in which norms and cultural factors about consultative and lobbying processes played an important role (Hocking, 2004; Woll, 2006)—analyses investigated the political struggles at the domestic level between various actors such as business groups, civil society representatives, state officials and diplomats, governments or parliaments, and showed how these were aggregated at the state level. These approaches shared the assumption that trade creates clearly identifiable winners and losers at the domestic level, shedding light on why states pursued certain interests at the international level, but not others. Following Fearon (1998), the literature on domestic-level analyses of trade policy can be divided into two groups: society-centred and state-centred approaches (see for a comprehensive review Conceição-Heldt, 2013).

Society-centred investigations highlight the impact on trade policy formulation of diverging societal interests and focuses on the distributional

---

6 Opponents to my approach would respond to this argument that political parties in Quebec were not able to make informed decisions because they lacked information. Yet, political parties reached different conclusions based on the *same*—albeit incomplete—information. Hence, the same conditions lend themselves to different positions.

consequences of trade, including domestic conflicts resulting from diverging interests. This literature includes theories that focused more either on sectors or factors of production. According to the literature focussing on sectors of production, the export-oriented production sectors have an interest in free trade, while import-competing sectors that operate on domestic markets face competitive threats. They therefore explained commercial relations as a function of the interests and capacity of influential interest groups (Dornbusch and Frankel, 1987; Frieden, 1988; Gourevitch, 1978, 1987; Kindleberger, 1951[7]). Against the background of a strong corporate tradition in Quebec (see for a critical review Montpetit, 1999, 2003), we might expect interest groups to play a dominant role in shaping Quebec's trade policy position.

Apart from the literature focussing on sectoral interests, another part of the society-centred body of literature highlighted the importance of classes or factors of production in explaining trade policy preferences. If certain factors were abundant and cheap in comparison to their trading partners, production sectors working with these factors were more likely to export a considerable portion of their production than sectors which relied upon rare factors. High-skilled workers, the argument goes, are more likely to endorse free trade, while low-skilled workers were more likely to fear the negative distributional consequences in capital-abundant economies. To the contrary, in labour-abundant economies, labour-intensive goods were more likely to be exported (Arndt, 2012; Rogowski, 1989). This relation might even bear upon socio-political cleavages (Kriesi, Grande et al., 2006, 2008). Yet, recent statistical analysis of individual attitudes failed to establish a correlation between education and attitudes towards trade, and instead suggested a correlation between exposure to economic ideas and attitudes towards trade (Hainmueller and Hiscox, 2006).

Apart from society-centred approaches in domestic analyses of trade policy, Conceição-Heldt (2013) identified **state-centred approaches** as a second influential body of literature. These approaches call attention to domestic institutions in determining trade policy positions. In general terms, authors associated with this body of literature argued that national political systems ought to be taken into account when analysing a country's foreign policy (Conceição-Heldt, 2011a; De Bièvre and Dür, 2005; Goldstein,

---

7 Kindleberger (1951) starts from the national level as his unit of analysis. However, he is one of the first scholars to acknowledge national subgroups or functional groups within the nation as well as their struggle for influence in national trade policies.

1988; Goldstein and Keohane, 1993; Karol, 2000; Lohmann and O'Halloran, 1994; Mansfield, Milner et al., 2002; Mansfield, Milner et al., 2007; Milner, 1999[8]; Milner and Kubota, 2005; Milner and Rosendorff 1996; Pahre, 2001; Rosenau, 1967;).

Another nascent but still very small body of the literature focuses on how political leaders or bureaucracies used discourse strategically to influence public opinion. One study investigated in how far trade policy was present in public discourse and how the politicisation of trade policy was used strategically (McKibben and Taylor, 2014). Another study showed how the European Commission's discourse on the EU-Korea bilateral trade agreement differed as a function of the arena in which it was deployed (Siles-Brügge, 2011). Despite their focus on discourse, these two studies worked with the assumption that actors *possessed* specific interests a priori, which they depicted strategically in their discourse in order to convince the public of the validity of their policy choice. However, the empirical puzzles described for Quebec, including sudden shifts in the development of their interests, cast doubt on the assumption of pre-existing interests.

2. The Problematic Status of Attributed Interests

Trade and investment agreements such as CETA, contrary to previous agreements, focus on tackling non-tariff barriers to trade, including regulations, market access, and property rights. While tariff barriers clearly fulfill a protectionist function for specific sectors, non-tariff barriers might not primarily bear a protective function, but they also promote area-specific technical standards related to risk assessment and management in production and consumption practices (Woolcock, 2011, p. 32-34). They can be explicitly anchored in domestic legislation or regulation, or they are implicit and arise from administrative procedures, market structure or institutional configurations (Saksena and Anderson, 2008). Hence, the effects of non-tariff barriers are more diffuse, not easily measurable and therefore not easily attributable to a specific societal group, which makes it more difficult to pinpoint the interests of specific groups according to their locati-

---

8 Milner develops a theory of relations between states in general and not specifically about trade policy. However, her case studies are drawn from the field of political economy, also including some studies on commercial policy (the North American Free Trade Agreement and the Anglo-American Oil Agreement) and multilateral trade cooperation (the International Trade Organization).

on in the economy and to project their effects. Furthermore, non-tariff barriers often concern administrative practices as well as ways of production, distribution and consumption that have historically grown and are thus anchored in political institutions, traditions and life-styles. (Deardorff and Stern, 1997). They foster deep —or "positive" (Scharpf, 1999, p. 43-83; Tinbergen, 1965)—economic integration through harmonisation or recognition of common regulatory standards and market access rights to investment markets, public procurement and trade in services (Bognar, 2011). Finally, the opposition between import-competing and export-oriented interests does not sufficiently take into account contemporary global value chains: imports *and* exports are intrinsic parts of many companies' production process, so that they cannot easily be allocated to import-competing or export-oriented interests; in fact, they might belong to both (van Assche, 2012). Therefore, actors' interests cannot simply be read off from macro-economic considerations or even ideological background.

Second, most trade policy theories start from a clear conceptual division between interests and ideas. However, non-tariff barriers may mirror historically grown administrative or production, distribution and consumption practices translated into economic public policies, which in turn often rest on worldviews or beliefs (Berger and Luckmann, 1966; Converse, 1964; Jobert and Muller, 1987; Sabatier, 1988). According to Skogstad, public policies "incorporate a society's shared beliefs about the ends to which it is striving collectively, as well as the means to achieve these goals" (Skogstad, 2000, p. 806). In fact, societal actors do not operate in a historical vacuum, and collectively shared experiences with trade might influence their interests in this area. In addition, given the diffuse effects of non-tariff barriers, it is nearly impossible to exactly pinpoint actors' interests before they enter a trade negotiation process. In turn, deducing trade policy preferences from theoretical assumptions as suggested by Jeffry A. Frieden (1999) might be compelling from a methodological perspective, but it fails to grasp the dynamics underlying the formation of trade interests. Drawing a clear line between interests and ideas is therefore empirically challenging and theoretically not desirable (Blyth, 2011). Outside the realm of trade policy, the suggestion that ideas and interests are co-constituted has already been taking ground in International Relations. Constructivist scholars have formulated a research programme that alleviates the shortcomings of methodological individualism and materialism (Checkel, 1998; see the review by Finnemore and Sikkink, 2001; see the review and theoretical considerations in Mehta, 2011).

Third, turning to the analytical process, the summative literature review presented above revealed that research strongly emphasises the *results* of trade policy-making. This procedure bears the risk of a research bias: in fact, these designs tended to neglect reflections on the policy options that were discarded, and on what grounds this happened (see for a similar argument Parsons, 2002). In other words: they are not very sensitive to the fact that some interests were favoured over others, and why this was so. What made political representatives think that some claims were more legitimate than others? How and against which yardstick did they evaluate what is "appropriate" for their economies? If we assume that trade interests do not exist a priori, then trade policy analysis needs to include the process through which some interests are discarded while others are legitimised, and the actors who undertake this process.

This leads to a final point of criticism, namely the striking absence, from most trade policy analyses, of actors beyond the role of carriers of (pre-existing) interests. Unlike in other fields of public policy, actors—how they formulated their agenda, formed coalitions and pursued their interests, or how these processes shaped trade policy—is largely absent from most accounts. However, as my introductory chapter highlighted, there were many groups of actors involved in a struggle for influence during the CETA negotiation. In doing so, they tried to legitimise their interests and delegitimise those of their opponents during a complex negotiation process in which they developed their interests and formulated their positions.

3. Overcoming the Great Divide: From Fixed Preferences to the Strategic Development of Interests

Bearing in mind the limitations of conventional trade policy theory regarding Quebec's trade policy position, and given my claim for the relevance of narratives and past experiences, I will resort to more constructivist approaches. Here again, the menu ranges from post-positivist frameworks unravelling truth regimes to the long-established tradition to measure the influence of ideas on policy choices. Within the vast array of possibilities, actor-centred constructivism[9] suggested a third way between rational

---

9 Rather than a theoretical field with clear boundaries, actor-centred constructivism is a label recently attributed to a group of constructivist scholars with shared assumptions that distinguish them from other streams in constructivism and public policy analysis (Saurugger, 2013).

choice and constructivist approaches. Although it has been deployed mainly in the context of European integration so far, striking similarities regarding issue and institutional complexity between European integration and
trade policy negotiations make actor-centred constructivism a compelling
framework for analysis.

In her review on different streams of contemporary constructivist literature, Sabine Saurugger maintained that "interests in ideational aspects of
policy-making processes make constructivist approaches particularly useful
at explaining policy outcomes in a context of high issue complexity"
(Saurugger, 2013, p. 889). Issue complexity is defined as a situation where
actors have unclear or contradictory interests that stem from their embeddedness in different values or worldviews and where the amount and nature of informal linkages is high, as for instance in the EU. As a consequence, integration is not even across sectors or issues (Zahariadis, 2003,
2013). The situation is similar in contemporary trade policy-making and
more specifically in the agreement between Canada and the EU. Actors
must pay attention to uneven economic integration across sectors and issues in a context where bi- and plurilateral agreements flourish alongside
multilateral integration. More specifically, the Canada-EU agreement is
comprehensive in nature, meaning that it covers a vast array of topics ranging from tariffs in agricultural, textiles and automotive trade, to intellectual property and regulatory convergence. While the comprehensive nature of CETA potentially allows for cross-sectoral bargains, it may also engender unintended cross-sectoral or cross-issue effects to which actors need
to be attentive.

Apart from issue complexity, the Canada-EU agreement also displays a
high degree of institutional complexity, which Saurugger identified as a second feature of constructivist accounts combining rationalist and constructivist thinking. She argued that a "high number of actors with overlapping
and often conflicting competencies increase the possibility of power
struggles for control of agendas and resources" (Saurugger, 2013). This institutional complexity complicates negotiations because it augments the
number of powerful actors. In fact, CETA stretches across two levels of jurisdiction in Canada. Both the provinces and the federal level have jurisdiction over areas pertaining to international trade, as highlighted in the introduction, and wanted to influence the outcome of the CETA negotiation
process according to their respective definitions of expected welfare gains.

What are the assumptions about how actors identify their interests and
pursue them? Actor-centred constructivism contests the long-standing opposition between rational choice and constructivism (for a review of the

tendency to dualistic thinking, Gofas and Hay, 2010). For scholars in this line of thought, interests and ideas are not fundamentally different. Rather, the material and the ideational are interwoven; they co-constitute each other (Blyth, 2002; Hall, 1989; Hay, 1999; Jenson, 1989). These authors criticize rational choice approaches for underestimating the power of ideas, while constructivist approaches underestimate the influence of material interests and the role of powerful actors. According to them, actors identify their interests as they interpret their environment and interact with each other (see the literature reviews by Saurugger, 2013; Surel, 2000). Thus, this approach does not discard interests, but rather wants to emphasise that interests do not exist independently of their carriers and that they change when their carriers re-evaluate their priorities and re-interpret their environment (Béland and Cox, 2011). Authors associated with actor-centred constructivism question the existence of direct causal mechanisms between policy choices and either material or ideational structures. Rather, analyses must take into account the way actors interpret these structures and develop their interests (Hall, 1993; Sabatier, 1988; Sabatier and Jenkins-Smith, 1993). Hence, interests are not clear-cut and stable, but instead ambiguous and subject to constant re-evaluation. They carry different meanings because pursuing them can serve various causes, and often coalitions form among actors who pursue different interests altogether. In that latter case, actors promote ambiguous interests in order to enter unusual coalitions or promote change against strong opposition (Jegen and Mérand, 2013).

This conception of interests changes the focus of empirical analyses from the discovery of the underlying interests that promote change to the processes that led actors carrying these interests to shift their perception of their own interests (Hay, 2011). In order to understand the choices that actors make, analyses need to consider how these actors interpret, organise and define their environment by drawing upon ideational structures that are available to them in their time and place. Such an approach allows accounting for the contingent and political nature of change. Consequently, actors do not simply possess a priori interests when they enter negotiations. Rather, they develop their interests in a political process in which they evaluate their interests (Blyth, 2002, 2011) and need to find coalition partners to promote them.

Furthermore, these approaches are conceptually well-equipped to document "legitimation strategies actors pursue in policy-making processes" (Saurugger, 2013 p. 899). Since the CUSFTA and NAFTA negotiations and the foundation of the World Trade Organization, the legitimation of international trade has increasingly been questioned both with regard to policies and governing institutions (Brunelle and Deblock, 1997; Dufour, 2006; Lemire, 2003). *That* Quebec continued to eagerly participate in this process of global economic integration and *how* it wanted to do so therefore required a legitimation strategy and building broad societal and political coalitions. In general, some narratives and themes lend themselves better to legitimation strategies, and they depend on time and place (Jenson, 1989):

> Politicians, officials, the spokesmen for societal interests, and policy experts all operate within the terms of political discourse that are current in the nation at a given time, and the terms of political discourse generally have a specific configuration that lends representative legitimacy to some social interests more than others, delineates the accepted boundaries of state action, associates contemporary political developments with particular interpretations of national history, and defines the context in which many issues will be understood (Hall, 1993, p. 289).

Rather than focusing on the distinction between interests and ideas and highlighting their respective influence in policy outcomes, analysts associated with theories of actor-centred constructivism pay attention to how ideas and interests matter, and not so much to the questions if and when they matter respectively (Mehta, 2011). Already in 1986, Peter Hall (1986, p. 4) made a similar comment about economic policy-making, in which he highlighted the political nature of economic policy-making :

> We must move beyond the view of policy-making implicit in most economics texts. They tend to see policy primarily as a response to prevailing economic conditions, and policy-making as the resolution of technical issues. To some degree, of course, this idea is quite valid: policy does respond to economic conditions. But such a view is far too incomplete. Economic policy is also made by governments, and governments are political creatures. [...] Economic policy-making must be seen as a highly political process.

Apart from a spotlight on the development of interests, another central focus lies on the forms and goals of the mobilisation ideas, common narratives and collective themes are subject to. According to Surel, they are deployed to produce identity, to allocate power, and to manage tension and conflict (Surel, 2000). In his study *Playing the Market*, (2006), Jabko documented that the European Commission skilfully deployed a large variety of market ideas to foster European integration through market integration—hence also the characterisation of this form of constructivism as *strategic constructivism*. These multiple facets of the market allowed for unusual coalitions, thereby promoting institutional change. These coalitions are not necessarily based on a convergence of interests or ideas, but they are necessary to carry out reform.

Actor-centred constructivism investigates thus when actors use certain ideas or interests strategically to legitimise their positions and to build coalitions with other actors. The forms of mobilisation ideas and representations can be subject to in policy-making becomes a central question. Despite the use of concepts such as strategy and interest, it is important to keep in mind that the approach remains a fundamentally constructivist one. First, the fact that this literature investigates how ideas and interests are mobilised does not imply that this use is purely rhetorical (Surel, 2000). To the contrary, various domestic actors enter into "argumentative competition" to shape representations of the national interests (Panke and Risse, 2007, p. 100). Second, the notion of strategy is different from the one used in game-theoretical accounts. It refers to a mode of collective and not individual action that focusses on the shared language actors deploy to form coalitions even if their interests differ (Jabko, 2006). In sum, actor-centred constructivism investigates how actors can partially mobilise the ideational background they evolve in to achieve their goals. This said, there is disagreement about the degree of independence actors enjoy when choosing a strategy. Some authors think that actors can mobilise ideational factors independently from their structural position (Blyth, 2002; Jabko, 2006). Others highlight that ideas only become visible if used by actors with a structurally powerful position making their ideas heard (Béland, 2009; Hall, 1993; McNamara, 1998; Parsons, 2003). I will come back to the notion of collective strategy in the next section.

Studies on international trade relations have overwhelmingly focussed on the outcome of trade-policy and have neglected the process that led to this outcome. Referring to President John F. Kennedy's assertion that the essence of a decision remains impenetrable to the observer, Majone (2008) speculates that this might be the reason for a lack of interest in processes and greater attention to outcomes. Actor-centred constructivism has already offered some insights into how actors mobilise ideas, narratives and themes to pursue their long-term visions. Yet, it has not yet fully acknowledged that the process through which interests are developed and coalitions are forged is crucial in understanding policy choices. This is all the more stunning since trade is a policy area where negotiation processes—at the international level, but also between domestic actors—are central to policy-making. Furthermore, since the literature on international trade has been strongly influenced by deductive theories, questions about the carriers of interests and ideas, policy entrepreneurship, hidden agendas or forum shopping are to a large extent not taken into account. Therefore, actor-centred constructivism needs to be adapted and extended. *First*, although these frameworks challenge the assumption that interests are attributed and instead assume that actors mobilise ideas strategically to construct their environment in a certain way, actor-centred constructivists have not suggested a conceptual toolbox to investigate how exactly interests are developed. *Second*, the origin of the ideas, narratives and themes mobilised have not been sufficiently theorised yet. For example, in *A Certain Idea of Europe*, Craig Parsons (2003) took into account competing ideas of European integration among French elites at the beginning of the European integration process which shaped France's interest in this process. Yet, he did not show the process through which the actors discursively developed these ideas in the first place.

Section 2: Analysing Trade Positions as a Discursive Strategy: A Conceptual Framework

This section proposes concepts that allow to reveal on which sets of ideas, narratives and themes actors can draw strategically to legitimise their own development of interests to the detriment of others'. In order to do so, looking at trade policy not from the perspective of trade policy literature, but through the lens of trade as a public policy, might help to understand the processual character of developing a position on trade policy, to account for the non-linearity of trade policy positions and to understand discursive issues such as problem definition or the evolution of policy positions across time.

1. Object of Research: Trade Positions as a Discursive Process

The object of research is the discursive process through which actors developed their interests and built coalitions through four processes of interest-construction and coalition-building at different moments in the policy-cycle and in three different fields of economic activity in Quebec. Given that actor-centered-constructivist frameworks have, so far, been largely absent from trade policy analyses, new research concepts and methods needed to be developed. Hence, my analyses do not only respond empirically to my research question, but also make a conceptual and methodological contribution to actor-centred constructivism by developing a systematic conceptual approach to the empirical analysis of discursive processes.

2. Trade Negotiations as a Policy Process

The transatlantic negotiation process of CETA can be divided into four negotiation stages: agenda-setting; policy formulation; decision-making; ratification and implementation. Even if, traditionally, the policy cycle is a process divided into *five* parts—agenda-setting, policy formulation, decision-making, implementation and evaluation (Howlett, Ramesh et al., 2009) —my analysis ends with the official conclusion of the CETA negotiation in 2014, given the relevance of the *development* of interests during trade negotiations, which comes to a conclusion when interests are formalised and anchored in a legal text (the decision-making).[10]

As the literature on public policy tells us, the agenda-setting and the ways in which issues are defined in the first place has an impact upon the policy choices that are being made (Rochefort and Cobb, 1993). At this stage, the rules of the game are set. According to John Kingdon (1995), policy agendas are necessarily narrow, so policy leaders need to make choices about which issue they want to address. In this process, ideas are particularly important (Béland, 2009). Therefore, the analysis of the agenda-setting process will shed light on the processes in which problems and solutions were identified. According to Page (2008), a central actor in this process is the policy entrepreneur who identifies and exploits the opportunity for a new policy agenda and needs to engage relevant audiences, including at the international and domestic levels. Depending on his positional power, he can even exert agenda control and select priorities for the political agenda (Majone, 2008).

The Canadian and European federal dynamics in trade policy-making might influence how the agenda setting stage unfolds. In fact, the Canadian federal government (Barrows and Jansen, 1991; Campbell, 1995; Hart,

---

10 After such a formalisation of interests, we might observe a re-evaluation of interests and a re-negotiation of the legal text—which happened, indeed, after the CETA negotiation was officially closed. This re-negotiation, however, is not part of this analysis which focusses on the initial construction of interests in Quebec.

2010; Robinson, 1995; Skogstad, 2012b), and the European Commission and the European Council (Conceição-Heldt, 2011b; Meunier, 2005; Meunier and Nicolaidis, 1999; Woolcock, 2010) represent the formal gate-keepers in opening trade negotiations. However, the prospect of provinces needing to implement provisions falling under their jurisdiction potentially makes them informal gate-keepers in the agenda setting process. Since they need to be convinced of the substantive benefit of such an agreement in order to ensure its implementation, and since the nature of CETA and its focus on non-tariff barriers involves a substantial number of issues falling under provincial jurisdiction, the provinces also need to be convinced of the importance of the new trade agreement (Kukucha, 2011b; Noel, 2006). Both levels of government therefore need to stay attentive to one another during the agenda-setting stage, as well as during the later stages of the negotiation.

Once a policy made it onto the agenda of central decision makers, the next important question is how the process of developing a policy position—which entails developing interests, defining a position, debating it and making a final decision about it—and updating this position throughout the negotiation process unfolds. During this process, actors try to maintain or create a monopoly on the understanding of a policy problem, as Baumgartner and his team showed (Baumgartner, De Boef et al., 2008). According to Baumgartner, actors' central task during this stage is to develop convincing frames that help them shape the understanding of a problem and, therefore, the suggested policy answers. In fact, frames are successful when their targets accept the problem and the solution they suggest (Polletta and Ho, 2006, p. 202). When actors define their policy position, they evaluate different possibilities to address the identified problem. This highly conflictual process has complex ramifications and involves struggles between actors advocating diverging policy alternatives. According to Brewer and DeLeon, this stage is likely to be the most political one: some policy solutions necessarily need to be excluded and this marginalisation needs to be legitimised (Brewer and DeLeon, 1983). A policy choice therefore includes winners and losers. It is not purely technical, even though actors try to convey their rationality in making choices.

In majoritarian parliamentary systems such as Quebec, the cabinet, backed by its bureaucracy and diplomats, is often solely responsible for making a policy decision. It is formally empowered to make authoritative decisions. According to article 20 of the *Loi sur le ministère des Relations internationales* (1988, 2002), Quebec's international agreements need to be signed by Quebec's Minister for International Relation[11] and endorsed by the government to come into effect. A similar procedure applies if Quebec endorses international agreements negotiated by the federal government including provisions falling under Quebec's jurisdiction. However, the provincial institutional design requires the deposition of *important* international agreements ("engagement international important")[12] in Quebec's legislative assembly, the National Assembly according to article 22.2. In addition, the National Assembly has to implement provisions requiring legislative changes falling under provincial jurisdiction. Hence, the executive needed to rely on the National Assembly' support.

Quebec's political spectrum is mainly defined by two cleavages: debates over national identity and sovereignty, on the one hand, and socio-economic policies, on the other hand (Noel, 2010, p. 105). Trade agreements and especially agreements including a high number of provisions on non-tariff barriers engage both dimensions of the political spectrum. In fact, they touch upon Canadian market integration, the participation of provinces in the negotiation process, hence engaging debates over Quebec sovereignty. They also considerably impact upon the provincial economic structure, hence potentially triggering debates about the socio-economic impacts of trade. As a consequence, the National Assembly engaged in debates about CETA during the negotiation process. Therefore, the analysis focusses on the way *political representatives* (the executive branch, deputies) identify provincial interests while they confront complex material realities and conflicting demands made by societal groups and their negotiation partners.

In international negotiations, we need to add another central actor to the policy-process, namely the chief negotiator (Putnam, 1988). Taking part in the decision-making at the national level as well as internationally, the chief negotiator has a pivotal role. He needs to stay attentive to the policy formulation at both levels at the same time. The chief negotiator and his team represent the objectives of the government he negotiates for and has his own motivations. His personal motivation cannot run counter to his government's position. Yet, he has considerable room to manoeuvre. He is compelled to present the deal he strikes at the international negotiation table as the best possible deal for the polity he represents and his audi-

---

11 Since 2016, the Minister for Economic Affairs, Science and Innovation exercises this function for international commercial agreements (Décret 31-2016 du 28 janvier 2016, (2016) 148 G.O. 2, 1256).

12 According to article 22.2, agreements on international trade are defined as important.

ences need to accept the negotiation results. What makes his role extremely complex is that the decisions taken at both levels need to be coherent and compatible. During the CETA negotiation, Quebec's chief negotiator represented Quebec at the international negotiation tables and at the federal level.

3. Repertoires, Frames and Strategies: Developing Trade Interests

As mentioned in the introductory chapter, actors again and again refer to specific themes when engaging in discourse on trade relations. In Quebec, recurring themes were, for instance, economic development, societal projects or the difference between Quebec and other Canadian provinces. Actors seem to interpret their interests against the background of their political community's past experiences with trade and other adjacent themes.

a) Repertoires: Connecting Interests to Collective Representations

Repertoires identify the themes, stories and past experiences of a political community and thereby provide us with a conceptual tool explaining which stories actors draw upon when constructing their interests. Repertoires define the economic and social assumptions that guide policy reform (Béland, 2009, p. 705). More specifically, in my analysis, a repertoire refers to a set of collective, non-homogeneous cultural, including national, ideas and political representations on which actors draw to develop their interests, define and legitimise their policy position, and acquire support from other actors. Hence, I aim to show that ideas do not emerge unexpectedly and unrelatedly to structural context—as some have argued (Blyth, 2002; Jabko, 2006)[13] —but that they are historically embedded and place-specific.

Repertoires include heterogeneous elements that can be related to each other in many different ways. They are therefore ambiguous: similar elements can be related to each other in multiple ways, thereby enabling multiple paths of action. Their status as floating signifiers makes them particu-

---

13 More recently, Jabko (2015) has departed from his initial position and now accords more importance to existing ideational frameworks.

larly suitable to be mobilised by various actors to different ends (Tilly, 1977[14]; Jabko, 2006; Jegen and Mérand, 2013).

First, repertoires vary with time and place. They draw upon a long history of previous struggles that are specific to a community (Tilly, 2006, p. 35). In other words, repertoires are bounded by space and time. Even though the boundaries of these repertoires may vary—they can be local, national, or transnational—*national* repertoires tend to remain very strong in setting the criteria of evaluation of political action (Lamont and Thévenot, 2000). Not every representation or claim is susceptible to be effective in every social setting, but political claims need to be made in accordance with historical and cultural contexts.

Second, according to Tilly, a repertoire operates like a script with which actors can engage creatively. In order to be effective, a claim needs to be recognizable, i.e. connected to a repertoire. Similar to a piece of music, every actor repeats the same template but adds variation to it. It is this delicate balance between repetition and innovation which allows proposals to be acceptable and yet to bring about curiosity and change.

The relation between stakeholders, instruments, and spaces defines the repertoire's structure and, in doing so, establishes political representations on which actors draw when developing their interests. Through these structures, actors *frame* the repertoire. Stakeholders include public authorities, societal groups or representatives of sectors of production. Instruments include public policy mixes, international agreements, or other public actions. Repertoires define the boundaries of the space in which stakeholders operate. These boundaries are in constant flux, and actors struggle to impose their interpretation of the space in which they want to operate; the process of naming spaces and mapping landscapes therefore has an impact upon the articulation of political, economic and cultural development projects (Jenson, 1991, 1995).

Repertoires are a concept to highlight the importance of common themes establishing a benchmark of reference against which actors evaluate their interests. However, actors might refer to these same benchmarks and still make contradictory or incommensurate claims. As mentioned in the introductory chapter, for example, political parties in Quebec pursued divergent policy objectives in the name of province-building. This is because repertoires can be structured in different ways through frames. Frames de-

---

14 Charles Tilly is best known for a theory on repertoires *of action* regarding social movements. However, he also developed a more general theory of repertoires that is applicable to political discourse.

fine the relationship between stakeholders, space and development goals, or between the various constituting entities of a federal polity and their constitutional vision.

Thus, frames are more than just rhetoric. They represent ordering devices in public policy-making (Bacchi, 2010; Baumgartner, De Boef et al., 2008; Benford and Snow, 1992, 2000; Chong and Druckman, 2007; Hajer and Laws, 2007; Marcankowski, 2014; Matthes, 2012; McAdam, 1996; Snow, 2004; Snow and Benford, 1992; Snow, Rochford et al., 1986). Actors who deploy specific frames align material structures, interests and policy-suggestions in a coherent and collectively legitimated way (McAdam, 1996; Steinberg, 1998). By doing so, they link their interests to their surroundings, previous experiences and collective values drawn from repertoires. Frames include a story both about what *has* happened, and what *should* and *will* happen next.

In Quebec's discourse on trade relations, two repertoires, structured by two frames respectively, were predominant. Figure 1 schematically lays out the relation between these repertoires and frames.

Figure 1 – Relation between Repertoires and Frames

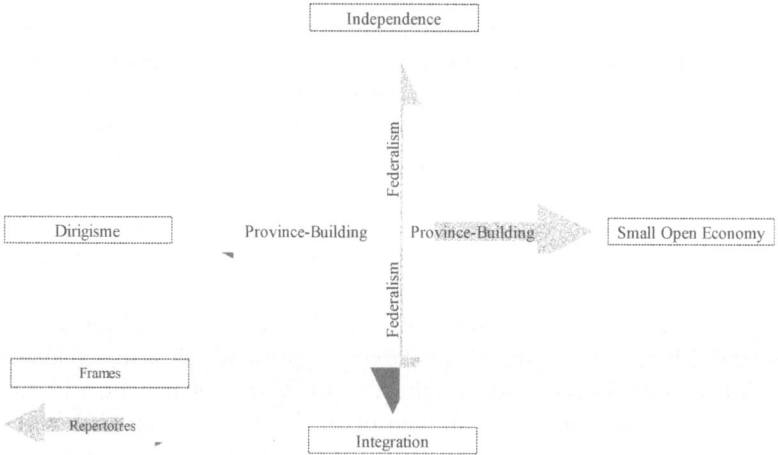

The **repertoire of province-building** relates stakeholders and spaces to specific economic, political, social and cultural development projects. Developed in the aftermath of Quebec's Quiet Revolution and the experience of activist governments in Ontario and Western Canada, the concept of province-building served to describe the role the provinces play in Canadian social integration and economic development (Cairns, 1971, 1977; Pratt, 1977; Stevenson, 2009 [1979]). More recent variations of it emphasise "the autonomy of provincial governments and their independent capacity for action" (Wilder and Howlett, 2016), highlighting the heterogeneity among provincial development paths and the expansion of the regulatory state at the provincial level. While one might criticize the concept of province-building for being "too vast and lurid" to carry analytical value (Young, Faucher et al., 1984, p. 783), no one would contest today that most provinces pursue their individual paths of provincial development (Atkinson, Béland et al., 2013; Smith, 2010a, p. 83-87). This repertoire has various pillars reflecting various development policies, including political, economic, social and cultural development (hence being more precise than the concept of nation-building, which I discarded as a repertoire). I coded data for this repertoire when deputies mentioned development policies and varying instruments to achieve it.

The **repertoire of federalism** defines the relation between federal and sub-federal levels of government in a federal political system as well as the nature of the relationship among sub-federal entities (intergovernmental relations). Throughout Quebec's modern history, the relation between the province and the federal level of government considerably shaped policymaking in the province, and continues to do so (Banting, 2005; Gagnon, 2014; Gagnon and Noel, 1995; Keating, 1997; Noel, 2006, 2010; Paquet, 2014; Stevenson, 1977, 2009 [1979]). During my empirical analysis, the theme of federalism was frequently present in the debates in the National Assembly when deputies discussed institutional configurations, intergovernmental relations or the internal Canadian market. Repertoires might also intersect and thereby re-enforce or weaken each other, for instance when the relation between Quebec and the other provinces has an impact upon its development policies.

The repertoire of province-building was structured in two different ways, reflecting the ways in which actors hoped to achieve different facets of provincial development. One possible structure is the **'small open economy'** frame—a term inspired by the work of Katzenstein (1985, 2003). Actors depicted Quebec as a small "trading nation" dependent on world markets and hence compelled to engage in international trade. When coding, I identified this frame when deputies mentioned the international activities of Quebec's companies abroad or the presence of international companies or foreign investments in Quebec.

That Quebec depends on international trade and investment is by no means a new idea. At least since the 1980s free trade debates on the North

American Free Trade Agreement (NAFTA), cross-party and societal consensus on the benefits of free trade for Quebec was strong. Pierre Martin (1995b) thoroughly reviewed several explanations to account for Quebec's vocal support for free trade at this time. He found that, even though structural conditions were conducive to Quebec's position, "structural conditions do not explain Quebec's support for continental economic integration" (Martin, 1995b, p. 7). In fact, Quebec's small size made it hugely trade dependent and therefore supportive of free trade, and it was true that Quebec strongly depended upon the US market. However, Martin argued, Quebec's structural position in the international economy and its dependency on the US market were not sufficient to explain continuous cross-party support for continental economic integration. In fact, the citizens of Quebec's neighbour Ontario, even more integrated in North American supply chains, voted in large numbers against Mulroney's free trade agenda. In the 1988 federal elections, which were fought almost entirely over free trade, Quebeckers' support for the pro-trade Progressive Conservatives (PC)'s free trade agenda became most evident. Mulroney's PC won far more seats in Quebec (63 seats, 52 % of the popular vote, total seats: 75) and in Alberta (25 seats, 52 % of the popular vote, total seats: 26) than in any other province, such as Ontario (46 seats, 38 % of the popular vote, total seats: 99) (Jackson and Jackson, 1990, p. 444).

A second way actors structured the repertoire of province-building was through the **'state dirigisme'** frame. In Quebec, practices of state dirigisme—a concept borrowed from French post-war economic practices (Dyson, 1980; Hall, 1986, p. 164-191; Schmidt, 1996, 1997; Shonfield, 1965) —refer to state activities, including by political executives and the bureaucracy, aiming to steer social, economic, and cultural activities in the province. I coded for this frame when deputies required the state or other public authorities to play an active role in promoting measures sustaining a common social, economic and cultural project. Inspired by the tradition of Western Europe and mainly France rather than the North American and British one, Quebec engaged in a development strategy which put the provincial state centre-stage in its modern development (Anderson, 2013; Averyt, 1989; Diekhoff 2014; Gagnon and Montcalm, 1992; McRoberts 2003; Noel, 2010; Wilder and Howlett, 2016 refer to "activist governments").

Finally, actors structured the federalism repertoire through the **'independence'** and **'integration'** frames as two opposed, yet complementary concepts identifying Quebec's position in the Canadian federal setting. While, according to the independence frame, Quebec should become more autonomous in economic, social and cultural policy-making, and aim for independence as the ultimate goal—a position usually associated with the Parti Québécois—the integration frame draws attention to the ways in which Quebec can increase its power within the Canadian federation—a position usually pursued by the Parti Libéral. According to the independence frame, there is an unwanted hierarchy between the federal and the provincial level in Canada's external relations. In this perspective, the provinces are not equal: contrary to Quebec, the other provinces are not nations, but functional administrative areas. In addition, being part of the Canadian federation represents an obstacle to Quebec pursuing its own policy objectives. Since the Quiet Revolution, independence has been given different meanings, ranging from traditional independence to sovereignty or sovereignty association (Keating, 1997, p. 698-699). According to the integration frame, to the contrary, all provinces are equal in status, even though some benefit from more resources. Also, there is an equality between the two levels of government and the relation between the federal and provincial levels is shaped by the distribution of jurisdictions. In this perspective, membership in the Canadian federation strengthens Quebec. The independence and integration frames often interacted with frames structuring the province-building repertoire, because the issue of free trade was often linked to the question of the relation between Quebec and Canada (Gagnon, 2003, p. 465).

b) Discursive and Coalitional Strategies

How can the individual claims by groups of actors be brought together to form the bigger picture of Quebec's trade policy position? What enables these conflicting and even incompatible claims to become compatible in a coherent framework for action? What brings frames and repertoires together in a specific combination to identify policy interests and acquire support for pursuing these interests? The need for change needs to be convincingly constructed to find suitable coalition partners, as Robert H. Cox claimed: "in a political environment the advocates of reform need to employ strategies to overcome the skepticism of others and persuade them of the importance of reform" (Cox, 2001, p. 475). In order to do so, actor-centred constructivist scholars have developed the concept of *strategy*: as Saurugger noted, "it is important to understand that actors must create broad coalitions around common strategies in order to carry out major reforms." (Saurugger, 2013, p. 897).

Nicolas Jabko's (2006) concept of political strategy in his study *Playing the Market* is the most prominent example of the use of a constructivist understanding of strategy in contemporary literature. Jabko documented that European market integration was a political strategy to foster European integration. The plurivalence of the market as a repertoire of ideas allowed actors with diverging or even opposed long-term goals to form coalitions in the short term, despite their awareness that their long-term expectations might be incompatible. Jabko thus explicitly departed from the convergence thesis predominant in large parts of political science. Rather, he showed how conflicting meanings of reality clashed and how political action was made possible nevertheless. He defined political strategy as "a socially constructed method of collective action that brings together actors with diverse motivations" (2006, p. 26). "In politics", Jabko observed, "actors do not just maximize and trade utilities in explicit bargains, nor do they consistently follow clear-cut ideas. They constantly have to make choices in the present while knowing that these choices will have unpredictable and contentious consequences beyond the short-term" (Jabko, 2006, p. 26).

The object of research of this study is the strategy deployed by political representatives in Quebec. This is an eminently political strategy, in the sense of Jabko's notion of "political strategy" (Jabko, 2006) and Brewer and DeLeon's notion of agenda setting as "political" (Brewer and DeLeon, 1983). In this sense, political does not refer to party-political behaviour, but to the struggle to impose a certain meaning of trade in discourse. Therefore, the process through which actors develop their interests and build coalitions to pursue them is the object of research rather than assigned interests organising behaviour. However, more than Jabko, the following empirical account focusses on the *discursive* processes which underlie political action: the deployment of frames, the embeddedness of policy positions in repertoires, and the way actors discursively construct alliances or opposition. As such, *discursive* strategy more specifically constitutes the object of research.

Conventional accounts of strategy (Lake and Powell, 1999; Frieden, 1999) usually assume that bargaining partners seek a compromise based on the lowest common denominator. Yet, as Jabko documented, actors might also pursue different goals altogether without settling for a compromise. Conventional accounts also overlook the possibility that strategies might be deployed not to maximise preferences concerning a specific policy, say trade policy, but something different. Negotiation partners might deliberately choose a certain way of common action that does not mirror a pre-existing preference on trade. As this chapter has already shown, trade policy in Quebec has sometimes been an instrument to achieve national unity, autonomy or power. It has also been used to differentiate the province from other provinces. These motivations largely exceed the kinds of answers we can get if we only look at pre-defined interests. Why actors ally around trade policy and what they wish to achieve by doing so are questions suggesting to look at trade policy through a different lens than that of stable and structure-dependent interests.

Section 3: Examining Political Positions on Trade

1. Disaggregating Trade Negotiations: Four Case Studies in Quebec

Although this analysis is grounded in the comparison of four case studies, the aim is *not* to insulate causal mechanisms or to show where interests come from—e.g. structural factors, learning effects, socialisation. Therefore, the following case studies are not designed as a set of varying relations between independent and dependent variables. Quite to the contrary, my case study design is cast against prevailing interest- or ideas-based accounts and wants to show that both remain eventually incomplete. Because they establish a direct relation between policy choices and material or ideational structures, they leave no room for individual choices.

a) Constructing the Cases: Four Discursive Processes

Given the centrality of actors in my framework, the boundaries of the four case studies were constructed inductively, based on the importance actors conferred on certain policy fields in their discourse.[15] As the following table shows, agriculture, foreign direct investment and public procurement were the topics occurring most frequently in the National Assembly after the negotiations were officially launched in 2009, while the agenda-setting was defined by general discussions about CETA.

---

15 Measured by the number of coding occurrences.

Table 1 – Coding Occurrences for Topics for Negotiation Stages

	12.2006-05.2009	06.2009-09.2012	10.2012-04.2014	05.2014-12.2014
CETA (general)	34	149	51	13
Agriculture	2	33	30	48
Public Procurement	0	89	19	0
Foreign Direct Investment	11	67	7	1
Culture	3	33	6	0
Trade Policy General	3	22	15	0
Labour Mobility	16	20	2	0
Intellectual Property	0	9	12	0
Internal Trade – Canada	9	3	2	4
Regulatory Cooperati-on	1	9	0	0
Rules of Origin	0	7	0	0
Tariffs	0	7	0	0
Alcohol	0	6	1	0
Transport	0	0	0	4
Telecommunication	0	2	0	0
National Security	0	1	0	0

Source: Analysis of parliamentary debates (plenary and committees, N= 159,527 words)

Figure 2 lays out the CETA policy process from a Quebec perspective and situates the four case studies. The agenda-setting stage begins in late 2006 with the first informal discussions in policy circles on a new EU-Canada trade agreement and ends with the beginning of the official negotiation process in May 2009 (2006-2009). The first negotiation stage in Quebec started in June 2009 and ended in September 2012, when general elections took place in Quebec. The second negotiation stage started in October 2012, when the 40th legislature was formed, and ended in April 2014, when the Assembly was dissolved. The decision-making stage started in May 2014, when the 41st Legislature was formed, and ended in December

2014, after CETA negotiations were officially closed in September 2014. As my analysis is concerned with the question of how a politically and strategically viable position was reached in Quebec, the timespan of empirical analysis ends with the closure of the negotiating process on 26 September 2014. Canada and the EU have since then published the final version of the negotiation text.[16] In order to cover debates following the immediate official closure, documents until the end of December 2014 were included.

Figure 2 –   Chronology of Empirical Case Studies (2006-2014, simplified)

In addition to being constructed inductively, the empirical case studies also bear theoretical relevance in varying along three relevant dimensions.[17] First, the cases represent both tariff and non-tariff topics. Second, they are also representative of various facets of opposition compelling political representatives to construct a discursive strategy to allow for collective action despite opposition. Third, the cases also represent different possibilities of pairing federal and provincial jurisdiction. Given that provinces might have more bargaining power in a situation where they have jurisdiction over the negotiated topic, one might assume that discursive strategies are mostly helpful when matters do not fall within their jurisdiction, requiring the provinces to justify their position and convince the federal government. Three cases are deviant cases, whose aim is to show that existing trade theory is not able to account for the outcomes we observe with CETA

---

16 This does not constitute the final version of CETA. The final version will be established after legal review and ratification by all the negotiating parties and the EU member states. Meanwhile, substantial parts of the agreement have been provisionally applied since 21 September 2017.

17 See also table 2 for an overview.

because considering structural factors alone is not sufficient to understand these cases. One case is a typical case whose aim is to demonstrate the usefulness of the novel theoretical and methodological framework even in settings confirming existing theories.

The *first case study* – the agenda-setting—investigates why Quebec's government developed an interest in launching a new agreement between Canada and the EU in the first place. The period of empirical investigation starts in winter 2006, when members of Quebec's government, the Quebec ambassador in Brussels and members of the Canada-EU Round Table for Business (CERT) discussed the opportunities related to a new trade and investment agreement under the leadership of Quebec's Premier, Jean Charest. This case study functions as a lens to observe how actors build discourse on a specific issue—trade policy—in order to constitute their interests and justify a change in the status quo. This period ends in May 2009, when negotiations were officially launched.

The *second case study* on public procurement investigates a non-tariff or new trade issue and does not correspond to a traditional sector. Provincial public procurement is an exclusive provincial competence, as is procurement by public authorities under provincial jurisdiction (municipalities, provincial crown corporations). Until the CETA negotiations, Quebec's provincial government successfully advocated the exclusion of their procurement practices from Canada's international commitments. Surprisingly for many observers, they actively suggested including them in the new trade and investment agreement.

The *third case study* on foreign direct investment (FDI) in Quebec investigates a non-tariff trade issue and has been key in the transatlantic negotiations. Although the screening of foreign direct investments is under exclusive federal jurisdiction, provinces retain adjacent competencies such as ownership of natural resources, regulatory jurisdiction over labour markets or, in general, contract law. Even though theories of economic nationalism might lead to assume that Quebec rejected the presence of foreign ownership in the province, its government has been arduously trying to attract foreign investments to the province at least since the 1970s. Hence, FDI represents a case where Quebec did not alter its position during the CETA negotiation.

The *fourth case study* on agriculture is the only sectoral analysis in a conventional sense, and one of the rare sectors where tariffs and tariff-free import quota were at the core of the negotiations, flanked, however, by some non-tariff issues such as sanitary and phyto-sanitary measures. Agriculture is under shared provincial and federal jurisdiction.

Table 2 – Case Design (Overview)

Cases	Key Questions	Logic of Selection
Agenda-Setting	Why and how did Quebec make a new transatlantic trade and investment agreement a political priority? How did its government acquire support to launch the agreement?	– New trade issues included; – Opposition (mainly) by actors outside of Quebec; – Sub-federal actor in international trade policy
Public Procurement	Why did Quebec offer European companies privileged access to provincial procurement markets? How did its government acquire support in Quebec and in the other provinces to do so?	– Non-tariff issue; – Opposition potentially high (municipalities, political opposition, trade unions, business) – Provincial jurisdiction
Foreign Direct Investment (FDI)	Why is Quebec eager to attract FDI? Why are cultural industries such a sensitive issue in Quebec? How did Quebec's government acquire support for a new chapter on FDI, despite mounting domestic opposition?	– Non-tariff issue; – Opposition potentially high (cultural industries, civil society, business); – Federal jurisdiction, adjacent provincial jurisdictions
Agriculture	How did Quebec come to consider that protectionism in agriculture might not be in the provincial interest, after almost 50 years of agricultural protectionism and investments in the modernisation of agricultural production? How did its government overcome strong domestic opposition?	– Tariff and tariff-rate import quota; – High opposition (political opposition, business groups, other provinces); – Shared jurisdiction

b) Focussing on Actors, not Structures: Selection Criteria for the Units of Analysis

Several groups of actors were key during the CETA negotiation in Quebec. *Quebec's representatives* refer to the provincial government, including its state apparatus and diplomatic representatives. According to Putnam, "[c]entral executives have a special role in mediating domestic and international pressures precisely because they are directly exposed to both spheres, not because they are united on all issues nor because they are insulated from domestic politics" (Putnam, 1988, p. 432-433). In addition, Quebec's political system is dominated by the executive (Brühl-Moser, 2012; Savoie, 2010). Given the central role public policy literature accords to authoritative decision-makers, I started by sampling members of government and the chief negotiator. Diplomats, and specifically the chief negotiator Pierre-Marc Johnson, occupied a central position, since they communicated Quebec's position to the other Canadian provinces and the federal government, as well as to the European negotiators when areas under provincial jurisdiction were involved. Johnson also contributed to elaborating coalitional strategies. On two occasions, Johnson appeared in public hearings organised by the National Assembly's Committee for Institutional Affairs (6 October 2010, 8 December 2011) and also gave numerous public conferences and press interviews.

Domestically, there were other *political actors* on the stage, including other political parties. Various *societal groups*, including representatives of business groups (lobbies), crown corporations, civil society groups and trade unions actively tried to influence their government's discourse, and therefore the interest, of their province. I sampled societal actors according to their relevance in representatives' discourse. Furthermore, Quebec's representatives also needed to react to the demands from their *negotiation partners*, i.e. the other provinces, the federal government and the EU. In the EU, the actors included the European Commission and the European Council as well as selected member states, mostly France, the United Kingdom and Germany.

Table 3 –   Conceptualisation of Actors at Aggregated Level and Corresponding Units of Analysis

Actors at Aggregated Level	Unit of Analysis
Representatives of Quebec	
	Provincial Government
	Chief Negotiator and diplomatic representatives
Political Actors in Quebec	
	Political Parties (PLQ, PQ, CAQ, ADQ, Québec Solidaire)
	Deputies in the National Assembly
Societal Groups in Quebec	
	Business Groups
	Crown Corporations
	Civil Society Groups
	Trade Unions
Negotiation Partners	
	Canadian Provinces
	Canadian Federal Government
	EU (including European Commission, European Council, member states)

2. Trade Policy Strategy as Discursive Data: Constructing the Corpus

Political discourse, by which I understand discourse produced either by political actors or directed at them, constitutes the empirical corpus.[18] Discourse refers to the conflictual process in which actors develop their interests, enunciate and legitimise their positions and thereby compete with others to impose a certain meaning of social reality.

To construct the corpus, I drew upon three sets of data. The *first data set* is constituted by parliamentary debates, which allow to trace the develop-

---

18 Discourses are thus *not* understood in the post-structuralist sense as truth regimes.

ment of discourse over a period of time. Parliamentary debates operate in-between policy communication and policy-making (Bara, Weale et al., 2007; Bicquelet, Weale et al., 2012; Sarcinelli, 1998). They are a forum where party political differences are most likely to be formulated directly, which makes them a relevant source for discourse analysis. Quebec's Llegislature, the National Assembly ("Assemblée nationale") is based on the Westminster model, which means that differences between parties are likely to be exacerbated. I sampled all plenary and committee debates between 2006 and 2014 that touched upon the topic of a trade agreement between Canada and the EU and relied on the Parliament's library indexation services to retrieve the relevant debates.[19]

The second data set is constituted by interviews with Quebec's representatives, political actors as well as societal groups in Quebec, negotiation partners and technical experts, conducted in Montreal, Quebec City, Ottawa, Brussels, and Paris between 2014 and 2016.[20]

Table 4 – Overview of Interviews Conducted

Interviews with Quebec representatives
- Deputy (PLQ), Quebec, 8.10.14
- Member of Quebec's government (PLQ), Montreal, 23.10.14
- Member of Quebec's government (PQ), Quebec, 1.10.14
- Member of Quebec's government (PLQ), Montreal, 20.10.14
- Diplomat, Montreal, 15.10.14
- Member of Quebec's government (PQ), Montreal, 24.04.15 (Skype)
- Diplomat, Brussels, 1.7.14
- Diplomat, Montreal, 9.10.14
- Interviews with Canadian representatives and representatives form other provinces
- Canadian (federal) diplomat, Brussels, 8.7.14.
- Member of Manitoba's government (NDP), Trier, 11.7.2017 (Phone)

---

19 Index topics: libre-échange; relations commerciales; commerce; Accord économique et commercial global entre le Canada et l'Union européenne.
20 See the following table for a complete list of interviews conducted.

Interviews with EU Civil Servants
- Official at European Commission, Directorate General for Trade, Brussels, 23.07.14
- Official at European Commission, Directorate General for Trade, Brussels, 14.07.14

Interviews with French representatives
- Diplomat, Montréal, 20.04.15
- Deputy in the National Assembly, Paris, 29.05.15
- Diplomat, Ottawa, 14.04.15
- Official, Ministère des Finances et des Comptes publics, de l'Economie, de l'Industrie et du Numérique Paris, 28.05.15
- Diplomat at the WTO, Trier, 23.1.15 (Phone)

Interviews with representatives of lobby groups
- Representative of the Union des producteurs agricoles, Longueuil, 14.10.2014
- Representative of the Union des producteurs agricoles, Dairy Producers, Longueuil, 17.10.14
- Representative of the Union des producteurs agricoles, Beef Producers, Longueuil, 15.10.14
- Representative of Coalition pour la diversité culturelle, Montreal, 24.10.14
- Representative of the Trade Justice Network, Montreal, 23.12.2015 (Skype)

Interviews with general experts
- International trade lawyer, Montreal, 16.04.15
- (Former) Quebec Diplomat to the US, Montreal, 15.9.14

Although interviews only mirror a snapshot of discourse at a certain moment in time, they allow us to understand how representatives developed provincial interests, which conflicts erupted out of diverging constructions and which alliances they tried to build. Interviews also supported research on partially classified information not necessarily displayed in parliamentary debates, such as the negotiation position of Quebec and its negotiation partners.

The sampling of interview partners[21] was a combination of purposive and snowball sampling (Tansey, 2009). First, I approached members of Quebec's Liberal and PQ governments respectively, also taking into account the relevance of non-responsiveness (Goldstein, 2002). Second, following the discourse of Quebec's representatives, I identified important actors behind the scenes in the state apparatus, diplomacy and business, civil society and trade union representatives. There were five key questions structuring the (semi-directed) interviews: (1) actors' role in the negotiation process, (2) reasons for their policy position, (3) negotiation process, (4) expected impact, (5) further documents and other informants.

Depending on the actor group of interview partners, I asked the following questions:

National Representatives

–   What was your role in the negotiation process?
–   What were the reasons for negotiating a new trade agreement between Canada and the European Union?
–   How did the negotiation process unfold? What were (actors) positions?
–   What will be the effects for (polity)?
–   Depending upon interviewee and time: How does CETA fit into (Quebec and NAFTA) and (Quebec and Canada)?
–   Can you refer me to another informant?

Lobby Groups

–   What is the role of (association) in general, what is its history?
–   What is the (association's) position on CETA?
–   How did you try to influence the negotiation process?
–   How do you prepare for the entering into effect of the agreement?
–   Can you refer me to another informant?

General Experts

Specific questions on the law of CETA and international commerce, and on the role of commerce in Quebec's province- or nation-building (phrased in accordance with actor's position on the question)

---

21 Given that trade negotiations were carried out behind closed doors, anonymity was crucial for most of the interviewees.

My *third data set* complements the first sets mostly to provide background information. It includes press releases, public speeches,[22] policy documents such as studies,[23] Summit Declarations,[24] the European negotiation mandate,[25] official statements,[26] and press releases from Quebec's government[27] and the Council of the Federation.

3. Looking for Patterns in Political Discourse: The Method of Analysis

I systematically coded for interests, frames and repertoires in the debates in the National Assembly. Whereas there is an abundant literature in political science on research design and sampling in qualitative research, the very few studies that employed systematic procedures of qualitative analysis (Baumgartner, De Boef et al., 2008) often remained at the level of reporting the coding scheme they developed.[28] Therefore, the methods developed by the social psychologists Miles and Huberman seemed more promising (Blatter, Janning et al., 2007; Miles and Huberman, 1994; Patton, 2002). They proceed in three steps: (a) systematic exploration and description, (b) systematic development of codes, and (c) description of patterns in the data. The organisation and analysis of empirical data was carried out by relying on the software NVivo, designed for in-depth analysis of qualitative data. Where appropriate, I will refer to the functions used in NVivo in footnotes (for a comprehensive overview of NVivo functionalities, see Bazeley and Jackson, 2013).

---

22 Refer for a complete list to the appendix.
23 European Commission, 2008, Assessing the Costs and Benefits of a Closer EU-Canada Economic Partnership; Canada, 2009, Joint Report on the EU-Canada Scoping Exercise.
24 Council of the EU, 2009, EU-Canada Summit Declaration. Prague`, 6 May 2009; EU, 2002, EU-Canada Summit Declaration. Joint Statement by the EU and Canada; EU, 2007, EU-Canada Summit Statement.
25 Council of the EU, 2009, Recommendation from the Commission to the Council in order to authorize the Commission to open negotiations for an Economic Integration Agreement with Canada.
26 Minister for International Trade Ed Fast, 2013, Letter to Ministre des Finances et de l'Économie Nicolas Marceau.
27 Available only on site at the Assemblée nationale's library services.
28 Contrary to statistical analysis, where the mode of correlating various variables is part and parcel of the method of analysis, political science has no clear expectation with regard to the establishment of patterns in the analysis of qualitative data.

a) Exploring and Describing

I first explored the empirical data by establishing systematic summaries[29] of parliamentary debates and interviews.[30] Carefully reading and summarising the empirical data was the first step in establishing a comparative overview of the data across the four cases (Angermüller and Schwab, 2014).

Table 5 – Template for Systematic Summary by Units of Analysis (Units A-Z)

	Public Procurement	**Foreign Direct Investment (FDI)**	**Agriculture**
Unit A	Summary Procurement A	Summary FDI A	Summary Agriculture A
...	...	...	...
Unit Z	Summary Procurement Z	Summary FDI Z	Summary Agriculture Z

b) Data Reduction Through Coding

These summaries guided the development of a coding scheme with the goal of data reduction and management. The coding of data involved the reduction of the data into small, structured and meaningful chunks carrying labels. A coding occurrence represented a chunk of data coded at a specific label. Assigning codes was based on semantic fields (hence codes refer to chunks of text grouped by meaning around the same topic).

---

29 The systematic summaries are variations of the Miles and Huberman "Prestructured Case" (1994).

30 In NVivo, summaries are generated as a framework matrix (Bazeley and Jackson, 2013).

I coded in two waves. The objective of the first coding wave was to organise data according to *cases* and *actors*. As coding units for the *cases*, I chose units of meaning with varying lengths. In total, I coded for the following cases (in order of number of coding occurrences):

i.   General CETA
ii. Agriculture
iii. Public Procurement
iv. Foreign Direct Investment
v.   Culture
vi. Trade Policy General
vii. Labour Mobility
viii.Intellectual Property

ix. Internal Trade – Canada
x.   Regulatory Cooperation
xi. Rules of Origin
xii. Tariffs
xiii.Alcohol
xiv. Transport
xv. Telecommunications
xvi. National Security

Then, each actor was assigned a code, a functional classification (elected office, diplomat) and political party (Parti Libéral du Québec, Parti Québécois, Coalition Avenir Québec, Action Démocratique du Québec, Québec Solidaire).[31]

During the second coding wave, I coded for topics, interests, frames and repertoires for each case respectively (i.e. for public procurement, foreign direct investment and agriculture).[32] I obtained these codes in an iterative way by going back and forth from data to theory (Fereday and Muir-Cochrane, 2006), so that my codes were firmly anchored in empirical data but also theoretically relevant. The codes apply *across* cases in order to allow for comparison between cross-case similarities and differences. As table 6 shows, I retained a large number of topics and interest codes, while the number of frames and repertoires was considerably lower. This was because topics and interests were descriptive, data-driven codes close to the text,[33] while codes for frames and repertoires conveyed a higher level of abstraction.

---

31 Refer to the appendix for a full list of actors coded for in parliamentary data.

32 I did not systematically code for agenda-setting: since the project was only in its infancy at that moment in time (2006-2009), the National Assembly was not used as a forum to display specific lines of argument. For the agenda-setting stage, I therefore relied to a large extent on interviews and press releases.

33 For example, when deputies talked about geographical indications, I coded this chunk of data as "Geographical Indications".

Table 6 – Coding Scheme

Topics, with sub-topics

- Geographical indications
- 'Gestion de l'offre' (Supply Management)
  - Cheese
- Quota (not Supply Management Products)
- Transport Routes
- Investment Protection & Conflict Resolution
- International Investment Agreement
- Natural Resources Exploitation
  - Water
- Negotiation Process
- Measures to Attract or Discourage FDI
- Rules of Origin
- American Recovery and Reinvestment Act (2009)
- Public Transportation
- Crown Corporations
  - Hydro-Québec
- Market Access
- Water & Waste Management
- Privatisation
- Internal Trade
- MASH sector
- Award Criteria and Process
- Tariffs
- Performance Requirements
- Culture

Interests
– Create Growth
– Honour Existing International Obligations
– Export
– Preserve Regulatory Capacity
– Increased Competition
– Award Contract to local Company
– Use Expertise
– Attract Capital
– Market Price and Price Transparency
– Contribute to CETA
– Fight Corruption and Collusion
– Reciprocity
– Protect Citizens
– Service Quality
– Social Economy
– Local Economic Development
– Establish Clear Rules
– National Treatment
– Preserve Public Monopolies
– Local Content
– Local Jobs
– Gain Votes

Frames
– Small Open Economy
– State Dirigisme
– Independence
– Integration

Repertoires
– Province-Building
– Federalism

c) Looking for Patterns

According to Miles and Huberman, "just naming or classifying what is out there [through coding] is usually not enough" (Miles and Huberman 1994, 69). In order to identify patterns across cases, I carried out a synchronic and a diachronic analysis. In the synchronic analysis, I observed the deployment of frames and repertoires at certain moments in time and focussed closely on discursive struggles. These moments were focal points when actors competed to impose their interpretation of reality, including potential effects on policy choices and power relations. In the diachronic analysis, I documented the evolution of repertoires and the way they were structured by frames throughout the negotiation process. I then compared these results to the discourses on NAFTA negotiation and other relevant international commitments taken by Canada, as reported in academic literature.[34]

Table 7 – Example of a Coding Matrix for Interests A-Z

	12.2006-05.2009	06.2009-09.2012	10.2012-04.2014	05.2014-12.2014	
Interest A	% coded "interest A"	% coded "interest A"	% coded "interest A"	% coded "interest A"	100%
Interest …	% coded "interest …"	% coded "interest …"	% coded "interest …"	% coded "interest …"	100%
Interest Z	% coded "interest Z"	% coded "interest Z"	% coded "interest Z"	% coded "interest Z"	100%

Conclusion

In this chapter, I constructed the discursive strategy through which actors developed their trade policy interests and build coalitions as my object of research. In this discursive process, actors defined, re-interpreted, re-defined and clarified their interests; declared, reconsidered and shifted their policy positions; and built coalitions around their projects. They deployed

---

34 The software NVivo calculated the relative percentages of text coded at different elements in terms of words. In order to see when different codes occurred, I ran coding queries for each case that allowed to observe the intersection of various codes, for example: negotiation stage and topic (or: interest, frame, repertoire), or actor and interest (or: topic, frame, or repertoire). The following table exemplifies a coding matrix for given interests A-Z at different negotiation stages. Coding matrices are included in the appendix and referred to in the empirical chapters where appropriate.

frames that underpinned their discursive action. These frames conferred meaning on the environment in which they acted and interacted, and structured the repertoires which embedded political action. Most existing theories in the literature focus on the results, rather than the processes, of trade negotiations, and underestimate the forms of mobilisation ideas, narratives and themes are subject to. Hence, they fall short in explaining the discursive process through which actors develop their interests, redefine them and represent them.

I argued that attributing interests as a function of an actor's or an economy's location in the domestic or international economy provides an incomplete account of contemporary trade negotiations. This is the case mainly because the effects of reducing non-tariff barriers, a focus of contemporary trade agreements, are much more diffuse, but also, from a theoretical perspective, because the choices actors made throughout the negotiation process when pursuing certain interests but not others ought to be included in the analysis of trade policy.

In order to empirically investigate actors' discursive strategy, I developed a method of qualitative analysis relying on systematic coding of parliamentary debates in plenary and committee sessions. I complemented these sources by interviews with key actors, press releases, government reports and studies, public speeches and official statements. This systematic coding process allowed me to highlight change and continuity in political discourse and to associate certain discursive patterns with groups of actors or time periods.

Chapter 2: Setting the Agenda—a Discursive Strategy to Launch CETA

The Comprehensive and Economic Trade Agreement CETA was by no means the first attempt to conduct comprehensive economic negotiations between Canada and the EU, nor is it to be understood as the result of steadily progressing integration between the two economies. In fact, since the 1990s, several attempts to reach a comprehensive economic agreement failed. Thus, enhancing economic relations between Canada and the EU is not a new idea. Especially in multinational business circles since the 1990s, expectations regarding a comprehensive agreement between the recently founded EU[35] and Canada were high. To business leaders' disappointment, however, several attempts did not produce the outcome they had hoped for. Just before the CETA negotiations were brought to political agendas on both sides of the Atlantic in 2007, negotiations towards a new Trade and Investment Enhancement Agreement (TIEA) were broken off in 2006. At this moment, the project to cement and foster economic relations between Canada and the EU through an economic agreement seemed buried.

Unexpectedly, however, the project of enhanced economic transatlantic cooperation re-emerged on Canadian and European trade policy agendas in 2007—only one year after the failure of the TIEA. Already in May 2009, Canada and the EU officially launched negotiations towards a Comprehensive Economic Partnership Agreement—the previous denomination for CETA—at their bilateral summit in Prague.

This swift and rapid appearance of a new economic agreement on the political agenda raises a number of questions: Why did Canada and the EU settle on these new negotiations despite the recently failed attempts to do so—and who or what made them think that these negotiations were to succeed? Who were the actors driving this process, and why were they doing so?

Quebec played a key role in promoting the project of a new transatlantic economic agreement. Although the provinces do not have jurisdiction over international trade—a prerogative which resides solely with the fe-

---

35 References to the EU also include the (former) European communities.

deral order of government—Quebec promoted the agreement in multiple venues. Under the aegis of the *Parti Libéral du Québec* (PLQ), Quebec's government and diplomats wanted to revive the old idea of an economic agreement between Canada and the EU. Quickly, they acquired domestic political support from the main opposition party, the *Parti Québécois* (PQ). For readers well acquainted with Quebec economic and political history, this cross-party support is not puzzling. In fact, both the Liberals and the PQ campaigned for trade liberalisation in the 1980s, making Quebec one of the strongest supporters of the North American Free Trade Agreement (NAFTA, 1994) among Canadian provinces. They did so to foster their respective province-building projects using free trade with the US and Mexico. In this way, the US became by far the most important trading partner for Quebec.

Despite the positive role free trade played in Quebec's recent province-building process across party lines, its action for launching a new agreement with the EU raises a number of questions. Why did Quebec's government suddenly develop such a strong interest in pushing a new economic agreement between Canada and the EU, committing considerable political and administrative resources to this new project? After all, the US was by far their most important trading partner. How did Quebec, a Canadian province, manage to bring a new economic agreement to the Canadian federal and provincial, and European political agendas?

In this chapter, I argue that the answers to these questions are intertwined. On the one hand, Quebec re-evaluated the province's economic interests and supported a higher degree of diversification in trade relations. At the same time, the government also discovered an opportunity for extending provincial paradiplomatic activity to the realm of international economic negotiations, as I will show in section 1, the first stage of the agenda-setting process—understood as the moment when decision-makers became convinced of its benefit. On the other hand, as I will document in section 2, Quebec's representatives, once convinced of the benefit of a new economic agreement, still needed to win over key decision-makers in Canada and the EU. To that effect, they fashioned coalitions with key European and Canadian actors.

Section 1: 'Un nouvel espace économique': Constructing an Interest to Launch a New Economic Agreement between Canada and the EU

1. Failing to Reach a Comprehensive Economic Agreement

Strong economic and political ties between Canada and the Canadian provinces, on the one hand, and the EU and the European member states, on the other hand have existed for a long time and were cemented in a number of both political and economic agreements at various levels of government and with varying scope. Canada and the EU signed the Framework Agreement for Commercial and Economic Cooperation in 1976—the first agreement on economic cooperation including the EU—followed by the Declaration on Transatlantic Relations in 1990. In parallel, Canadian provinces as well as European member states and their sub-federal states pursued bilateral relations in accordance with their constitutional competencies. Against this backdrop, Canada and the EU seemed natural partners for closer economic ties when inter-connectedness between the world's leading economies progressed in the mid-1980s and especially since the foundation of the World Trade Organization (WTO), of which both economies were founding members.

In the 1990s, the project to further economic relations between Canada and the EU was inscribed in the context of global developments and North American economic integration. Although regionalism was not Canada's favourite option, gridlock at the multilateral level finally made Canada embrace North American continental integration through the Canada-US Free Trade Agreement (CUSFTA, 1989) and its successor, the North American Free Trade Agreement (NAFTA, 1994) (Cameron and Tomlin, 2000; 2003; Keating, 1999; Morici, 1985, 1997). In the early 1990s, Canada felt that continuous European integration and substantive advancements in the multilateral arena had set the stage for an economic agreement between the NAFTA countries and the EU. The US and the EU indeed began reflecting on economic negotiations. As both were engaged in continental integration processes, they hoped economic agreements would counter possible transatlantic estrangement resulting thereof. The Canadian government, led by Trade Minister Roy Maclaren, quickly joined in these reflections, both because of fear to be left out and because these plans mirrored Canada's long-standing plan to conclude a Transatlantic Free Trade Agreement (TAFTA) between the NAFTA members, and the EU and its member states (Donges, Freytag et al., 1997; Frost, 1997). Though strongly committed to free trade in North America (Finlayson and Bertasi, 1992;

Hart, 2004, 2010), Canada also pursued its historical vision of transatlantic economic integration through a "euro-American construct" (Stairs, 1999, p. 229).

However, both the US and the EU lacked the commitment to pursue these talks. In fact, the US favoured multilateral and plurilateral agreements within the WTO and OECD (Organisation for Economic Co-operation and Development) frameworks. In the EU, France's opposition to TAFTA outdid German and British support. At the supranational level, the European Trade Commissioner Sir Leon Brittan advocated bilateral negotiations with the US, excluding Canada and Mexico. Canada thus found itself in an impasse. Since the TAFTA avenue was not available, Canada engaged in the less ambitious bilateral road with the EU. Again, Germany became an ally among European member states. In 1996, Canada and the EU made a *Joint Political Declaration* and presented an *Action Plan*, mirroring developments in bilateral EU-US relations. This Action Plan suggested stronger cooperation on a number of issues, including product certification and regulatory standards, competition policy, government procurement, financial services, intellectual property rights, veterinary, sanitary and phyto-sanitary co-operation, and energy. Subsequently, Canada and the EU concluded a number of sectoral agreements. However, they did not reach a cross-sectoral economic agreement similar to NAFTA (Potter, 1999, p. 209-218; Stairs, 1999).

In Canada and the EU, business leaders of multinational companies very much supported closer economic cooperation between the two economies in order to ease trade and investment relations (Cameron and Loukine, 2001; Hübner, 2011; Woolcock, 2011). After the conclusion of the multilateral Uruguay Round of the GATT (1986-1993), regional economic integration between Canada and the EU resembling that in North America seemed a promising avenue to them. Dissatisfied with the current state of things, yet not discouraged by recent throwbacks during the mid-1990s, multinational business leaders continued to support bilateral economic and trade relations between Canada and the EU. In 1998, under the influence of business lobbies, Canada and the EU launched the Euro-Canadian Trade Initiative (ECTI), by which they hoped to give form to their commitments in the Action Plan mentioned above. However, the ECTI did not produce the effects business circles had hoped for. The publication of a legally non-binding Canada-EU Partnership Agenda (2004), two bilateral sectoral agreements[36] as well as the failure of an agreement on investment were its meagre results. In this regard, Stairs pointed out that one reason for this lack of success was that Canada and the EU committed to these negotiations as a reaction to EU-US relations, not genuinely bilateral EU-Canada interests (1999). Under the aegis of Trade Commissioner Pascal Lamy, the EU committed to an informal moratorium on bilateral trade agreements, in 1999, in order to pursue the multilateral avenue. The aim of this moratorium was to allow the multilateral Millennium Round of the WTO to be concluded successfully (Meunier, 2007).

Subsequent to gridlocked negotiations between the two economies, the leaders of multinational companies decided to re-organise the representation of their interests. In 1999, they founded the Canada Europe Round Table for Business (CERT) to channel their interests (Canada Europe Round Table for Business, 1999a). This umbrella organisation was launched in Brussels in the presence of Canadian Minister for International Trade Sergio Marchi, the European Commissioner for Trade Leon Britton and the Canadian Ambassador to the EU Jean-Pierre Juneau (Canada Europe Round Table for Business, 1999b). CERT pursued a vigorously liberal agenda. According to the CERT, "it is important to convince all people that liberalised trade and investment improves the prosperity and quality of life for all people" (Canada Europe Round Table for Business, 1999b). The CERT was initially chaired by Paul de Keersmaeker, a Belgian politician and business man. In 2000, former Canadian Trade Minister Roy Maclaren, then High Commissioner for Canada in the United Kingdom, became its Co-chair (Canada Europe Round Table for Business, 2000). A first issue constantly addressed by multinational business leaders were non-tariff barriers hampering foreign direct investment (FDI). According to the CERT, existing regulations significantly impeded the establishment of foreign direct investments in the host economy, for example in the energy sector (Canada Europe Round Table for Business, 2004). They pressed for increased establishment rights for investors and advocated reciprocal access to public procurement markets (Canada Europe Round Table for Business, 1999c). CERT leaders also addressed issues related to the absence of common regulatory norms and standards. They contended that different production norms and standards hindered trade between the two economies.

---

36 Agreement on trade in wines and spirit drinks (September 2003), Agreement in the form of an Exchange of Letters pursuant to Article XXVIII of GATT 1994 for the modification of concessions with respect to cereals provided for in EC Schedule CXL annexed to the GATT 1994 (March 2003).

Furthermore, they highlighted losses engendered by remaining tariff barriers in certain sectors such as spirits, newsprint, and aluminium ingots. From the beginning, Canadian policy makers were receptive to arguments developed by the CERT. In fact, the Canadian federal government hoped to mobilise business representatives in order to convince the EU to relaunch trade negotiations.

In addition to growing support by business communities, recent developments on the global level set the scene for Canada and the EU to re-enter bilateral talks. Foreign direct investment (FDI) was becoming a pressing issue, and both the EU and Canada were dissatisfied with the failure of multilateral talks on FDI, which they attributed to the US pursuing a plurilateral OECD-avenue (Smythe, 2011).[37] At their summit in Brussels in 2002, Canada and the EU therefore launched negotiations on a new Trade and Investment Enhancement Agreement (TIEA). This agreement's aim was to "design a new type of forward-looking, wide-ranging bilateral trade and investment enhancement agreement covering, inter alia, new generation issues and outstanding barriers" (EU and Canada, 2002). Yet, faltering from the beginning, the project was suspended in 2006 after some years of negotiations. Retrospectively, diplomats asserted that the TIEA's restricted scope did not allow for cross-sectoral bargains, contributing to the negotiations' failure.[38] Others highlighted that the European Commission sought reciprocity in market access provisions which the Canadian federal government was unable to commit to because of the distribution of competencies among levels of government (Woolcock, 2011, p. 27). Finally, in the mid-2000s, the EU's priority had shifted to the successful conclusion of the multilateral Doha Development Round.

2. Reviving the Project of an Economic Partnership: A New Space for Economic Development

Despite this history of failure, the idea to launch negotiations on a comprehensive economic agreement between Canada and the EU resurfaced again in Quebec in the mid-2000s. Why did a Canadian province, without jurisdiction over international trade, develop an interest in committing resour-

---

37 The relation between trade and investment and the failure to regulate investment thoroughly at the WTO will be described in more detail in the chapter on foreign direct investment.

38 Interview with Canadian diplomat, Brussels, 8 July 2014.

ces to convincing Canadian and European authorities to embark on this project? In this process of mobilisation, the interests of business groups played a key role, although they cannot account alone for Quebec's entrepreneurship.

Transatlantic business actors and Quebec's existing paradiplomatic network were indeed decisive in bringing an economic agreement to the attention of Quebec's provincial government.[39] However, the process through which the interests of business groups were channelled to Quebec's government exemplified, albeit counterintuitively, that business leaders did not have a direct effect upon the agenda of political leaders. In fact, their previous attempts to do so had been ineffective, as showed previously.

Capitalising on existing ties established by Quebec, the diplomats of the Quebec Delegation in Brussels were open to the suggestions advanced by business leaders operating in the EU and Canada. In mid-2006, Quebec's General Delegate in Brussels, Christos Sirros, realised during a meeting organised by the Canadian ambassador in Brussels that the CERT still supported a bilateral agreement between Canada and the EU, despite several failed attempts.[40] According to diplomats' analysis, multinational business leaders had lobbied for their demands in the wrong venue by addressing the Canadian federal governments and not the provinces. However, a growing number of areas targeted by international trade agreements fall under provincial jurisdiction. Insofar as the Canadian federal government cannot force the provinces to implement international provisions falling under their jurisdiction, bilateral negotiations between Canada and the EU had become gridlocked when substantive provisions falling under provincial jurisdiction became increasingly important. A diplomat in Brussels therefore suggested that business leaders approach *provincial* instead of the *federal* government:

> Alors moi je dis à un moment donné qu'il me semble que vous [les entreprises] cognez à la mauvaise porte. Vous vous plaignez du fait que le Canada ne peut pas négocier avec l'Europe, et c'est vrai, mais pourquoi

---

39 Quebec has a large network of international representations supporting ist paradiplomatic activities; in 1972, Quebec founded a delegation in Brussels which promoted the province's interests in Belgium, the Netherlands, and Luxembourg, as well as to the EU.

40 Interview with Quebec diplomat, Montreal, 9 October 2014.

accepter ça comme ça? Pourquoi ne pas aller approcher les provinces [...]?[41]

Through the paradiplomatic networks of the Quebec Delegation in Brussels, diplomats transmitted their demands to Quebec. Quebec's government then became the main advocate for re-launching bilateral negotiations:

> Le premier ministre du Québec, rapidement, achète l'idée. Il devient un peu le porte-parole de l'idée.[42]

Still, the question remains why Quebec supported a new transatlantic agreement so strongly.In the following, I will argue that its historic support for free trade combined with a strong belief of the Liberal government that Quebec can channel its interests best through membership in the Canadian federation, was at the root of a new discursive strategy.

3. A Discursive Strategy for Province-Building and Strengthening the Federation

During the 1980s, both the PQ and the PLQ came to strongly support North American economic integration. However, each political party did so for partially different reasons (Campbell, 1995; Robinson, 1995). For the PQ—whose members promoted NAFTA earlier than the Liberals—economic development, a certain degree of independence from the Canadian market, the promotion of francophone control and ownership in the economic realm and the emergence of a corporate elite close to the state underpinned the party's independence project (Keating, 1997; Paquin, 2001). This position lead some Canadian nationalists to argue that North American economic integration could actually threaten Canadian national unity (Schwartz, 1998). In fact, the PQ advocated redirecting Quebec's economy to prepare for political independence and isolate Quebec from economic retaliation by Canada (Bélanger, Brunelle et al., 1999; Brunelle and Deblock, 1997; Jockel and David, 1997). In this way, the PQ's conception of Quebec as a small and open economy became instrumental to its pursuit of Quebec independence; in this way, two frames interacted and engendered a specific course of action. In the mid-1980s, the go-

---

41 Interview with Quebec diplomat, Montreal, 9 October 2014.
42 Interview with Quebec diplomat, Montreal, 9 October 2014.

verning PQ, led by René Lévesque, therefore considerably altered its discourse and encouraged free trade with the US, Quebec's Southern neighbour, even though Lévesque in particular had opposed high degrees of economic integration before. This shift made the PQ endorse free trade before the Liberals did (Paquin, 2016, p. 156). In fact, at that time, when Robert Bourassa led the Liberal opposition in Quebec, the Liberals were less convinced than the PQ to fully embrace free trade (Rocher, 2003, p. 467). When the Quebec Liberals finally endorsed free trade, they did so because they were convinced that economic interdependence would make the question of political independence irrelevant. In a situation where Quebec was too small to sustain its economic development without international commercial exchange, the Quebec Liberals opted for economic openness to support economic development while remaining part of the Canadian federation. In this way, the Liberals' conception of Quebec as a small and open economy interacted with its representation of Quebec's interest to promote further provincial integration into the Canadian federation. At the beginning of the 1990s, a strong pro-trade consensus united both political parties in the name of economic development, even though they held very different motivations. In this process, the US became Quebec's most important trade partner (Kresl, 1997). Hence, Quebec's choice for free trade was driven by its province-building project rather than mere liberal ideology.

Building the provincial state was a second pillar of province-building to which the 1980s and 1990s free trade agendas contributed, which seems counterintuitive if one considers the link between free trade and reduced state activity in the economic realm. At the Canadian federal level, free trade was associated with rationales of economic competitiveness and a drastic reduction of state intervention. However, unlike at the federal level of government, Quebec's free trade agenda was not entirely rooted in a rationale of reducing state activity in the market and social relations. To the contrary, Quebec's leaders across party lines at that time conceived of the trade agenda as a way to promote domestic francophone business, which was considered a key actor in provincial economic development. In a situation where the federal state retreated from the organisation of economic and social policy developments, Quebec's political elite seized the opportunity to require autonomy over state levers of economic development, including public procurement and social policies, so that "the social and economic situation of the Québécois will not only be administered but fashioned by the Quebec state" (Jenson, 1995, p. 107). Furthermore, the institutions of Canadian federalism mediated the effects of free trade on Quebec to a large extent, because the provinces were not subjected to all provisions of international trade agreements (Keating, 1997, p. 706). In this way, free trade became instrumental to the practices of state dirigisme, supporting the provincial state in its efforts to steer the direction of the province's economic development. By promoting free trade, the province could direct economic development and secure economic opportunities for its companies without relying on federal policies. In this process, the provincial state claimed the right to oversee the structural effects of free trade. Quebec and other provinces sought to fill policy spaces left by the federal government when it retreated as a consequence of neo-liberal ideologies in the 1980s (Jenson, 1991). Through the control of policies such as education, unemployment insurance, and public procurement, and of large companies, it actively supported the francophone entrepreneurs of "Québec Inc.", a group of successful Quebec-based companies that contributed to provincial economic development and were part of a well-integrated "state-private sector business class" (Keating, 1997, p. 706). They were considered national economic champions (Bélanger, 1994; Keating, 2003; Smith, 1994) and in turn supported free trade and engaged in international activities (Martin, 1995a). Apart from extending the role of provincial states in shaping provincial economic and social policies, Canada's adherence to international trade agreements had an additional effect on provincial autonomy. Control mechanisms built into multilateral agreements, but even more so into NAFTA, considerably reduced the potential for unexpected policy actions, policy actions against the provincial interests or even economic sanctions by Canada in the event of Quebec independence. In fact, building a body of supranational rules and enforcement mechanisms could contribute to absorb such federal policy decisions—the Trudeau federal Liberals' economic policy in the 1970s bearing negative effects on Quebec was well-remembered. In this way, Quebec became less exposed to policy shifts promoted by the federal government as a consequence of NAFTA prohibiting certain protectionist practices.

Thus, during the 1980s, Quebec's representatives of the two main political parties did not only support a free trade agreement with the US because the provincial economy depended so much on the US. They did so because free trade contributed to two pillars of province-building: developing the provincial economy and building the provincial state. This convergence allowed for a cross-party coalition despite varying conceptions of province-building. Both parties strongly encouraged embedding Quebec's economy in global economic networks: instead of fostering an East-West axis corresponding to Canada's internal market, they wanted to make the North-

South axis more important for the province. By doing so, they considerably altered the space in which they envisaged economic development: from an East-West configuration (the Canadian market), they shifted towards a North-South configuration (with the US and later Mexico) (Balthazar, 1988; Bernier, 1988; Latouche, 1988, 1995, 2011; Martin, 1995a, b; Rocher, 2003) in order to expand the Quebec state's scope and competences in the economic realm and manage the insertion of the national economy into the global economic order. This was an important pillar of province-building because it promoted functional independence from the federal government (Gagnon and Montcalm, 1992; Keating, 1997, p. 705-708).

In sum, the PQ and the PLQ both supported free trade with their North American partners. Yet, the frames underpinning their respective decisions were different. Both parties oriented their practices according to the small open economy frame with regard to province-building, yet they differed with regard to the evolution of the Canadian federation they promoted: while the Liberals used free trade as a means to strengthen Quebec's role in the federation, the PQ saw free trade as an instrument to prepare independence. Hence, they promoted free trade as a consequence of divergent, and to some extent even opposed, interests. However, they coalesced around the free trade project because it served their common province-building objective. Therefore, both parties entered a political bargain without knowing which structure of the repertoire of federalism would eventually prevail—Quebec as a stronger member of the Canadian federal setting, embedded in global economic networks, or an independent Quebec state. The repertoire of province-building allowed for an ad hoc coalition between the two parties, yet their divergent conceptions of federalism had this coalition stand on hazardous grounds for future global economic integration processes.[43]

In Quebec, CETA's agenda-setting process took place against the backdrop of these discourses, structured mainly through the repertoires of province-building and federalism. Hence, when Quebec's Liberal government advanced its project of new economic agreement between Canada and the EU in late 2006 and early 2007, it did so because its members were convinced that a new trade agreement would contribute to the Liberals' province-building and federalism projects. They came to this conclusion on the basis of the interaction between the repertoire of federalism, structured by

---

43 For instance, the PQ did not support Canada's investment agenda in the 1990s on the grounds that it jeopardised the role of the state in the economy, see also chapter 4 on foreign direct investment.

the integration frame, and the repertoire of province-building, structured by the small open economy frame. Against this backdrop, the Quebec Liberals' support for furthering global economic integration through a new economic agreement between Canada and the EU was not puzzling per se. Creating new export opportunities, and attracting investment and qualified labour to Quebec were essential in a situation where the province's economy had been oriented to a very large extent towards the US, making its economy vulnerable to economic developments South of its border.[44]

In promoting a new transatlantic agreement, the Quebec Liberals updated their conception of the space in which they embedded Quebec's province-building project. In this altered discourse, the US lost in importance, while the EU acquired a new relevance as an economic space. Why did Quebec's government decide to re-orient economic relations from North America to Europe?

In his speech opening the National Assembly's session on 10 March 2009, Premier Charest presented provincial economic development as the most important issue for his government.[45] Noticing an increasingly strong economic recession in the US since 2007, the appreciation of the Canadian dollar vis-à-vis the US dollar as well as mounting competition by emerging economies on global markets, the Quebec's liberal government re-evaluated Quebec's relation to the US and updated its discourse. Reiterating its conviction that Quebec is a small and open economy, its new strategy was designed to diversify export opportunities, thereby contributing to province-building, as Charest explained in an article published by the Quebec daily *La Presse* (Charest, 2008):

> Le marché américain devient de plus en plus difficile alors nous allons exporter davantage de produits Québécois vers l'Europe et les autres provinces canadiennes. Nous allons y arriver avec le lancement de négociations visant un accord transatlantique entre le Canada et l'Union européenne et avec la négociation d'un nouvel accord sur le commerce avec l'Ontario.

Even though trade has been part and parcel of Quebec's province-building strategy since the mid-1980s, the current government needed to explain its

---

44 Jean Charest (PLQ), Assemblée nationale du Québec, 10 March 2009.
45 In this speech, Jean Charest asserted that: "L'enjeu central de ce mandat, c'est l'économie. Tout mon gouvernement, chaque ministre, chaque député, chaque ministère, chaque société d'État est mobilisée pour aider nos travailleurs et nos entreprises à traverser cette crise sans précédent.".

shift away from the US and towards Europe as a new space for provincial economic development. It did so through a discursive strategy in which it reorganised the space in which economic development was situated, advertised as a "nouvel espace économique". Through this strategy, they discursively constructed the need to reform Quebec's economic development policy while preserving a strong outward orientation. To construct the need for reform, the government continued thus to draw upon the frame of Quebec as a small and open economy. In a speech about a new provincial budget, Minister Jérôme-Forget highlighted that protectionism was not an option in her government's eyes. Rather, Quebec needed to capitalise on its positive position in the global economy:[46]

> Le monde est devenu un village global. Certains y voient une menace. Nous, au contraire, nous croyons que nous devons saisir les occasions extraordinaires qui se présentent aux Québécois. Nous avons démontré notre capacité d'être des leaders mondiaux [...].

The liberal government's discursive strategy was to be sustained by five agreements: a labour mobility agreement with France, an agreement between Quebec and Ontario, an economic partnership agreement between Canada and the EU, several amendments to the Canadian intergovernmental Agreement on Internal Trade (AIT, 1995), and the recognition of professional qualifications acquired outside of Quebec, as the government underscored on many occasions. This discursive strategy encompassed thus agreements on different scales: an agreement between a province and a European member state, several inter-provincial agreements and a transatlantic agreement between two federations. That they served a common goal, namely fostering the Quebec Liberals' vision of province-building and Canadian federalism, highlighted the spatial multiplicity and flexibility in which Quebec operated. Premier Charest mentioned these agreements in a speech to the Assembly's Committee on Institutional Affairs on 16th April 2008,[47] and summarised how he wanted to implement this project of a new economic space as follows in 2009:[48]

> Cet espace, nous le créerons avec l'entente France-Québec sur la mobilité des travailleurs. Cet espace, nous le déploierons dans un accord entre le Canada et l'Union européenne. Cet espace, nous le développe-

---

46 Monique Jérôme-Forget (PLQ), Assemblée nationale du Québec, 13 March 2008.
47 Jean Charest, Assemblée nationale du Québec, Commission des institutions, 16 April 2008.
48 Jean Charest, Assemblée nationale du Québec, 10 March 2009.

rons par de nouvelles alliances au sein de la fédération canadienne. Et, ce nouvel espace, nous l'occuperons en nous donnant un plan pour développer le Nord québécois.

When the economic recession fully hit the US in 2008, Quebec's representatives updated their discourse once again and highlighted the US recession as a threat to economic development. As Premier Charest pointed out in his opening speech to the National Assembly in 2009, Quebec as a small and open economy was directly exposed to the negative effects of the US economic recession, hence threatening its province-building project in which the US occupied a key role:[49]

> Je me présente à vous et à tous les Québécois à la tête d'un nouveau gouvernement ayant obtenu le mandat de traverser une tempête économique qui secoue le monde entier, y incluant le Québec. […] Depuis trois mois, l'économie américaine a perdu plus de 2 millions d'emplois. Pendant la même période, le Canada a perdu 200 000 emplois. Il y a dans ces chiffres un lien de cause à effet puisqu'au Canada un emploi sur trois dépend directement de l'économie américaine.

This new argument—that Quebec needed to diversify its export partners—also conferred meaning on the American Recovery and Reinvestment Act (ARRA, 2009), a stimulus package designed as the political response to the recession in the US. In this stimulus package, provisions required that infrastructure projects funded through this package utilise mainly iron, steel and other goods manufactured in the US, a measure deemed protectionist by Canada. For example, the Canadian Manufacturers and Exporters lobbied strongly against the ARRA (Nossal, Roussel et al., 2015, p. 151). Similarly, Quebec's deputies highlighted in the National Assembly the negative effects of this legislative package on their economy, thereby uncovering the high exposure of Quebec to economic and political developments in the US, making it necessary to diversify export destinations.[50]

Why did the Liberals consider the EU a key economic partner? So far, even though trade and investment relations with the EU and its member states were strong, the structuring role North America took in Quebec's province-building repertoire absorbed competing frames, such as the importance of Europe as an economic partner for Quebec. The declining role

---

49 Jean Charest, Assemblée nationale du Québec, 10 March 2009.
50 Jean D'Amour (PLQ), Clément Gignac (PLQ), Assemblée nationale du Québec, Commission de l'économie et du travail, 6 May 2010.

of the US in Quebec's province-building repertoire allowed the EU to take a more prominent position. By giving Europe a more prominent economic meaning, the Liberal government conferred sense on their growing interest to foster economic relations between Canada and the EU. According to the government, Quebec already entertained strong ties with several European member states and sub-federal entities. Also, the project to enhance trade and investment relations had been on the table for quite a while. At the same time, the EU was Quebec's second most important trading partner and gaining in importance (Québec, 2007). Furthermore, the existence of strong multinational business interests also played a key role in investing Europe with an economic meaning in the PLQ's new discourse. Multinational business leaders had already highlighted in which areas a trade agreement could generate welfare gains. The existence of these interests, paired with the prominent role Quebec's Liberal governments have accorded to multinational business in province-building, suited Quebec's needs in shifting the space of provincial economic development. In the Quebec Liberals' visions, large business has been the backbone of provincial development. Business leaders have traditionally been a key support base : for instance, the Liberal Premier Bourassa reflected the party's social basis by appointing three cabinet members who held senior corporate positions before (McRoberts, 1993, p. 392).

In this discursive process, the European space acquired a new meaning: from a space of cultural and historical significance, it was transformed into a space for economic development. Until then, Europe was invested mostly with a cultural meaning (Keating, 1997, p. 708), despite the existence of strong commercial links, as can be seen in Quebec's international activities. For example, Quebec engaged with France and Belgium regions through the Francophonie, an international organisation which focusses on cultural and creative industries as well as media and telecommunication.[51] Looking at Quebec's international agreements, for example with France, a focus on culture and education stands out as well: as of 2006, Quebec and France had concluded 46 agreements, 7 of them were in the field of education, and 11 in the field of culture, 9 in the field of health and social security, 3 on finance and fiscal relations, 3 on environment, but only 3 in the field of economic development (Québec, 2016).

Through this strategy, Quebec's government gave meaning to its interest to launch negotiations on a new economic agreement between Canada

---

51 In fact, out of four Francophonie agencies, two operate in the academic realm, one in the media and one on the municipal level.

and the EU. Preoccupied by Quebec's small size, the provincial government promoted the position that commercial exchange was essential to provide the provincial economy with the necessary resources to spur economic development.

Casting a new trade agreement with the EU against the backdrop of economic development paved the way for support by the PQ. In their discursive strategy, members of the government capitalised on the history of cross-party support for free trade in the 1980s. According to the Liberals, both the federal government and the PQ would support them in their endeavour to enhance economic relations with the EU and its member states, as a senior member of Quebec's Liberal government reported on their strategy to acquire support:[52]

> La réalité qui sous-tend cette vision-là, c'est qu'il y a une reconnaissance que nous sommes que trente-cinq millions d'habitants. Que notre marché intérieur est modeste. Et que notre niveau de vie est élevé. Et qu'à défaut d'avoir accès à des marchés il est impossible pour les Canadiens de maintenir le niveau de vie que nous avons. Donc, il y a une réalité qui s'impose, qui transcende les philosophies de partis et les paliers de gouvernement, qui fait en sorte que l'adhésion devient une chose qui – sans être automatique – est assez spontanée.

For the PLQ—and in this they differ strongly from the PQ's position—economic development did not only take place through international activity, but also through inter-provincial trade and investment relations. Fragmented along provincial borders, a heterogeneous inner-Canadian market represented an obstacle to Quebec economic development and to trade with the EU (Whalley, 1983, 2009). In fact, the same issues that had to be addressed by a new trade agreement between Canada and the EU also obstructed trade relations among provinces, mainly concerning labour mobility, investment relations and public procurement (Finbow, 2013; Hinarejos, 2012). Against the backdrop of the integration frame structuring the Liberals' representation of Canadian federalism, the Quebec Liberals actively promoted their vision of Canadian federalism as an intergovernmental forum, and of Canadian market integration as inter-provincial cooperation during the CETA agenda-setting stage. For them, both processes were mutually beneficial. In this way, the Liberals' representation of economic development, a pillar of province-building, and of Canadian

---

52 Interview with member of Quebec's Liberal government, Montreal, 23 October 2014.

market integration boosted each other. Accordingly, Premier Charest also promoted Canadian internal market integration in his opening speech in the National Assembly in 2009:[53]

> Ce nouvel espace économique, c'est aussi une mise en valeur de notre appartenance à la fédération canadienne.

In this way, the Liberals also underlined that Quebec's economic development would best be served as a member of the Canadian federation. As a diplomat from Quebec asserted, political independence was less important than economic relations for them:[54]

> L'Etat-nation, donc une nation, un Etat, c'était bon en 1800, mais aujourd'hui, tu parles de quelle indépendance de toute façon?

Quebec addressed these issues first with the government of Ontario, the largest Canadian province. Convincing Ontario was a crucial step, since the two central provinces had considerable weight in the federation. On 2 June 2008, the governments of Quebec and Ontario held their first Joint Cabinet Meeting. In this meeting, economic integration was one of the key topics. Both governments hoped to strengthen economic exchanges in Central Canada, and by tackling similar issues to those of CETA showed that transatlantic economic integration was not so different from internal Canadian economic integration. In addition, the Charest Liberals promoted internal market integration through the Council of the Federation (Council of the Federation, 2004b). More specifically, the Quebec Presidency of the Council in July 2008 made inter-provincial labour mobility a priority.[55]

Similar to the Quebec Liberals' conviction that global economic interdependence made Quebec's political independence an obsolete question, they encouraged altering the institutions of Canadian federalism to create sufficient opportunities, for Quebec, to pursue its provincial development goals as a Canadian province within Canada and internationally. In this way, current processes of global economic integration provided the Liberals with the opportunity to make new claims, including representation in Canada's trade negotiations (see for this argument also Jenson, 1995). The Quebec Liberals, led at that time by Jean Charest, hoped to introduce this

---

53 Jean Charest, Assemblée nationale du Québec, 10 March 2009.
54 Interview with Quebec diplomat, Montreal, 9 October 2014.
55 Jean Charest (PLQ), Assemblée nationale du Québec, Commission des institutions, 16 April 2008.

new mode of intergovernmental conflict resolution in Canada's policy-making through founding a new intergovernmental institution: The Council of the Federation.

In 2003, shortly after Liberals had won the provincial elections, provincial and territorial Premiers founded the Council of the Federation, an institution which allowed them to meet twice a year in a formal context (Brown, 2003). This Council promoted a particular vision of the Canadian federation as being composed of provinces and territories with different interests and histories, whose positions on political issues might differ from the federal government's. Before the institutionalisation of the Council, there was no formal forum where the provinces could meet and deliberate. The Council mirrored the view that the Canadian federation was a mode of cooperation and conflict resolution among equal provinces and territories in their respective domains of competency. Premiers affirmed that "it is important for provinces and territories to play a leadership role in revitalizing the Canadian federation and building a more constructive and cooperative federal system" and that they wan to "[p]romote interprovincial-territorial cooperation and closer ties between members of the Council, to ultimately strengthen Canada (Council of the Federation, 2004c). Unlike a "top-down" view of federalism where provincial action depended upon federal spending—the vision of federal level during Canada's Fordist years of economic policy-making—this more dynamic approach asserted that the growing complexity of government tasks required cooperation between different orders of government.

The PQ did not support this institution; its stance mirrored the party's structuring of the repertoire of federalism, in which federal institutions should reflect the recognition of Quebeckers as a sovereign nation—not merely a province— of its own. A setting of equality among provinces would "forestall the granting of special status for Quebec" (Rocher and Smith, 2003, p. 32), as Bernard Landry, leader of the PQ, highlighted in the National Assembly during a discussion preceding the foundation of the Council of the Federation:[56]

> Est-ce que ça veut dire qu'il [Jean Charest, Premier] admet que le Québec, dans ce Conseil de la Confédération, irait s'asseoir avec les Territoires du Nord-Ouest, d'égal à égal, puis avec l'Île-du-Prince-Édouard, d'égal à égal? Est-ce que ce n'est pas la négation même de la notion

---

56 Bernard Landry (PQ), Assemblée nationale du Québec, Commission des institutions, 2 July 2003.

centrale des relations entre Québec et Ottawa pour l'instant que le Québec forme une nation et qu'il recherche l'égalité avec les autres nations et ne pas aller s'asseoir dans une instance de plus, d'égal à égal, avec des endroits éminemment respectables comme l'Île-du-Prince-Édouard ou le Manitoba mais qui ne sont ni des nations et qui n'ont pas l'importance économique, politique et sociale du Québec?

In a later discussion in the National Assembly on the role of the Council of the Federation, Liberal deputy Alain Paquet summarised the different conceptions of Canadian federalism in the following words:[57]

Et là une chose qui nous distingue [the PLQ] fondamentalement, je crois, de ce côté-ci de la Chambre et nos amis des deux oppositions : les amis de l'opposition souvent prennent le reste du Canada comme le ROC, "the rest of Canada", le bloc monolithique, c'est eux contre le Québec, alors que le reste du Canada, les différents partenaires dans le reste du Canada, ce n'est pas un bloc monolithique.

The creation of the Council of the Federation as well as Quebec's government's endeavour to develop common positions among the provinces on a new economic agreement with the EU demonstrated that Quebec's representatives from the Parti libéral constructed Quebec's interests against the backdrop of the integration frame structuring their perspective on Canadian federalism. In trying to institutionalise the Council of the Federation as prime arena for building a compromise among the provinces, and sometimes the territories if they were concerned, the Quebec Liberals acknowledged that each province had different interests concerning the economic agreement. However, these different interests could only surface once channelled through the Council of the Federation.

4. Provincial Para-Diplomacy and Intergovernmental Relations

The project of a new economic agreement also contributed to conferring a new ambition on Quebec's paradiplomatic activities (Balthazar, 2003; Bélanger, 1995; Kirkey, Paquin et al., 2016; Paquin, 2004, 2006). Even though the Mulroney era (1984-1993) had been a "golden age" for extending Quebec's international activities under the PQ (Bernier, 2001), the federal government had not yet actively included the provinces in the 1980s free tra-

---

57 Alain Paquet (PLQ), Assemblée nationale du Québec, 11 June 2007.

de negotiations with the argument that free trade was of exclusive federal jurisdiction. In general, however, the PLQ engaged more actively in para-diplomatic activities than the PQ; in fact, the latter focused on promoting sovereignty and reassuring US investors that sovereignty did not pose a threat to them. As Keating documented, Quebec mostly engaged in external activity targeted at specific objectives including in the trade and investment realm, but not so much in traditional diplomacy (Keating, 1997, p. 708).

Yet, with the new economic negotiations, Quebec's provincial government aimed at becoming actively involved in a project that clearly fell under federal jurisdiction: international trade agreements. Thereby, it tried to considerably alter the mode of Canadian diplomacy and treaty-making. The Liberal provincial government, backed by the PQ, supported the active involvement of Canadian provinces in the negotiation process. The provincial government had two reasons to do so. First, it hoped to extend the scope of a new transatlantic economic agreement by including the provinces. If an agreement was to reach beyond the mere question of tariffs, the provinces needed to be included, as a member of Quebec's government asserted by referring to education, research and development, environment and culture, all under exclusive provincial or shared jurisdiction:

> Il fallait déborder de la stricte question des tarifs, la stricte question du commerce pour déborder vers des domaines qui touchent vraiment les relations entre les peuples. L'éducation, la recherche et le développement, l'environnement, la culture.[58]

Since Quebec's government hoped to foster provincial economic development through reducing non-tariff barriers to trade and investment, including the provinces was part of their strategy to make negotiations succeed.

The second reason why the Quebec Liberals supported a more active role for the provinces during the negotiations of a new transatlantic economic agreement was related to the way they structured the repertoire of Canadian federalism. Contrary to the PQ—which supported a higher degree of provincial influence on Canada's trade negotiations, but which would prefer that Quebec negotiated its own agreements as a sovereign nation—the Liberals hoped to alter the mode of intergovernmental relations in Canada during trade negotiations and increase provincial participation

---

58 Interview with member of Quebec's Liberal government, Montreal, 24 October 2014.

in the negotiation process.[59] In contributing to setting the agenda for a new economic agreement between Canada and the EU, Quebec's representatives managed to discursively construct an imperative for high provincial participation in the negotiation process. In order to legitimise their claims, they drew upon Quebec's practice to extend issues under provincial jurisdiction to the international stage. Their objective was to establish a new way to coordinate Canada's trade policy negotiations that reflected the changing nature of international trade agreements and mirrored the Liberals endeavour to acquire more influence for Quebec within Canada.

The changes Quebec tried to bring about reflected that the governing Liberals structured the repertoire of federalism using the integration frame. According to this structuring, Canada consisted of autonomous but interdependent political, economic and social communities. Each pursued its own interests but also cooperated to achieve compromise in a setting of "equality of the provinces" (Rocher and Smith, 2003, p. 23-28). Given that each province was too small to pursue its interests effectively on an international scale, they were compelled to find compromises. In this view, intergovernmental relations in Canada were highly political: they were not entertained behind closed doors by public officials, but addressed among provincial Premiers, sometimes joined by the federal Prime Minister. While this vision has become increasingly entrenched in Canadian constitutional affairs since the 1960s, it had been less present in day-to-day policy-making (Jackson and Jackson, 1990, p. 246-250).

Trade was a particularly useful area to attempt to include the provinces in Canada's international activities, since many of the issues negotiated fell under their competency and therefore opened a window of opportunity for the Quebec Liberals to promote their particular vision of Canadian federalism. In their discourse, the Quebec Liberals continuously highlighted that core issues of international trade negotiations fell under provincial jurisdiction: many non-tariff barriers were of exclusive provincial or shared federal/provincial jurisdiction, including access to sub-federal procurement

---

59 Until the negotiations between Canada and the EU, the provinces had not been systematically included in trade negotiations; the federal government consulted and informed them as they deemed fit (Kukucha, 2008, 2016; Skogstad, 2012b). In the event of trade disputes, the provincial and federal governments tended to pool their sovereignty when areas under provincial jurisdiction were involved (Atkey, 1971; Jackson and Jackson, 1990, p. 632-634; Johannson, 1978; Skogstad, 2012a, p. 228-230; 2013; VanDuzer, 2013). During CETA negotiations, the inclusion of issues under provincial jurisdiction, required their participation in the negotiation process (Fafard and Leblond, 2012; Leblond, 2010; Paquin, 2013).

markets, certain establishment rights and limitations on foreign investments, environmental regulations, labour rights, technical barriers and regulatory standards, or services. By highlighting the relevance of these issues, all of which were contentious at the multilateral level, they constructed
CETA, at this preliminary stage of the negotiations, as an agreement that
very much concerned Canadian provinces' jurisdiction. Quebec's representatives could represent the new economic project in such a way that it involved provincial competencies adjacent to international trade, thereby
forcing the province's way into international trade and investment negotiations. This combination conferred meaning and legitimacy on the province's paradiplomatic activity in the area of international trade. Quebec discursively constructed the need to involve provinces in trade negotiations
from the preliminary stages of the project. Through this strategy, the governing PLQ paved the way for support by the PQ. In fact, stronger involvement of Canadian provinces in Canada's international trade negotiations has usually been a request made by the PQ (Skogstad, 2012a, p. 235).

In sum, business groups did not *trigger* the provincial government's
commitment to a new agreement, even though their interests converged to
a large extent with Quebec's project (see also Woll, 2011). In the Liberals'
development strategy, multinational businesses played a key role, yet they
were attributed a specific role in Quebec's province-building. Thus, the Liberal government did not just blindly follow liberal ideology including the
wishes of business representatives. Rather, it assumed that such an agreement would support economic development as well as its conception of
Canadian federalism. Early attention to issues relating to provincial jurisdiction also prepared the ground for an element that would become central to the Liberal government's strategy: the mandatory participation of
Canadian provinces in trade-policy negotiations with the EU. Thus, political and business leaders' interests might have converged and fed into each
other, and the government instrumentalised business demands in its discursive strategy.

Section 2: Building Coalitions—a Strategy based on Provincial Jurisdiction

Despite fading political interest on both sides of the Atlantic, the idea of
enhancing economic relations between Canada and the EU resurfaced in
the mid-2000s. Even though there is no "single hero in this complicated
story"—to use the language developed by Nicolas Jabko (2006)—Quebec
was a pivotal actor during the agenda-setting stage. Quebec developed a

strong interest in the project and tried to bring it to the agenda of key decision-makers, the Canadian federal government and the EU. According to Quebec's representatives, the province played a crucial role in constructing a re-newed interest in a common economic agreement. From the province's perspective, Quebec was able to convince the European Commission, important European member states, the Canadian federal government and the Canadian provinces of the comparative benefits of such an agreement. Most external actors confirmed this perspective[60] (see also Woll, 2011, p. 52-54), with some giving more or less credit to Quebec's representatives. In the following analysis, the focus will not be on who was right or wrong. Rather, the aim is to show how Quebec constructed its interests in a complex environment and how it convinced others with equally complex motivations to join its efforts. This process was a complex interplay between many different actors and their (sometimes unclear) motivations.

In order to pursue Quebec's interest to engage considerable resources to launch this new trade project, its government did not confine itself to the boundaries of the province, nor Canada. From the beginning, it engaged with existing transatlantic networks, both formally and informally. The very fact that Quebec was not an institutionally powerful actor in international trade relations, helped its leaders overcome existing gridlock between Canada and the EU, and establish a new path for cooperation.

When putting their updated province-building project into action, Quebec's representatives faced the obstacles that international trade was not under provincial jurisdiction, and that the EU and Canada had abandoned the project of a comprehensive economic agreement between their two economies. They had to find a way to make their voice heard as a Canadian province without jurisdiction over international trade. To do so, they needed to convince the key gate-keepers of trade negotiations: the European Commission and the Canadian federal government, as well as European member states. Reflecting the integration frame structuring the Liberal government's conception of federalism, they also addressed the other Canadian provinces, even though the provinces were not gatekeepers. In late 2006, Quebec's representatives had already realised that building transatlantic and internal Canadian coalitions prior to launching negotiations was essential, as one diplomat recounted. He specifically referred to the

---

60 European interviewees tended to confirm this story about CETA, while the Canadian federal representatives tended to see the role of Quebec as important, yet less crucial in the overall process.

Canadian federal government, the other provinces, and the EU as key partners:

> Parce que ce n'est évidemment pas le Québec qui peut négocier avec l'Union européenne, c'est le Canada qu'il faut amener. [...] Le Québec entreprend une démarche auprès des autres provinces ici. On entreprend aussi des démarches en Europe.[61]

Building the right coalitions was thus key. The following analysis documents how Quebec's representatives explored potential coalitions across the Atlantic and domestically, and how the various streams of their coalitional strategies connected during the Canada-EU summit meetings.

1. Exploring and Attracting Attention

To create momentum for a new transatlantic economic agreement, Quebec's first step consisted in exploring the opportunity for a new agreement and attracting the attention of key stakeholders and political decision-makers. In fact, the Canadian federal government and the European Commission were reluctant to launch new economic negotiations. This represented a major obstacle to the Liberal government's province-building project and its conviction that Quebec as a small and open economy needed to seek out new commercial opportunities abroad. At the same time, the Liberal government needed to explore avenues to advocate its new project in a way consistent with its representation of Canadian federalism.

At the early stages of the agenda-setting, Quebec's representatives needed to demonstrate the extent to which business representatives supported their new project and consequently a genuine potential for economic growth. Since the current government accorded a prominent position to multinational business as the backbone of provincial economic development, a pillar of province-building, it needed to secure their support. By showcasing business support, it hoped to attract relevenat political decision-makers' attention.

---

61 Interview with Quebec diplomat, Montreal, 9 October 2014.

a) Networking Dinner in Quebec City (December 2006)

During this exploratory stage, Quebec's Premier Charest arranged a first demonstration that business leaders were interested in supporting such an agreement. In December 2006, he organised a dinner designed to showcase the new trade project and the support from business leaders, including Bombardier, the Canadian Chamber of Commerce, the Business Council of Canada, and the Canadian Council of Chief Executives. In organising this meeting, the Canada-Europe Round Table for Business (CERT) played a key role.[62] In the presence of the Ambassador of the EU to Canada, Quebec's representatives exhibited their new trade project. They hoped the ambassador would transmit their plans to the European Commission, which he did, resulting in a first encounter in Davos.

b) Exploiting the Myth of Davos (January 2007)

After this informal exploratory meeting in Quebec City, Premier Charest and the Minister for Economic Development, Raymond Bachand, took their project to the international stage: they announced their government's intention to support a new agreement between Canada and the EU on 26 January 2007 during the World Economic Forum in Davos (Bergeron, 2007). This venue was not chosen randomly. Quite to the contrary, it was part of Quebec's representatives' discursive and coalitional strategies.

Regarding *discursive strategy*, the World Economic Forum in Davos allowed Quebec's representatives to anchor their new project in a specific setting of global economic integration: the World Economic Forum, established in 1971, brings together political representatives, business leaders, journalists and academics for the promotion of entrepreneurship and free trade. It is best known for its annual meeting in January in Davos, Switzerland, where selected leaders discuss pressing global issues. The Davos meetings are highly mediatised events, attracting senior political and business decision-makers, but also increasingly criticism (Chesters and Welsh, 2005; della Porta, 2016). This choice of venue acknowledged the role global economic integration played for Quebec economic development.

In his Davos speech, the Quebec Premier embedded his new trade project in the Quebec Liberals' province-building project. By encouraging glo-

---

62 Interview with member of Liberal Government in Quebec, Montreal, 23 October 2014.

bal economic integration, the Liberals wanted to advance economic prosperity in their small and open economy:

> Le Québec est ouvert sur le monde et c'est pourquoi les Québécois ont appuyé la mise en place d'un accord de libre-échange nord-américain. Nous avons la responsabilité de consolider et de développer ces liens, nécessaires à notre croissance et à notre prospérité. Nous avons des niveaux de développement comparables et nous partageons les mêmes valeurs. Nos économies ont besoin de marchés développés pour prospérer, et nos chercheurs ont besoin de travailler au sein des meilleures équipes. Nous pouvons ensemble agir plus efficacement face aux grands enjeux, tels le réchauffement de la planète, la sécurité internationale, l'aide au développement ou la lutte contre la pauvreté (Jean Charest, 2007).

The Liberals' discursive strategy, combined with references to Quebec's long-standing support of free trade and the exclusion of sensitive sectors, aimed at ensuring domestic provincial support and therefore fed into their *coalitional strategy*. In fact, references to the benefits of past trade relations that the PQ supported allowed the Liberal government to develop a discourse to which the PQ could easily adhere. This discursive strategy allowed Quebec's current government to set the scene for collective action in the sense that all major parties potentially supported the project. In fact, the Liberal government's project was discursively constructed as non-partisan. Even though the Liberals and the PQ had in the past pursued free trade with different, sometimes even opposed, objectives, their common project to open Quebec to international exchanges enabled collective action despite Pauline Marois' PQ favouring more interventionist economic policies (Séguin, 2012).

In his speech, Charest also identified key sectors of potential cooperation: investment, trade in goods and services, sustainable development, free movement of people, the recognition of professional qualifications and scientific and technological cooperation. In addition, he also underlined that Quebec wished to preserve the status quo of international trade provisions concerning Canada's system of agricultural supply management and the protection of cultural industries:

> Par ailleurs, le secteur agricole devra être exclu des discussions devant mener à un tel accord. Les gouvernements québécois et canadien ont exprimé à plusieurs reprises leur intention de continuer à défendre le système de gestion de l'offre actuellement en place. Un éventuel ac-

cord devra également accorder une attention spéciale à la protection et à la promotion de la diversité culturelle.

Hence, the World Economic Forum in Davos allowed Quebec's government to bypass the venues of traditional state diplomacy and detour the restrictions of Canadian federalism with regard to jurisdiction for trade policy. As part of the government's coalitional strategy, announcing Quebec's support for a new economic agreement at this occasion attracted the attention of the international business community. In his speech, Premier Charest introduced the province as a legitimate actor in promoting this new agreement by asserting that the province had been a key driver behind Euro-Canadian economic relations. Davos provided the Premier with an international stage for the government's project and privileged informal access to key political decision-makers, including German federal Minister for Economic development, Michael Glos.[63] After the Canadian Ambassador to the EU informed the European Trade Commissioner Peter Mandelson of Quebec's plan to support bilateral economic negotiations, Jean Charest and Peter Mandelson met personally in Davos in January 2007. Mandelson's positive reaction prompted Charest to make his first public announcement of the new trade project in Davos.

2. Finding Partners across the Atlantic

After making a first public announcement of the new trade project to the global business and political community gathered in Davos and securing initial support from the Trade Commissioner, Quebec's new trade strategy required convincing the necessary coalition partners in the EU. Quebec's representatives simultaneously acted on two fronts: they addressed the European Commission, more specifically the Trade Commissioner, and the European member states, meaing that they addressed, as a diplomat from Quebec phrased it, "anything that moved".[64]

When approaching these partners, representatives' task was twofold: they needed to convince potential partners that the agreement was in their interest, and to bring it to relevant political agendas in a form that benefitted their province-building project. In proceeding with their ambition, re-

---

63 Interview with member of Quebec's Liberal government, Montreal, 23 October 2014.
64 Interview with Quebec diplomat, Montreal, 9 October 2014.

presentatives needed to devise a discursive strategy to promote their interests and a coalitional strategy to align a large variety of other actors' interests. At the same time, these alliances served them in their domestic coalitional strategy to demonstrate that they supported a promising project.

a) Convincing the European Commission: From 'Global Europe' to Bilateral Relations with Canada?

Quebec's representatives identified European Trade Commissioner Peter Mandelson as a key coalition partner in promoting their new project.[65] However, persuading the Trade Commissioner was not an easy task. In fact, Mandelson was reticent to embark on new negotiations with Canada: under his aegis, the EU had developed the new trade policy strategy *Global Europe* (2006), which identified key bilateral partners to prepare for a potential failure of the Doha Round. Canada was not among these potential partners. At the same time, the EU was also reluctant to embark on bilateral negotiations with a member of the G8, which might compromise multilateral negotiations, while the Doha negotiations were still ongoing, as a Canadian diplomat reported:[66]

> Around 2007 to 2008, when we started pushing this, the EU was not fully committed to the bilateral process at that point. They were still, I think, very much hoping that the Doha Round would still produce results. So, they were not fully committed, I think, to the idea of "bilaterals" at that point.

In addition, Peter Mandelson's analysis of the failure of the TIEA negotiations proved to be an obstacle to re-launching bilateral economic negotiations: according to the Commissioner, Canada's federal institutions were among the key reasons for the failure of bilateral negotiations. According to a Quebec diplomat, the Trade Commissioner suggested that Quebec's Premier assure provincial support for the project before launching negotia-

---

65 There is a large body of literature on the question of European Commission autonomy in Trade Policy: (Conceição-Heldt, 2011a, b; Elgström and Frennhoff Larsén, 2010; Meunier, 2005, 2007; Woolcock, 2012) According to most analyses, the European Commission cannot fundamentally alter member states' preferences or act against them. However, its role as sole negotiator often seemed to grant the Commission a high degree of autonomy. From Quebec's perspective, it was an important gate-keeper.

66 Interview with Canadian diplomat, Brussels, 8 July 2014.

tions. The Quebec diplomat quoted the Europan Commissioner (in English) and gave his interpretation of the Commissioner's position (in French)[67]

> "When you get your house in order, come and see me." En voulant dire que si les provinces ne sont pas là, alors ça ne nous intéresse pas.

In this, Mandelson referred to the institutions of Canadian federalism in trade policy-making. According to Canada's dualist legal tradition, international treaties—even if ratified—are not directly enforceable under Canadian law. Before they can constitute legal obligations, they need to be implemented by domestic legislation. In this process, the provinces implement provisions that fall under their jurisdiction.[68] At the same time, the Canadian government cannot force the provinces to implement international provisions under their jurisdiction according to provincial procedures[69] (Atkey, 1971; Campbell, 1995; Delagran, 1992; Kukucha, 2003; Paquin, 2010; Robinson, 1995, 2003). During previous economic negotiations, the federal government's hands were tied by the Canadian provinces' refusal to cooperate with the Canadian federal government on trade issues under provincial jurisdiction.

Quebec's government and its diplomatic team drew upon two key arguments in their coalitional strategy to convince the Trade Commissioner of the existence of an economic interest for the EU.[70] Their first argument consisted in presenting negotiations with Canada as a key step in the EU's trade policy, and more specifically the EU's long-established project of an economic agreement with the US, as a diplomat from Quebec related:[71]

---

67 Interview with Quebec diplomat, Montreal, 9 October 2014.

68 In the 1937 *Labour Conventions* Case, the Privy Council held that the federal government cannot use the need to comply with international treaties as justification for encroaching on areas of provincial jurisdiction (1937).

69 According to the Loi sur le Ministère des relations internationales, Quebec needs to ratify important international agreements. According to article 20 (1988, 2002), "les ententes internationales visées à l'article 22.2 doivent, pour être valides, être signées par le ministre, approuvées par l'Assemblée nationale et ratifiées par le gouvernement." In urgent cases, the government can ratify an international agreement without seeking the National Assembly's approval and without previously informing them, according to article 22.5 (2002).

70 Mandelson was more attentive to economic arguments in trade policy than his predecessor Pascal Lamy, who attached more importance to larger political objectives, see (Meunier, 2007).

71 Interview with Quebec diplomat, Montreal, 9 October 2014.

Et l'argument fondamental était de dire : avant que vous essayiez de négocier une entente de libre-échange avec les États-Unis, il ne serait pas bête, pour vous, de négocier quelque chose avec le Canada, qui est plus facile, plus près des Européens au niveau des valeurs. Et cela vous permettrait par la suite d'envisager la suite des choses.

According to the analysis made by Quebec's representatives, negotiating an agreement with Canada could be a European test case for a future negotiation with the US both in terms of substantive results and negotiation processes; regulatory choices were fairly similar in Canada and the US, as were their negotiation practices in international trade. A new Canada-EU agreement could therefore be a blueprint for negotiations with the US.[72] At the same time, this suggestion promoted the Liberals' conviction that Quebec and Canada could be a point of entry to the North American market, thereby attracting high levels of foreign direct investment to the province, as Premier Charest asserted on many instances.[73] Strong in natural resources, Quebec and Canada were attractive for foreign direct investors, who could build plants in Canada and export relatively easily to the US.[74] Concluding an agreement with a NAFTA-member would give European companies privileged access to the US market via Canada. For example, CETA would allow to integrate Canadian plants into global value chains and export intermediate or final goods to the US without facing WTO tariff rates. The Canadian federal government shared this perspective:[75]

> We also offer now, once the agreement's in place, sort of a tariff free, investment-friendly window into North America. So, for European companies looking for broad access to the North American market, we think we now offer a really good location to do that.

Their second argument regarded the economic advantage the EU could gain by concluding an agreement with an economy whose internal market was ten times smaller in terms of GDP. Quebec's offer was in provincial public procurement markets. In Canada, federalism had shielded the provinces to some degree from the effects of international trade law; therefore, some markets under provincial jurisdiction remained fairly closed to international competition, even for US companies. As a politically influential

---

72 Interview with member of Quebec's Liberal government, Montreal, 23 October 2014.
73 E.g. Jean Charest, Assemblée nationale du Québec, 10 March 2009.
74 Interview with European Commission official, Brussels, 23 July 2014.
75 Interview with Canadian diplomat, Brussels, 8 July 2014.

province, Quebec advocated that the Canadian provinces agree to fully cooperate to create competitive advantages for European companies exporting to or investing in Canada, and Charest created the credible expectation in the European Commission that they would do so. In this way, Quebec offered what the federal government was not able to provide without provincial cooperation, namely market access rights falling under provincial jurisdiction, as a member of Quebec's Liberal government reported:[76]

> Dans le fond, le prix à gagner est au niveau provincial plus qu'au niveau fédéral.

b) Finding Allies among Member States

Among European member states, the government of Quebec identified three main countries to include in their coalition: Germany, the United Kingdom and France.[77] The economic recession and financial crises of 2008 and 2009 played an important role in paving the way to reflect about new ways to organise global economic exchanges.[78] Germany instantly supported the project, mainly because it saw a trade agreement with Canada as an instrument to foster transatlantic relations and prepare a future agreement with the US. Quebec's coalitional strategy consisted in highlighting the transatlantic nature of a new agreement, as a diplomat from Quebec related:

> On a pris un plaisir à rappeler à madame Merkel que le transatlantique inclut le Canada.[79]

Quebec also tried to include the United Kingdom (UK) in its strategy. The UK seemed a natural partner both because it supported free trade and because it had close ties with Canada. However, Quebec's government disco-

---

76 Interview with member of Quebec's Liberal government, Montreal, 23 October 2014.
77 If not otherwise indicated, the following account is based on an interview with a Quebec diplomat, Montreal, 9 October 2014, and a member of Quebec's Liberal government, Montreal, 23 October 2014.
78 Interview with a Canadian diplomat, Brussels, 8 July 2014.
79 Interview with Quebec diplomat, Montreal, 9 October 2014.

vered with astonishment that the UK was at best lukewarm to its new plan, as a member of Quebec's Liberal government recounted:

> De manière intéressante, l'Angleterre a été plutôt indifférente. [80]

Quebec also turned to France. Including France in its coalition was particularly important for Quebec's strategy: insofar as France was not among the traditional supporters of free trade in the EU, its support lent further credibility to the project. In the past, France had not been a fierce advocate of free trade among European member states. Although its position has become more nuanced since the mid-1990s, France remained more cautious than other member states with regard to the benefits of global economic integration (Gordon and Meunier, 2001; Meunier, 2013). A member of Quebec's Liberal government reported that France's support therefore astonished the Trade Commissioner:

> À la Commission, [le soutien de la France] a été un sujet d'étonnement. Les Français sont typiquement sur les freins pour les ententes, alors que là, les Français poussaient. [...] Mettez-vous dans les souliers de Mandelson : [...] tout d'un coup, Chirac dit : moi, ce projet-là, je veux le faire avec le Canada. [...] Alors, il y a comme un étonnement. [81]

Apart from playing a part in Quebec's coalitional strategy, France was also important in Quebec's discursive strategy, Hence, discursive and coalitional strategies fed into each other. To demonstrate the reality of this special relation and its positive effects on provincial economic development, Quebec's representatives drew attention to a recent bilateral agreement on labour mobility concluded in 2008, the *Entente France-Québec sur la reconnaissance mutuelle des qualifications professionnelles*. This agreement established a common framework for a procedure to recognise professional qualifications with the aim to accelerate mutual recognition of qualifications concerning regulated professions or trades. In the representatives' discursive strategy, this agreement served two purposes. On the one hand, it demonstrated that provinces have jurisdiction over central issues of contemporary economic integration. In this instance, provincial jurisdiction over educational matters impacted upon labour mobility and international tra-

---

80 Interview with member of Quebec's Liberal government, Montreal, 23 October 2014.
81 Interview with member of Quebec's Liberal government, Montreal, 23 October 2014.

de in services; in fact, services were in many cases delivered in the host territory and therefore required a high degree of labour mobility. This served the Quebec government's demonstration that tackling non-tariff barriers involved provincial jurisdiction. The agreement also emphasised the Quebec Liberals' ability to successfully negotiate and conclude international agreements, which was important because they promoted the integration of Quebec in the Canadian federation. Thereby, they underscored that Canada as a federal union of different provinces acting in their respective areas of jurisdiction did not keep Quebec from concluding beneficial international agreements, as the members of the PQ suggested. In a speech in the National Assembly, Premier Charest highlighted that it was not the constitutional status that determined Quebec's international activity, but its standing:

> Voilà la preuve que l'influence du Québec n'est pas affaire de statut mais plutôt de stature.[82]

Hence, this agreement legitimised provincial participation in EU-Canada negotiations. In addition, Quebec's representatives used the agreement with France to influence the scope and coverage of a new Canada-EU bilateral agreement. According to them, the France-Quebec agreement demonstrated the success of enhancing labour mobility. Therefore, similar provisions should be included in the transatlantic agreement, as Premier Charest highlighted in the National Assembly:

> Ce premier corridor de mobilité entre deux continents facilitera le recrutement d'une main d'œuvre qualifiée. [83]

In the government's discursive strategy, this agreement helped to attract more qualified labour to Quebec, an essential step towards improving the province's economic development which, due to its small size, lacked qualified labour. With this agreement, France and Quebec preluded two issues they deemed relevant in global economic relations: services and education. Therefore, the government also used the France-Quebec agreement on labour mobility to justify the need for a new trade agreement tackling issues related to services and education. By the same token, this agreement could also be a positive example for transatlantic negotiations, as a diplomat from Quebec asserted:

---

82 Jean Charest (PLQ), Assemblée nationale du Québec, 10 March 2009.
83 Jean Charest (PLQ), Assemblée nationale du Québec, 10 March 2009.

> Le Québec avait conclu un accord avec la France sur la mobilité de la main d'œuvre, qui était quand même assez spectaculaire [...]. Le Québec voulait aussi inclure un chapitre sur cette question-là dans l'accord Canada-Union européenne. Ce qui a été fait à la fin. [84]

Why did France commit to further trade relations between the EU and Canada? First, they had substantive economic interests, mostly attracting investors:

> C'est clair qu'il y a actuellement un gros effort chez nous, chez nos gouvernants, de développer l'attractivité de la France pour faire venir des entreprises étrangères en France. Le Canada fait bien sûr partie des pays-cibles, donc on essaie d'intéresser les investisseurs, enfin les entreprises qui veulent investir en Europe et de les amener vers la France. [85]

France hoped to become the point of entry for Quebec and Canadian commercial exchanges to the EU, building on existing economic interdependencies. In addition, the French government promoted a trade agreement with Canada to enhance French companies' development opportunities beyond Quebec: according to French diplomats based in Ottawa, France drew upon its diplomatic relations with Quebec to launch new negotiations, yet hoped to be able to extend commercial and investment relations to Canada's Western provinces through a new agreement.[86] Furthermore, according to a senior member of Quebec's Liberal government, French support could also be explained by the exceptional diplomatic relations they entertained with Quebec:

> [Les Français] poussaient parce qu'ils y croyaient, mais ils y poussaient aussi par amitié envers le Québec et le Canada. Notre relation était tellement exceptionnelle. C'est une belle histoire, parce que ça nous dit que les relations entre les peuples font une différence. La qualité de la relation fait une différence. Et en voilà un exemple très concret. Et franchement, sans ce leadership français, je ne suis pas sûr que le projet serait fait. [87]

Apart from economic interests, transatlantic economic integration was also part of the strategy of the French government under Sarkozy to "fashion

---

84 Interview with Quebec diplomat, Montreal, 9 October 2014.
85 Interview with French diplomat, Montreal, 20 April 2015.
86 Interview with French diplomats, Ottawa, 15 April 2015.
87 Interview with member of the Quebec Liberal government, Montreal, 23 October 2014.

the global economic order" (Meunier, 2013, p. 236): considering the Euro-Canadian agreement a blueprint for future economic agreements conclu-ded by the EU, the French government hoped to influence the shape and pace of future global economic integration. According to this vision, the Euro-Canadian agreement would regulate and direct, rather than deregula-te and liberalise, international trade flows, as President Sarkozy unders-cored during a press conference with Canadian Prime Minister Harper and European Commission President Barroso (Sarkozy, 2008a).

By highlighting the positive effects of the bilateral relations with France, representatives also lent credibility to the project domestically and paved the way for the PQ's support. In fact, the PQ attached an important role to the state in directing global economic integration, similar to France. Fur-thermore, several of Quebec's Premiers entertained "direct and privileged" relations with French Presidents, contrary to Quebec-US relations which to a very large extent were strictly limited to relations between Ottawa and Washington, given that the US did not want to treat Quebec as an interna-tional actor (Paquin, 2006; 2016, p. 150).

3. Securing Domestic Support: Convincing the Federal and Provincial Governments

Even though Quebec's government and Brussels-based diplomats had been highly successful in capturing the EU's and key member states' attention and support for a transatlantic trade agreement, domestic Canadian sup-port was not a fait accompli in 2007. While Quebec's government was sure to obtain provincial support for its project, insiders anticipated opposition from the federal government. Therefore, its members needed to devise a strategy to ensure the federal government's commitment. When facing the federal government, Quebec's government needed to convince the Prime Minister and the Minister for International Trade to support negotiations and to give the provinces a stronger voice in the process.

a) Ensuring the Federal Government's Commitment

As international trade falls under federal jurisdiction, only the federal go-vernment could open international trade negotiations. Therefore, Que-bec's government was compelled to seek Ottawa's support. However, Ca-nada's federal government did not enthusiastically endorse Quebec's new project at first, as a member of Quebec's Liberal government reported (see for a review of Canadian trade interests Leblond and Strachinescu-Oltea-nu, 2009).[88] This position stemmed mainly from the ambiguous position the EU occupied in Canada's trade strategy at that time. In the mid-2000s, after the failure of the Doha Round at the WTO and the TIEA with the EU, Canada's federal government was reconfiguring its trade strategy. At that moment, it had not yet established its strategic partners in trade. Espe-cially with regard to the EU, Canada had not yet developed a clear posi-tion, as Peter Cook, business columnist at the Canadian daily newspaper *The Globe and Mail*, asserted:

> It is hard to identify what Canada's strategy is. And this is especially true in relation to Europe, by far its largest trade and investment part-ner after the US. [89]

That the EU was not a main target for increasing trade and investment re-lations was evident from the orientation of trade missions led by the Mi-nistry for International Affairs at that time. Between 1998 and 2000, after launching the Euro-Canadian Trade Initiative, four of eight federal-led tra-de missions went to states in Europe. Yet, there was not a single mission organised to a European member state between 2000 and 2010.[90]

Quebec's government therefore needed to convince the federal govern-ment to re-prioritise economic relations with the EU. In this, Quebec had an ally in the federal bureaucracy, with which the provincial government had previously established contact.[91] The bureaucracy's positive recom-mendation to the government, in a setting of high bureaucratic influence (Savoie, 2010), contributed to convincing the federal government. Further-more, the existence of strong European interests to launch negotiations on a new economic agreement also played a key role. As a Canadian diplomat reported, the 2008 economic crisis eventually convinced the federal go-vernment that a new strategy for economic growth had to be developed, with the aim to diversify the Canadian export market and make Canada less dependent on the US in the long run:

---

88 Interview with member of Quebec's Liberal government, Montreal, 24 October 2014.

89 http://www.theglobeandmail.com/report-on-business/europes-winning-trade-strat egy-doesnt-include-canada-peter-cook-says/article765371/ [access: 03.02.2016].

90 See appendix.

91 Interview with member of Quebec's Liberal government, Montreal, 24 October 2014.

> I think the idea overriding this was really diversification of our export market. We are very heavily dependent on the US, as our chief trading partner. At the time, over 80-85% of our trade was with the US. With the crisis, it became clear – although the US is a very good market, they will always be, frankly, our primary trade partner – there was no guarantee the access would always be easy. So, we had to diversify.[92]

Once the federal government had taken the decision to diversify export markets for Canadian companies, they represented the European market as a main target, referring to cultural similarities and a long-standing relationship at the political level, paralleled by private links between Canada and European states which would be important for Canadian companies when making the choice to invest in or export to the EU:

> You know, a lot of us have European background [...] A free trade agreement does give the impetus, [...] but companies now have to take the next step, which is to actually look at the market, get partners, look for opportunities, do their homework, see if they want to invest or export. [The agreement] gives companies some comfort to take the effort to look at the market more carefully. [93]

Finally, the federal government also regarded a new transatlantic agreement as a way to foster internal market integration. Using the momentum created by the new economic agreement with the EU, the federal government hoped to convince the provinces to reduce inter-provincial barriers to trade and investment. As a Canadian diplomat asserted:

> A big positive out of CETA, for both the EU and Canada, is that it was not only a negotiation between us, to open our bilateral trade, but it was an opportunity for each side to encourage more internal openness. [94]

Having secured federal commitment to launch negotiations, Quebec's representatives faced a second obstacle in pursuing their strategy: their discursive strategy to alter intergovernmental relations in Canada was not met with enthusiasm at the federal government. To the contrary, the Harper Conservatives refused to expand provincial participation in the negotiation process at first: as a member of Quebec's Liberal government reported:

---

92 Interview with Canadian diplomat, Brussels, 8 July 2014.
93 Interview with Canadian diplomat, Brussels, 8 July 2014.
94 Interview with Canadian diplomat, Brussels, 8 July 2014.

L'Etat fédéral canadien n'a pas l'habitude d'inclure les provinces et ne voulait pas inclure les provinces. [95]

However, extending provincial participation in Canada's trade negotiations was part and parcel of the Quebec Liberals' discursive strategy, as explained above. In order to pursue its project to alter intergovernmental relations in trade negotiations, the government and its diplomatic team entered a coalitional strategy with the European Commission. In this strategy, the European Commission supported Quebec's demand to increase provincial participation during trade negotiations because it sensed that a far-reaching trade agreement would only be possible if supported by the provinces, as a member of Quebec's Liberal government explained:

> Mais l'Europe avait une réponse toute faite qui a été formidable pour nous. L'Europe a dit à l'Etat fédéral : c'est un deal breaker. C'est-à-dire que, pour les négociations, si les provinces ne sont pas à la table, nous on ne négocie pas. [96]

Therefore, by constructing the new trade agreement as a comprehensive one, Quebec's Liberal government could pursue and foster its particular view of Canadian federalism through the new trade negotiations. As a consequence, the provinces were included as active partners in the negotiations from the beginning—a first in Canadian trade negotiations.

b) Gaining Provincial Support

Quebec launched domestic provincial and inter-provincial processes to ensure support for the new trade project. The government approached the deputies in the National Assembly as early as June 2008 on an economic partnership agreement with the EU. Underlining cross-party support for the trade project, Raymond Bachand (PLQ), Minister for Economic Development, Innovation and Export, Nicolas Marceau (PQ), and Gilles Taillon (ADQ) presented a joint motion on 13 June. Adopted unanimously, this motion underscored that deputies supported the government in its new trade project. Furthermore, the motion also underlined Quebec's motivation to participate in these negotiations, namely enlarging its export markets

---

95 Interview with member of Quebec's Liberal government, Montreal, 24 October 2014.
96 Interview with member of Quebec's Liberal government, Montreal, 24 October 2014.

and establishing Quebec as a point of entry for European companies to North America:

> Que l'Assemblée nationale appuie les négociations en vue d'un parte-nariat économique plus étroit et de nouvelle génération avec l'Union européenne visant à favoriser le commerce des biens et services, ainsi que la circulation des capitaux et des travailleurs qualifiés, permettant au Québec d'atteindre de nouveaux marchés et de le confirmer comme principale porte d'entrée de l'Europe en Amérique du Nord. [97]

Apart from securing support from the deputies of all parties in the National Assembly to launch negotiations, it was also crucial to convince the provincial legislature because of its institutional role in the ratification process. Quebec is the only Canadian province to require executive and sometimes legislative ratification prior to implementation. Usually, the Minister for International Affairs—jointly with the Minister for Economic Development in the case of trade agreements—ratifies an international agreement.[98] If the Minister judges an international agreement to be important, he needs to refer it to the National Assembly for further scrutiny. According to the *Loi sur le ministère des affaires étrangères* (1988, 2014), the Minis-

---

97 Assemblée nationale du Québec, Motion *Appuyer les négociations en vue d'un par-tenariat économique avec l'Union européenne*, 13 June 2008 (adopted).

98 Art. 22.1 specifies that "Le gouvernement doit, pour être lié par un accord inter-national ressortissant à la compétence constitutionnelle du Québec et pour don-ner son assentiment à ce que le Canada exprime son consentement à être lié par un tel accord, prendre un décret à cet effet. Il en est de même à l'égard de la fin d'un tel accord."

ter for International Affairs is obliged to file an important international agreement with the National Assembly[99] and seek approval from it.[100]

Even though the other Canadian provinces were not essential actors in *launching* trade negotiations with the EU, they would need to *implement* provisions in the future agreement falling under their jurisdiction. As explained above, international agreements need to be implemented into domestic law before they become effective. Insofar as many of the areas intended to be included in a new economic agreement fell under exclusive or shared provincial jurisdiction—provincial public procurement, property rights, services, education—the provinces needed to be included to ensure successful implementation. The memory of the WTO Agreement on Government Procurement (1994) and provincial refusal to implement provisions falling under their jurisdiction was still vivid.

In general, convincing the other Canadian provinces to support the project was not a troublesome task. In this process, the Council of the Federation served Quebec's government as a facilitating venue and they used the it as a forum where provincial Premiers developed a common position in their areas of jurisdiction, in a manner consistent with Quebec's Liberal government's conviction that the Canadian provinces could shape Canadian policy as equals in their areas of jurisdiction, and that they would develop a trade policy position upon which the federal government would base its negotiation position. Through regular meetings with provincial Premiers, Quebec's government communicated its project and encouraged its

---

99 Art. 22.2 specifies this obligation : "Tout engagement international important incluant, le cas échéant, les réserves s'y rapportant, fait l'objet d'un dépôt à l'Assemblée nationale, par le ministre, au moment qu'il juge opportun. Le dépôt du texte de cet engagement international est accompagné d'une note explicative sur le contenu et les effets de celui-ci. L'expression "engagement international important" désigne l'entente internationale visée à l'article 19, l'accord international visé à l'article 22.1 et tout instrument se rapportant à l'un ou l'autre, qui, de l'avis du ministre, selon le cas:

1° requiert, pour sa mise en œuvre par le Québec, soit l'adoption d'une loi ou la prise d'un règlement, soit l'imposition d'une taxe ou d'un impôt, soit l'acceptation d'une obligation financière importante;

2° concerne les droits et libertés de la personne;

3° concerne le commerce international;

4° devrait faire l'objet d'un dépôt à l'Assemblée nationale."

100 Art. 22.4 provides that : "La ratification d'une entente internationale ou la prise d'un décret visé au troisième alinéa de l'article 22.1 ne peuvent avoir lieu en ce qui concerne tout engagement international important qu'après son approbation par l'Assemblée nationale."

colleagues to endorse it. Quickly, most Premiers supported the project, as a member of Quebec's government reported:[101]

> Au Conseil de la Fédération, qui est le forum où nous nous retrouvons, l'adhésion a été assez spontanée. Ça n'a pas été problématique.

As a consequence, championed by Quebec, almost all the provinces supported opening procurement markets during CETA's agenda-setting phase, except for Newfoundland and Labrador, which did not agree with the nature of intergovernmental interaction at that time.[102] On 20 February 2009—three months before the official opening of negotiations between Canada and the EU—the Council of the Federation endorsed the project at its summit meeting in Quebec City (Council of the Federation, 2009b).[103] In its statement, the Council announced full support for the negotiation of a new and comprehensive economic agreement with the EU. Premiers highlighted that the inclusion of the provinces in the negotiation process was key to assuring negotiation success. They drew attention to consultations between the federal and provincial governments on issues falling under provincial jurisdiction, thereby suggesting that early involvement of the provinces would considerably ease the conclusion and implementation of a new trade agreement.

For Quebec's government and the Quebec Liberals, this announcement equalled a negotiation mandate by the provinces to the federal government, similar to the mandate given to the European Commission by the

---

101 Interview with member of Quebec Liberal government, Montreal, 24 October 2014.
102 Interview with member of Manitoba's government (2007-2009), by phone, 11 July 2017.
103 Support in the Council of the Federation was not unanimous, however: the province Newfoundland and Labrador did not endorse the Council's announcement. Instead, the provincial government issued a statement of its own on 20 February 2009. In this statement, the government expressed concerns with the negotiation process of a new trade agreement. According to Newfoundland and Labrador's Premier Williams, "a track record of a lack of substantive and inclusive consultation on federal-provincial issues gives Newfoundland and Labrador great cause for concern, particularly in light of the far-reaching implications of a possible Canada-EU trade agreement." In particular, the Premier underlined provincial interests in the fisheries and seal sectors, which it feared the federal government would not support in transatlantic negotiations. Unlike the Council of the Federation, Newfoundland and Labrador suggested that the dynamics of cross-level interaction did not satisfy provincial interests (Newfoundland and Labrador, 2009).

member states.[104] This endorsement of the new trade agreement project by the provinces reflected the way the Quebec Liberals structured the repertoire of federalism along the lines of the integration frame. The Council's statement referred to "a partnership respectful of their respective jurisdiction and responsibilities" between the two levels of government, thereby highlighting the distribution of competencies between levels of government as well as the absence of a hierarchical order between them. Because of the inclusion of areas under provincial jurisdiction in a new trade agreement, the Quebec Liberals could encourage their own vision of Canadian federalism. At the same time, obtaining support from the other provinces was crucial to assure the European Commission of provincial consent to implement future provisions falling under their jurisdiction.

4. Bringing a New Economic Agreement to the Policy Agenda

Once Quebec's representatives had convinced key policy makers across the Atlantic and domestically, the ball was in the court of the Canadian federal government and the European Commission. To discuss their goals, affirm their commitment and undertake the necessary steps leading to the official launch of the negotiations, they drew upon existing institutions. In particular, they capitalised on the summit meetings established by the Declaration on Canada-European Community Transatlantic Relations (1990) to bring together the Prime Minister of Canada, as well as the President of the European Council and the President of the European Commission. During the agenda-setting process, these summit meetings were an opportunity to consult with each other, demonstrate political commitment to a new trade and investment agreement and reflect upon the scope and coverage of such an economic agreement.

a) The Prelude: the Canada-EU Summit in Berlin (June 2007)

With the strong support of the German Council Presidency (Hübner, 2011), the Canadian federal government and the EU's leaders announced, at their summit in Berlin in June 2007, their intention to re-open bilateral economic negotiations for the first time after the failure of the TIEA nego-

---

104 Interview with member of Quebec Liberal government, Montreal, 24 October 2014.

tiations. In their Summit Statement, they stated their intention to pursue negotiations on a new economic agreement. At this stage in the agenda-setting process, the scope and coverage of such a new agreement were still in flux. Political leaders on both sides of the Atlantic highlighted the potential for increased commercial relations, mostly through the reduction of non-tariff barriers, and cooperation reaching beyond commercial exchange through enhanced cooperation in the areas of science and technology, energy and the environment. In their wording in the Summit Statement, leaders referred to "a closer economic partnership" as well as to a "balanced and closer EU-Canada economic integration." In order to determine the costs and benefits of such an agreement, Canada and the EU commissioned a Joint Study. Jointly drafted by the Government of Canada, led by Foreign Affairs and International Trade, and the European Commission, led by DG Trade, this study should be presented at their next summit scheduled in October 2008.

b) The Overture: the Canada-EU Summit and the bilateral France-Quebec visit in Quebec City (October 2008)

In October 2008, several events took place in Quebec City: the EU-Canada summit under the rotating French Presidency of the Council of the EU, a bilateral visit to Quebec by French President Nicolas Sarkozy, as well as the summit of the international organisation *La Francophonie*. Furthermore, Quebec City celebrated its 400th anniversary. The convergence of these events created momentum and international attention for Quebec, including its project of a new trade and investment agreement. In a situation where Quebec as a Canadian province did not have jurisdiction to launch bilateral negotiations or even meet with EU leaders in the formal context of a summit, capturing international attention was key for Quebec's representatives. These events allowed its government and diplomats to showcase their intention to launch a new trade and investment agreement, as well as their success in convincing key gatekeepers on both sides of the Atlantic. As a Quebec diplomat pointed out, October 2008 was a key moment in launching negotiations:

> C'est un peu comme si tous les astres étaient alignés à ce moment-là.[105]

---

105 Interview with Quebec diplomat, Montreal, 9 October 2014.

Two events were particularly important for the agenda-setting process: the Canada-EU summit and the French bilateral visit to Quebec.

The *EU-Canada summit in 2008* represented a crucial moment in the agenda-setting process: unlike the exploratory 2007 summit, the 2008 summit held in Quebec City expressed strong political commitment. During this summit, decision-makers publicly endorsed a new trade agreement in their Summit Statement:

> Based on the results of the study and the interest demonstrated by our business communities, and in order to provide crucial impetus to creating a stronger, ambitious and balanced economic partnership, [...] [we] are prepared to initiate before the end of the year the steps to obtain the mandates necessary to launch negotiations as early as possible in 2009. We will endeavour to complete these negotiations quickly, [...] (EU and Government of Canada, 2008).

They also reviewed the results of the Joint Study commissioned in Berlin in June 2007 (European Commission and Government of Canada, 2008). In their study, the Government of Canada and the European Commission shortly recapitulated their existing bilateral economic relations, thoroughly reviewed the factors affecting Canada-EU trade and investment relations, and identified existing and potential areas for bilateral cooperation. In their assessment of the costs and benefits of remaining tariff and non-tariff-barriers to the flows of goods, services and investments, the Canadian federal government and the EU reached the conclusion "that there is scope for deepening the EU-Canada economic relationship and that bilateral trade and investment flows have not reached their full potential (European Commission and Government of Canada, 2008, p. 28)" This broad approach very much reflected the project promoted by Quebec's Liberal government aiming to widen the space of Quebec's economic activity. According to the study's projections, direct gains in GDP from a trade agreement would reach €11.6 billion in the EU and €8.2 billion in Canada by 2014, in addition to indirect gains from cooperation in less-quantifiable areas. Although the study refrained from providing the possible scope and coverage of a new agreement, it already provided a comprehensive review of possible sectoral and cross-sectoral areas of cooperation. Apart from trade obstacles related to the reduction or abolition of tariffs and tariff-rate import quotas, it identified potential benefits arising from the reduction of non-tariff barriers related to market access rights, labour regulations, intellectual property rights, telecommunication and electronic commerce. In addition, the study identified areas in which cooperation could be enhanced: science and technology, energy, environment, regulatory cooperation, transport, customs cooperation and trade facilitation, employment and social affairs, movement of people, investment promotion, competition, taxation matters, and fisheries.

As revealed by the Joint Study, several of the issues with potential economic benefit fell under Canadian provincial or European member state jurisdiction to varying degrees —including labour, environment, social and educational regulation. As the Summit Statement highlighted, the sub-federal level—the Canadian provinces and territories and the European member states— would therefore play a key role in the negotiation process:

> Canada and the EU agree to work together to define the scope of a deepened economic agreement and to establish the critical points for its successful conclusion, particularly the involvement of Canada's provinces and territories and EU Member States in areas under their competencies. This agreement will address key issues for both parties (EU and Government of Canada, 2008).

During this summit, leaders also commissioned a Scoping Report in order to determine the scope and coverage of the new trade and investment agreement. While the Joint Study on the costs and benefits of the new agreement intended to illustrate economic growth potential and therefore served as a tool for building a coalition in support of launching negotiations, the Scoping Report was technical in nature: it provided the future negotiation teams with negotiation indications by highlighting the potential areas to be covered and the depth of reciprocal market access.[106] This report was to be rendered in early 2009.

For Quebec's representatives, the *bilateral visit by French President Sarkozy* to Quebec was probably the most important in these series of events, because it served to build domestic support by feeding into representatives' discursive and coalitional strategies respectively. Reminding Quebeckers of their strong ties with France and Europe, and of the positive effects of these ties on province-building in Quebec, the provincial government depicted France as an actor supporting Quebec's province-building project by contributing to economic and cultural development. Through this visit, the Liberal government also underscored its specific understanding of Canadian federalism, which was one where Quebec successfully engaged in

---

106 Interview with European Commission official, Brussels, 23 July 2014.

flexible relations with key international partners, among which France, and thereby shaped Canadian trade policy.

In addition, the French visit to Quebec also served Quebec's representatives' coalitional strategy. In fact, the visit demonstrated French support for the government's economic development project and therefore underscored its credibility. French President Sarkozy fully endorsed the government's project on several occasions during his visit. For instance, he gave interviews to the Canadian national and Quebec provincial press. In all his contributions, Sarkozy highlighted the special relationship between France and Quebec and insisted on the need to have a bilateral trade agreement between Canada and the EU. He was also the first French President to deliver a speech to the National Assembly. In this speech, he endorsed the project of a new trade agreement and argued for an extension of the long-standing relation between France and Quebec—often only depicted in cultural terms—to the economic realm. In particular, he highlighted the need to strengthen cross-Atlantic investment relations:

> Il faut renforcer notre coopération économique. C'est un sujet de préoccupation du Premier ministre [Charest]. Les investissements croisés et partenariats d'affaires sont la clé de voûte. La France est aujourd'hui le deuxième investisseur étranger au Québec, et les entreprises et investisseurs du Québec sont très présents en France. Il nous faut aller beaucoup plus loin, car c'est sur la base de ces relations économiques que nous inscrirons durablement nos relations fraternelles. Et c'est sur cette base-là que nous serons à la hauteur de ceux qui nous ont précédés (Sarkozy, 2008b).

Similar to French presidents' previous interventions in Quebec, such as President De Gaulle's famous address to Quebeckers in 1967, Sarkozy's speech attracted a lot of attention, confirming the prominence of France in Quebeckers province-building projects. Contrary to De Gaulle, however, Sarkozy explicitly rejected Quebec independence, thereby aligning himself with the current government's discursive strategy on Canadian federalism. According to him, Quebec needed to pursue its provincial development project as a member of the Canadian federation, which was why Sarkozy's speech was very well received by Quebec federalists, as a diplomat recounted:

> C'était de la musique aux oreilles de tous les fédéralistes québécois. [107]

---

107 Interview with Quebec diplomat, Montreal, 9 October 2014.

Finally, Sarkozy also participated in a press conference with Canadian Prime Minister Harper and President of the European Commission Barroso in Quebec City on 17 October 2008. By giving a conference with the Canadian Prime Minister in Quebec City, Sarkozy bridged the gap between the different levels of government in Canada, the provincial and the federal one. Even though he appeared in two different capacities—French president and rotating President of the Council of the EU—the symbolism of France supporting Quebec's government's economic project at different scales reinforced the Liberals government's discursive strategy. During this press conference, Sarkozy underlined once again that a new bilateral economic agreement aimed at regulating and supervising economic flows, rather than liberalising them. According to his analysis, the current economic crisis was rooted in the absence of international rules; a new economic agreement should represent a blueprint for future global economic governance.[108] Barroso suggested a similar analysis, also highlighting the need for a coordinated global response to the economic crisis.[109]

Yet, Sarkozy's bilateral visit to Quebec was more important for the discursive and coalitional strategies deployed by Quebec's representatives than it was for France. Although Quebec diplomats suspected—and hoped—that Sarkozy would make this new trade agreement a key topic of the French rotating Presidency of the Council of the EU,[110] this did not happen. Although France supported it, a new economic agreement did not figure high on the French list of priorities, as can be seen for instance in the Policy Report on the French Council presidency.[111] Sarkozy's support for a trade agreement between Canada and the EU was probably part of his transatlantic strategy vis-à-vis the US, which he suggested in his speech de-

---

108 "Il s'agit de bâtir la gouvernance mondiale du XXIème siècle, le système capitaliste du XXIème siècle.", see Sarkozy (2008a).

109 "La crise financière a des effets globaux, elle nous met tous à l'épreuve et ce ne sont que des réponses coordonnées à l'échelle globale qui pourront, dans un premier temps, stabiliser le système financier international, regagner la confiance et, dans un deuxième temps, refonder les bases de ce système pour une meilleure gestion, c'est-à-dire au service de nos citoyens et de nos entreprises." (Sarkozy, 2008a.)

110 Interview with Quebec diplomat, Montreal, 9 October 2014.

111 For example, in the policy report on the French Council Presidency, the bilateral economic relations with Canada project took a mere half page in a 50 pages-document (Secrétariat général des affaires européennes, 2008).

livered to the Quebec National Assembly when referring to including the US into France's perception of global economic integration.[112]

c) Launching Negotiations: the EU-Canada Summit in Prague (May 2009)

Subsequent to the EU-Canada summit meeting and the French visit to Quebec, leaders on both sides of the Atlantic agreed to initiate their respective formal processes for obtaining negotiation mandates in order to officially launch negotiations at the beginning of 2009. On the European side, the Council of the EU authorised the Commission to open negotiations concerning "an economic integration agreement with Canada, which will contain provisions on trade", on 27 April 2009, following Commission recommendations to do so on 7 April 2009. On the Canadian side, although the federal government did not need a mandate from the provinces, the statement issued by the Council of the Federation mirrored provincial Premiers' support for launching negotiations and represented the dynamics of Canadian cross-level interaction promoted by the Quebec Liberals. It also assured European leaders of provincial commitment.[113]

In their *Joint Report on the EU-Canada Scoping Exercise* rendered on 5 March 2009, Canada and the EU set out the scope of their negotiations. This report was more specific than the *Joint Study* of 2008 and provided initial negotiation recommendations. The report was the first step in delineating a future agreement's provisions: it put an emphasis on enhanced trade and investment relations, and mostly non-tariff barriers. Other areas that had been at the forefront of discussions before, including labour mobility, environmental and scientific cooperation, and culture, were reduced to secondary issues.

In their report, Canada and the EU also stressed the importance of provincial support for and participation in the negotiation process. They sug-

---

112 "Permettez-moi de vous dire que dans toute ma vie politique, j'ai suffisamment été un ami des Etats-Unis d'Amérique, cette grande nation. [...] Mais ils doivent comprendre aussi qu'ils ont des partenaires, qu'ils ne sont pas seuls dans le monde et qu'ensemble nous devons regarder l'avenir, que chacun ait sa place, parce que nous avons besoin de tout le monde pour garantir la paix et la prospérité au XXIème siècle." Nicolas Sarkozy, Discours du Président de la République devant l'Assemblée Nationale du Québec, Quebec City, 17 October 2008.

113 See 2.3 *Gaining Provincial Support* for an analysis of intergovernmental dynamics in Canada.

gested the establishment of an internal Canadian process to include the provinces and territories in the negotiations:

> While the federal government negotiates and enters into international treaties, the provinces and territories are responsible for implementing the treaty obligations that fall within their jurisdiction, including through enacting legislation, as required. For this reason, the Government of Canada will provide a process for the participation of the provinces and territories and ensure that their views are fully taken into account in the development of Canadian negotiating positions, both before and during these negotiations (Canada and EU, 2009, p. 2-3).

Furthermore, the Report also stressed that provincial participation in the negotiations should yield provincial commitment to ensure the smooth implementation of the international agreement into domestic law:

> A successful negotiation will include explicit commitments from provincial and territorial governments. These commitments will be incorporated into the agreement and provinces and territories will take the necessary steps to implement the provisions falling in their areas of competence. The provinces and territories will participate in the negotiations with a view to making binding commitments in all areas falling, wholly or in part, in their jurisdiction in any agreement to the full extent that European undertakings warrant (Canada and EU, 2009, p. 3).

Quebec representatives' discursive strategy of constructing an imperative for provincial involvement was thus highly successful. Negotiators on both side of the Atlantic accepted the reasoning that the Canadian provinces ought to be more present in the negotiations in order to make them succeed. In this discursive strategy, timing was crucial: Quebec's team first convinced the European Commissioner for Trade of the necessity to increase provincial presence during the negotiation process. Once it had acquired support from the European Commissioner, the Canadian federal government was left with no choice but to accept an increased participation of the provinces in the negotiation process. The Canadian federal diplomacy was aware of this strategy. Yet, they needed to comply if they were to launch negotiations with the EU, as a Canadian diplomat strongly involved in the CETA negotiations related:[114]

---

114 Interview with Canadian diplomat, Brussels, 8 July 2014.

External policy, like trade policy, really is the responsibility of the federal government. It tends to be a clear line on things like that. Now, on trade, with CETA, that line has become blurred again, because the EU requested that the provinces be more engaged in the CETA discussion. In areas of their competencies, they were very engaged. In that instance, we did develop a bit more of a collaborative approach to the negotiations, much more so than previous discussions. [...] With CETA, the EU really pushed to have provinces more involved.

At their summit in Prague in May 2009, leaders announced the launch of negotiations towards a "comprehensive economic partnership agreement". Through their *Summit Declaration*, they defined the outlines of the new agreement. While earlier declarations also highlighted the potential for more cooperation between the two economies beyond commercial exchange, leaders now focused to a large extent on trade and trade-related barriers to economic exchange. The *Joint Declaration* specified the areas that a new agreement should cover: trade in goods and services, market access, investment and other trade-related issues. After officially launching negotiations in Prague, the negotiation process started quickly. From 19-23 October 2009, the first negotiation round was held in Ottawa.

Since the very beginning of economic negotiations, provinces had thus been part of the process. To represent them in the negotiations, most provincial governments chose to name senior executive officers as chief negotiator for their province. Quebec embarked on a slightly different path by making Pierre-Marc Johnson chief negotiator. Johnson was a former provincial Premier, albeit only for the short period from October to December 1985. More importantly for the Liberal representatives' coalitional strategy, their government appointed a member of the PQ. Thereby, Quebec underlined the non-partisan nature of its position. Furthermore, Johnson was an experienced international negotiator. In 1991, he was appointed special advisor to the Secretariat of the United Nations Conference on Environment and Development. In 2001, Bernard Landry's government appointed Johnson as chief negotiator and advisor during a trade dispute between Canada and the US. After the launch of the official negotiations between Canada and the EU in May 2009, Johnson very actively engaged in negotiations with the Canadian federal negotiator, Steve Verheul, as well as the EU's negotiator, Mauro Petriccione. He also represented Quebec at the negotiation tables when it came to issues under provincial jurisdiction. Domestically, he reported to the Minister of International Relations under the Liberal government, and the Minister of Finance under the PQ government. On two occasions, Johnson appeared for public hearings at the National Assembly's Committee for Institutional Affairs (6 October 2010, 8 December 2011).

Conclusion

In this chapter, I argued that Quebec's government pursued the new economic agreement between Canada and the EU as part of their province-building project. They did so as a consequence of re-evaluating the provincial economic interest along the lines of the small open economy frame: in a situation where Quebec as a small and open economy depended on external economic developments, representatives concluded that the province needed to diversify its economic partnerships to foster province-building. Therefore, they updated their discursive strategy for provincial economic development. At the same time, representatives also discovered an opportunity for extending provincial paradiplomatic activity to the realm of international economic negotiations, an important pillar of the Quebec Liberals' representation of Canadian federalism. Since they structured the repertoire of federalism along the lines of the integration frame, they interpreted negotiations between Canada and the EU as an opportunity to extend their international activities as a Canadian province. Quebec's support for the new economic agreement in the mid-2000s was thus a story of continuity and change: continuity in cross-party support for free trade, yet change related to its preferred trade partner, which shifted from an almost exclusive focus on the US towards the EU.

Subsequently, Quebec's representatives convinced the European Commission that provincial participation in trade negotiations with Canada would lead to further-reaching provisions than in previous negotiations. Through this discursive process, they also provided the European Commission with a rationale to re-start economic negotiations with Canada. Their strategy constructed the new agreement as a far-reaching economic agreement that enabled, for the first time, comprehensive economic integration between Canada and the EU. In this way, the Canadian federal government felt compelled to accept European demands to include the provinces in the negotiations to a higher degree than in previous negotiations.

The story of CETA's agenda-setting was thus mainly about building unlikely coalitions in support of a project many considered implausible. In order to gain their partners' backing for the project, the Quebec government along with its diplomats in Brussels needed to deploy a coalitional strategy appealing to all essential partners. This strategy aligned actors who promoted a new trade agreement for a variety of reasons.

This chapter allowed to make three theoretical observations. First, in trade relations, interests are not stable but evolve when actors re-interpret the complex realities in which they are embedded. Although Quebec's embeddedness in North American value chains could have led the province to reinvigorate its relations with the US, its representatives chose to embark on a different path. Against the backdrop of two key elements of province-building—economic development and international activity—the government led by the Liberal party constructed the provincial interest in furthering this new project of transatlantic economic integration.

Second, in constructing these interests, political representatives act within the limits of important repertoires in place. They can restructure these repertoires by deploying new frames, but they need to justify these alterations. The agenda-setting of CETA, in Quebec, is thus an instance of discursive continuation, flanked by several discursive adaptations.

Third, representatives draw on discursive interactions of repertoires in their discursive and coalitional strategies. As a consequence of an interaction between the repertoire of province-building and the repertoire of federalism, representatives altered the structure of the repertoire of province-building. A discourse of market diversification allowed them to update the space in which Quebec's representatives embedded economic development, integrating Europe as an important space besides North America. Accordingly, the new structure given to the repertoire of province-building led Quebec's representatives to reconsider their interests deriving from Quebec's position in the global economy. In addition, this restructuring also established a new link between economic development and para-diplomatic activity in an area which had so far been considered to be under exclusive federal jurisdiction, namely international trade negotiations. Through the interaction of representatives' conception of provincial international activity as a pillar of Canadian federalism and their representation of economic development as a pillar of province-building, they constructed the need to be included as negotiation partner in transatlantic negotiations.

In May 2009, Canadian and European authorities launched negotiations on the (so far) most comprehensive economic and trade agreement, covering a vast array of remaining tariff barriers and non-tariff issues, and reaching beyond the scope of traditional trade agreements. The following chapters will closely examine Quebec's representatives' discourse associated with three topics covered during the negotiations, namely public procurement, investment and agriculture. At the end of these analyses, readers will understand why the project of a trade agreement became so important to Quebec's representatives that they abandoned provincial prerogatives on public procurement, encouraged foreign investment on Quebec territory, and reconsidered agricultural support policies. In these processes, Quebec's representatives mobilised the discourse established during the agenda-setting of CETA to underpin their evaluation of Quebec's interests.

Chapter 3: Public Procurement—a Promise Made, a Promise Kept?

When approaching the European Commissioner for Trade Peter Mandelson in 2007, Quebec's Premier Jean Charest committed to opening provincial public procurement[115] markets to European competitors. Given Canada's small consumer market, the promise to open the valuable provincial procurement markets was a key reason for the EU to initiate negotiations. Quebec thereby promised European businesses privileged access to bid on lucrative public contracts at the provincial level.[116] Despite this initial promise, negotiators on both sides of the Atlantic projected, when they started official negotiations in 2009, that the chapter on public procurement was going to be among the most contentious issues in the overall negotiation process. Both Europeans and Canadians expected difficulties against the background of long-standing provincial opposition to opening their procurement markets to international competitors. More specifically, Quebec had a well-established tradition of supporting vital sectors through the use of public contracts. Against the backdrop of the state dirigisme frame prevalent in discourse on public procurement in Quebec, many commentators projected that Quebec's Liberal government would face strong internal opposition after desisting from the provincial position of shielding procurement markets from international competition.

Therefore, success of the overall CETA negotiations hinged on the willingness of Canadian provinces to cooperate with the federal government

---

115 The WTO refers to *government* procurement, while the CETA language refers to *public* procurement. In the following, I will use the term 'public procurement' except for the names of specific agreements. Apart from remaining close to the CETA negotiation language, "public" also reveals the wide scope of the Canada-EU agreement, which includes authorities established under public law in addition to governments.

116 Provincial public procurement includes procurement by provincial governments, municipalities as well as by public and para-public companies under provincial authority, such as school boards and hospitals. The latter are often referred to as the 'MASH sector' (municipalities, municipal organisations, publicly-funded academic institutions, and social and health services entities). It includes a variety of contracts, including commercial contracts, construction contracts, service contracts and public-private partnerships.

in the implementation of procurement provisions. Both the Canadian federal government and negotiators on the European side were concerned that the provinces could refuse to implement provisions pertaining to public procurement under their authority once the agreement was ratified, as permitted by constitutional practice: European negotiators were in fact aware that Canadian provinces had refused, over several decades, to embrace the global trend—initiated by the OECD and further pursued by the WTO—of opening their procurement bids to foreign companies.

While the Canadian federal government had fully engaged in the international trend to include public procurement in international trade agreements, the provinces, to the contrary, managed to restrict access to their markets by refusing to implement these provisions. Before CETA was inscribed on the European and Canadian policy agendas in 2007, Canada's provincial procurement markets had not been opened comprehensively to international competition through any international agreement, which represents an exception both to the contemporary trade context and Canada's overall strong commitment to international trade.[117] As a consequence of provincial opposition, international agreements encompassing provincial procurement contracts, such as the WTO's 1994 *Agreement on Government Procurement*, remained void domestically in that respect. Others, such as NAFTA, only included provisions on federal, yet not on sub-federal, procurement.

In Quebec, the Liberal government's promise was therefore met with astonishment; in fact, the shift in Quebec's position with regard to provincial public procurement and trade could not be directly related to societal influences. On the one hand, Quebec's new position broke with successive government's usual stance on procurement, which advocated a logic of state dirigisme in the awarding of public contracts. In fact, provincial governments across party lines had used public procurement as a tool to steer Quebec's economic and social development, a common practice among Canadian provinces. As a consequence, procurement had become an instrument to support certain vital economic sectors or companies. Among provinces, Quebec had championed the use of procurement contracts as an

---

117 In parallel to CETA negotiations, new developments took place on provincial public procurement in Canada. In 2010, Canada and the US signed a new Agreement on Government Procurement which includes provincial procurement. Subsequently, provincial procurement was also included in the 2014 revision of the WTO's Agreement on Government Procurement. Yet, the scope of these agreements is more limited than CETA's. I will come back to these agreements in the course of this chapter.

instrument to encourage local companies without directly subsidising them, acting according to the logic of the state dirigisme frame. On the other hand, it was met with criticism from societal groups. Business representatives feared increased competition for local companies, and argued that this might challenge local economic development. In addition, the representatives of some large companies also refrained from fully supporting their government's position. When public employees' unions, and civil society movements in Quebec and at the Canadian level became aware of the inclusion of provincial procurement in CETA, they strongly and actively opposed the provincial government's position. Civil society's opposition to CETA's procurement chapter was equalled only by their rejection of agricultural provisions.

Against this background, Quebec's promise to open provincial procurement to foreign competitors was difficult to understand, and it could prove hard to implement. Negotiators and commentators anticipated challenging negotiations, all the more so with the provinces being fully involved in the negotiation process.

Yet, surprisingly, the chapter on procurement provisions was relatively easy to negotiate, and both sides were highly satisfied with the result. In the final negotiation text, the scope, including the coverage and depth of the provisions, was unexpectedly far-reaching.[118] Not only did the provinces commit to open their procurement markets, but they also included municipalities, crown corporations[119] and the entire MASH sector in CETA's chapter on public procurement.[120] CETA's scope on public procurement extended beyond other agreements reached on provincial contracts in parallel to the CETA negotiations, namely with the US (2010) and, subsequently, in the framework of the WTO (2012). Also, value thresholds above which CETA provisions apply were equal or lower in comparison to other similar agreements. Nevertheless, Quebec also wanted to include some exemptions, which was counterintuitive to its overall free trade strategy.

This chapter is a case where representatives considerably altered their discursive strategy and their subsequent position on CETA's procurement

---

118 Scope refers to coverage (entities or sectors covered) and depth (level of penetration of domestic economy, for instance through thresholds).

119 Crown corporations are entities owned by the Canadian provincial state and carrying out state services, but benefitting from a high degree of autonomy. In Quebec, the state company ("entreprise d'Etat") is more common.

120 See footnote 116.

chapter. It focusses on why Quebec changed its position with regard to public procurement and international trade against the backdrop of high domestic opposition, and how its government acquired domestic legitimacy to endorse CETA's provisions on provincial public procurement, which were unexpected both in scope and depth.

Section 1: Canadian Federalism and Provincial Public Procurement

When public authorities purchase services, construction works and supplies from private companies,[121] they need to follow certain rules and procedures in choosing their contractors. Rules and procedures applicable today are in large parts the result of international trade agendas: since public procurement contracts represent a substantial part of the global economy, restricting them to domestic contractors represents a sizable non-tariff barrier. In Canada, the internationalisation of public procurement practices considerably challenged the institutions and practices of Canadian federalism. Until CETA negotiations, the federal and provincial governments pursued incommensurate public procurement practices, which lead to inter-governmental tensions. The object of the following section is to depict the origins and consequences of these tensions, focussing first on the Canadian federal level and then on Quebec.

1. International Trade and Provincial Jurisdiction over Procurement

In Canada, each level of government has the authority to award public contracts in its own areas of jurisdiction and according to its respective rules of public expenditure. From a purely constitutional perspective, authority over public contracts at both levels of government is thus clearly separated. Since sectors with high-volume investments such as energy, transport and healthcare are under provincial jurisdiction, expenditures at the provincial level have been quite substantial. As the following table indicates, the share of provincial expenditures in total Canadian procurement has increased considerably since the mid-2000s. Their share increased because provinces spent more in volume, but also because federal expenditures diminished. While both levels of government spent roughly equal

---

121 Construction work contracts are usually regulated by specific rules due to their high value, and far-reaching impact on several economic actors.

amounts on public contracts before the mid-2000s, provinces now spend a larger sum than the federal government. In substantive terms, procurement by the federal level represented CAD 9 billion per year on average between 2000 and 2009. In comparison, Quebec's procurement represents slightly less than CAD 3 billion per year for the same period (Marketplace Canada (Marcan), 2017).

Table 8 – Evolution of Share of Total Public Procurement by Procuring Entity (1995-2012)

Source: Marketplace Canada (Marcan) (2017)

Both levels of government kept their procurement markets fairly closed to foreign competitors, as did most economies, until international trade agreements gradually opened them to foreign competition. Until the mid-1990s, public procurement was regulated to a large degree through internal budgeting rules, such as anti-corruption or integrity laws, so that governments could procure goods and services without necessarily resorting to public calls for tender. In this period, public procurement at the Canadian federal level was regulated by the budgeting rules of the *Financial Administration Act* (1985). Accordingly, individual bidders had no right to be considered eligible for a contract and public authorities were not obliged to guarantee a selection process based on objective and transparent criteria such as quality or pricing. Rather, they relied on criteria such as geographical location, personal contacts, or (in the case of Quebec) language background of the company's management. These practices sometimes favoured protectionism, fraud, and corruption, and created a situation where

127

public authorities used public procurement contracts to protect local industries (Anderson and Arrowsmith, 2011).

The Organisation for Economic Co-operation and Development (OECD) was the first international organisation to raise awareness of the economic benefits of subjecting government spending to transparent procedures and national treatment provisions among its members. In 1976, the OECD published its non-binding Draft Instrument on Government Purchasing Policies, Procedures and Practices. The first binding plurilateral agreement on procurement, the Tokyo Round Agreement on Government Procurement, was concluded in 1979 in the framework of the GATT. Since many considered public procurement to relate closely to state sovereignty, the Tokyo Round Agreement remained at the plurilateral level and was not regulated at the multilateral level (Collins, 2008). With the diffusion of international standards of public procurement through international trade negotiations, binding rules imposing objective and transparent criteria and foreign competition on procurement markets were introduced for the first time. By making public authorities accountable for the awarding of public procurement bids, practices of favoring companies based on their geographical origin, language or personal contacts became more difficult. In this way, members of the GATT hoped to allow foreign competitors to participate in public tenders. In this logic, welfare gains could be expected because governments could procure the best and cheapest goods, services and construction works (Hoekman and Mavroidis, 1995).

Yet, international trade law only began to truly permeate domestic procedures of government spending in the late 1980s and early 1990s against the backdrop of an increasing relevance of non-tariff issues for international trade agendas and a general political inclination to shrink public spending. From mere internal administrative rules, procurement procedures developed into public tendering procedures conferring certain rights on individual bidders by establishing clear benchmarks for awarding contracts. They introduced binding rules on transparent, non-discriminatory and competition-led procurement processes at the domestic level. In Canada, this process was launched in the early-1990s as an effect of NAFTA and its procurement chapter covering the federal, yet not the sub-federal, level of government. According to the logic of this new free trade area, public authorities should not favour their own companies to the detriment of companies based in the neighbour state. As a consequence of NAFTA provisions and the conclusion of the plurilateral Agreement on Government Procurement (GPA, 1994) among some members of the WTO, including Canada, the Canadian federal government passed the *Department of Public*

Works and Government Services Act (1996). Through this process, public procurement at the federal level was subjected to provisions on transparent, merit-based and competitive selection procedures, which conferred the right to bid on public contracts on foreign competitors covered by Canada's international commitments (Graham, 1983).

As so often before, the institutions and practices of Canadian federalism created a challenging situation for the federal government's external activities. While the federal government has an explicit constitutional mandate for foreign trade policy, the increasing appetite of foreign investors for provincial procurement markets and the international momentum to open government procurement to foreign competition in the late 1980s and early 1990s rendered provincial procurement contracts a topic of international trade negotiations. The provinces were surprisingly successful in shielding their procurement contracts from international processes introducing principles of trade law into domestic procurement procedures. This contrasted with the EU, where Single Market integration fuelled the process of opening national procurement markets to inter-member state competition (Garrett, 1992).

Subsequently, the interplay between expanding international trade and public procurement challenged the clear separation of competencies between levels of government. While the federal government opened its procurement market almost completely to foreign competitors as part of its liberal trade policy,[122] Canadian provinces continued to award procurement contracts to achieve social, economic or other collective goals (McMurtry, 2014). Thus, the once clear boundary between federal and provincial jurisdictions became blurred, creating a "new arena for federal provincial conflict" (Delagran, 1992). While the Canadian constitution does not explicitly foresee a modus operandi for trade relations and provincial procurement, various practices responding to the challenge brought by the new link between government procurement and trade have been carved out over the last decades (Paquin, 2013). Conflicts between the federal and provincial governments arose on several occasions when the provinces' refusal to allow foreign competitors blocked Canada's trade agenda. This process started with the North American economic integration, and was accelerated by a growing intervention of the WTO in government procure-

---

122 International provisions on procurement procedures tolerate, within clear limits, a certain degree of favouritism, typically for national security or for the protection of minorities.

ment practices in the mid-1990s, on both of which I will comment in the following.

NAFTA negotiations initially targeted Canadian provincial procurement, which the provinces vigorously and successfully opposed. Therefore, provincial and territorial procurement markets were not covered by chapter 10 in the *North American Free Trade Agreement* (1994), which only applied to federal procurement contracts being bid on by US or Mexican bidders. According to Paquin, the dynamics of the CUSFTA and NAFTA negotiation processes, which excluded the provinces from the official negotiation rounds, was the prime reason why provincial procurement was excluded from the scope of the North American Agreements (Paquin, 2013). Despite the failure to include sub-federal procurement in NAFTA, Canada, the US and Mexico did not lose sight of their goal to open these markets to companies based in member economies when NAFTA was signed. When the negotiations were concluded, the negotiating parties agreed that they would consult with state and provincial governments to revise the coverage of their procurement markets under NAFTA until the end of 1998, as set out in NAFTA art. 1024. Yet, they never reached an agreement on this contentious issue (Greenwold, 1994, p. 105). The Canadian provinces' refusal to open their procurement market irritated the US, which retaliated by refusing to open their state and local procurement markets to Canadian companies.

Deadlock on sub-national procurement between Canada and the US was only broken with the 2010 *Canada–United States Agreement on Government Procurement* (AGP). Through this agreement, Canada and its provinces permanently extended, for the first time in their trade relations, the scope of sub-federal procurement contracts to bids by foreign companies. These negotiations were triggered by the restrictive provisions on the participation of foreign companies in sub-national public procurement in the *American Recovery and Reinvestment Act* (ARRA, 2009), but also by the prospect of CETA's far-reaching procurement provisions (Global Affairs Canada, 2013b). ARRA was interpreted as the US response to Canadian provinces' reluctance to open their calls for tender to US companies. Even though an agreement was reached in 2010 before CETA was concluded, CETA's procurement chapter had a wider coverage and depth than the AGP.[123]

Tension between the Canadian federal government and the provinces also arose during the negotiation of a new agreement on government procurement among several WTO members. Canadian federal representatives

---

123 See section 2.1. in this chapter.

agreed to include provincial procurement in the list of covered Canadian sub-federal entities, listed in Annex II. According to the WTO's GPA (1994,[124] 2012[125]), Canada's federal level of government as well as the provinces were bound to establish an open, fair and transparent process of awarding government contracts,[126] which included accepting foreign bidders if contract values exceeded a certain threshold.[127] Yet, the Canadian provinces never acquiesced to the provisions negotiated on their behalf by the federal government, and refused to implement the GPA provisions. Even though the WTO's Committee on Government Procurement questioned Canada, in October 1995, about its failure to commit sub-federal entities to the GPA, an obligation specified in Annex II of the agreement, Canada never complied (Grady and Macmillan, 1999). As a consequence of Canadian federal institutions, the provisions Canada negotiated and ratified internationally remained void domestically.[128] Analyses of these incommensurate positions pointed to Canadian negotiation leverage—the country wanted to secure access to procurement markets in which its own companies have a comparative advantage—but also to diverging economic strategies at the federal and provincial levels. Rather than following the federal government's conviction that foreign competition on public contracts would increase welfare, the provinces resisted this strategy in order to pursue their own economic development strategy (see for a critical overview of the argument Collins, 2008, 2011a). As a consequence of provincial commitments to the US in 2010, Canada extended the scope of its subnational obligations in the GPA in 2014, a measure with which Quebec also complied. In comparison to CETA, however, the GPA's thresholds were considerably higher, which means that a smaller number of contracts were covered. Also, several procuring entities in the area of education, health

---

124 Entered into force in January 1996.

125 Entered into force in April 2014.

126 Exceptions to this general rule include, among others, crown corporations, as well as the most lucrative contracts in the areas of shipbuilding and repair, urban rail and urban transportation equipment, as well as contracts related to national security.

127 Thresholds of application represent the value of a contract above which international provisions apply. In other words, contracting parties only commit to submit their calls for tenders to the provisions of international trade agreements if they exceed a certain value threshold. In principle, there are different thresholds for goods, services, and construction work.

128 Many commentators document that the GPA does not cover provincial procurement. This is not accurate, however, since the agreement does cover them, even though the provinces never implemented the respective provisions.

and social services, as well as public companies and municipalities, were excluded from the scope of the agreement.

Domestically, public procurement also remained fairly closed among Canadian provinces, though to a lesser degree than internationally. Similar to the reluctance to open their procurement markets at the international level, provinces also preserved their right to favour companies based in their territory, and to discriminate against companies from other provinces. With the *Agreement on Internal Trade* (AIT) (1995, 2015), provincial first ministers were finally able to reach an intergovernmental agreement on provincial procurement practices. In the first text of the AIT (1995), chapter five on public procurement covered a large number of ministries and agencies, yet excluded municipalities, the MASH sector and crown corporations. After fourteen amendments, the AIT (2015) lowered applicable thresholds to CAD 25,000 for goods, and CAD 100,000 for services and construction works respectively,[129] and considerably reduced exceptions.[130] However, several procurement activities remained excluded from the principles of the AIT, including independent public corporations, entities whose objective was national security, businesses of a commercial nature or in competition with the private sector, and state monopolies involved in the transformation and distribution of goods and services. For Quebec, the *Caisse de dépôt et placement du Québec, Hydro-Québec* and the *Société des alcools du Québec* were among the excluded companies.[131] Procurement in the area of energy also remained excluded from AIT amendments.[132]

In sum, when the CETA negotiations were put on the official agendas of Canada and the EU in 2008, the EU's request to open Canadian procurement markets to European competitors reached beyond the scope of any other agreement on public procurement concluded thus far. In parallel to the CETA negotiation process, the provinces made some concessions to the US with the Canada-US Agreement on Government Procurement (2010) and, subsequently, to the signatory states of the WTO's Agreement on Government Procurement (2012), to which the EU was also a signatory. Still, the scope of these agreements did not extend to municipalities, school boards, and some crown corporations. Why provinces and more particularly Quebec offered to extend coverage and depth of CETA will be

---

129 AIT, art. 502.
130 Consolidated AIT, 2015, Annex 502.2A.
131 AIT, Annex 502.2A.
132 In the 2015 amendment, the chapter on energy contains only the provision that parties agree to negotiate in the future.

documented in section 2. Before that, however, I turn to Quebec's procurement practices more specifically. In Quebec, government procurement has played an important, albeit controversial, role ever since the Quiet Revolution. Public procurement has been deployed as an instrument for Quebec's province-building project along the lines of the state dirigisme frame, which is why Quebec tried for a long time to exclude it from the scope of its international commitments.

2. The Legacy of the Quiet Revolution: Quebec's Procurement in the Tradition of State Dirigisme

In Quebec, the institutions of Canadian federalism shielded the provincial state's procurement practices from international processes restricting states' ability to use public procurement contracts as a tool to achieve local economic, social or political objectives. Since the *Quiet Revolution*, Quebec's public spending practices have been an important instrument in achieving the provincial state's province-building goals by awarding contracts to companies which best reflected their respective province-building project. By the mere expansion of its role as a purchaser on the provincial market, the provincial state steered economic activity in the province (McRoberts, 1993, p. 361).

These dirigiste practices were grounded in a discourse of state dirigisme and province-building. For political leaders across the board, province-building would be best achieved by deploying dirigste practices. They wanted to direct economic development by supporting specific companies in strategic sectors. In an era without binding rules on government procurement—except for general rules of state budgeting—state officials and elected politicians could champion some companies at their discretion. On the governments' choices with regard to their procurement practices, McRoberts (1993, p. 361) reported that there was "the general disposition of government officials to favour Francophone bids". Public procurement played a crucial role in providing Quebec's Francophone companies with business opportunities. Many of these companies emerging in the early and mid-1970s became part of "Québec Inc.". At the core of this group were Québecor, Lavalin and Bombardier. The mass transit equipment company Bombardier and the engineering company Lavalin provide examples here.

Bombardier was founded in 1942 under the name L'Auto-Neige Bombardier Limitée as a producer of snowmobiles in the Eastern Townships of

Quebec by Joseph-Armand Bombardier. McRoberts documented that there was a strong link between provincial government procurement and the development of Bombardier into a leading multinational transportation equipment and aerospace company with headquarters in Montreal, registering revenues of around USD 18bn per year (McRoberts, 1993). The provincial government actively promoted Bombardier's production activities within the province and continues to do so today, mostly by awarding public contracts to the company, but also by intervening through loans and subsidies to correct for decreasing international orders (Milke, 2014). In this process, the large-scale and publicly-funded investments in the development, construction and maintenance of Montreal's metro system played a crucial role. While the contract for the first metro trains in the early and mid-1960s had been awarded to the Montreal-based Canadian Vickers—a subsidiary of the UK engineering company Vickers—the following contract in the early and mid-1970 was awarded to Bombardier. The aim was to build technological expertise in Quebec and subsequently enable the company to participate in international competition. This CAD 117 million contract included building 423 type MR-73 trains put to use in 1976 for the Olympics in Montreal (Société de transport de Montréal, 1997-2016) and allowed Bombardier to enter the international realm of mass transit equipment.

Apart from strategic state spending, the Quebec provincial state also steered economic development through the establishment of a large number of state companies.[133] State companies played an important role in the province's industrialisation. The mission of these public companies was to develop provincial industrial capacity in strategic sectors and regions. Public companies were mostly installed by nationalising existing industries. The government also launched a number of public companies specifically geared towards economic development. As Bernier noted, the leading political class conceived of Quebec's state companies as an instrument to catch up with overall Canadian levels of development (Bernier, 2012, p. 482). Over time, their development goal diminished to the benefit of commercial goals. Through its public companies, the provincial state took an active role as an economic player and used this leverage to strategically direct economic development, either by fostering provincial industrial capacity or by steering investments in the province. In this regard, the energy sector played a significant role, both because it was investment-intensive—thus requi-

---

133 Contrary to other provinces, Quebec avoided naming its public companies "crown corporations", the legal term used in other provinces.

ring a high volume of procurement—and because it carried a provincial development mission which continues in contemporary discourse. What distinguished Quebec's public companies from those in other Canadian provinces, although they were equally numerous, was that they were carriers of Quebec's national project; thus, challenging their status inherited from the Quiet Revolution was an inadvisable strategy for any political party (Bernier and Garon, 2003, p. 227, 242).

The energy generating, transmitting and distributing public company Hydro-Québec was emblematic of these dirigiste practices. Energy being under exclusive provincial jurisdiction, the provinces jealously kept their energy markets closedand used investment-intensive facilities to promote strategic sectors of their choice. Each province developed its own energy mix, which encouraged the contemporary heterogeneity of the Canadian energy market as well as the considerable isolation of these markets from inter-provincial procurement.[134] Energy sources ranged from fossil fuels in Alberta to nuclear power in Ontario and hydro-electric energy in Quebec. In the 1960s, the Lesage government chose to invest in water-powered plants, thus exploiting the natural resources of the province. The provincial government continuously invested in the development of expertise and equipment depicting Hydro-Québec as a symbol for provincial energy autonomy and engineering capacity as well as a driver of the development of peripheral areas in the province (Faucher, 1989; Faucher and Bergeron, 1986). In its procurement practices, it was common for Hydro-Québec to favour local Francophone companies. Energy being a sector under exclusive provincial jurisdiction, the provinces heavily invested into the development, conservation and management of sites and facilities in their territories. In addition, the creation of Hydro-Québec and the choice to invest in hydro-electric energy involved large infrastructure projects, which fuelled the activity of private companies, notably Lavalin, contributing to these construction works. Also, one of its aims was to generate energy at comparatively low rates which in turn attracted energy-intensive industries, supporting the creation of jobs in the province. Many of these investments in Quebec's Northern regions were in contradiction to the interests of rural or peripheral communities, and especially First Nations, and have been criticized for not taking objections seriously (Martin, 2008; 2010; Prémont, 2014; Slowey, 2008).

---

134 The chapter on energy in the Agreement on Internal Trade (1995) remained blank.

While Hydro-Québec's mission clearly lay in social and spatial development of peripheral areas during the Quiet Revolution, the company has taken an increasingly commercial role since the 1980s, even exporting to the US and other Canadian provinces (Bernard, 1982; Bernard and Doucet, 1999). By becoming profitable, Hydro-Québec evolved into an important source of revenue for the provincial government (Bernard, 2014; Bernier, 2014). Therefore, even after internal operational and strategic modernisation, the legitimacy of the public status of Hydro-Québec has never truly been challenged in spite of suggestions on privatising the company (see Lanoue and Hafsi, 2010 for a comprehensive overview). Recently, Hydroelectric energy represented around 40% of the province's total energy consumption and was generated almost entirely by Hydro-Québec (Gouvernement du Québec, 2007-2013).

Against the backdrop of directive state action through state spending and Quebec's resistance to internationalisation, Quebec's practices of dirigisme could survive longer than internationalisation would generally have permitted had Quebec been a sovereign state. Until the CETA negotiations, public procurement practices were underpinned by the state dirigisme frame structuring the repertoire of province-building. Therefore, provincial general budgeting rules applying to public procurement set out in the law on the *Secrétariat du Conseil du Trésor* (1971) were replaced by the *Loi sur les contrats des organismes publics* only in 2006. For the first time, this new law adopted, in its article 2, procedural principles similar to those established at the international level, without, however, granting foreign companies any access rights to provincial procurement markets. These legal principles included transparency, integrity, fairness and accountability. Importantly, the recent law conferred the right to participate in tendering procedures on qualified competitors. The law also explicitly referred to the intergovernmental agreements Quebec concluded comprising public procurement. This new law also set the scene for the internationalization of Quebec's procurement markets, albeit with some exceptions.

Section 2: Re-evaluating Public Procurement as an Instrument for Provincial Development—the Small Open Economy Frame

Against this backdrop of provincial resistance to opening their procurement markets to foreign bidders—couched in a long tradition of state dirigisme, particularly in Quebec—CETA negotiators on both sides of the Atlantic expected laborious negotiations. Beyond the possibility of provinces' refusal to implement procurement provisions under their jurisdiction, Canadian federal negotiators were unaccustomed to brokering a deal on a key area of provincial competency. Similar to the doubts raised by negotiators, voices in the academic literature during the early negotiation stages also evaluated provincial procurement as potentially hazardous for CETA. According to these analyses, CETA provisions on procurement were unlikely, for economic and internal political reasons, to deviate substantially from the agreement reached in 2010 between Canada and the US on government procurement (Hübner, 2010; Kukucha, 2010, 2011b, 2013).

In these circumstances, the Quebec Liberals' active promotion of opening their procurement markets to foreign competitors, albeit with some exceptions, stood out. Even more remarkable was their key argument for their position: opening procurement markets would foster provincial development. At the beginning, Quebec's Liberal government faced opposition, including from the other provinces (except for Alberta), the PQ, municipalities, and public employees' trade unions. It had to develop a coalitional strategy. Doing so with regard to the other provinces allowed the Quebec Liberals to strengthen the integration frame of the repertoire of federalism. Furthermore, province-based companies, including to some extent Bombardier, feared increased competition on public bids. They were joined in their claims by civil society organisations opposing the intended pace of global economic integration in general. Yet, in the end, even the PQ aligned with the Liberal government's reasoning—a puzzling stance with regard to Quebec's and especially the PQ's long-time adherence to practices related to state dirigisme. How Quebec came to fundamentally alter the relation between procurement and provincial development will be the object of this section. This section depicts the process through which Quebec's representatives constructed their position on public procurement. In this process, they re-evaluated the role of public procurement as a tool for province-building.

1. A Keystone of the Agreement: Public Procurement in the Overall Negotiation Process

In a context of low tariffs and a small Canadian consumer market, potential access to the lucrative procurement markets under provincial authority triggered European interest in a trade agreement with Canada in the first place. Opening provincial public procurement contracts to European companies was a prime reason to launch negotiations with Canada, and a key demand of the European side during the negotiations,

When CETA negotiations were officially launched at the EU-Canada summit in Prague in May 2009, delegations endorsed the Joint Report by the European Commission and the Government of Canada on the EU-Canada Scoping Exercise in which public procurement played a key role (Canada and EU, 2009). According to the scoping report, a new agreement should aim "to achieve full coverage of central and sub-central government procurement in all sectors, to ensure *inter alia* treatment no less favourable than that accorded to locally-established suppliers". Similarly, the 2009 mandate of the European Council to the European Commission left no doubt about the European ambition to gain privileged access for their companies to public calls for tender on the Canadian provincial level. According to the mandate:

> The Agreement should aim for maximum ambition complementing the Government Procurement Agreement in terms of coverage (procuring entities, sectors, thresholds, services contracts). The Agreement will ensure mutual access to public procurement markets at all administrative levels (national, regional and local) in the traditional sector as well as in the field of public utilities, ensuring treatment no less favourable than that accorded to locally-established suppliers. Market access provisions will extend to the relevant bodies governed by public law and to undertakings operating in the field of utilities (Council of the EU, 2009).

A deal including an extended scope on procurement would secure European companies privileged access to highly lucrative business opportunities: on the one hand, government procurement represented a high share of overall government expenses in industrialised countries, and even more so in Canada where it was above the OECD average (Organisation for Economic Cooperation and Development, 2015); on the other hand, provincial procurement contracts represented more than half of Canadian overall procurement, as shown above. The WTO estimated the value of provincial and territorial procurement at USD 20 billion per year and federal procurement at USD 15 billion in 2015 (World Trade Organization, 2015).[135] In 2009/10, provincial and territorial procurement represented CAD 19.6 bil-

---

135 These figures are quite volatile across years. There are also measurement differences among various statistical publications. For example, some publications include below-threshold contracts while others do not.

lion (of a total of CAD 31.8 billion in Canada) (Marcan (Marketplace Canada), 2017). Quebec's procurement market represented around 15 percent of overall Canadian procurement contracts on average, with an annual value of around CAD 5 billion in recent years (Québec, 2013). In 2014-15, Quebec public contracts individually worth over CAD 25,000 represented a total of CAD 9.3 billion (Gouvernement du Québec, 2016d). Additionally, according to Quebec chief negotiator Pierre-Marc Johnson, several large European companies relied on public procurement markets to sell their goods and services.[136] Privileged access to a lucrative market seemed a promising outcome to the European Commission, as interviewees from the EU, the Canadian federal and the Quebec provincial level reported.[137]

As documented in the previous chapter on agenda-setting, Euro-Canadian trade and investment relations had lost impetus after the failure of bilateral negotiations in 2006. Then, in early 2007, appetite for these markets was stimulated by Quebec's government when it offered to open provincial procurement markets to European competitors. It is therefore important to bear in mind that Quebec was not forced to endorse CETA provisions on public procurement, but actively participated in their inclusion in CETA.

Its government did so with two arguments. The first one was directly related to public procurement: Premier Charest promised Peter Mandelson that the other provinces supported his project and agreed to opening their procurement markets, even though they had not done so yet at that moment.[138] From their previous experience with the Agreement on Government Procurement (1994) concluded between several members of the WTO—where provinces refused to ratify the provisions under their jurisdiction negotiated by the federal government—both the Canadian federal government and the European Commission were well aware that the provinces' support for the procurement provisions in CETA was essential if these markets were to be opened to European companies. The second argument was only loosely connected to public procurement, but concerned knowledge about the involvement of the state in the economy, of which

---

136 National Assembly, Committee on Institutions, 6 October 2010 (= first public hearing of Pierre-Marc Johnson).

137 Senior Canadian diplomat, Brussels, 8 July 2014, French public official, Ministère des Finances et des Comptes publics, de l'Economie, de l'Industrie et du Numérique, Paris, 28 May 2015, senior French diplomat, January 2015.

138 Interview with member of Quebec's Liberal government (2008-2012), Montreal, 23 October 2014.

public procurement was an instrument. Quebec's government represented CETA as a first attempt for negotiating a bilateral comprehensive trade agreement between two developed economies involving a large number of behind-the-border issues. Given Canada's comparatively small size, CETA could be a test case for future negotiations between the EU and the US.[139] Since procurement by government entities mirrors traditions of state interventionism, the argument went, procurement negotiations might provide the European Commission with knowledge about the state's role in the economy in North American traditions. In this process, Quebec wanted to play the role of a facilitator in mediating between the European and North American traditions, as several interviewees from Quebec and beyond affirmed. According to a diplomat from Quebec, for instance,

> Il y a une sensibilité dans le fond, ce que j'appelle l'interventionnisme étatique en Europe, notamment dans le secteur de l'économie, et qui est particulièrement aiguë au niveau du Québec. A cause de ses sociétés d'Etat, à cause de ses programmes de stimulation et de développement économique. Le Québec s'est inspiré de l'Europe dans beaucoup de ses approches administratives. Quand on arrivait par exemple à des enjeux touchant le rôle des sociétés d'Etat, on pouvait chevaucher facilement entre la vision canadienne et la vision européenne. Et je pense qu'on a réussi à faciliter le dialogue.[140]

Quebec considered itself to be an interface between the European and North American economic traditions and wanted to provide consultancy on state companies and economic development strategies. By doing so, Quebec's government sought to increase the Canadian provinces' and particularly Quebec's bargaining power.

In sum, the success of the public procurement chapter reached beyond the mere topic area and concerned the agreement as a whole. If procurement negotiations were to fail, the continuation of the CETA negotiation and the conclusion of the overall agreement would be very unlikely. The-

---

139 This argument would prove to be true. In 2013, the EU launched negotiations with the US on similar topics as the ones covered by CETA. Also, Chrystia Freeland, the Canadian Trade Minister at the time, reported in an interview with Karen Smith on 14 July 2016 ("Growing Trade the Progressive Way") that the European Commission tried to hire Steve Verheul, the lead Canadian negotiator for CETA, as a consultant for their negotiations with the US, the prime reason being his knowledge on the European and US modes of negotiation, see (Freeland, 2016, time sequence at 1:21:27).

140 Interview with senior Quebec official, Montreal, 15 October 2014.

refore, procurement was in the spotlight and a satisfactory result was crucial.

2. An Unexpected Negotiation Outcome

When the CETA negotiation was closed in August 2014, negotiators had achieved a procurement chapter of considerable and quite unexpected scope (van Overmeire and Nychay, 2016). In cooperation with provincial governments, Canadian negotiators had succeeded in offering coverage of all government entities, the MASH sector, and provincial and territorial crown corporations. As a comprehensive agreement with a negative-list approach, CETA's procurement chapter covered all existing sectors and sub-sectors by default, although all parties included a number of exceptions.[141] Both in coverage and depth, CETA reached thus beyond what had been offered to foreign competitors from outside the EU. A Canadian diplomat reported that the Canadian sub-federal procurement offer represented "certainly the best agreement Canada has ever offered."[142] According to the same diplomat, public procurement was

> An area where we sort of thought it was going to be difficult and a problem to begin with, [but which] has actually turned out to be one of the really good things about the agreement, for both the EU and Canada.

As negotiators from the EU reported, both sides were extremely satisfied by the results obtained on procurement.[143] Even though CETA and the Agreement on Government Procurement concluded among several WTO

---

141 Negative lists are a negotiation technique in which the parties agree upon the sectors and sub-sectors they wish to exclude from their commitments. All other sectors and sub-sectors are included in their commitments by default. According to the European Commission, the negative list approach is more transparent than the positive list approach, a technique by which parties need to list all the commitments they wish to make, establishing a list of exclusions in the second step, see (European Commission, 2016a) From a more general perspective, it may also foster liberalisation, since new sectors would automatically be subject to the commitments set out in the agreement, although this effect has been contested, see (Adlung and Mamdouh, 2013.)

142 Interview with Canadian diplomat, Brussels, 8 July 2014.

143 Interview with French public official, Ministère des Finances et des Comptes publics, de l'Economie, de l'Industrie et du Numérique, Paris, 28 May 2015; Interview with high-ranking French diplomat, by phone, January 2015.

members (GPA, 1994, 2012) followed similar principles in their approach to procurement markets—an international trade lawyer reported that CE-TA is almost a "copy and paste" of the GPA[144]—its scope differed.

Particularly in comparison to the recent Canada-US Agreement on Government Procurement (AGP, 2010), modelled on the WTO GPA principles and modifying Canada's and the US' obligations under the WTP GPA, CETA's provisions stood out with regard to the entities covered and thresholds. Therefore, the prediction that provinces would not grant European competitors substantively different access rights than Canadian or US companies through the Canada-US AGP (Kukucha, 2010, 2011b) proved to be only partially true. In fact, there were substantive differences between the two agreements. First, the covered entities differentiated CETA from the Canada-US AGP. The AGP explicitly excluded purchasing contracts awarded by some municipalities, and the crown corporations of the provinces and territories.[145] CETA provisions, to the contrary, also applied to provincial crown corporations and the entire MASH sector, as the following table highlights. Second, value thresholds were higher in CETA than in the Canada-US AGP. For goods and services, CETA provisions applied to provincial government and agencies above thresholds of 200,000 SDR,[146] and 5,000,000 SDR for construction, excluding exceptions specified in the annexes. In the AGP, these thresholds were fixed at 355,000 SDR for goods and services and 5,000,000 SDR for construction. The following table specifies the detailed general thresholds for the respective public authorities and agreements. Thresholds varied between government entities and crown corporations, with thresholds for crown corporations being generally higher.

---

144 Interview with international trade lawyer, Montreal, 17 April 2016.
145 Except for construction works above the threshold of CAD 8,500,000, see the following table.
146 Special Drawing Rights (SDR) is an international reserve asset, created by the International Monetary Fund (IMF) in 1969 to supplement its member countries' official reserves. In addition to its role as a supplementary reserve asset, the SDR serves as the unit of account of the IMF and some other international organisations. The value of the SDR fluctuates and is based on the U.S. dollar, euro, the Japanese yen, and pound sterling. The Chinese renminbi has been added as the fifth currency in October 2016. Providing value thresholds in SDR permits to adapt them to current currency values. On 2 September 2014, 1 SDR equalled CAD 1.65.

Table 9 – Comparison between General Value Thresholds in CETA's Public Procurement Provisions and the Canada-US Agreement on Government Procurement[147]

		Government Entity			Crown Corporation		
		Goods	Services	Construction	Goods	Services	Construction
Federal Ministries & Specified Agencies	CETA	130,000	130,000	5,000,000	355,000	355,000	5,000,000
	AGP	n.a. (WTO GPA thresholds apply)					
Provincial and Territorial Ministries & Specified Agencies	CETA	200,000	200,000	5,000,000	355,000	355,000	5,000,000
	AGP	355,000	355,000	5 million/ 8,500,000 CAD*	excluded	excluded	8,500,000 CAD
MASH Sector	CETA	200,000	200,000	5,000,000	n.a.		
	AGP	excluded	excluded	Municipalities: 8,500,000 CAD*	n.a.		

* The agencies and municipalities to which the threshold of 8,5 million CAD applies are specified in Appendix C Part B – Market Access.

Source: Consolidated CETA Text (September 2014), Canada-US Agreement on Government Procurement (2010)

This table summarises *general* procurement thresholds. Exceptions to this general rule are not documented in the table above.

The inclusion of the crown corporation Hydro-Québec's procurement activities in CETA was particularly stunning if compared to its coverage in Canadian inter-provincial agreements. On energy procurement, the EU demanded a level of access to provincial energy procurement markets which provinces had not even granted to each other in the Agreement on Internal Trade (1995). Contrary to the EU energy market whose integration proceeded quickly in the framework of the Single Market between 1996 and 2007 (Jabko, 2006, p. 91-120), the Canadian inter-provincial energy markets remained fairly closed. In fact, provincial jurisdiction in the sector,[148] paired with highly diverse natural circumstances and economic de-

---

147   Values in special drawing rights, except if otherwise specified (see also footnote 146).

148   Constitution Act 1867, 1982, art. 92A (1). In matters of energy production, the federal level only manages international energy transfers and matters pertaining to national safety. Since the 1970s and rising interest in energy supply and growing awareness for international environmental concerns, the federal level has

velopment projects, led to a high degree of heterogeneity in energy policies and energy landscapes. With the provinces procuring goods, services and construction works to invest in the development, conservation and management of energy sites and facilities in their territories, these markets were very lucrative but also very difficult to access. In some provinces, energy industries represented a considerable part of provincial GDP, reaching 20-30 percent in Newfoundland and Labrador, Alberta, and Saskatchewan, as the following graph shows. Energy accounted for CAD 53bn of the total Canadian GDP in 2002 (Government of Canada – Statistics Canada, 2003). Quebec excluded procurement by Hydro-Québec from all interprovincial agreements it committed to, the only exception being in its relations with its neighbour Ontario. In the framework of the *Agreement on Labour Mobility and Recognition of Qualifications, Skills and Work Experience in the Construction Industry (2006) Between the Government of Ontario and the Gouvernement du Québec* and the *Trade and Cooperation Agreement Between Ontario and Quebec* (2009), Quebec gave Ontario-based companies access to Hydro-Québec's construction contracts.

Table 10 – Percentage of Energy GDP in Total Province GDP (selected provinces, 2007 – 2014)

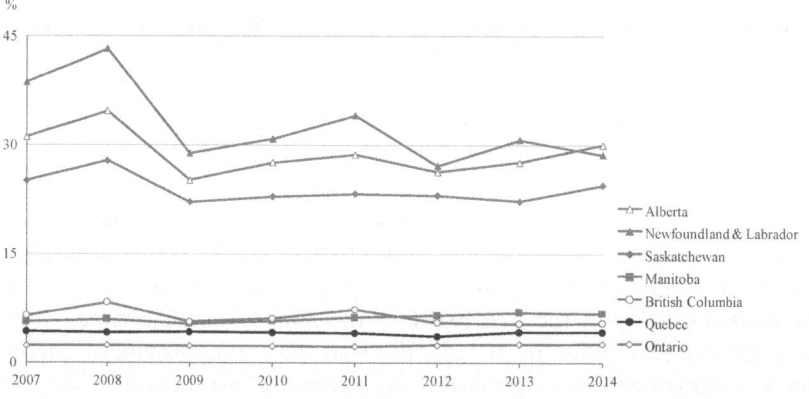

Source: Data from Statistics Canada (Government of Canada – Statistics Canada, 2015b).

---

become increasingly involved in the energy sector. The federal government has created two main regulatory agencies, the National Energy Board and the Canadian Nuclear Safety Commission, see The Standing Senate Committee on Energy, the Environment and Natural Resources (2012).

The EU had a clear demand: including procurement in the energy sector in the agreement.[149] Yet, opposition in several provinces made it difficult for Canada to meet this demand at first. In fact, at the beginning, only Alberta's government supported Quebec's position of including energy markets in CETA's procurement provisions. Not only were the other provinces reluctant to follow Charest's plan, but he also met with considerable resistance within Quebec: a Quebec diplomat reported for instance that Quebeckers opposed opening Hydro-Québec's procurement markets despite their overall support for free trade:

> Dans le cas de l'hydro-électricité, au niveau des marchés publics, la tendance des provinces c'était la fermeture. Ne pas ouvrir, sauf une province, qui était tout à fait ouverte, qui est toujours ouverte, c'est l'Alberta, donc, ça ne surprend pas [...] Mais toutes les autres provinces, en matière des monopoles d'Etat, en matière d'énergie, c'était, Don't touch. Et, le paradoxe c'est qu'au Québec ce sentiment-là est aussi très puissant. Le Saint Graal de l'Hydro-Québec-là, c'est qu'on ne touche pas à ça.[150]

Despite these far-reaching sub-federal commitments, the Canadian procurement offer also listed a number of exceptions. They were particularly interesting with regard to the aims of Canadian provinces when negotiating procurement. Indeed, these exceptions traced the boundaries of provinces' willingness to subject procurement to CETA provisions and therefore deserve special attention. Exceptions included measures relating to national security, protection of public morals, order or safety, as well as human, animal or plant life or health, intellectual property or the purchase of goods or services from persons with disabilities, philanthropic institutions or prison labour.[151] In addition, the purchase—yet not the production itself—of drinking water, energy, or fuels for the generation of energy was excluded.[152] There was also a list of specific exceptions: shipbuilding and repair for certain entities; agricultural goods that were part of support programmes; transportation services; certain goods or services purchased for representational or promotional purposes; programme material by broadcasters

---

149 Interview senior Quebec official, Montreal, 15 October 2014.
150 Interview senior Quebec official, Montreal, 15 October 2014.
151 CETA consolidated version (2014), Chapter 21 Government Procurement, art. 3 "Security and General Exceptions".
152 Canadian Government Procurement Market Offer, Notes to Annex X-03, Section B. This means that foreign direct investments in these areas are possible if provincial legislation permits it.

and contracts for broadcasting time; cultural industries in Quebec; some parts of drinking water, energy, transport and the postal sector; procurement by Aboriginal communities; and procurement in relation to an international crossing between Canada and another country.[153]

Another exception in goods was in the public transit sector. In this sector, Quebec and Ontario successfully advocated the inclusion of several quite far-reaching exceptions on mass transit procurement, as reported by government members involved in negotiations.[154] Contrary to Quebec's general inclination to open procurement markets, its position on mass transit equipment therefore stood out as an exception. According to the CETA text,[155] procuring entities in Quebec and Ontario may require that the successful bidder contract up to 25 percent of the contract value in Canada for mass transit vehicles. This means that 25 percent of the value contained in the procured vehicle needs to be of Canadian origin, which is a domestic content requirement. Furthermore, within these 25 percent, Quebec may include the performance requirement that the final assembly of these vehicles take place in Canada. Given that Quebec advocated opening its procurement markets to benefit from the effects of higher competition, why did its government defend several exceptions as well as a certain degree of favouritism in its mass transit equipment procurement?

3. Reconfiguring the Role of the Provincial State: The Unfolding of the Negotiation Process in Quebec

The challenge Quebec's representatives faced during the negotiation of provincial public procurement provisions lay in aligning two conflicting priorities, both anchored in the repertoire of province-building: on the one hand, they re-evaluated public procurement as a tool to further province-building and gave opening these markets to foreign competitors a positive

---

153 Canadian Government Procurement Market Offer, Notes to Annex X-07. This note also specifies the conditions for applying these exceptions, namely: the procurement needs to be of a total value estimated at one million Canadian dollars or less, it needs to support small firms or employment opportunities in non-urban areas, the derogation is limited to ten times per year and per province or territory, the measure cannot be funded by the federal government, and certain notification rules apply.

154 Interview with member of Quebec's PQ government (2012-2014), Skype, 24 April 2015.

155 Annex X-04, Goods.

quality; on the other hand, they also wished to preserve an important instrument of provincial economic development without federal interference.

The start of negotiations on provincial procurement was not auspicious. Opposition to opening procurement markets was substantial. Provincial procurement remained one of the last instruments for provincial governments to single-handedly steer economic development within their borders. In addition, the other provinces, except for Alberta, did not fully back Charest's plan at the beginning of the negotiations.[156] Initially, the other provinces were quite uncertain about their position. Moreover, Quebec's representatives had tied the overall success of CETA to provincial procurement during the agenda-setting stage. This link between success on procurement provisions and CETA created a hazardous situation in which the success of CETA depended upon Quebec's government's ability to form a coalition around their project both among Canadian provinces and within Quebec. Conflict among those hoping to open public procurement and those opposing this measure therefore seemed inevitable. If Quebec as the instigator of the idea of opening provincial procurement markets did not find an internal agreement, the chances for the other provinces to accept European demands would decrease considerably. Conflict and the necessity to reach an agreement made procurement a hotly debated topic in political discourse in Quebec's National Assembly.

On the whole, public procurement was one of the most discussed topics in Quebec's National Assembly, as the following table shows. The relative importance of discourse on public procurement mirrored internal cleavages in political discourse, but also the importance of successful negotiations on public procurement for the CETA negotiations as a whole. In the whole discourse on CETA in the Assembly (2006-2014), discourse on procurement represented 14 percent. While public procurement was absent in the agenda-setting phase, in the first and second negotiation stages, procurement was a very important topic, representing between 15 percent and 16 percent of the overall discussions on CETA. Nor was it discussed during the decision-making stage. In fact, an agreement on procurement was only reached when negotiations were officially closed in autumn 2014, with both sides being exceptionally satisfied by the result.

---

156   Interview with senior Quebec official, Montreal, 15 October 2014.

Table 11 –   Total Coding on Public Procurement per Negotiation Period (Percentages of total discourse on CETA, 2006-2014)

Negotiation Stage	Policy Cycle	Government in Office	Discourse on public procurement in total discourse on CETA[157] (% of total)
12.2006-05.2009	Agenda-Setting	PLQ	0
06.2009-09.2012	1st Negotiation Phase	PLQ	15
10.2012-04.2014	2nd Negotiation Phase	PQ	16
05.2014-12.2014	Decision-Making	PLQ	0

Source: Analysis of parliamentary debates (plenary and committees, N=159,127 words)

a) From State Dirigisme to a Small Open Economy (2009-2012)

Part of the explanation for Quebec's positive stance towards opening a substantial part of its procurement markets can be found in the dynamics of international negotiations. During the negotiation, negotiation partners sometimes exchanged their respective ambitions to acquire further market access for granting negotiation partners access to formerly protected sectors. Acquiescence to opening their public procurement markets to an unseen degree provided Quebec in particular with negotiation leverage to ask for European concessions in return. According to a Quebec diplomat, the province's negotiations tactics consisted in trading public procurement for concessions in agriculture. In return for European companies' privileged access to bidding on provincial public contracts and the backing of this cause in inter-provincial debate, Quebec asked for higher market access to

---

157   Measured in relation to parliamentary plenary and committee sessions in Quebec's National Assembly. Percentages represent the number of words coded as "Public Procurement" as ratio of the total discourse coded as "CETA". I coded the sections manually and inductively, guided by the indexes provided by the National assembly. Coding was therefore inductive and not based on word searches. The software NVivo counted the words coded and displayed the corresponding percentages.

European beef and pork markets and, most importantly, hoped to maintain the existing level of openness for European dairy, poultry and egg exporters.[158] In sum, the comprehensive nature of CETA allowed Quebec to engage, albeit with limited success as will become clear in the analysis of agricultural trade in chapter 5, in cross-sector bargains. Furthermore, Quebec and the other provinces considered public procurement as a necessary offer to acquire privileged access in general to the European consumer market.[159]

A second part of the explanation lay in the active involvement of the provinces in the negotiation process (Fafard and Leblond, 2012; Paquin, 2010, 2013). A combination of external factors created a situation which empowered the Canadian provinces. In fact, the EU's understanding that the Canadian federal government could not force the provinces to implement provisions in their areas of jurisdiction, its explicit request to involve the provinces as active negotiation partners, and its ambition of gaining privileged access to provincial procurement tenders for its companies strengthened the position of the provinces in the Canadian federal setting. In this situation, the provinces had the institutional power to block the negotiation of a comprehensive agreement, given that provincial public procurement was such an important issue. This represented an opportunity, for the provinces, to require a more active involvement in Canada's trade negotiations. In this context, they made their constitutional prerogative to allow or block the liberalisation of provincial public procurement a bargaining chip for acquiring access to the negotiation table. Subsequently, the federal government felt compelled to accept their request. This situation allowed the Quebec Liberal government to advance its discursive strategy promoting the integration of Quebec in Canada by encouraging its understanding of the repertoire of federalism as a cooperation among equal governments in their respective areas of jurisdiction.

This argument was not only taken up in the academic reflection on public procurement; Quebec's government and negotiation team equally highlighted that the positive outcome of the CETA negotiations on provincial procurement were directly related to the opportunity given to provinces to participate in the formal negotiations process in Brussels and Otta-

---

158 Interview with Quebec diplomat, Montreal, 15 October 2014. See chapter 5 for a more detailed account of the agricultural negotiations.
159 Interview with member of Manitoba's government (2007-2009), by phone, 11 July 2017.

wa.[160] Contrary to other trade negotiations, provincial negotiators were actually sitting at the negotiation tables.[161] Pierre-Marc Johnson, Quebec's chief negotiator, and his team, underlined that the federal design in Canada accounted for the EU's insistence to include Canadian provinces in the negotiations:

> Connaissant la complexité constitutionnelle canadienne, l'UE exigea que les provinces et territoires soient présents dès l'amorce des pourparlers afin de s'assurer notamment que leurs marchés publics figurent bel et bien dans l'offre canadienne (Johnson, Muzzi et al., 2013)

Similarly, a senior member of Quebec's government depicted provincial jurisdiction over their own procurement as a key asset for the provinces to require a more active mode of participation in the negotiation process. According to his analysis, the federal government had no choice but to accept the provinces' requirement of a more collaborative approach to trade policy if it expected them to open their public procurement markets to European companies. [162]

Still, the academic and empirical accounts mentioned above underestimate domestic political constraints which interfered with international trade negotiations during the ratification and implementation processes.[163] In fact, despite Premier Charest's initial promise to European Trade Commissioner Mandelson, Quebec's government still had to surmount domestic opposition to its new discursive strategy. Since Quebec's parliamentary opposition parties were excluded from the negotiation process, there was a chance that they would jeopardise ratification and implementation if they entered government shortly before or during the ratification and implementation stages. Among political parties, the Parti Québécois (PQ) was most likely to form a future government, which made its support essential for the future implementation of CETA's provisions. Among members of the PQ close to trade unions, opposition was highest.[164] Still other factions in the party condemned the potential inclusion of the public company Hy-

---

160 Interview with high-ranking Canadian diplomat, Brussels, 8 July 2014.
161 Interview with senior Quebec diplomat, Montreal, 15 October 2014.
162 Interview with member of Quebec's Liberal government (2008-2012), Montreal, 23 October 2014.
163 Quebec is the only province which foresees a formal ratification process for international agreements through its *Loi sur le Ministère des Relations internationales* (1988, as last amended in 2014).
164 Interview with Quebec representative of the Canadian Union of Public Employees, Montreal, 23 June 2016.

dro-Québec in the Quebec offer, given its role in fostering provincial development in remote areas and in providing energy-security.[165] When the PQ was elected in 2012, the *Globe and Mail* for instance asked, "whether Quebec's openness toward free trade will survive the election of a PQ government" (Cousineau, 2012). In the same vein, *La Presse* reported on Premier Marois' threat not to implement CETA provisions in areas of provincial jurisdiction if the latter contravened her government's expectations (Larocque, 2013). Support for opening procurement on behalf of the PQ—the political party championing dirigisme in the economy in order to foster Quebec development—was highly unexpected and therefore requires further attention.

In addition, a comparison to the Canada-US AGP (2010) provides a counterfactual to the argument that involvement in the negotiation process accounted for the negotiation outcome. Contrary to CETA, this negotiation process was led by the federal government alone and the provinces were not part of the official delegations. According to a report by the Library of Congress (Clarke, 2015), citing an article published in the *Financial Post*, Stephen Harper contacted the provinces in June 2010 to acquire their consent to open their procurement markets to US companies. At first, all provinces *except for Quebec* opposed this measure—an example of Quebec supporting opening their procurement without participating in the negotiations. Eventually, however, provinces felt compelled to accept the agreement, even though the federal government holds no formal power to force them to implement provisions from international agreements which fall under their jurisdiction (Kukucha, 2008; Paquin, 2010). This outcome can be read in several ways. Provinces could have acted under pressure from the federal government. According to the federal level, provincial reluctance to include US companies in their public procurement provisions had damaged the overall economic diplomatic relation between Canada and the US. Provinces were also exposed to business pressures, mainly from the steel and manufacturing industry. As a consequence of domestic content provisions at the state level included in the ARRA (2009), Canadian producers had suffered losses. Although ARRA did not contravene US obligations under international trade law, many interpreted these practices as retaliatory measures directed against Canadian provinces

---

165 This argument was dominantly suggested by Louise Beaudoin, for example in the Committee on Institutions, 6 October 2010 (= first public hearing of Pierre-Marc Johnson) and 8 December 2011 (= second public hearing of Pierre-Marc Johnson).

refusing to open their procurement markets to their Southern neighbour. In the overall Canadian interest, the federal government tried to resolve this "trade war" at the sub-federal level by negotiating an agreement with the US that would include provincial procurement markets.

In sum, challenged by long-established practices of provincial public procurement and recent development in international procurement agreements, an institutional argument based on sub-federal participation in international trade negotiations alone cannot account for provincial acquiescence to CETA's procurement provisions. Therefore, the process through which members of the PLQ, and later also of the PQ, came to conceive of Quebec's interest as lying in opening procurement markets to foreign competitors deserves further attention.

The following analysis shows how representatives re-evaluated their interest on public procurement and represented opening these markets to foreign competitors and acquiring privileged access to European markets as a key step in economic development, a pillar of province-building. As a positive side effect for Liberal representatives, they also promoted the integration frame of the repertoire of federalism by strengthening Quebec's role in Canada's trade policy-making. In its new discursive strategy, the Liberal government reconfigured the repertoire of province-building using the small open economy frame. By doing so, it depicted restrictive procurement procedures as an obstacle for province-building and, conversely, promoted foreign competition as a driver for provincial development. Hence, representatives constructed opening public procurement to foreign competition as an asset—not a hindrance—for provincial development. Convinced of the beneficial effects of increased competition on provincial development in Quebec and the creation of new export opportunities for Quebec-based companies, they actively suggested opening these markets to foreign competition.

Quebec's representatives, including their negotiation team, depicted three ways in which opening public procurement could foster province-building. In their discursive strategy, the small open economy frame played a central role in legitimising representatives' new position. The *first* argument in support of increased competition joined liberal market assumptions. According to this discourse, increasing competition would encourage efficiency and the development of new goods and services. This process would enhance companies' competitiveness on international markets in general. Referring to the competitiveness of Quebec production, and thereby legitimising increasing competition, chief negotiator Pierre-Marc Johnson related the case of a business leader in Quebec who was not alarmed by increased competition from Europe, given the higher quality and lower price of his products in comparison to European equivalents.[166]

Their *second* argument promised new business opportunities for Quebec companies in the EU. In a situation where Quebec depended upon exports to generate business opportunities for its domestic companies, acquiring access to the vast EU procurement market was a key ambition. Central to the dynamics of CETA procurement negotiations, reciprocity was thus a key driver for Quebec to suggest opening its procurement markets. A member of the Liberal government asserted for instance that opening procurement created business opportunities and incentives, for Quebec companies, to become more competitive,[167] thus contributing to provincial economic growth and welfare. Furthermore, procurement markets were considered attractive especially for small- and medium-sized businesses since they were more predictable than other markets. Based on CETA's procurement provisions, Quebec companies would acquire privileged access to tendering procedures in the EU, going well beyond the 2014 WTO GPA, as the following table published on the Quebec government's web page shows. Some thresholds were indeed lower for CETA than for the revised GPA (2014), and CETA also covered more entities including the MASH sector, public utilities and public services. In sum, market penetration especially at lower levels of government and at the municipal level was higher in CETA, while coverage of central entities was the same. From a Quebec perspective, CETA provided thus multiple opportunities for Quebec companies which were not given by the GPA. CETA would therefore give Quebec companies an advantage on European public procurement markets in comparison to other third countries.

---

166 National Assembly, Committee on Institutions, 6 October 2010 (= first public hearing of Pierre-Marc Johnson).

167 Interview with member of Quebec's Liberal government (2008-2012, 2014), Montreal, 20 October 2014.

*Table 12 –   Value Thresholds for Quebec Companies on the EU's Public Procure-
ment Market: The Agreement on Government Procurement (GPA)
and the Comprehensive Economic and Trade Agreement (CETA)
(Goods and Services)*

Entities	GPA (1996)	Revised GPA (2014)	CETA (2016)
Central EU entities (Council of the EU, European Commission) Ministries and public entities in member states	130 000 €	130 000 €	130 000 €
Sub-central government entities	excluded	355 000 €	200 000 €
Municipalities, hospitals, schools, universities	excluded	excluded	200 000 €
Public utilities	excluded	excluded	355 000 €
Public services (water, electricity, airports, and urban transport)	excluded	excluded	400 000 €

Source: Based on Gouvernement du Québec (2016b)

Translation by author, Special Drawing Rights (SDR) converted into euros by the Government of Quebec[168]

Representatives' *third* argument related to political development, another pillar of province-building. According to this argument, opening procurement to European competitors would contribute to strengthening the provincial state. By complying with the provisions of CETA, representatives hoped to employ the rules of international trade and public procurement to promote transparency, integrity and competition in the awarding of public contracts. On the one hand, increased competition would lead to lower prices in government purchases, thus contributing to reducing the existing differences, in the provinces, between the price index for the public sector and that for GDP (Mou, Atkinson et al., 2014). In this way, the government would contribute to a more careful handling of the taxes they collected, which was in line with the Liberals' overall ambition to reduce state spending during their term in office. On the other hand, opening

---

168   See footnote 146 for a definition of SDR.

procurement was also seen as a way to contain the risk of price collusion or favouritism. By subjecting tendering procedures to international competition, bureaucracies could assure that the criteria for tendering processes that they established with the *Loi sur les contrats des organismes publics* (2006) were observed. In addition to their domestic law, CETA would confer individual rights on bidders, so that bureaucracies could be held accountable more easily when distributing public contracts. This would add an additional layer of accountability. Through international trade law, Quebec's government could tie the hands of future governments in this regard. Chief negotiator Johnson summarised this ambition to strengthen the provincial state in a public hearing:[169]

> Mais l'ouverture des marchés publics, au Québec comme ailleurs, qu'est-ce qu'elle vise? Elle vise à donner des meilleurs prix aux institutions qui achètent, premier objectif; deuxième objectif : de rendre visibles ces prix; troisième objectif : de réduire les occasions de collusion entre les pouvoirs publics puis les pouvoirs privés.

Why did Quebec's representatives deem this necessary? In Quebec, the long-standing entanglement between private and public interests encouraged complicity between political decision-makers and private businesses in the awarding of public contracts in the past. In 2009, controversies on public procurement contracts resurfaced, fuelled by Charest's refusal to launch a public enquiry into the construction sector and donations made to the Liberal Party. Two years later, political pressure compelled the government to take action against potential collusion, corruption and fraud related to public procurement. The same year, the government invested the Commission of Inquiry on the Awarding and Management of Public Contracts in the Construction Industry, also referred to as Charbonneau Commission, to examine practices of collusion and corruption, as well as of organised crime infiltrating the construction industry. With respect to the high-profile cases investigated, their findings disparaged municipal practices of awarding contracts, and three mayors from major cities resigned as a consequence (Saint-Martin, 2016). In this context, many representatives, including from the PQ, considered internationally agreed and controlled procedures of government tendering as an antidote to these practices.

---

169 National Assembly, Committee on Institutions, 8 December 2011 (= second public hearing of Pierre-Marc Johnson)

Representatives hence fundamentally altered the dominant discursive strategy: while representatives argued, before the CETA negotiations, that they could strengthen the province's economy by favouring local contractors, they now upheld that they could pursue economic and political development through increased competition and new export opportunities for Quebec's companies. For the first time, a leading party suggested that the opportunities offered on foreign markets outweighed potential domestic drawbacks *and* that these drawbacks might even contribute to provincial development by forcing domestic companies to become more competitive. As table 13 illustrates, representatives from both leading parties shifted to the small open economy frame between 2009 and 2014, with the share of discourse coded as 'state dirigisme' declining steadily and being absent altogether since 2014.

Table 13 – Frames by Political Parties at Different Negotiation Stages (Percentages of Total Discourse at a Certain Negotiation Stage)

PQ	12.2006-05.2009	06.2009-09.2012	10.2012-04.2014	05.2014-12.2014
Small Open Economy	0	1	79	0
State Dirigisme	0	99	21	0
	(100%)	100%	100%	
PLQ	12.2006-05.2009	06.2009-09.2012	10.2012-04.2014	05.2014-12.2014
Small Open Economy	0	49	100	0
State Dirigisme	0	51	0	0
	(100%)	100%	100%	(100%)

Source: Analysis of parliamentary debates (plenary and committees, N=30,743 words)

It is thus crucial to underline that Quebec's representatives did not merely acquiesce to European demands because they were pressured, but because they reconsidered provincial interests. In fact, they were previously quite successful in shielding their procurement markets from internationalisation, as demonstrated in this chapter's first section. As a result of restructuring the repertoire of province-building using the small open economy frame, Quebec's representatives now encouraged that Quebec as a small economy needed to secure market access to other economies in order to preserve economic welfare. In addition, they also constructed this step as a way to pursue the development of their provincial state. As a consequence of this discursive restructuring, representatives interpreted opening procurement markets as an opportunity for Quebec to generate new wealth and contribute to provincial prosperity and state-building, two pillars of province-building.

However, Quebec's government's new discursive strategy met with some opposition in the other provinces and considerable opposition domestically, compelling it to develop a coalitional strategy to bring important partners in line with its interpretation of provincial interests. During the early negotiation stages, the government's altered strategy was most strongly criticized.

Some degree of opposition to Quebec's new discursive strategy could be found in other Canadian provinces. Apart from Alberta, the provinces were not very eager to open their procurement to competing European companies,[170] even though their reasons to do so might have differed from those of opponents in Quebec. In general, the provinces' stance on government procurement provisions in CETA was ambiguous and sometimes contradictory. The most difficult issue was procurement in the energy sector, given that European companies were eager to penetrate this formerly highly protected and often state-led sector. However, Quebec's government quickly convinced the other provinces of the benefits of a trade agreement with the EU and in particular highlighted new export opportunities.[171]

When including the provinces in their coalitional strategy, the Quebec Liberals acted according to the integration frame of the repertoire of federalism. Unlike the PQ, the Quebec Liberals wanted to strengthen Quebec's position in the Canadian federation. They used the setting of the Council of the Federation to develop provincial support for opening procurement contracts to European companies. In this setting, the federal government was obliged to acknowledge provincial jurisdiction on this issue,[172] which contributed to altering the mode of intergovernmental inter-

---

170 Interview with Senior Quebec official, Montreal, 15 October 2014.
171 Interview with member of the Manitoba government (2007-2009), by phone, 11 July 2017.
172 Interview with member of the Manitoba government (2007-2009), by phone, 11 July 2017.

action in Canada. Hence, the consequences of the shift in Quebec's position on public procurement were not limited to Quebec's province-building project. Building a coalitional strategy with the other provinces allowed Quebec's Liberal government to strengthen the integration frame to the detriment of the independence frame structuring the repertoire of federalism.

In opposing their government's new discursive strategy, domestic opponents drew upon the former structure of the repertoire of province-building using the frame of state dirigisme. They highlighted the necessity to direct economic development by consciously favouring some companies over others and thus rejected opening procurement to European competitors. For them, province-building depended on public authorities' capacity to channel market forces and exploit them for the overall benefit of the province. In this perspective, they claimed that public procurement was a redistributive tool: through directing state spending according to overall development goals, the provincial state could correct market deficiencies, such as environmental degradation or social inequalities. In a situation where the provinces had already surrendered many tools of provincial development either to the federal government, to international organisations during the process of international economic integration or through complying with international agreements, preserving public procurement was an essential instrument for province-building in their eyes. This dirigisme frame was shared initially among the members of the PQ, the CAQ,[173] and Québec Solidaire, but also among some members of the PLQ, who highlighted that Charest was contested in his own ranks. Political parties con-

---

173 A new political player entered the stage in the period from 2012 to 2014, the newly formed party Coalition Avenir Québec (CAQ). The CAQ is a political party founded in November 2011, originating from a social and political movement that published a manifesto on Quebec's future ("Coalition pour l'avenir du Québec") in February 2011. The CAQ wants to suggest a third way between the PQ's sovereign and the PLQ's federal programmes and calls itself a "nationalist" party. It emerged partly out of a critique of the PQ's politics formulated by former eminent PQ member and now CAQ leader Jean-François Legault, a businessman and co-founder of the airline Air Transat. According to Legault, the PQ has become too focused on the question of independence, thereby losing track of the more imminent problems Quebec faces in healthcare, education and economic development. Since the foundation of the party in 2011, the CAQ attracted former members of the PQ and merged with the Action démocratique du Québec (ADQ), with whose members the CAQ shares a common position on the status of Quebec within Canada.
.

testing the government's new discursive strategy aggregated claims from various social groups, including unions, social movements, and business, but also from public entities such as public companies or municipalities. After the following overview of the most contentious issues, I will come back to these claims in detail.

Since public procurement did not represent an economic sector in the conventional sense but cut across sectors, deputies discussed a large variety of specific issues alongside more general discussions. The following table gives an overview of the most important topics during the first negotiation stage, ranked according to their comparative relevance in representatives' parliamentary discourse. The most important topic was the CETA negotiation process. Opponents criticized the secrecy surrounding the negotiations and called for more involvement (see also Trew, 2013). In Quebec's Assembly, this discourse was embedded in the repertoire of federalism. While PQ deputies argued that the current negotiation dynamics were not sufficient to defend Quebec's interests, Liberal deputies upheld that the current mode of intergovernmental interaction served Quebec's interests best. There was thus a conflict around the frame that structured the repertoire of federalism. While the PQ used the independence frame and threatened not to implement CETA if negotiation dynamics were not altered, the Liberals drew upon the integration frame.

In Quebec, mirrored by the debates in the Assembly, three topics shaped the discourse on public procurement in particular: the procurement of mass transit equipment for public transportation; the generation, transport, and distribution of energy (mostly public companies, including Hydro-Québec); and the delivery of municipal public services (mostly water and waste management, including their potential privatisation), as table 14 documents. Overall, opposition to the government's discursive strategy was organised in three cross-provincial networks. First, there was an alliance of Quebec and Canadian municipalities acting against opening procurement contracts at the municipal level. Second, social movements grouped together in pan-Canadian networks opposing the current pace of trade negotiations led by the Trade Justice Network.[174] For them, public procurement was a key issue demonstrating that contemporary trade agreements such as CETA were, in essence, not about trade, but about reducing state regulatory capacity and its ability to provide public services to citizens. Third, public employees' trade unions also engaged in cross-provincial alli-

---

174 Interview with representative of the Trade Justice Network, Montreal, 23.12.2015 (Skype).

ances, although they did so to a lesser degree in Quebec. While the Quebec section of the Canadian Union of Public Employees (Syndicat Canadien de la Fonction Publique) fully embraced the pan-Canadian Union movement's opposition to opening procurement contracts, the Syndicat de la Fonction Publique et Para-Publique du Québec acted, for historical reasons, mainly in Quebec.[175]

Table 14 – Topics during the First Negotiation Stage (Percentage of Discourse on Public Procurement, 2009-2012)

Negotiation Process	24
Award Criteria	13
Public Transportation	12
Hydro-Québec	10
Water/Waste Management	8
Other topics*	33

Source: Analysis of parliamentary debates (plenary and committees, N=22,682 words)

*See the appendix for a complete list of other topics

aa) Diverging Conceptions of Provincial Interests: Mass Transit Equipment and Bombardier

Among contentious issues, mass transit equipment was the one most discussed in Quebec's National Assembly. The importance of this topic was first related to the high value of contracts for vehicles such as trains or busses. For example, the metro contract for the renewal of a part of Montreal's metro fleet was worth CAD 1.2 billion, and was thus among the largest contracts awarded in 2010 (Société de Transport de Montréal, 2010). In addition, public transportation traditionally involved mainly provincial and municipal sources of funding. Although jurisdiction for public transportation was, like other areas pertaining to transportation, shared between the federal and provincial levels of government,[176] urban public transportation

---

175 Interview with Quebec representative of the Canadian Union of Public Employees (CUPE/ SCFP), Montreal, 23 June 2016.
176 See for Quebec's jurisdiction in transportation Gouvernement du Québec, (2016c).

only had a short history of federal investments: the first federal government-led transportation strategies were only launched in 1998 (Roschlau, 2008). As a consequence, long-term investments in transportation equipment depended to a large extent on provincial, including municipal, funds. Success of CETA negotiations on provincial procurement thus depended to some extent also on the mass transit negotiation offer each province was willing to make. Furthermore, in Quebec more specifically, the public transportation equipment company Bombardier figured among the province's economic champions of the Quiet Revolution. New provisions with regard to the procurement of public transportation equipment would therefore have an impact on Bombardier, a company that has benefitted on several occasions from state support, as explained in section 1.

Despite its active support for opening procurement markets, Quebec nevertheless insisted on including high domestic content and imposing performance requirements for mass transit procurement activities, which were far-reaching exceptions. In explaining these exceptions, we might look at producer interests. Bombardier indeed kept several production plants in Quebec, so its interest could have led the government to preserve market shares for the company. Europe being home to specialised companies in mass transit equipment,[177] Bombardier could lose privileged access to these contracts awarded in most cases by provincial governments. At the time of negotiation, Bombardier was also exposed to fierce competition on the international mass transit procurement market, especially on the train and road transportation equipment sector for which tariffs were likely to be diminished with CETA.[178] During negotiations, Quebec's government seemed indeed to lean in the direction of protecting their ability to supply Bombardier with public contracts and thereby protect production plants in Quebec. In parallel to CETA negotiations, Quebec's Liberal government demonstrated how important preserving market shares for Bombardier was to it: representatives tried to exclude competition by the French rail vehicles and signalling equipment company Alstom and the Spanish Construcciones y Auxiliar de Ferrocarriles for a metro car renewal contract in Montreal at the expense of paying higher prices for the new cars (Corriveau, 2010).

---

177 For example, competition to Bombardier in replacing a part of Montreal's metro cars came from a Spanish and a French company. The Chinese offer was not considered admissible.

178 Interview with senior Quebec official, Montreal, 15 October 2014.

Bombardier's position in the global economy could well explain the government's insistence on including a number of exceptions in the mass transport equipment provisions. According to such a reading based on the influence of business interests, Bombardier wanted to preserve market shares on the Quebec and Canadian procurement markets through the inclusion of domestic content and performance requirements in CETA provisions. This plan could have translated into higher market shares for the company. In a framework of import-competing versus export-oriented interests, one might have argued that a more protective setting would be in the interest of Bombardier, since it might shield the company from European competition. As a matter of fact, a member of Quebec's government confirmed that the province wanted to preserve a certain market share for Bombardier in mass transit procurement:

> Et aux marchés publics des provinces. Dans le cadre de cet accès, il y avait des enjeux quant à ce qu'on appelle le " matériel roulant " c'est-à-dire les autobus, les trains, ce type de matériel. Donc les sociétés de transport dans les différentes municipalités achètent des autobus, achètent des trains et les Européens voulaient pouvoir accéder à ce marché. Et nous, comme vous vous en doutez, on voulait protéger une part de marché pour nos entreprises, entre autres pour Bombardier.[179]

Yet, surprisingly, Bombardier did not support such exceptions in CETA. Quite to the contrary, Bombardier's reluctance to accept domestic content requirements prompted the reduction of the domestic content requirements from initially 50 to 25 percent.[180] Even though Bombardier did not openly oppose the exceptions advocated by Quebec's representatives, interviews with members of Quebec's governments and diplomats revealed that Bombardier interpreted these exceptions as a hindrance rather than as a business opportunity. Contrary to what theories based on business interests would expect, Bombardier did not protect its production activities in Quebec and Canada. A member of Quebec's government confirmed that exceptions on mass transit were not included as a consequence of Bombardier's influence on the government:

---

179 Interview with member of Quebec's PQ government (2012-2014), Skype, 24 April 2015.
180 Interview with senior Quebec official, Montreal, 15 October 2014.

> Du côté de Bombardier, je vous dirais que [l'inclusion d'exceptions] n'est pas venu de Bombardier non plus. [...] Je ne vous dirais pas que Bombardier était enchanté de [l'inclusion d'exceptions].[181]

Why did Bombardier not endorse the Quebec government's position? The answer lay, to a large extent, in the nature of contemporary global value chains and their effect on trade (Young, 2016). As a multinational company, Bombardier strongly participated in contemporary practices of producing the different parts of its final products in various countries in order to benefit from competitive advantages associated with different places (van Assche, 2016). Therefore, domestic content and performance requirements represented constraints on Bombardier's production strategy and restricted its use of global value chains. Through CETA, Bombardier wished to liberalise rather than geographically restrict its activity, hoping to benefit from more flexibility in organising its production chains, as a member of government reported:

> Bombardier, c'est très simple à comprendre, Bombardier, d'une certaine façon, préfère plus de flexibilité. Alors d'imposer des contraintes dans l'accord, en vertu desquelles Bombardier ou les contrats de fournitures à des compagnies de transport doivent avoir un certain contenu québécois [...] qu'elle peut ne pas vouloir avoir à satisfaire.[182]

Bombardier did therefore not influence the provincial government to impose restrictions on opening public procurement contracts, but the company rather wanted to emancipate itself from the provincial government's influence with the help of a new trade agreement. These tensions are not new. Since the Quiet Revolution, the extent to which the interests of Quebec's various governments and national economic champions converged for the benefit of overall Quebec development have been disputed and debated. The consensus that the government supported these champions rested upon the conviction that business contributed to provincial development. As McRoberts documented, this is a common pattern found among internationally active Quebec-based companies. On several occasions, they resisted the role as national champion ascribed to them by the provincial government's development strategies. In the mid-1980s, large Francophone businesses, which had an ambivalent attitude about state intervention

---

181 Interview with member of Quebec's PQ government (2012-2014), Skype, 24 April 2015.
182 Interview with member of Quebec's PQ government (2012-2014), Skype, 24 April 2015.

although they benefited from it, started supporting the contraction of the Quebec state. After the 1985 general election, they strongly backed the Bourassa Liberals' project to reduce the size and activities of the provincial state. They did so because state intervention restricted their flexibility (McRoberts, 1993, p. 404-423). Similarly, during the CETA negotiations, Bombardier hoped that CETA would reduce public intervention in its production activities. During the CETA negotiation, Bombardier's opposition did thus not stem from fear of increased competition, but from a rejection of state intervention in the economy.

As demonstrated, protectionist business interests were not the main source of procurement provisions on mass transit equipment. Hence, the question remains why Quebec's representatives insisted on including these exceptions in the procurement chapter despite their support for opening procurement procedures to European companies. Again, the answer lay in the structure of the repertoire of province-building Quebec's representatives used in their discursive strategy. In a situation where Bombardier, a national economic champion, fostered economic development, Quebec's representatives wanted to retain a market share for the company in order to preserve existing production plants in the province. By supporting the large engineering and manufacturing plants of Bombardier in Dorval, La Pocatière, Mirabel, and Saint-Laurent, as well as administrative sites situated in Dorval, St. Bruno and Montreal, provincial representatives hoped to maintain employment in the area, even though Bombardier might have preferred to transfer production plants elsewhere; therefore, representatives wanted to impose local content and performance requirements in CETA's mass transit provisions. Eventually, Quebec's government supported Bombardier in spite of the company's wish. A government member asserted for instance that the government wanted to preserve some constraints on mass transit equipment production to retain leverage over local employment:

> Et nous [le gouvernment], on voulait avoir des contraintes, de façon à pouvoir nous assurer qu'un certain contenu canadien soit fabriqué au Canada ou au Québec dans ce cas-ci.[183]

Within Quebec, the contradictions and ambiguities inherent in the relation between the provincial governments and national economic champions materialised with Bombardier's opposition to the restraints imposed on its

---

183 Interview with member of Quebec's PQ government (2012-2014), Skype, 24 April 2015.

production activities. This conflict revealed that large Quebec-based businesses obstructed governments' dirigisme-style strategies of provincial development, thus rejecting the role governments assigned to them. A member of the provincial government reported, for instance, on the discrepancy between Bombardier's wish to obtain public contracts from the Quebec government and the company's willingness to contribute to the economic development of the province:

> Dans le monde idéal de Bombardier, il n'y a pas de contraintes [concernant un certain contenu canadien] puis il y en a plein de contrats.[184]

In sum, domestic content and performance requirements requested by the provincial government, yet not by Bombardier, elucidated that some structuring elements of the state dirigisme frame survived in the Liberals' discourse, in spite of business representatives' interests. While the exceptions advocated by Quebec's representatives did not represent tools to steer the economy because they terminated governmental favouritism for national economic champions, they were a way to assure that at least a part of public funds in mass transit contracts supported provincial employment and sector-related expertise in the province. Hence, mass transit procurement revealed to what extent Quebec's government was selective in its pursuit of opening procurement markets at the provincial level, thus documenting the complexity of its discursive strategy.

bb) Opposition to Opening Energy Procurement: "Le Saint-Graal de l'Hydro-Québec"

Energy procurement and procurement pertaining to energy generation, transport and distribution was a second topic which shaped discourse on provincial procurement in Quebec. Energy generation, transport and distribution falls largely under provincial competency and is carried out by state-owned companies to a very large extent, as documented above. Given the high level of domestic opposition and the importance of successful procurement negotiations for CETA, the government had a particularly challenging task. Across political parties and provinces, including in Quebec, political leaders resisted opening procurement by energy generating

---

184 Interview with member of Quebec's PQ government (2012-2014), Skype, 24 April 2015.

public companies to foreign competition. Pierre-Marc Johnson reported in the National Assembly:

> Je dois vous dire que les provinces, l'ensemble des provinces, avec le Québec, ont exprimé des réserves à l'ouverture des marchés publics de l'hydro, et cela va probablement, aux yeux des Européens, réduire le niveau d'ambition de cet accord.[185]

Until CETA negotiations began, energy procurement markets were even closed among Canadian provinces, and the Canadian energy market was very heterogeneous. According to the Liberal government's understanding, this heterogeneous market hindered the Canadian market in achieving its full economic potential,[186] even though provincial governments in other provinces refrained from openly contesting the Quebec government's position. Yet, in their practices, they pursued energy policies which rejected the purposes of prospective CETA provisions. For example, a set of procurement measures in Ontario developed in parallel to the unfolding of the CETA negotiation was particularly likely to jeopardise Quebec's discursive strategy including energy procurement as an area where increased competition could enhance domestic efficiency and competitiveness. In 2009, Ontario passed the *Green Energy Act*, a piece of legislation aiming to support local economic development. Wishing to promote green energy and industrial capacity in the province, Ontario wanted to address climate change by phasing out energy from coal and, at the same time, support the development of a local economy in sustainable energy production. The province did so through local content provisions in its public purchasing policies. In this project, domestic content requirements were paired with a guaranteed feed-in tariff for public energy procurement from renewable sources. Thus, Ontario's government agreed to pay above-market prices for its energy procurement as long as producers met local content requirements and produced energy in an environmentally sustainable way. Key to their development strategy was thus a combination of investment in renewable energies and job creation in a situation where many manufacturing jobs were lost as a consequence of the 2008 recession.

Ontario's legislation triggered three international trade disputes in parallel to the CETA negotiation. In 2010 and 2011 respectively, Japan[187] and

---

185 Pierre-Marc Johnson, National Assembly, Committee on Institutions, 8 December 2011 (= second public hearing of Pierre-Marc Johnson).
186 Interview with Quebec diplomat, Montreal, 15 October 2014.
187 Dispute DS412.

the EU[188] requested consultations with Canada on this act at the WTO. Unlike Ontario, which tried to build its case as an issue of provincial procurement—at the time of the disputes, Canadian provinces were not yet subjected to the WTO GPA (1994)—Canada's opponents argued that the Green Energy Act was an issue of foreign direct investment, regulated by international trade law and subjecting the federal government.[189] According to both complaints, Canada violated GATT 1994, Subsidies and Countervailing Measures and TRIMS provisions with regard to most favourable treatment, domestic content requirements, national treatment and state subsidies. The Dispute Settlement Body found part of the Green Energy Act inconsistent with international trade law. It circulated its report on both claims on December 19, 2012. Subsequently, Ontario amended its legislation. Apart from these two challenges at the WTO, Ontario's Green Energy Act was also challenged under NAFTA by the Mexican company Mesa Power Group for violation of national treatment, most-favoured nation treatment, minimum standard of treatment, performance requirements and stipulations relating to state enterprises. Mesa Power claimed over CAD 6 million in compensatory damages. On March 31, 2016, the arbitration tribunal dismissed Mesa's claim and confirmed that Canada was in compliance with its NAFTA obligations.

These disputes related to Ontario's Green Energy Act had consequences on the discourse in Quebec. Trade unions' and civil society movements' opposition to CETA drew upon this case to formulate their claims. Overall, opponents argued that these disputes showed that international trade harmed provincial development in several ways. First, these disputes represented an instance where provincial procurement used as a tool for provincial economic development was challenged by international trade law. These law-suits therefore bolstered the arguments put forward by networks opposing CETA procurement provisions. Second, it was interpreted as a case showing that international trade was at odds with the protection of the environment, also considered a pillar of sustainable development. A pending dispute between Canada and Lone Pine Resources Inc., under NAFTA, concerning Quebec's 2011 moratorium on fracking in the St. Lawrence River basin and Gulf reinforced opponents' claim that trade agreements and sustainable energy generation are at odds with each other

---

188 Dispute DS426.
189 See chapter 4 on Foreign Direct Investment for the distribution of jurisdiction pertaining to foreign direct investment between levels of government.

(Council of the Canadians, 2013).[190] Third, it also showed that the EU did not refrain from legally challenging Canada when its companies were restricted in business opportunities. As the following figure shows, opponents directly linked the Green Energy Act case to the CETA negotiations, which were interpreted as an instrument to generate corporate profits for European companies at the expense of Ontario.

Figure 3 –   Green Energy and International Trade

Source: Trade Justice Network (2010)

Ontario's Green Energy Act and related trade disputes also fueled opposition among Quebec's deputies. In the National Assembly, energy procurement and the fight against climate change became intertwined issues. According to those opposing opening public procurement, public authorities needed to be able to play a significant role in promoting the development of industrial capacity in the area of sustainable energy production. They presented a case for the protection of the environment in generating energy through environmentally-friendly public procurement activities. Energy procurement was a particularly cumbersome negotiation issue in Quebec. Although energy represented less than 5% of provincial GDP in Quebec in

---

190   The dispute between Canada and Lone Pine Resources Inc. will be analysed further in the chapter on investment, since it was disputed as an issue pertaining to investment protection.

2003 (Government of Canada – Statistics Canada, 2003), it figured high among Quebec's political priorities. In fact, the choice by Jean Lesage's government to invest in hydro-electric energy production played an important role in provincial economic development and continues to do so until today. Procurement by the crown corporation Hydro-Québec and electrical facilities in other provinces, including in the area of wind energy, was among key demands of the EU.[191] Given that Canadian crown corporations were excluded from other international trade agreements at that point, CETA would grant European companies privileged access to these markets alongside Canadian companies, which put them in a very competitive position.

Negotiations on opening Hydro-Québec's procurement revealed the contradictions of Quebec's position which oscillated between the structure of the small open economy frame and the state dirigisme frame. No single frame structuring the repertoire of province-building for energy had been firmly established yet. Paradoxically, despite Quebec's strong support for free trade in general, state companies continued to play a crucial role in the economic landscape of the province, particularly in the energy sector with Hydro-Québec. During the CETA negotiation, the leaders of the crown corporation Hydro-Québec strongly opposed being constrained in its choice of procurers, arguing that it contributed significantly to economic and spatial development.[192]

The heterogeneity of the Canadian energy market and in particular the autonomous status of Hydro Corporations in several provinces was related to the role they played in province-building projects and particularly in the different energy mixes they supported, as Pierre-Marc Johnson explained during a hearing in the National Assembly:

> J'ai toujours dit, moi, que, si j'avais été ministre fédéral, je n'aurais pas voulu être ministre de l'Énergie, parce que c'est probablement le plus grand casse-tête qu'il y a dans la fédération canadienne, entre les intérêts de l'Ouest autour du pétrole et du gaz, les intérêts de l'Ontario autour du nucléaire [...] puis les intérêts du Québec, qui est essentiellement largement hydroélectrique, et réconcilier tout ça n'est pas toujours simple.[193]

---

191 Interview with Quebec diplomat, Montreal, 15 October 2014; Interview with member of Manitoba's government, by phone, 11 July 2017.

192 Interview with senior Quebec official, Montreal, 15 October 2014.

193 Pierre-Marc Johnson, National Assembly, Committee on Institutions, 6 October 2010 (= first public hearing of Pierre-Marc Johnson).

In Quebec, Hydro-Québec played an important role in province-building. Regarding the role of Hydro-Québec, the state dirigisme frame structures the repertoire of province-building. As a crown corporation, i.e. a state-owned company owned by the Quebec state, it abides by the rules and standards of public procurement when procuring goods and services. It does so for almost CAD 3 billion annually as the following table highlights. According to the company, almost 90 percent of procurement contracts went to Quebec-based companies, thereby creating around 18,000 jobs and contributing to economic and spatial development (Hydro-Québec, 2010). In the National Assembly, PQ deputy Cloutier referred to Hydro-Québec's role in rural economic development and therefore opposed liberalising their contracts:

> Dans le cadre des projets d'énergie éolienne, par exemple, octroyés par Hydro-Québec, on a obligé les fournisseurs à fournir 60 % des dépenses sur le territoire québécois, 30 % juste dans le comté de Matane. Alors, M. le Président, j'aimerais savoir du ministre si ce genre de clause là va être exclue et si, oui ou non, Hydro-Québec fait partie ou non de l'accord.[194]

Hydro-Québec enjoys a high degree of autonomy from the provincial government despite its statute as a public company. In addition, it is deeply anchored in Quebec's culture, as the following quote by a Quebec member of government underlined:[195]

> Si j'avais à identifier la société d'État dont sont le plus fier les Québécois, ce serait probablement Hydro-Québec.

Table 15 – Procurement Value (Goods and Services) by Hydro-Québec (CAD billion per year)

Year	2005	2006	2007	2008	2009
Procurement Value (bn)	2.4	2.7	2.6	2.7	2.9

Source: Hydro-Québec (2010, p. 43).

---

194 Alexandre Cloutier, National Assembly, Plenary Session, 6 December 2011.
195 Interview with member of Quebec's PQ government (2012-2014), Skype, 24 April 2015.

How could Quebec's government ensure support both in the other provinces and within Quebec, despite strong opposition and in a situation where the state dirigisme frame dominated the repertoire of province-building? To some extent, the concessions from provinces to open their energy procurement markets were related to internal Canadian dynamics of inter-provincial competition. The market for the procurement of goods related to energy production has remained one of the least integrated interprovincial markets. For this reason, concessions made by individual provinces to European companies would weaken the competitive position of the other provinces. In this situation, provinces supporting the opening of their energy procurement markets to European competitors—led by Quebec—placed the other provinces in a situation where they felt compelled to follow. The dynamics among provinces therefore shaped the offer Canada was able to make to European negotiators, as a Canadian diplomat reported:[196]

> There was also sort of an internal competitive aspect to it, I think: provinces not wanting to lose their own competitive position in relation to neighbours or other provinces and things.

In Quebec, the Liberal government promoted change despite strong opposition. When evaluating Quebec's interests, it re-interpreted the status of closed energy procurement markets against the backdrop of an interaction between the province-building and the federalism repertoire. Its shift from the dirigisme frame to the small open economy frame was in fact strengthened by the Liberal government's use of the integration frame. According to the government, the current structure of Canada's energy market represented a hindrance to inner-Canadian market integration, which weakened Canada's overall economic performance. Since the Quebec Liberals promoted further integration of the Canadian internal market, CETA provided them with an opportunity to further internal Canadian market integration.

Quebec's representatives, led in this instance by Pierre-Marc Johnson, deployed a coalitional strategy on the topic of hydro-electricity which allowed them to include opposition in their discourse. In this strategy, representatives demonstrated the need for more openness in energy procurement to foster province-building. First, they reminded their opponents that Quebec depended upon supplies from Europe for its energy sector. The province already procured services of European origin related to the construction, transport and distribution networks, as well as the procure-

---

196   Interview with Canadian diplomat, Brussels, 8 July 2014.

ment of equipment related to renewable and nuclear energy.[197] Therefore, CETA would only legally entrench existing practices. Hence, a change in procurement law would contribute to ensuring Hydro-Québec's continuous access to the best equipment and services. Second, they underscored that opening procurement to foreign competitors would strengthen Hydro-Québec's commercial role, thereby generating revenues for the provincial state, an important instrument of political development and a pillar of province-building. While the company had been founded through the nationalisation of several energy-producing plants with a clear economic, social and spatial development aim, a more commercial interpretation of the public company's role had emerged in the 1970s and 1980s (Bernard, 2014; Bernier, 2014).[198] Hence, the discursive strategy involved a slight threat related to the company's profitability as well as a suggestion to increase profits by allowing foreign competition: by increasing competition on procurement markets, Hydro-Québec potentially would pay less for similar equipment and services, so that its revenues would increase. Through this discursive strategy, representatives put existing discourses, which had not prevailed so far, to the forefront, aligned them with the benefits of free trade and used them to legitimise their position.

Despite substantive opposition, this discursive strategy eventually allowed Quebec to open its energy procurement market to a considerable degree.[199] Quebec acquiesced to submitting contracts from Hydro-Québec to public tenders including from European companies. Yet, the province, jointly with other provinces, also insisted on adding some exceptions to the chapter.[200] According to a member of Quebec's government, their main concern was to maintain expertise on hydro-electric power generation in Quebec.[201] Thus, by deploying a discursive strategy on the benefits for province-building of procuring internationally, apprehensions against

---

197 Pierre Marc Johnson, National Assembly, Committee on Institutions, 8 December 2011 (= second public hearing of Pierre-Marc Johnson).

198 In its annual report, Hydro-Québec highlights that the company generates revenues for the provincial government on top of high-volume acquisition and construction activities fuelling economic development in Quebec.

199 The exact percentage of coverage is not known. Estimates by the Canadian government surmise that 75-85% of procurement by energy companies in Canada is covered by the CETA provisions, see Government of Canada (2016c).

200 Notes to Annex X-04. The annex lists certain goods, and representatives confirmed that these goods were of strategic importance.

201 "c'était carrément une volonté du gouvernement, là, de s'assurer du maintien de l'expertise, que ce soit – enfin je vous l'ai dit, là – pour les biens stratégiques", Member of Quebec's PQ government (2012-2014), Skype, 24 April 2015.

opening procurement markets shifted from a focus on the development of peripheral areas to the maintaining of expertise. This shift had consequences for the type of provisions acceptable to Quebec's representatives. Instead of rejecting these new provisions, they supported them and focused their opposition on their established know-how that provided them with a competitive advantage on world markets.

cc) Municipal Water and Waste Management: For Sale?

Public procurement by municipalities was at the origin of a lot of contention in Quebec and other Canadian provinces. Since municipalities fall under provincial jurisdiction, the provinces were entitled to offer opening municipal procurement markets to European competitors. According to the offer from the provincial governments, municipalities would be required to accept bids from European companies above applicable thresholds,[202] should they decide to issue a public call for tender for the procurement of goods, services or construction works.

The Canadian offer on procurement was submitted in July 2011,[203] during the first negotiation stage, so the PQ was not officially involved in the elaboration of the Quebec offer in this regard. In the National Assembly, the Liberal deputies rarely mentioned municipal procurement. During their time in the opposition, PQ deputies did not pursue a coherent party position. While some deputies, led by Martine Ouellet, stayed close to the trade unions in their assessment of municipal services procurement, others partially aligned with the Liberal discourse. PQ deputies only agreed on a coherent position during their term of office (2012-2014), as will become clear in my analysis of that period.

The most vocal opposition to opening procurement markets for municipal services came from a coalition formed between public employees' labor unions and civil society organisations. They mainly had three objections to opening municipal contracts to foreign competitors: municipalities provide public services such as water and waste management which need to be carried out by companies that are aware of local needs; municipalities are a large employer; many municipal services represent business opportunities for small and medium local companies. Opponents' con-

---

202 See for the outcome of the negotiation process part 2 in this section.
203 Pierre-Marc Johnson, National Assembly, Committee on Institutions, 8 December 2011 (= second public hearing of Pierre-Marc Johnson).

cerns pertained to the quality, sustainability and local impact of subjecting these services to CETA provisions. Members of the Syndicat de la Fonction Publique et Parapublique du Québec (SFPQ) and the Canadian Union of Public Employees/ Syndicat Canadien de la Fonction Publique (CUPE/ SCFP) felt threatened by the consequences of potential outsourcing of their areas of employment to private companies. They formed a stable co-alition with civil society movements contesting the current pace of liberali-sation efforts, led by Attac-Québec and the Réseau Québécois d'Intégration Continentale (RQIC). They sometimes formed coalitions with movements from Anglophone Canada, in the case of procurement mostly the Council of Canadians and the Trade Justice Network. Public employees' criticism was rooted in concerns about the indirect effects of international tenders on the municipal job market. According to them, specialised European companies might become contractors for public municipal services, offe-ring lower prices than municipalities currently pay for these services when carried out by public employees. Therefore, accepting foreign tenders could entail major layoffs in the municipal sector.[204]

Yet, the unions mostly refrained from formulating their claims by refer-ring to their own interests. Rather, they adhered to a more general discour-se about the drawbacks of opening procurement markets for public ser-vices, and more specifically in the drinking water and waste management sectors. Civil society movements in Quebec and Anglophone Canada could rally behind them to equally oppose opening procurement by muni-cipal authorities. The largest movements in terms of members and visibili-ty, the RQIC, the pan-Canadian Trade Justice Network, Attac-Québec, and the Council of Canadians coalesced with public employees' unions. For the purpose of defending water treatment and distribution, they formed an alliance with the issue-specific alliance *Coalition Eau Secours!*. While waste management was an equally important topic in the National Assem-bly, civil society movements and unions focused their public campaigns on drinking water supply. In 2010, the CUPE and the Council of Canadians published a common study on the prospective dangers of privatisation re-lated to drinking water management (Syndicat canadien de la fonction pu-blique and Conseil des Canadiens, 2010). This alliance between public em-ployees and civil society movements focused their claims on a potential de-terioration of public services as a consequence of outsourcing them to pri-vate operators in Europe, as the following two figures illustrate. Through

---

204 Interview with Quebec representative of the Canadian Union of Public Em-ployees (CUPE/ SCFP), Montreal, 23 June 2016.

this alliance with civil society organisations, the unions were able to avoid structuring their discourse around an opposition between workers (the unions) and employers (the municipalities). They rather constructed a discourse opposing the public and the private sectors. In this way, their discourse could be easily adopted by social movements claiming to represent civil society interests.

Figure 4.1 – "Special Offer"

Source: Syndicat canadien de la fonction publique & Conseil des Canadiens (2010, p. 1).

Figure 4.2 – "CETA Threatens Municipal Water Services"

Source: Trade Justice Network (2010, p. 2).

Municipalities themselves also engaged in the discussions about opening municipal procurement contracts. The Quebec municipalities did not embrace the discourse the workers' unions had established—unlike some municipalities in other provinces—despite the unions' efforts to make them adhere to their coalition against opening municipal procurement for foreign competition. Torn between diminished local authority in buying practices—an argument supported by alternative-trade movements and think thanks—and lower prices—an argument brought forward by the Liberals and the CETA negotiation team, the municipalities' position was ambiguous throughout the negotiation process.[205], A resolution by the City Council of Montreal voted in January 2012 mirrored this ambivalence. In this resolution, the Montreal City Council endorsed the benefits engen-

---

205 Despite several attempts, the organisations of Quebec and other Canadian municipalities respectively did not respond to my interview requests, which might be a sign of their ambiguous position. The analysis of their position is based only on documentary sources and on reports from other interviewees, mostly with trade unions.

dered by trade for local development, while also highlighting the dangers of provisions limiting regulatory capacity, forced privatisations, and incomplete access to information. It also reminded negotiators to keep municipal rights and interests in mind, and it called for thorough information on the effects of CETA on the municipal level (Conseil Municipal de Montréal, 2012). In general, Quebec municipalities were aware, on the one hand, of their missions to deliver high-quality public services to their inhabitants. Thus, they partially endorsed some claims formulated by the coalition opposing opening procurement markets, which led some of them to call upon the government to proceed with caution. On the other hand, municipalities also considered the positive effects of increased competition for their procurement bids, mainly a broader choice of service providers with the potential to increase service quality and decrease prices.

At the Canadian level, some major cities opposed the provisions in CETA, while others remained more cautious. The Toronto City Council in particular passed a motion asking the government of Ontario to "issue a clear, permanent exemption of the City of Toronto" from CETA (Toronto City Council, 2012). Overall, however, Canadian municipalities were divided on the procurement provisions and never established, during the CETA negotiations, a clear position encompassing all Canadian municipalities. The Federation of Canadian Municipalities issued a declaration on CETA in which its members subscribed to the following seven principles: reasonable thresholds, simplified administrative procedures, progressive application, Canadian content requirements for strategic sectors or sensitive projects, dispute resolution mechanisms, consultation and communication with municipalities, and reciprocity (Federation of Canadian Municipalities, 2010, 2013). Similar to the Montreal City Council's resolution, this one reflected municipalities' inability to find a common position. While opponents' fears were somewhat taken into account by asking for the protection of sensitive sectors and dispute resolution mechanisms, the resolution also refrained from fully rejecting opening municipal procurement markets, as did Toronto's. The following table summarises opponents' claims as documented above.

Table 16 – Overview of the Most Prevalent Topics, Actors and their Claims

Topics	Key Actors in Quebec (Excluding Political Parties)	Claims (Simplified Overview)
Mass Transit	Bombardier	Global value chains are compromised.
	Municipalities	Better prices or regulatory capacity?
Energy	Provinces	Provincial autonomy is threatened. Provincial development is threatened.
	Hydro-Québec	Autonomy of State companies is endangered.
Water & waste mgmt.	Municipalities	Service quality and pricing are core. Regulatory capacity needs to be preserved.
	Syndicat de la Fonction Publique et Parapublique du Québec (SFPQ)	Service quality is endangered by CETA.
	Syndicat Canadian de la Fonction Publique (SCFP)	Service quality is endangered by CETA.
	Trade Justice Network	CETA concerns regulatory capacity, not trade.
	Attac-Québec	Service quality is endangered by CETA.
	Coalition Eau Secours!	Water services are essential public services.

Source: based on documentary and interview analysis, see chapter 2 for more details.

In sum, during the first negotiation stage (2009-2012), the discourse on CETA's procurement provisions, including on the procurement related to the three contentious issues of mass transit equipment, energy generation equipment, and water and waste management services, showed that for the Liberal government and deputies in the Assembly, opening procurement was not a goal per se, nor was it pursued only against the background of (neo-)liberal ideas or business interests. To the contrary, Quebec's representatives evaluated the effect of liberalisation against the backdrop of their understanding of the repertoires of province-building and federalism.

It is also important to note that by doing so, they did not merely accept European demands under negotiation pressure or in exchange for concessions from the European side. Rather, they actively promoted the offer to open provincial procurement markets to the EU because this fed into their (new) conception of province-building and Canadian federalism. In addition, they were able to meet the claims from various key actors and integrated them into their discursive strategy.

Analysing the discursive processes on these three issues documented that the Liberals restructured the repertoire of province-building along the lines of the small open economy frame, which conferred importance on the benefits of increased competition for fostering economic and political development as two pillars of province-building. Representatives upheld that opening procurement was an imperative to strengthen the provincial economy and state, two important pillars of province-building. In fact, opening large parts of provincial procurement contracts contributed to the Liberals' conception of Quebec as a small and open economy. Quebec's representatives therefore argued that it was in the provincial interest to pursue the liberalisation of public procurement, except for some parts where they considered that protectionism served province-building best. At the same time, opening provincial public procurement also supported the Quebec Liberal's representation of Canadian federalism. By opening procurement bids to European competitors, the Liberal government triggered an inner-Canadian reflection on internal barriers established by provincial procurement law. In fact, provisions on provincial procurement would grant European companies better access to some provincial contracts than Canadian companies from other provinces.[206] In this way, international trade also encouraged the Liberals' endeavour to strengthen the integration of the Canadian market and hence fed into their discursive strategy to support their representation of Canadian federalism.

Confining the agreement's ambit, non-tariff barriers within Canada concerning procurement represented a hindrance to fully enact the new strategy. When CETA negotiations began in 2009, the Canadian inter-provincial procurement market was far from fully integrated. Contrary to the European member states whose procurement markets had been integrated in the Single Market framework through three consecutive legislative packages in the late 1990s, mid-2000s and late 2000s (Jabko, 2006), inter-provin-

---

206   Interview with Canadian diplomat, Brussels, 8 July 2014.

cial procurement in Canada was integrated to a lesser extent (Dawson, 2013, p. 9-11). The inadequate integration of the internal Canadian procurement market posed an obstacle to the government's new discursive strategy in two related ways. First, provincial resistance to opening inter-provincial procurement markets reduced the overall ambition of the CETA agreement. In fact, the fragmentation of the Canadian procurement market along provincial lines decreased the potential of economies of scale, competition and innovation. Overall, it reduced the appeal of the Canadian market for European companies. Second, from the provinces' perspective, CETA might grant European companies better market access to provincial contracts than other Canadian companies. Barriers to inter-provincial procurement markets therefore decreased Canadian companies' competitive advantage considerably. A Quebec diplomat reported on this asymmetry between European and Canadian companies on procurement in the energy sector:[207]

> C'est intéressant de voir qu'en vertu de l'AECG, l'accès au marché public des sociétés d'Etat dans le secteur de l'énergie est plus favorable à l'Europe, dans le cas du Québec, l'Ontario ou n'importe qui d'autre, qu'il ne l'est aux autres résidents canadiens qui ne sont pas issus de cette province.

The government's new discursive strategy also fed into the process of opening procurement contracts among provinces that had been simmering since the mid-1990s (Gouvernement du Québec, 2009). The provinces Quebec and Ontario reacted first to the new market conditions projected by the implementation of CETA. In October 2014, the Premiers of Ontario and Quebec subscribed to a memorandum in which they confirmed their intention to reinvigorate and strengthen the trade relations between the two provinces. Subsequently, in May 2015, they signed an amendment to their Trade and Cooperation Agreement (2009). Their amendment on public procurement entered into force in January 2016 for Ministries and agencies and in September 2016 for other public entities.[208] Quebec and Ontario were not the only provinces to reduce access barriers to provincial procurement markets among themselves. British Columbia, Alberta, and Saskatchewan also included procurement in their New West Partnership Agreement (2010).

---

207 Interview with senior Quebec official, Montreal, 15 October 2014.
208 School boards, academic, health and social services entities, and municipalities, entities of a commercial or industrial nature.

Then, through the Council of the Federation, provincial Premiers reached an agreement in principle replacing the Agreement on Internal Trade with a new Canadian Free Trade Agreement (2016). In this agreement, opening procurement markets among provinces was among the main achievements (Gouvernement du Québec, 2016a). Both the Ontario-Quebec Agreement and the Canadian Free Trade Agreement will grant Canadian companies equal or better access to provincial procurement markets than European ones.

Thus, CETA procurement positions also fuelled existing discourses, in Canada, about the reduction of inter-provincial access barriers to public procurement contracts. A Canadian diplomat reported, for example, that CETA was meant to encourage further integration of the internal Canadian procurement markets:[209]

> And also, in Canada, it should have the effect of encouraging [...] dropping the interprovincial trade barrier that exists. [...] Because there is going to be sort of this perverse outcome, where a European company will have a better access to procurement and other issues in Ontario than a Quebec company will. You know, I mean, it doesn't make a lot of sense, internally, when you think about this.

As documented above, the Liberal government's new discursive strategy met with considerable opposition from trade unions, civil society movements, and state companies in Quebec, as well as with reluctance in other provinces. Yet, the most challenging opposition was to come with the election of the Parti Québécois as majority party in the National Assembly. After the PLQ's defeat in the 2012 elections, the position advocated by the PQ with regard to public procurement would show if the Liberals' strategy had also restructured the PQ's discourse, or if the new government would return to its former strategy and advocate favouring local companies for provincial procurement contracts.

b) The PQ's Alignment to the Liberals' Strategy (2012-2014)

When the PQ took office after general elections in 2012, public procurement was among the most challenging negotiation issues for them, paralleled only by agriculture. While the Liberals also had to remind Quebeckers of the need for the province to engage in international trade, thus ad-

---

209 Interview with Canadian diplomat, Brussels, 8 July 2014.

justing the role the state played in the economy, the PQ had a more difficult discursive reworking to undertake. In addition, the party's potential
influence on the chapter was limited by the unfolding of the negotiation
dynamics. Offers for procurement had been submitted in June 2011,
which left the PQ with little substantive room for influence when they
took office in Quebec. Yet, the government it led still had to assume responsibility, given that negotiations were officially still on-going and that
it was not known publicly at that moment which substantive chapters of
the negotiations had been closed.

One reason why the PQ faced challenging discursive adjustments was
that they could not connect a new discourse as easily as the Liberals to existing discourses. In fact, the Liberals' new discursive strategy connected
their position on public procurement to existing—even if not prevailing
—discourses on rolling back state intervention in the economy established
since the Bourassa Liberals and even more so since the Charest Liberals.
Although the PQ had also engaged in the process transforming public
companies into private enterprises or making them more efficient in the
mid-1980s and 1990s,[210] they had done so in order to preserve, not reduce,
the legitimacy of these public companies. In fact, as Bernier and Garon noted, these transformative processes made public companies stronger, so
that their role in steering the economy despite the integration of Quebec
in the global economy increased. Their international activities even contributed to their autonomy (which they needed in order to become market
actors) and legitimacy (because they generated revenues for the provincial
government). Hence, the PQ could easily connect its dirigisme discourse
to the integration of public companies in the global economy. Bernier and
Garon concluded that:

> Les sociétés d'État demeurent un outil d'intervention flexible puisqu'il
> apparaît possible de l'adapter en fonction de la conjoncture économi-
> que, légale et idéologique qui prévaut dans un environnement mon-
> dialisé (Bernier and Garon, 2003 p. 243-248).

However, the suggestions made during the CETA negotiation were potentially incommensurate with the PQ's previous discourses. In fact, for the

---

210 Commissioned by the PQ government, the rapport Facal (1997) was the most
comprehensive recent review of Quebec's public organisms and triggered far-reaching transformative processes among Quebec's state-owned companies, such
as a reduction of public organisms, and the establishment of profitability as a
primary goal (Bernier and Garon, 2003 p. 242-243).

PQ more than for the Liberals, state companies were an instrument of local economic development. Even though the internationalisation of state companies made them more profitable and therefore legitimised their existence, CETA brought this internationalisation process to a new level by requiring them to open their procurement markets. Therefore, the local impact of state companies would be diminished, which did not suit the current PQ leadership discourse well. In fact, Premier Marois has been associated with the social-democrats and dirigiste traditions in the PQ when she served as Minister in various PQ cabinets, which differentiated her from the previous PQ leader Landry, who was closer to business circles (Tanguay, 2003, p. 268). In addition, the PQ did not promote further integration of the Canadian procurement market: especially in the energy sector, its members believed that each province should retain maximum autonomy for their crown corporations.[211] These factors made it discursively more challenging for the Marois government to adhere to the Liberals' strategy than it might have been for previous PQ leaders. These differences demonstrated that, contrary to the Liberals, the PQ was characterised by internal cleavages on socio-economic policy. They were thus compelled to carve out a new discourse and decide which frame they wanted to follow.

Moreover, the traditional PQ electoral basis complicated the PQ's task of establishing a legitimate and coherent discourse on procurement. In the 1970s, the PQ had established itself as the party representing public employees and trade unions. In fact, even when Bouchard's government had to considerably cut back on state expenses to reduce Quebec's budgetary deficit, they did so in concertation with trade unions and tried to keep reductions to a minimum (Tanguay, 2003, p. 257-267). Yet, as documented above, these two groups were the most vocal and influential opponents of opening procurement contracts to European competitors. For electoral reasons, and aspects related to party history and its current leadership, the PQ could therefore not disregard demands to exclude certain provisions such as the coverage of municipalities and crown corporations as easily as the Liberals.

Between the first and the second negotiation phases, the PQ deputies considerably altered their discourse on public procurement. At the beginning of the negotiations, deputies of the PQ argued that provincial procurement was one of the last available instruments for steering economic development and a necessary instrument to contribute to province-building.

---

211 Interview with member of Quebec's PQ government (2012-2014), Skype, 24 April 2015.

Thus, they opposed the PLQ's new discursive strategy. As table 13 depicting the frames that the two major parties deployed in the National Assembly highlights, state dirigisme was the main frame deployed by the PQ in the first negotiation phase (2009-2012). Overall, the PQ tried, more than the Liberals, to engage with social movements, even though social activists reported that they did not feel that their position was influential in political discourse.[212]

Between 2012 and 2014, the PQ deputies considerably re-worked their discourse on public procurement. In this second stage of the negotiations, they not only desisted partially from using the state dirigisme frame to reflect their position on public procurement, but they also adopted the small open economy frame previously introduced by the Liberals in the discourse on procurement. In this process, they re-evaluated Quebec's interests and realigned a large part of their discourse according to the structure of the small open economy frame, in which they highlighted the benefits of increased competition on public procurement markets. By doing so, they connected their position on procurement to the party's overall support for free trade. Yet, they did not completely abandon their representation of the role of the state in developing the provincial economy. In fact, a considerable portion of their contributions in the National Assembly maintained references to state dirigisme as the structure of reference when they were in office. How could these two frames coexist in the PQ's discourse, and how were the Liberals able to open the way, for the PQ, to take up the small open economy frame in their discourse on public procurement, as they did in more general terms during the NAFTA debates?

The discursive strategy deployed by the Liberals in the first negotiation stage spotlighted provincial development through increased competition on procurement contracts. This ingenious way of legitimising the government's plan resonated not only with Liberal party members and their electorate, but also with their main political opponent, the PQ. The Liberals' new discursive strategy therefore paved the way for their coalitional strategy: through the skilful references to provincial development, the Liberals provided the new PQ government with favourable circumstances to align with their new position—that opening procurement supported provincial development. When they took office, the PQ could align with this new discourse: emphasising their own enthusiasm for free trade, the PQ government could also draw upon the repertoire of province-building, as it did

---

212 Interview with Quebec representative of the Canadian Union of Public Employees (CUPE/ SCFP), Montreal, 23 June 2016.

183

during previous free trade debates. This new discourse allowed accommodation of both the state dirigisme and the small open economy frames to structure the issue of public procurement. Subsequently, market access and privatisation became more important topics for PQ deputies, as table 17 documents.[213] While market access and privatisation were not placed high on the Liberals' agenda, they were key innovations in the PQ's updated discourse, highlighting the relevance its government and deputies attached to the role public actors assume in the economy. In addition to the three contentious issues of Hydro-Québec, mass transit equipment and water and waste management commented on above, additional topics for the PQ were market access and the negotiation process.

In public procurement provisions, market access is established or denied by way of value thresholds. These thresholds determine whether a public contract is subjected to international trade rules. Insisting on value thresholds allowed the PQ to deploy two incommensurate discursive structures, one aligning with the Liberals and their enthusiasm for free trade, and one remaining in line with their previous dirigiste discourse. By doing so, they used thresholds to constitute the boundary between the two frames they deployed. In their discourse, including in the interviews conducted, members of the PQ were inclined to deploy the frame of state dirigisme for contracts below the thresholds established by CETA, and the small open economy frame for those above the thresholds. In this discursive strategy, the negotiation of appropriate value thresholds remained essential in the eyes of the PQ: it allowed them to assure the benefits of increased competition for large contracts, while also preserving the ability to support small companies through low-value contracts.

The second topic PQ deputies accorded increased attention to was privatisation, mostly of municipal services, including water and waste management. Influenced by the discourse suggested by the coalition of social movements and public employees' trade unions, the PQ had to address their argument that CETA would be conducive to privatisations in the area of public services, leading to a loss of public oversight and lesser service quality.

---

213 Other important topics were award criteria for public contracts, the negotiation process, see appendix.

Table 17 – Evolution of Importance of the Topics "Market Access" and "Privati-
sation" for PQ and PLQ (Share of Topic in Total Discourse on Pub-
lic Procurement at Respective Negotiation Stage)

PQ	2009-2012	2012-2014
Market Access	0	30
Privatisation	6	19
Other *	94	51
Total	100%	100%

PLQ	2009-2012	2012-2014
Market Access	6	0
Privatisation	6	0
Other**	88	0
Total	100%	0%

Source: Analysis of Parliamentary Debates (Plenary and Committee Sessions).

*Including award criteria, negotiation process, water & waste management, Hydro-Québec, and the MASH sector.

**There were considerably fewer coding occurrences for the PLQ than for the PQ. The most important issues apart from privatisation and market access were the American Reinvestment and Recovery Act (ARRA) and the negotiation process.

Note: Refer to Appendixfor detailed coding occurrences.

As in the case of procurement by public companies, the PLQ had successfully paved a way for the PQ to partially adhere to its discourse, albeit for different reasons than their own. While the Liberals had restructured their discourse and by now referred almost exclusively to public procurement against the backdrop of the small open economy frame, the PQ continued to structure its discourse according to the state dirigisme frame by tying the effects of CETA back to local development. Minister for International Relations, the Francophonie and External Trade Jean-François Lisée spoke in the National Assembly on the topic of the much-feared privatisation of municipal water services on two occasions.[214] In his discursive strategy, he adopted some elements of the small open economy frame to structure his

---

214 National Assembly, Plenary, 6 November 2013, National Assembly, Committee on Institutions, 15 February 2013.

discourse, but not others: on the one hand, he followed the Liberals in highlighting the benefits of international competition for the promotion of expertise and high-quality services; on the other hand, he also explained how even contracts carried out by foreign companies could create local economic development by drawing upon local workforce and content. In addition, and more than the Liberals, the PQ government stressed that opening procurement contracts on the municipal level did not equal privatising these services. According to the PQ, conferring the management of water and waste services on private providers did not correspond to selling the facilities and services associated with them. Therefore, the PQ stressed, the benefits of increased international competition only played out if public authorities remained the owners of public services. In this regard, civil society groups and labour unions distanced themselves from the PQ discourse. According to them, the danger of opening procurement lay in a potential spill-over between the investment protection chapter in CETA and the opening of procurement markets. Investment protection provisions, this argument went, make it difficult, for municipalities, to reverse failed privatisations or to expand public services. Hence, this creates an asymmetry between privatisation and public services. This argument was backed among others by the Canadian Union of Public Employees, the Réseau Québécois sur l'Intégration Continentale and Attac-Québec. The Canadian Center for Policy Alternatives, an Ottawa-based think tank, joined in this line of argument and supported social movements with analytical reports (Trew, 2014).

Despite these updates, the PQ's discourse remained anchored in the state dirigisme frame. With this discursive strategy, the PQ tried to preserve the provincial state's capacity to intervene in the economy, a central pillar of province-building for the PQ. At the same time, the PQ also tried to strengthen Quebec's economy by developing opportunities for local business. However, unlike the PLQ, the PQ insisted more on local contracts and less on export opportunities.

The PQ's attention to market access and to thresholds, as well as privatisation and public services was partially successful. While municipal services, electricity generation and mass transit have not been excluded from CETA provisions, as opponents had advocated, they were subjected to higher thresholds. In this way, market access was restricted. In the Canadian Government Procurement Market Access Offer,[215] Annex X-02 in conjunction with section B of Annex X-03 specified that the public drinking water

---

215   Consolidated CETA text, 2014, Annexes X-01 – X-08.

management services were subject to higher thresholds than foreseen for other procurement contracts. Similarly, higher thresholds would also be applicable to mass transit contracts and electricity production, transport and distribution networks. As table 18 comparing general and specific thresholds shows, CETA provisions would only apply to these exceptions for contracts twice the value of those falling under the general procurement rules. These results were made possible by a successful coalitional strategy between the PLQ and the PQ. On the one hand, the Liberals' discursive strategy paved the way for the PQ to join their coalitional strategy and, on the other hand, the PQ's discursive strategy successfully addressed some of their opponents' claims.

Table 18 – General and Specific CETA Thresholds for Procuring Activities under Provincial Jurisdiction (SDR)

General Thresholds Applicable to Procurement by Sub-Central Government Entities[216]		Thresholds Applicable to Specific Procurement Activities by Sub-Central Government Entities: drinking water, mass transit, electricity generation	
Goods	200,000	Goods	400,000
Services	200,000	Services	400,000
Construction	5,000,000	Construction	5,000,000

Source: Canadian Government Procurement Market Access Offer, CETA (2014), Annex X-02 and X-03.

Conclusion

When negotiations on CETA's public procurement chapter were closed in August 2014, Quebec committed to an unprecedented opening of its public procurement markets to European bidders, although its representatives also managed to carve out some exemptions. Nevertheless, their offer on provincial procurement markets reached beyond the coverage offered to US bidders under NAFTA (1994) and the Canada-US Agreement on Go-

---

216 For Quebec, these are, as specified in Annex X-02: departments, governmental agencies, and para-public organisations (municipalities, municipal organisations, and other public bodies).

vernment Procurement (2010), or other international bidders under the updated WTO's Agreement on Government Procurement (1994, 2014). In some instances, their offer even exceeded inter-provincial levels of openness. At the same time, Quebec wanted to protect some areas, including mass transit equipment, strategic areas managed by public companies, and the drinking water management area.

This shift in the way they interpreted the provincial interest on public procurement was the result of a complex discursive strategy. Both the Liberals and the PQ promoted opening procurement markets to foreign competitors to spur economic development and to strengthen the provincial state, two crucial pillars of province-building for the two parties. By introducing the small open economy frame to the discourse on public procurement, Quebec's representatives partially re-evaluated the province's interests, even though they did so for partially different reasons. These reasons were related to the different frames that underpinned their respective discourse.

Overall, two frames dominated the discourse: the small open economy frame and the state dirigisme frame. Despite their differences, both frames were part of the repertoire of province-building. This common set of references allowed the Liberals and the PQ to support subjecting provincial public procurement procedures to CETA provisions, thereby relinquishing a central instrument of provincial policy-making. Their discursive oscillation between these two frames revealed the contradiction inherent in Quebec's position. This became particularly obvious in the water and waste management, energy and mass transit sectors. These sectors represented cases where the provincial state traditionally played a strong directing role, which challenged Quebec political leaders across parties to stay true to their pledge to opening procurement markets in spite of contradiction with their past discourse.

The Liberal government successfully reworked its discourse on public procurement and stressed the importance, for Quebec's manufacturers, of acquiring access to new export markets. Representatives also established the small open economy frame as the basic structure of the repertoire of province-building which embedded provincial public procurement. The results of this re-structuring were far-reaching and also impacted upon the repertoire of federalism.

At the beginning of the negotiation, the Liberal government developed its discourse in terms of the small open economy and, albeit to a minor extent, the integration frames. In its discursive strategy, the interaction between the promotion of international activity and the benefits of opening public procurement allowed the Liberal government to restructure the repertoire of province-building and to firmly anchor its representation of Quebec as a small economy committed to and dependent on international trade. At the same time, it also pursued internal market integration through its discursive strategy, an important pillar of the federalism repertoire for the Quebec Liberal party. The PQ had a more difficult discursive task. Although major processes of rolling back the Quebec state had taken place under a PQ government, the party nevertheless continuously stressed, in its discourse, that these measures were necessary to preserve the Quebec model of province-building and a strong role of the provincial state in the economy, two essential pillars of province-building. It also believed that energy market should remain under provincial control, given that it promoted the independence frame of the repertoire of federalism. During CETA negotiations, it highlighted that CETA provisions did not interfere with the role of the state in the economy. In fact, through the inclusion of value thresholds and several exemptions in key areas—sometimes against business interests—the PQ succeeded in safeguarding a directive role for the state, thereby continuing to draw upon the state dirigisme frame. This mixed discourse accounted for both opening public procurement and for including a list of exemptions in the agreement.

Through their coalitional strategy that gave them the opportunity to legitimately promote both openness and closure with regard to procurement, the PLQ and the PQ could delegitimise some claims made by trade unions and civil society from their discourse, and pursue a similar negotiation position in support of European demands. Societal opposition in Quebec largely embraced a non-territorial conception of the CETA provisions on procurement. Unions as well as civil society movements embedded their action in pan-Canadian networks. By highlighting cross-provincial interests in keeping procurement markets closed and organising common campaigns,[217] a cross-provincial alliance opposing Quebec representatives' strategy was able to underline the drawbacks for all citizens and workers, rather than single provinces. Hence, these movements contested the boundaries structuring their representatives' discourse and thereby challenged the very foundation of their province-building strategy. The coalitional strategy between the PLQ and the PQ, based on ambiguity in the frames underpinning their discourse on province-building, allowed the Quebec governments at different moments in the negotiation to overcome opposi-

---

217 Interview with Quebec representative of the Canadian Union of Public Employees (CUPE/ SCFP), Montreal, 23 June 2016.

tion by trade unions and civil society movements. By defining Quebec's interest in the trade negotiation as an objective of province-building, they could legitimately shift their position towards support for opening provincial procurement contracts.

Chapter 4: Attracting Foreign Direct Investment—a Discursive Conciliation for Province-Building

Foreign direct investment[218] was at the core of the CETA negotiation: Since Canada and the EU had not been able to reach a multilateral consensus at the WTO on international investment rules, they hoped to establish a set of standards for their respective investors at the bilateral level. Until CETA, several recent attempts to establish an agreement on their investment relations failed. Although foreign direct investment is under exclusive federal jurisdiction, the provinces retain adjacent competencies and participate in Canada's overall attractiveness for investors. Foreign direct investment was one of the many non-trade issues: investment rules influence intra-industry trade, and they also offer the opportunity to ease trade in services. Contrary to mere commercial exchanges, however, investment activities participate in and may even notably influence a country's economic structure because they constitute a lasting interest of the investor in the host economy. Cutting across industrial sectors, investments reach thus to the core of national economies. Foreign direct investment is therefore a case to highlight how national representatives engaged with processes of deep economic integration. Might the reason for the recent success in reaching a comprehensive agreement on investment in the CETA negotiation lie in novel provincial participation and a reinterpretation of provincial interests, as the public procurement case was?

Even though an outside observer might have suspected that Quebec would resent the presence of influential foreign investors in the province—in Quebec's Quiet Revolution, a main objective was to reclaim ownership of Quebec's industrial basis from Anglophone Canadians—both the Quebec Liberals and the PQ have historically been strong supporters of

---

218 The following empirical analysis draws upon the preliminary CETA text according to the agreement reached during the official negotiation period extending from 2009 to 2014. On 29 February 2016, the European Commission and the Canadian government released a new version of the provisional CETA text after legal and linguistic revision. In this version, the investment dispute settlement mechanisms between states and investors have been altered considerably in comparison to the 2014-version. How Canada and the EU came to argue that their interests lay in the development of a new investor-to-state dispute mechanism is, however, beyond the scope of the current chapter.

attracting foreign investments to the province in the name of province-building. Convinced that Quebec is too small to generate the resources necessary to restructure its industrial basis and generate growth, provincial political leaders promoted investor-friendly policies, often against the Canadian federal government's stance on the issue. Quebec's negotiation position on CETA's investment chapter was no exception. Provincial representatives supported including investment in Canada's negotiation offer and they also accepted the final negotiated chapter. Yet, in Quebec, this political consensus was briefly challenged during the CETA negotiations. In fact, some members of the National Assembly as well as civil society organisations claimed that the way CETA regulated investment relations would interfere negatively with province-building. Thereby, they challenged the small open economy frame which had been part of the political consensus thus far. Suggesting an alternative appreciation of the relation between foreign investment and province-building, this discourse was most influential with several members of the PQ and Québec Solidaire. Members of the PLQ, too, drew upon it to define certain limits to investment rights, such as in the cultural industries. How, then, did the Liberal government react to this challenge and what were the effects of opposition on their representation of Quebec's interests?

Section 1: Foreign Direct Investment in Quebec and Canada before CETA

Over the last decades, the Canadian federal government and Quebec's provincial government witnessed many political debates on the desirability of foreign direct investment. Overall, in these debates, Quebec and Canada sometimes took opposite stances on foreign investment hosted on their territory. While Canada often exhibited caution towards accepting or even attracting foreign investors to its territory, albeit to varying degrees, Quebec mostly favoured foreign investment in the province, as did several other Canadian provinces.

Since the beginning of the new millennium, the federal government's and Quebec's positions have converged, so that they both started CETA negotiations with a generally positive attitude towards hosting international investment. Smythe argued that "to understand how investment interests are defined, we need to look at both ideas about investment and the context in which negotiations take place" (Smythe, 2011, p. 409). The following account sets the scene in which CETA negotiations unfolded.

1. Overlapping Jurisdiction over Foreign Direct Investment: Institutional
   Developments

In Canada, both the federal and the provincial levels of government have jurisdiction over matters related to foreign direct investment. Legislation on investment can be divided into two groups of policies: legislation on the procedure of acquiring business ownership for foreign citizens and legislation contributing to the overall attractiveness of a host country for foreign investors. The federal level *alone* passes legislation on the procedure for foreign nationals acquiring ownership on Canadian territory. In general, the federal Minister for Economic Development monitors, reviews and regulates non-Canadian investors who acquire control of a Canadian business or establish a new business in Canada. In specific sectors, special legislation applies and other ministries administer foreign investment. The provinces, for their part, do not have any power to influence the legal procedure for foreign direct investments made in their territory.

However, the provinces hold a number of competencies that are adjacent to investment and allow them to actively participate in shaping their own and Canada's investment environment. For one thing, provinces' exclusive power over property and civil rights provides them, in general, with the constitutional tools to establish a specific investment regime in their province. They are also competent for labour market regulation in most sectors, except for specific labour groups such as the federal bureaucracy, the personnel of federal state-owned companies and personnel in the banking sector. Furthermore, provinces' fiscal autonomy allows them to develop incentive programs to attract foreign direct investment (Van Biesebroeck, 2010). Fiscal incentives often consist in direct subsidies, or grants, loans, loan guarantees, venture capital, or tax credits. Finally, provinces also own the natural resources in their territory and are in charge of environmental legislation (Bushnell, 1980). Given that Canada is to a large extent a resource-based economy with the natural resources sector accounting for 17 percent of its GDP in 2015 (Government of Canada – Natural Resources Canada, 2016b), ownership of natural resources makes the provinces influential political actors in shaping Canada's attractiveness for international investors. At the same time, the expanding provincial role in environmental legislation, often related to the extraction of natural resources, adds to provincial activity in the field of investment (Harrison, 2003).

Two developments related to international trade policy increased the role of the provinces in shaping Canada's foreign investment environment. These processes created a situation in which the federal level increasingly depends on provincial willingness to contribute to their overall investment policy plans. *First*, the relevance of areas under provincial jurisdiction expanded as the range of policy instruments under federal jurisdiction narrowed. Since investment review and screening procedures were gradually reduced through public international law, the potential effects of investment-related federal jurisdiction also gradually declined (Prince Agbodjan and Rousseau, 2016). In this context, domestic regulatory measures including at the provincial level acquired all the more relevance in shaping a jurisdiction's attractiveness for foreign investors.

Second, investment-related provisions under provincial jurisdiction have spread onto the negotiation agendas on foreign investment rules. As a result of these effects, the provinces' policy space and regulatory capacity expanded: they are concerned when it comes to several investment provisions included in the international agreements Canada signed, both with regard to access rights and protection clauses (Thakur, 2012). Regarding access rights, the provinces control several aspects of legislation adjacent to investments, as mentioned above. Therefore, they need to implement the provisions included in Canada's international commitments or refrain from taking policy actions that might inhibit the settlement of foreign investors. Regarding investment protection, provincial regulatory choices might be targeted by international investors referring to investment protection clauses. In this regard, WTO regulations are less relevant for provinces, since they mostly target trade-distorting measures that are administered by the federal executive. NAFTA, to the contrary, has created provisions on the protection of investments and the expropriation of investors that are particularly relevant for the provinces.[219] In fact, a provincial action may constitute a direct or indirect expropriation in the sense of NAFTA's chapter 11. Yet, the provinces are not signatories to Canada's international agreements. This raises the questions of provincial liability and provincial responsibility for compensatory damages in case of an infringement. This mostly concerns indirect expropriations, which refer to policy measures having an effect similar to a direct expropriation in substantially reducing the investments value (Luz, 2000-2001; Luz and Miller, 2002).

With investment agreements increasingly targeting domestic policy measures, provinces do not only become actors in international investment policy. They are also increasingly concerned by the effects of foreign investment provisions included in investment treaties. Unlike trade relations in a strict sense, foreign direct investments establish a long-term rela-

---

219 Chapter 11, articles 1101-1139, annexes 1120-1138.

tionship between the direct investor and the host economy. Since ownership of assets gives the investor influence over the company's management, the investor has a direct influence on production processes. As a consequence, the foreign investor is responsible for vital decisions such as the transfer of technology and management skills, the strategic positioning of the production processes in global value chains, or corporate culture and management styles. Therefore, an investment grants the investor a significant degree of influence on the management of the acquired enterprise. Eventually, ownership structures and management styles impact upon established ways of production, distribution and consumption. In addition, by forbidding trade-distorting measures, investment agreements reduce policy makers' capacity to steer investments in specific directions and therefore limit provincial government's ability to direct foreign direct investment flows to further their economic development project. For example, a host country must not require the use of local input for production. Furthermore, investment protection provisions may keep provincial legislatures from taking certain policy actions.

2. Canada's Changing Foreign Direct Investment Interests: There and Back Again

Canada's federal post-war foreign direct investment policy has been a politically salient and sensitive topic. Depending on governments' overall economic strategy, foreign direct investment took different roles in Canada's economy. In a nutshell, debates oscillated between the fear of exposing Canada's economic basis to foreign interests and the perceived need to attract foreign investments to stimulate growth and economic development. As a consequence of these diverse interpretations of the drawbacks and benefits of FDI, Canada's federal foreign investment policy underwent three major changes after the Second World War, with 1974, 1984 and the 2000s representing major turning points in public policy. The following account briefly documents these periods and the political thinking underpinning them, reflects the evolving nature of Canada's economic interests and shows why and how the discursive relationship between Canadian sovereignty and foreign direct investment has been reconfigured various times (the following account is based on Collins, 2011b; Hale, 2008; Raby, 1990; Smythe, 2011).

Until the late 1960s, membership in the British Empire and then the Commonwealth established a consensus on the contribution of foreign direct investment to developing Canada's vast territory. As a consequence, there were almost no federal measures to steer, let alone discourage, foreign investment. In this encouraging environment, both federal and provincial governments welcomed the influx of foreign capital, mostly from the UK, but also increasingly from the US, to develop manufacturing, exploit Canada's natural resources, complement fiscal policies, support the growth of the welfare state and spread industrial development. This policy did not remain without challenge—the Royal Commission on Canada's Economic Prospects chaired by Walter Gordon suggested in its report (1957) a more restrictive investment policy to the image of Germany, France or Japan. But critical voices were kept back.

In the late 1960s, this consensus on the benefits of FDI started to vanish. Expanding US ownership of Canadian companies alarmed political decision-makers as well as societal actors (Murray and Gerace, 1972; Murray and Leduc, 1976). Debates about unfettered access rights granted to foreign investors were taking place against the backdrop of the election of Pierre Trudeau's Liberals at the federal level (1968-79; 1980-84), which initiated a period of wariness vis-à-vis the free movement of goods, services and capital. Influential civil society groups such as the Committee for an Independent Canada (1970-1981) advocating the reduction of foreign influence on Canadian economic development further fuelled the governing Liberals' anxiety about foreign ownership structures in Canada. Preluding a fundamental policy shift, the government ordered three reports related to foreign investments and ownership.[220] These reports highlighted the extent to which existing investment policies might compromise Canadian sovereignty. By referring to the US tendency to assert jurisdiction over branches of its companies established abroad, the reports gave a very tangible example of Canada's reduced rights of control over companies' establishment in the country. Furthermore, the reports highlighted that foreign ownership made Canadian companies dependent on US innovations, while at the same time preventing them from developing innovative skills necessary to Canada's economic development (a process often referred to as the 'hollowing out' of Canada's economic basis). Based on this interpretation, the three reports suggested introducing review mechanisms and excluding companies in strategic sectors from foreign ownership. The last of the

---

220 Foreign Ownership and the Structure of Canadian Industry (=Watkins Task Force Report, 1968); The Eleventh Report of the Standing Committee on External Affairs and National Defence Respecting Canada-US Relations (=Wahn Report, 1970); Foreign Direct Investment in Canada (=Gray Report, 1972).

three reports, known as the Gray Report (1972) after its chairman Herb Gray, was the most influential. By highlighting the share of Canadian businesses owned by foreigners and outlining their detrimental effect on Canada's economy, the report recommended the creation of a review process for foreign direct investment. This momentum against increased foreign ownership of Canadian companies culminated in the enactment of the *Foreign Investment Review Act* (1973), which initiated a period of limiting foreign presence in Canada's economy. In 1974, the Foreign Investment Review Agency (FIRA) began screening foreign investments (both acquisitions and new establishments) and advised the government if action should be taken against planned foreign investments.

Trudeau's foreign investment policy, and his government's economic policy in general, were short-lived. Even before the election of Mulroney's Progressive Conservatives in 1984, domestic and international processes induced policy reversals. At the domestic level, the early 1980s recession prompted many Canadians to question Canada's restrictive investment policy. Also within the executive, the external affairs department started to challenge Canada's investment policies in light of their overall trade policy strategy (Government of Canada, 1983, p.15-17). At the international level, Canada's trade partners increasingly criticized the FIRA's inconsistent and unpredictable decision-making (Globerman, 1984) and exposed the contradictions between Canada's review process and its commitments to multilateral trade. In this regard, the US challenged Canada's investment laws before a dispute settlement panel of the GATT in 1982.[221] The panel's landmark ruling not only considerably narrowed the scope of Canada's review procedure,[222] but it also established, for the first time, the international community's stance on the relation between trade and investment. It also attracted international attention towards Canadian practices.

With the election of the Mulroney's Progressive Conservatives in 1984, Canada's policy makers to some extent overturned Trudeau's economic po-

---

221 BISD 30S/140, 1984.
222 The panel ruled that Canada's review process partially infringed GATT provisions. According to its ruling, local content requirements were inconsistent with national treatment obligations under the GATT, but that export performance requirements did not interfere with Canada's obligations under the GATT. This ruling was significant in that it established that commitments made by governments in terms of trade also extend to their investment policies. However, GATT obligations do not extend to investment policies in general, which is why the panel rejected the U.S. position that export performance requirements contravene Canada's GATT obligations.

licy and took a clear stance for the free movement of goods, services and capital. Mulroney's government attempted to invite foreign investments by creating an attractive domestic policy environment. Among its first policy reversals, in 1985, the new government replaced the FIRA with the *Investment Canada Act* (ICA). Although this new act restricted the government's ability to control investment influx, it remained firm on the need for a screening procedure for investments of significant size. In some regards, Canada's foreign direct investment policy remained therefore restrictive within the limits imposed by the GATT's FIRA panel ruling (1984). The extent to which the FIRA's and the ICA's review procedures vary has been subject to discussion. Even though the structure of the new law remained essentially similar to the FIRA screening procedure, thresholds for application were increased considerably and review procedures were shortened (see Raby, 1990 for specific thresholds and areas of application). Above thresholds, a review procedure needs to take place according to the ICA. In this review, the "net benefit" resulting for the Canadian economy according to a number of factors specified in advance was established as the criterion for accepting direct or indirect investments made in Canada. This procedure is still applicable today, although it has been significantly altered by various legislative packages (Prince Agbodjan and Rousseau, 2016).

Although Canada' federal government preserved the right to submit foreign investment hosted in Canada to the "net benefit" test, the federal government also committed to new limits on governmental control over foreign direct investment in the 1980s (Deblock, 1988). At that time, it did so mostly because it acknowledged the role of FDI in the development of large infrastructure projects supporting Canadian economic development (Government of Canada, 1983). The conclusion of the free trade agreements between Canada and the US (CUSFTA, 1988) and later Mexico (NAFTA, 1994) gave the government the opportunity to further curtail the review procedures (Raby, 1990, p.409-419). Indeed, by adhering to NAFTA, Canada committed to investment provisions with Mexico and the US which exceeded by far their multilateral investment obligations in the 1990s.[223] NAFTA provisions altered the Canadian screening procedure for US and Mexican investors. Canada accepted a ban on performance requirements and raised thresholds of application for its screening procedure. Canada mostly agreed to these provisions not to protect its own investors abroad, but to render Canada attractive to foreign investments. Still, NAFTA

---

223 Including obligations in the GATS, the TRIMs, the TRIPs, the GPA and the ASCM.

did not exempt US and Mexican investments made in Canada from review under the Investment Canada Act.

Until the late 1990s, the Canadian federal government's strategy thus focused mostly on its domestic attractiveness for foreign investors. In this logic, attracting foreign investors was more important than being the source of outbound investment. Then, in the 1990s, the federal government became more attentive to the beneficial effects of *out*bound investment flows, when Canada became a net capital exporter by 1997 (Smythe, 2011 p.409). In fact, increasingly globalised supply chains required Canadian companies to make investments abroad to remain internationally competitive. As a consequence of their changed interests, Smythe argued, "Canadian negotiators became interested in protecting outward investment" (Smythe, 2011, p. 411). Alongside the EU and Japan, Canada became an active *demandeur* at the WTO for the introduction of multilateral investment establishment and protection laws. As a consequence of changed investment interests and discourses underpinning them, several major take-overs in the mid-2000s did not lead to critical public debate, as one could have expected against the history of Canada's take-over debates (Hale, 2008).

In parallel to becoming a net exporter, the Canadian provinces also eased inter-provincial investment relations through the Agreement on Internal Trade (AIT, 1995). In the AIT, a full chapter on inter-provincial investment relations (articles 600-616, 1995 version) guaranteed for instance non-discrimination and a ban on performance requirements. Unlike many other investment agreements, the AIT explicitly forbids waiving environmental protection measures to encourage investors to establish their company in the respective province. In addition to the AIT, the provinces also concluded a Code of Conduct on Incentives, which was included as an annex in the AIT (annex 608.3), and aimed at reducing the use of subsidies to poach companies from other provinces (Thomas, 2011). An integrated Canadian market should make the economy more attractive to foreign investors.

3. 'L'apport déterminant des investissements étrangers dans la croissance économique québécoise'[224]

Discourses and policies in Quebec unfolded in parallel and in reaction to federal FDI policies. Contrary to the federal levels' story of FDI, Quebec's position remained relatively stable. Given the significant influence foreign investors have on host economies, Quebec could have opposed reducing barriers to international investment inbound flows, as the federal government did on several occasions. In fact, regulatory capacity, state authority and local ownership were issues that figured high on Quebeckers' agenda to become "maîtres chez nous": Quebec's efforts to expand francophone ownership of Quebec's economic basis was indeed a key part of province-building efforts during the Quiet Revolution. Rolling back an increasing (anglophone) US presence in Quebec's economy might seem the logical step to avoid undermining the provincial economy, even more so with the backing of the federal government in this regard.

However, Quebec' representatives did not select this path. To the contrary, the province has historically been a strong supporter of reducing barriers to foreign direct investments as well as of easing investment flows among Canadian provinces. Over the last decades, Quebec's and Canada's overall investment policy plans have therefore often diverged. At the beginning of the 1970s, when the federal government felt alarmed about foreign ownership, Quebec's provincial government not only continued to pursue investment-promotion activities, but also strongly and overtly objected to the federal government's plans to establish a new screening procedure for foreign direct investments hosted in Canada. According to Rocher, they did not conceive of foreign direct investment through the "prism of economic nationalism", as did the federal government (Rocher, 2003, p. 462, author's translation). Quite to the contrary, attracting foreign investment to the province has been part and parcel of Quebec's paradiplomacy since the Quiet Revolution (Paquin, 2004). Overall, Quebec has been a strong supporter of establishment rights and protection of foreign investment *because* and not *despite* of its province-building project.

Some governments even made this policy a key priority of their time in office, albeit to different degrees and sometimes reluctantly. Political leaders actively promoted Quebec as a destination for foreign investments, for

---

224 This is a quote form a letter sent in 1972 by William Tetley, Quebec Minister of Financial Institutions, Companies, Cooperatives and Consumer Protection, to Herb Gray, the Canadian Minister of Revenue, see Tetley (1972).

example by opening delegations abroad or by organising regular commercial relations trips led by high-ranking members of the provincial government. Mainly, they targeted investors from the United Kingdom, the United States, and France (Cornut, 2016; McCulloch, 2016; Paquin, 2016). When the Liberals were elected in 1970, they made the attraction of foreign direct investment a key governmental priority in order to spur the creation of employment opportunities. For example, Premier Bourassa visited the United Kingdom in 1971 and 1972, and again in his second term in 1994. Unlike the federal government, Quebec's leaders did not perceive an opposition between attracting foreign investments and asserting control over their own economy, as François Rocher highlighted:

> En d'autres termes, on a constamment essayé de démontrer que le nationalisme québécois pouvait être compatible avec une grande ouverture à l'égard des capitaux provenant de l'extérieur. Ainsi, le gouvernement du Québec s'est toujours refusé à attribuer l'origine de tous ces problèmes économiques à la présence des investisseurs étrangers (Rocher, 1994, p. 471)

Why did provincial representatives actively promote Quebec as an investment-friendly jurisdiction? Provincial leaders hoped to spur growth and economic prosperity at a higher degree than internal resources would otherwise permit. FDI thus supported economic development, an important pillar of province-building. Furthermore, by actively promoting Quebec as an investment-friendly jurisdiction, the provincial government acquired an additional instrument of economic development that it could deploy in accordance with the provincial development strategy. By doing so, it acquired a higher degree of autonomy from federal economic policy-making (Kirkey, Paquin et al., 2016; Vormann and Lammert, 2014).

As a reaction to federal plans to introduce a foreign investment review procedure, William Tetley, Quebec Minister of Financial Institutions, Companies, Cooperatives and Consumer Protection, sent letters to the federal Ministers for Industry and Commerce (Tetley, 1973) and of Revenue (Tetley, 1972). Furthermore, the provincial government established an inter-ministerial committee on foreign direct investment in 1971, chaired by Minister Tetley, to reflect upon the effects of the new Canadian federal legislation. The committee's report was rendered in 1973 and revised in 1974 (Tetley, 1973, revised 1974). In their report, committee members stressed the negative effects of the review process foreseen by the new legislation on Quebec. According to them, the presence of multinational companies did not impede Quebec companies' business opportunities. To the contrary, the presence of large businesses provided them with the opportunity to become a part of the international trade network. They advanced two arguments against the new federal legislation which explained the crucial development role FDI played for Quebec as a small economy. First, the new federal legislation would deprive Quebec of an instrument to support large-scale provincial industrial restructuring and economic development. In the letter sent to the Canadian Minister of Revenue, Minister Tetley made a similar argument and highlighted the provincial economic development opportunities related to foreign investments, through the creation of jobs as well as the transfer of technology and management skills:

> Mes collègues et moi avons déjà eu l'occasion d'indiquer publiquement et en plusieurs circonstances au cours des derniers mois l'apport déterminant des investissements étrangers dans la croissance économique québécoise tant par les emplois qu'ils procurent et les activités indirectes qu'ils suscitent que par les indispensables connaissances techniques et managériales qu'ils véhiculent (Tetley, 1972).

In addition, the inter-ministerial committee highlighted the extent to which the new Canadian legislation of the 1970s was also an issue of Canadian federalism. Quebec not only opposed the substance of the new federal legislation, but it also made a constitutional argument about federal interference with provincial matters. According to the committee, the FIRA review procedure established by the federal government unilaterally deprived the provinces of their constitutional prerogatives related to investment. In fact, the review procedure nullified potential provincial initiatives to attract foreign investments in accordance with their respective provincial legislation and development projects. Therefore, the new legislation did not respect regional disparities (Tetley, 1973, revised 1974, p. 23). Furthermore, the committee argued that the federal review procedure artificially reduced competition among provinces to attract foreign investment. In the case of Quebec, the new legislation deprived Quebec of development opportunities to reduce its lag behind the Canadian average. In his letter to the Canadian Minister of Industry and Commerce, Minister Tetley (1973) also wrote that

> [Les critères de la loi] privilégieraient l'industrie canadienne telle qu'elle existe et donc tendrait à figer la structure industrielle au profit des régions présentement favorisées mais au détriment du Québec dont le principal objectif est la transformation de sa propre structure industrielle.

After provincial elections in 1976, Quebec's commitment to international trade and investment faced a short interlude with the PQ in government, when international investors feared a lesser influence of business on the provincial government and briefly reduced their investments in Quebec (Tanguay, 2003 p. 257-258). However, already in 1982, the PQ shifted back to highlighting Quebec's dependency on foreign investments—a forecast of the PQ's future support of NAFTA (Paquin, 2016). A more serious challenge to Quebec's positive stance on FDI occurred at the beginning of the 1990s: the 1990's *indépendantistes* increasingly challenged the positive discursive link between FDI and province-building (Rocher, 2003, p. 473-477). Cast against the backdrop of renewed debates about Quebec sovereignty, the change was induced by a combination of change in party leadership and Quebec's first experiences with NAFTA's chapter 11 as well as developments in international investment agreements. The positive link between investment and province-building became weakened and was increasingly challenged. In particular, Quebec opposed the *Multilateral Agreement on Investment* (MAI), negotiated by the members of the OECD after the failure to reach a satisfying agreement on investment in the framework of the WTO (Blackhurst and Otten, 1996; Lowenfeld, 2003).[225] Quebec joined France in rejecting this agreement, and it eventually failed. For the PQ led by Jacques Parizeau and later Lucien Bouchard,[226] the MAI threatened Quebec's sovereignty. In this discourse, they dissolved the previously established structure of the repertoire of province-building and restructured it along the lines of the dirigisme frame (Brunelle and Deblock, 1997; Parizeau, 1997, 1998). More specifically, they debated three issues related to investment, which will also reappear in the CETA debates: cultural diversity, performance requirements, and investment protection.

The effects of investment liberalisation on cultural diversity have been an extremely contentious topic (Gattinger and Saint-Pierre, 2010; Goff, 2000; Rocher, 2003, p. 476). In an article published in *L'Action Nationale*, Parizeau[227] (1999, p. 49) referred to the threat NAFTA's investment provi-

---

225 Although the agreement was called 'multilateral' and was meant to be open to non-OECD members, it still was, in fact, a 'plurilateral' agreement.

226 Jacques Parizeau led the PQ from 1988-1996 (Premier from 1994 to 1996). Lucien Bouchard led the PQ from 1996-2001 (Premier from 1996 to 2001).

227 In order to further research on that topic, he founded the Montreal-based Institut de recherche en économie contemporaine (IREC) in 1999. In economic policy-making, the Institute's studies still play an important role. They are frequently cited in the National Assembly and influence the way some political representatives interpret contemporary trade relations.

sions and the suggested multilateral investment agreement posed to national sovereignty in his eyes:

> Le cadre étant ainsi tracé, il est clair que pour un nouveau pays en émergence qui deviendrait membre du Club, ou même pour plusieurs pays développés mais de petite taille, comme le Québec, qui ont adopté leurs propres formules de développement de leurs centres de décision, l'adhésion à l'AMI marquerait la fin de tout espoir d'infléchir leur développement, y compris dans le domaine culturel.

A second contentious issue was, and still is, performance requirements. These "are government measures that require or encourage specific behavior by private investors" (Edwards and Lester, 1997, p. 170; Parizeau, 1999, p. 50-51). Typically, they consist in prescriptions aiming to foster local development, such as the achievement of a certain level of domestic content, the export or import of a certain percentage or volume, trade balancing requirements, ownership requirements, research and development requirements, technology transfer requirements, supplier requirements or employment and training prescriptions. Sometimes, they also relate to the capital structure and management of companies. Many states used performance requirements to steer investment in the direction of their respective development strategies, particularly after commercial measures to support local industries became increasingly challenged by multilateral agreements (see Fredriksson and Zimny, 2004; Shenkin, 1994). Considered a trade distortion, performance requirements were banned in several WTO agreements for specific areas. In bilateral agreements, bans on performance requirements were sometimes generalised (Edwards and Lester, 1997; Lowenfeld, 2003; Salacuse, 2010). NAFTA imposed an almost absolute ban on such measures.

Investment protection was a third issue that challenged Quebec's overall ambition to be an investment-friendly jurisdiction. Opposition in Quebec mainly targeted the effects of NAFTA's chapter 11, which became visible at that time (see for a general review Brunelle and Deblock, 1995). Even though Quebec had strongly supported the investment chapter during the NAFTA negotiations, including investment protection mechanisms, leading PQ members soon re-evaluated Quebec's interests after NAFTA came into force. In fact, several high-profile cases had brought NAFTA's investment protection provisions to the forefront of political attention. *Ethyl Corporation v. Government of Canada (1997 [Notice of Arbitration, settled])*, one of the first cases filed against Canada under NAFTA and referring to national treatment, performance requirement and expropriation clauses, caused upheaval against NAFTA's chapter 11 (Lemire, 2003, p. 294).

When the Liberals were elected in Quebec in 2003, investment remained an important topic. Even though NAFTA continued to play a predominant role in Quebec's economic development because it offered Quebec companies access to the US markets (Rocher, 2003, p. 467), the Liberals increasingly searched for new investment opportunities and investors from outside the US. They turned to inter-provincial investment relations, with Quebec and Ontario being the main driving political forces. In their *Trade and Cooperation Agreement* (2009), they noted "the need to reduce investment distortions arising from government support in the context of this Agreement" (Article 2.6, paragraph 2b) and established a working group to do so. In fact, the Liberals promoted Canadian market integration in order to strengthen the provinces' economic basis, not to confer more powers on the federal government (Rocher, 2003, p. 467).

Section 2: Negotiating A Comprehensive Investment Chapter

Foreign direct investment was at the core of the CETA negotiation. In fact, increasing bilateral investment flows was one of the main reasons why Canada and the EU launched bilateral negotiations in the first place. As noted in the preceding section, Canada and the EU were both, on an international scale, on the side of *demandeurs* for stronger international investment rules and protection.

In the negotiation process, Quebec fully supported the aim to increase market access rights and investment protection. Quebec's representatives made investment relations one of their main interests during the negotiations. They based their discursive strategy on the conviction that Quebec as a small economy needed to be investor-friendly to stimulate economic development., At the same time, they also supported reducing internal barriers to investment flows among the Canadian provinces in order to ease the reception of European investment in Canada. However, some provincial representatives and several societal groups also wanted to include certain safeguards with regard to cultural industries, performance requirements and investment protection clauses. These were important issues in the overall negotiations: provincial jurisdiction over matters pertaining to investment made the provinces necessary partners to create a transatlantic barrier-free investment market as Canada and the EU intended. Therefore, Quebec's representatives were compelled to devise a coalitional strategy allowing them to bridge the gap between these two apparently incommensurate interests. Thus, on many occasions, they had to update and adjust their discourse, without, however, significantly changing its underlying structure.

1. Reinvigorating Investment Relations between Canada and the EU: Exploring the Bilateral Avenue

Regarding their future foreign direct investment relations, Canada's and the EU's interests converged to a large extent. In a nutshell, they wanted to create a transatlantic space where investments could flow more easily. However, previous attempts to advance in this area had failed in several regards. In the mid-2000s, Canada and the EU broke off their negotiations on the *Trade and Investment Enhancement Agreement* (TIEA) (2004-2006).[228] This raises two questions. First, this recent failure had left political leaders reluctant to conduct negotiations on a new investment agreement, although easing investment relations had been a top priority for transnational business for many years. In fact, the Canada-Europe Round Table for Business (CERT) had been asking for better investment opportunities since its foundation in 1999,[229] thus raising the question why Canada and the EU were willing to launch new comprehensive investment negotiations only at this point. Second, the CETA parties drafted an investment chapter which exceeded their ambition in the TIEA and their current multilateral and also, largely, bilateral commitments. In the TIEA, parties merely agreed to engage in a political dialogue on investment and explore future avenues of facilitating investment relations (Global Affairs Canada, 2013a). This raises the question why and to what extent CETA's approach to foreign direct investment was so broad.

Canada and the EU had already tried to find a multilateral agreement on comprehensive investment rules: alongside Japan, both had been highly active in the WTO's working group on trade and investment (founded in 1996), but they ultimately failed to reach an agreement, which was initially related to opposition by some WTO members (the US and developing countries) (Smythe, 2003; Smythe, 2011), but also increasingly to oppositi-

---

228 See also chapter 2 on the agenda-setting.
229 For instance, in its first policy recommendation issued to Canada and the EU, the CERT supported finding a multilateral agreement on investment in the framework of the WTO, see Canada Europe Round Table for Business (1999c).

on from social movements (see Fredriksson and Zimny, 2004 for an overview of the intellectual history; Young, 2016). Therefore, they both engaged in bilateral investment treaty-making.[230]

Between 2007 and 2009, continuously stagnating growth rates on both sides were among the main reasons to launch bilateral negotiations. Since domestic resources were limited, policy makers hoped to spur growth by attracting foreign capital, a suggestion business leaders across the Atlantic had been making for over a decade. In addition, a looming economic recession convinced both parties to speed up this process. At the same time, the increasing importance of global production chains provided a complementary argument to enhance investment relations for both parties. In their joint study on the feasibility of a new trade and investment agreement, the Canadian government and the European Commission argued that

> Global foreign direct investment (FDI) outflows have grown exponentially over the last 25 years, reaching US$1.2 trillion in 2006. This development has been one the key drivers of globalisation as foreign investment has facilitated links between companies, global value chains and new economic opportunities (European Commission and Government of Canada, 2008, p. 45).

For the EU, in particular, gaining privileged access to Canada's wealth of natural resources, mostly fossil fuels, energy and minerals, was a key motivation,[231] as was privileged investment access to a NAFTA member (European Commission and Government of Canada, 2008, p. 48). These European demands directly concerned the provinces, which own the majority of Canada's natural resources. Quebec for instance has a high potential for mining operations. In a Canadian study, it was cited among the most attractive jurisdictions for investments in this sector (Fraser Institute, 2008?). For Canada, a main motivation lay in the diversification potential for its investment relations in order to acquire more independence from the

---

230 After the failure of the Havanna Charter in 1948—in which investment provisions were included—leaders of the GATT countries issued, in 1955, a non-binding *Resolution on International Investment for Economic Development* in which they suggested the use of bilateral investment treaties instead of a multilateral solution. The negotiation of comprehensive investment rules at the WTO has not been successful so far, and many economies have engaged in a bilateral avenue (Smythe, 2003; World Trade Organization, 2016a).

231 Interview with European Commission official, Brussels, 23 July 2014.

US.[232] Furthermore, Canada and the EU observed that their respective levels of FDI in the partner country did not reflect the respective size of their economies. According to the European Commission, Canada had outward stocks in the EU evaluated at 135.5 billion euros, while the EU's total outbound stock in Canada had a total value of € 234.7bn in 2013 (European Commission, 2016b). Therefore, Canada hoped to attract more European investment (European Commission and Government of Canada, 2008, p. 48). Also, European member states differed in their degrees of investments made in Canada. For instance, France had a high level of investment (but a smaller share of trade in goods), while Germany had a lower level of investment, as related by a French diplomat in Quebec:

> La France, par exemple, on la compare souvent avec l'Allemagne. Parce que la France a plutôt fait le choix d'investir ici, alors que nos échanges commerciaux sont assez faibles. L'Allemagne a relativement peu – ou enfin moins – d'investissements au Québec, par contre elle a beaucoup plus d'échanges commerciaux.[233]

Both parties were aware that the significance of CETA's investment chapter reached beyond the treaty itself: CETA was the first comprehensive trade and investment agreement negotiated by the European Commission with an exclusive European competence for foreign direct investment, which had been introduced with the Treaty of Lisbon (2009).[234] Thus it was also a way to reflect the EU's own internal integration potential. A Canadian diplomat based in Brussels asserted that CETA was an instrument for the EU to push its member states to display their respective degree of openness to cross-border investment flows:

> On services and investment, forcing the member states to do a negative-list approach forced them to look at their services and investments markets and decide what's open and what isn't. I think CETA will help push the development of the single market. [235]

CETA negotiations were therefore a test case for the EU's ability to successfully find a common negotiation position satisfying all the members states in their bilateral relations. Furthermore, CETA's investment chapter reflected the form and nature of an agreement between a North American econ-

---

232 Interview with French diplomat, by phone, 23 January 2015.
233 Interview with French diplomat, Montreal, 20 April 2015.
234 Interview with European Commission Official, Brussels, 23 July 2014.
235 Interview with high-ranking Canadian trade official, Brussels, 8 July 2014.

omy and the EU, which have different investment traditions. CETA could therefore serve as a potential benchmark for future agreements.

Embedding investment relations in a trade agreement also mirrored a particular understanding of the relationship between trade and investment. Since the 1990s, leading trade elites asserted that this relationship was threefold (Vandevelde, 1998): Investments made in host countries allow circumvention of existing trade barriers, they increase the factor endowment for production processes in the host country and they reduce transaction costs between affiliated companies in global production chains. Indeed, the highest potential for new trade relations between Canada and the EU did not lie in market access, but in the enhancement of the efficiency of global value chains, including intra-industry trade. Competitive advantages of different economies pushed companies to localise their production sites in different jurisdictions. CETA's investment chapter should reduce transaction costs in intra-company value chains, and allow easier exchange of intermediate goods among different manufacturing sites (van Assche, 2012). In order to deploy its full potential, foreign direct investment needed to be complemented by processes of regulatory recognition and harmonisation so that primary or secondary products could be exported more cost-efficiently, which was also a driving thought behind CETA's comprehensive design. With CETA, both parties recognised that all these elements interlock.

This ambition translated in the EU's negotiation mandate, which targeted the highest level of market access. Yet, it also allowed for (a limited number of) sectoral exceptions:

> The Agreement shall provide for the progressive and reciprocal liberalisation of establishment and of trade in services with the aim to ensure the highest level of market access opportunities. [...] This is without prejudice to the possible exclusion of a limited number of sectors from the liberalisation commitments (Council of the EU, 2009).

In its mandate, the European Council explicitly excluded audiovisual and other cultural services, as well as services supplied in the exercise of governmental authority. The guiding principles of the investment chapter were set out to be transparency, non-discrimination, market access, stability and general principles of protection, national treatment, as well as most-favoured nation status. In the mandate, there was no particular mention of the Canadian provinces with regard to investment. Although the provinces have jurisdiction over investment-related issues such as natural resources, labour standards or environmental regulations, the European negotiators did not expect opposition from their part. On the Canadian side, the provinces highlighted in a release by the Council of the Federation that Canada's attractiveness for investors depended on provincial cooperation:

> Ongoing collaboration between provinces, territories, and the federal government on shared strategic approach to the global economy is critical, and provinces and territories have numerous international strengths that can facilitate development of international trade and investment linkages (Council of the Federation, 2011).

While not expecting the provinces to cause complications during the negotiations, the European Commission anticipated that the Canadian federal legislation on investment, the Investment Canada Act, might present an obstacle. In fact, the EU asked for a more privileged access than foreseen by the Investment Canada Act, while Canada did not want to offer European investments better access than US investors who are bound by the Act despite NAFTA.[236] Investment negotiations were thus taking place in the shadow of NAFTA, which was the benchmark for CETA's investment chapter.

2. A Comprehensive Approach to Investment in CETA

To a large extent, negotiators achieved what they had set out to do during the agenda-setting. CETA includes a full chapter on foreign direct investment. Including investment as an issue in its own right represented a significant change in comparison to other agreements.[237] In WTO agreements, investment is conceived as an aspect related to trade, but not as a commercial issue per se (see for a discussion on the differences between bilateral and multilateral agreements Gestrin and Rugman, 2005; see for a similar argument McBride, 2006).[238] For the EU, CETA is the first bilateral trade

---

236 Interview with French diplomat, by phone, 23 January 2015.
237 As explained in footnote 217, the following account is based on CETA's *provisional* chapter on investment of the consolidated text published in September 2014 after the conclusion of the negotiations between Canada and the EU.
238 In WTO agreements and most Bilateral Investment Treaties (BITs), there is no general right of establishment and no guarantee of non-discrimination, except for situations in which domestic regulation on investment interferes with the provisions relating to trade in goods and services, intellectual property rights, public procurement or subsidies and countervailing measures.

agreement that includes a comprehensive chapter on investment,[239] assuring broad coverage of all sectors except those explicitly excluded. In fact, the previously negotiated EU-South Korea Free Trade Agreement (2011) only regulates foreign direct investment related to trade. This agreement does not include a dedicated investment chapter. Rather, investment relations are referred to mainly in the chapters on services (chapter 7), and payments and capital movements (chapter 8).

In addition to wide and generalised coverage, CETA provides a very broad definition of investment. The consolidated 2014 version of CETA defines an investment, in article X.2, as "[e]very kind of asset that an investor owns or controls, directly or indirectly, that has the characteristics of an investment, which includes a certain duration and other characteristics such as the commitment of capital or other resources, the expectation of gain or profit, or the assumption of risk." The forms investments may take are defined broadly, for example, as taking control over or interest in an enterprise, equity participation in that enterprise or loans given to the enterprise; intellectual property rights or other moveable rights; or claims to money or performance which do not arise solely from commercial contracts. Therefore, investments refer to the acquisition of assets with the aim to participate in the production, transformation and distribution cycles of goods and services on the partner's territory. Subsequently, they exceed the interactions related to commercial exchange and represent an instance of deep economic integration.

CETA's logic is very similar to NAFTA's, despite minor differences. Both agreements define investments in broad terms and from a business perspective as (almost) every kind of asset used to generate future profits. Both agreements are also constructed around four rights given to investors: establishment, treatment, protection, and access to dispute resolution. I will review these in turn.

First, in terms of investment establishment rights, NAFTA and CETA provide for market access rights, although CETA is more explicit than NAFTA in this regard. CETA spells out measures that are not allowed with regard to reviewing incoming investments, such as imposing limitations on the number of companies that can carry out a specific activity. NAFTA, to the contrary, does not include such a list, but refers to establishment rights in relation to other provisions, for example in non-discrimination clauses. Both NAFTA and CETA impose an almost absolute ban on performance requirements. Since there is no global definition of performance re-

---

239   Interview with European Commission official, Brussels, 23 July 2014.

quirements, most Bilateral Investment Treaties (BITs) banning them establish a positive list with measures the parties wish to prohibit. CETA prohibits—in a language similar to that of NAFTA—most of the currently used performance requirements with regard to the establishment *or* the reception of an advantage in connection with the investment: export or import requirements, domestic content requirements, and technology transfers.[240]

Second, NAFTA and CETA prohibit discrimination against foreign investors. Accordingly, both agreements guarantee national treatment (treatment no less favourable than accorded to domestic investors in similar situations) and most-favoured nation treatment (treatment no less favourable than accorded to investors from any other third country) within the limits of the chapters' scope. The conjunction of these two clauses is significant in the context of the heterogeneous internal Canadian market; in fact, the two clauses commit the provinces to offer a foreign investor the highest internal and international standards of protection. In the EU, the effect of the combination of both clauses is less relevant given the high openness to cross-border investment flows within the Single market . CETA and NAFTA also forbid specific requirements for the composition of a company's board of directors, such as citizenship. With regard to treatment clauses, the Investment Canada Act constituted a specific challenge for Canadian negotiators. Under NAFTA, investments are subjected to the Act, which is why Canada refused to abolish the procedure for European investors.[241] In addition, according to CETA's Annex X.43.1, decisions made under the Investment Canada Act (ICA) are not subject to dispute settlement provisions. However, Canada agreed to raise the threshold for review to CAD $1.5 billion (except when the European investor is a state enterprise). Furthermore, future amendments made to the ICA must not decrease the conformity of the ICA with CETA.

Third, both agreements have a section on investment protection. This section organises compensation for losses and expropriation, as well as the transfer of funds. In terms of protection, NAFTA and CETA go beyond existing WTO agreements. The WTO agreements offer almost no protection beyond the respective national legislation and courts.[242] To the contrary, NAFTA's protection standards reach further: they foresee fair and

---

240 Performance requirements are regulated in article X.5.
241 Interview with French diplomat, by phone, 23 January 2015.
242 There is one exception: the GATS includes a provision on an international means of dispute resolution.

equitable treatment, include provisions on compensation, and provide protection against expropriation. Again, CETA follows a similar logic.

A fourth element, connected to investment protection, lies in the establishment of a specific method of dispute resolution in both NAFTA and CETA. Even though CETA's dispute resolution mechanism has undergone significant change after the treaty was signed in 2014, it still establishes a unique dispute resolution mechanism allowing investors to pursue governments in another forum than domestic or multilateral courts.

With regard to investment protection and Canadian federalism, CETA's investment chapter raises the question of provincial liability which has already been debated in the past, as noted in section 1.1. of this chapter. While provinces have so far not been held accountable internationally for their breaches of Canada's investment obligations, the strong involvement of the provinces in the negotiation of CETA triggered the long-standing debate of provincial liability again.[243] So far, it has not yet been clearly established if the Canadian provinces are liable if they violate obligations from an international agreement signed by Canada. From the perspective of public international law, CETA is concluded among sovereign states; therefore, liability only extends to Canada. Internally, however, Canada might devise a mechanism to transfer the costs of the legal process, including legal fees and compensatory payments, to the province which committed an infringement. Currently, there is no such mechanism.[244] Probably, cost sharing will be decided on a case by case basis in the event of an infringement.[245]

CETA includes a list of exceptions to which the investment chapter's provisions do not extend. Article X.1 specifies two exceptions, promoted among others by Quebec. First, measures concerning air services and related services are partially excluded from provisions on the establishment of investment and non-discriminatory treatment.[246] Second, Canadian cultural industries are excluded, while the EU only reserves itself the right to exclude measures with respect to audio-visual services. According to the PQ's Jean-François Lisée, the exclusion of cultural industries was a key condition set by Quebec. According to him, refusal to exclude cultural industries

---

243　Assemblée nationale du Québec, 6 October 2010.

244　Interview with trade lawyer, Montreal, 17 April 2016.

245　As discussed at Round Table " The EU-Canada Comprehensive Economic and Trade Agreement (CETA): Building Competitive Advantage for Canada", Montreal, 2 June 2016.

246　A list of reservations specified in the agreement applies to this exception.

could have resulted in Quebec rejecting the agreement. According to Lisée, Quebec exchanged the exclusion of cultural industries from the investment chapter against broad access to provincial procurement markets.[247]

3. A More Autonomous Provincial Investment Policy for Quebec

Reducing transatlantic barriers to foreign direct investment was among Quebec's top priorities for engaging in CETA negotiations in the first place. As the negotiations went along, Quebec's political leaders across party lines and members of its diplomatic corps generally supported the Canadian offer and the final negotiation outcome on investment. Thus, the province stayed in line with the support it had given to foreign direct investment over the last decades, highlighting the positive role foreign direct investment played in province-building. In addition, CETA allowed Quebec's Liberal government to further their Canadian market integration agenda by reducing non-tariff-barriers among the provinces. Overall, the investment chapter was therefore not among the issues considered contentious in the province.[248] It contrasted with more contentious issues such as public procurement or agriculture.

Overall, Quebec's negotiation position on investment was similar during the agenda-setting stage and at the end of the negotiations. Considering the province's historic inclination to create an investor-friendly environment, this position does not represent a major empirical puzzle. Yet, although it did not engender as much controversy as other issues in the CETA negotiations, investment was still a predominant topic in the National Assembly during the negotiations, mostly during the agenda-setting and early negotiation stages. Then, investment represented around 10 percent of the overall discourse on CETA (in terms of words), as the following table shows. Towards the end of the negotiations, the relative importance of discourse on investment declined. This was a counterintuitive process which needs more explanation, given the PQ's inclination to promote state dirigisme in international investment, as it did during the MAI negotiations. Eventually, however, the PQ deputies accepted the provisions suggested by the Liberals. How the Liberals included them in their coalitional strategy and how they might have updated their discursive strategy to do so therefore requires further attention.

---

247 Jean-François Lisée, Assemblée nationale du Québec, 15 February 2013.
248 Interview with Quebec diplomat, Montreal, 15 October 2014.

Table 19 – Total Coding on Investment and Investment Protection per Negotiation Period (2006-2014)

Period	Policy Cycle	Government in Office	Discourse on investment in total discourse on CETA (%)
2006-2009	Agenda-Setting	PLQ	12
2009-2012	1st Negotiation Stage	PLQ	10
2012-2014	2nd Negotiation Stage	PQ	5
2014	Decision-Making	PLQ	1

Source: Analysis of parliamentary debates (plenary and committees, N=159,127 words)

a) Setting the Agenda for Attracting Foreign Capital (2006-2009)

Representatives of business groups were one basis for Quebec's move to launch and support a new investment agreement with the EU. Above, I described the influential role played by the Canada-Europe Round Table for Business in supporting an agreement including broad investment provisions. In addition, in Quebec, the Quebec Federation of Chambers of Commerce strongly supported measures to attract foreign investment. They conceived of foreign direct investment as an instrument to spur production and therefore growth in the province. Continuously, they underlined the importance of international trade and investment agreements to spur investments to Quebec (Fédération des chambres de commerce du Québec, 2008?, p. 14). Furthermore, the Federation repeatedly highlighted the role foreign direct investment has played in the province's economic development, for instance in their comments on the PQ's 2013-14 budget:

> Historiquement, les investissements directs étrangers (IDE) ont joué un rôle majeur dans le développement économique du Québec et il faut s'assurer d'être capable de continuer à attirer ces investisseurs (Fédération des chambres de commerce du Québec, 2013, p. 5).

In its 2010 report, the Federation of Quebec's Chambers of Commerce noted that the economic recession led to a decrease of foreign direct investment in Quebec. As a remedy, it suggested to increase the attractiveness of Quebec as a jurisdiction for foreign direct investment. Additionally, it highlighted the extent to which the EU has developed into an increasingly important partner for Quebec's companies (Fédération des chambres de commerce du Québec, 2010?, p. 14). Therefore, it vigorously opposed a suggestion made by the leader of the provincial political party Action démocratique du Québec (ADQ)[249] to have the Caisse de dépôt et de placement hinder foreign ownership in the province.

However, relating Quebec's support for reducing barriers to transatlantic investment relations merely to business interests leaves a number of questions unanswered. In fact, business representatives promoting the liberalisation of investment relations existed for a long time. Yet, provincial governments did not make themselves champions of promoting this position through an international trade agreement before. Also, there were specific exceptions promoted by Quebec which cast doubt on the assertion that business representatives were the main driver, in Quebec, behind the governments' respective positions. These exceptions represented specific industries which the government wanted to protect, at the risk of compromising their entire support for CETA, particularly in the cultural sector.

In addition, looking at the interests of business groups as if they were homogeneous underestimates their variety and how political parties integrated them into their respective discursive strategies. Sometimes, indeed, the PQ evaluated the effects of CETA's investment provisions on province-building differently than the Liberals. While the Liberals consistently followed the logic of the small open economy frame, the PQ was torn between the state dirigisme and the small open economy frame.

Overall, as table 20 shows, 'measures to attract foreign direct investment' was the most important issue discussed in the National Assembly during the agenda-setting stage; 86 percent of the total discourse on FDI during the agenda-setting stage concerned this topic. Quebec's natural resources were considered a way to do so, which was why 14 percent of the discourse concerned this topic. Adhering to the logic of the small open economy frame, Quebec Liberal representatives promoted the attraction of foreign

---

249 Founded in 1994 by a group of former members of the Liberal Party of Quebec supporting the conclusions of the "Rapport Allaire" contrary to their former party colleagues, the Action démocratique du Québec supported increased transfer of powers to Canadian provinces after the failure of the Meech Lake Accord (1990). Economically, they supported Liberal policies and suggested to reduce the role of the State in the economy. After electoral defeat, the ADQ merged with the newly founded Coalition Avenir Québec in 2012.

investment to the province to spur economic development, particularly but not only in the scarcely populated North. Structuring the repertoire of province-building according to the small open economy frame, the Liberal government promoted three processes underpinning their interest to attract foreign investors: generating growth without increasing state expenses, diversifying the origin of foreign investments into the province, and attracting European investors' attention to Quebec. A systematic examination of the Liberal deputies' discourse in the National Assembly confirmed that, during the agenda-setting stage, CETA was constructed as an instrument to attract foreign investors' attention to the province. As negotiations advanced, as table 21 shows, measures to attract FDI became less important. Natural resource extraction surged after the official beginning of the negotiation process, and I will explain later why it did. During the agenda-setting stage, the Liberals' discursive strategy had three dimensions: making Quebec an investor-friendly jurisdiction, drawing attention to the province, and creating investment opportunities.

Table 20 –   Most Important Topics during Agenda-Setting Stage (Percentage of Total Discourse on FDI, 2006-2009)

Measures to At-tract FDI	Natural Resour-ces Extraction	Others	Total (%)
86	14	0	100

Source: Analysis of parliamentary debates (N=1,612 words)[250]

Table 21 –   Evolution of the Relative Importance of 'Measures to Attract FDI' and 'Natural Resource Extraction' at Different Negotiation Stages

	2006-2009	2009-2012	2012-2014	2014	Total percentage
Measures to Attract FDI	56	33	11	0	100
Natural Resources Extraction	9	91	0	0	100

Source: Analysis of parliamentary debates (N=2458 words)[251]

---

250   See appendix for full table.
251   See appendix for full table.

Making Quebec an investor-friendly jurisdiction was the first dimension of the provincial representatives' discursive strategy. Through this strategy, they wanted to spur economic growth, a pillar of province-building, as explained in the chapter on the agenda-setting stage. Their discursive strategy consisted in bolstering the investment relations between Quebec and European investors. In fact, declining growth rates, amplified by the economic recession since 2007, forced the government to devise a plan to relaunch Quebec's economy while staying true to its promise to reduce state expenses considerably. In this period, which corresponded to CETA's agenda-setting stage, the Liberal government constructed foreign investment as a remedy to currently stagnating or declining growth rates and showed how FDI contributed to economic development, a pillar of province-building. Since the government accorded such a prominent role to FDI in economic development, declining levels of US investment in Quebec posed a major threat for Quebec's economic growth in their eyes. In fact, the bulk of foreign investments in Quebec are of US origin, as table 22 documents.[252] However, capital investments from US companies in construction, and machinery and equipment in companies based in Quebec have declined around 35 percent between 2004 and 2011.[253] According to the government and think tanks (e.g. Gendron, 2005), Quebec therefore needed to become considerably more attractive for foreign investors outside the US. In order to stimulate investments in the province, the government announced in its 2008 budget the abolition of tax on capital to increase Quebec's comparatively low ratio of investment to GDP.[254] The capital tax is a type of tax levied from financial and non-financial companies on their

---

252 Foreign direct investment to Canada is not documented for every province. Yet, experts agree that investments of US origin prevail in Quebec. Interview with French diplomat, Montreal, 20 April 2015: "les entreprises américaines [sont] de loin le premier investisseur étranger au Québec.".

253 Statistics Canada does not produce statistics on volumes of FDI broken down by province. An exact measure of foreign direct investment made in Quebec is impossible to establish empirically. Upon request, *Statistiques Québec* suggested to use data on capital investments (e.g. in machinery or infrastructure) made in Quebec by foreign-owned companies as a proxy. They provided me with the necessary data, on which table 22 is based.

254 According to Finance Minister Monique Jérôme-Forget, investment stimulates companies to develop and export competitive products, thereby contributing to the creation of new jobs. In this way, Quebec can overcome the economic recession. On 13 May 2008, the Minister announced in the National Assembly: "Nous allons stimuler l'investissement. J'annonce l'abolition immédiate et complète de la taxe sur le capital pour toutes les entreprises manufacturières.".

capital reserves, reserves and their long-term debt regardless of their income. Generally, the tax on capital is conceived to be a hindrance to investments (Institut Économique de Montréal, 2005).

Table 22 – Capital Investment to Quebec in Machinery, Equipment and Non-residential Construction by Country of Company Ownership (2004-2011)

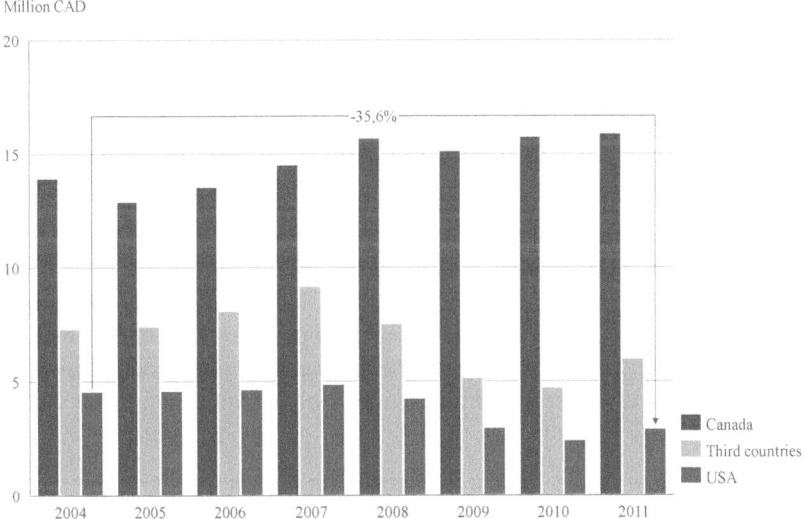

Source: Gouvernement du Québec (2012b)

This budget expressed the Liberal government's conviction that governments should create an investment-friendly environment through regulation rather than through subsidies. In fact, when they came into office in 2003, the Liberals cut state subsidies by almost 30 percent. It was their conviction that investor attractiveness depends on policy, not subsidies (Thomas, 2011, p. 351). In a speech in the National Assembly, Premier Jean Charest highlighted, for instance, that the policy think tank Fraser Institute mentioned Quebec as one of the most investment-friendly jurisdictions in the mining sector because of its public policies, implying that they outweigh subsidies.[255] In fact, the exploitation of natural resources and the

---

255 Jean Charest, Assemblée nationale du Québec, 16 April 2008.

need of foreign investments to do so played an important role in debates in the National Assembly during the agenda-setting stage.[256]

In addition, the representatives' discursive strategy making Quebec an investor-friendly jurisdiction also contributed to strengthening the Liberal government's representation of Quebec in the Canadian federal setting. Increasing provincial attractiveness would allow Quebec, within the limits of federal legislation, to pursue an investment policy independently from federal policies. In fact, they argued that international agreements were more resistant to political change than domestic legislation. Therefore, CETA could insulate Quebec from new policy orientations at the provincial or federal level. To a large extent, Quebec's diplomatic corps shared this assessment. In the National Assembly, Pierre-Marc Johnson asserted for instance that CETA would institutionalise existing investment practices:

> Et il faut être conscients que souvent ces accords visent à figer dans un texte juridique, qui donne des certitudes, des pratiques qui existent déjà. Et une des vertus de cette négociation, c'est précisément de donner un niveau de certitude et de prévisibilité sur le plan des pratiques entre le Canada et l'Union européenne pour assurer celles et ceux qui prennent des risques d'investissement et qui prennent des investissements pour exporter ou importer qu'ils ont et qu'elles ont un cadre qui est stable.[257]

This discursive strategy supported Quebec's representatives' representation of Canadian federalism and province-building. Sometimes, these two repertoires interacted. As far as Canadian federalism was concerned, Quebec's Liberal government tried to further integrate the inner-Canadian market. In line with the integration frame structuring the repertoire of federalism, a more independent investment policy would contribute to making Quebec independence obsolete. This argument was similar to the Quebec Liberals' reasoning during the 1980s free trade debates (Rocher, 2003). On the one hand, this ambition contributed to their province-building objectives (in particular economic development) and the easing of investment relations among Canadian provinces by decreasing inter-provincial barriers to trade. On the other hand, the internal integration of the Canadian market also added to the overall attractiveness of the Canadian market for foreign investors. In addition, the CETA investment negotiati-

---

256 See full tables in appendix.
257 Pierre-Marc Johnson, Assemblée nationale du Québec, 8 December 2011 (=2nd hearing).

on was also an opportunity to remind the provinces of their jurisdiction pertaining to international investment relations: as a consequence, the Council of the Federation reflected on ways to reduce barriers to investment activities among Canadian provinces. Provincial Premiers did so explicitly with the aim to prepare negotiations of an economic agreement with the EU. Their twofold aim was to prepare a common Canadian position where provincial jurisdiction was involved, and to allow CETA provisions to achieve their full potential in an integrated Canadian market (Council of the Federation, 2011).

Apart from creating an investor-friendly environment in Quebec and Canada, the second dimension of provincial representatives' strategy involved creating momentum for attention by the international business community for Quebec as an investor-friendly jurisdiction. Against the background of declining US investments, the government adjusted its discourse and accorded European investors a more prominent position in its economic development strategy. It devised policies to diversify Quebec's investment partnerships. Highlighting the low level of European investments in Canada in comparison to Canadian investments made in Europe, representatives constructed an interest for Quebec in the attraction of higher volumes of European investments to the province.[258] In this discursive strategy, CETA was conceived of as an instrument to draw attention to Quebec. Investment therefore played an important role in crafting the raison d'être of CETA in the eyes of Quebec representatives. In their view of CETA, Quebec would be a point of entry for European investment made in Canada. They based their understanding on the practices of French companies, which tended to use Montreal and Quebec as a point of entry for their activities in North America, as a French diplomat asserted:

> Vraiment, on le voit, c'est très souvent un tremplin de venir à Montréal et au Québec pour aller ensuite vers l'Amérique du Nord anglophone. [...] Pour les entreprises françaises c'est très net, c'est vraiment la porte d'entrée du marché nord-américain.[259]

Based on this conception, Quebec's representatives hoped to make Quebec a hub for European companies in general by means of CETA.

The third dimension in Quebec's representatives' discursive strategy consisted in devising a substantive plan to generate investment opportunities,

---

258 Interview with Canadian diplomat, Brussels, 8 July 2014; Pierre-Marc Johnson, Assemblée nationale du Québec, 8 December 2011 (=2nd hearing).
259 Interview with French diplomat, Montreal, 20 April 2015.

an instrument for economic and spatial development and an important pillar of province-building. They did so mainly through the *Plan Nord*: after the Liberals won the 2008 elections in which they had promoted spatial development in the province's Northern regions (Plan Nord), the Liberal government made the Plan Nord a centre-piece of its discursive strategy. It created a ministry coordinating the new economic, social and environmental development plan and presented it in 2008, not without criticism (Robitaille, 2008). By investing into the development of a sustainable industry based on natural resources and tourism, the government aimed at invigorating the scarcely populated North to the benefit of the province as a whole. In Quebec and even more so in its Northern regions, the low ratio of population to land explained the need for foreign investments to keep the Northern regions inhabited and economically well-developed. At the same time, Quebec's low ratio of investment per capita illustrated existing investment opportunities. Thus, CETA also became an instrument through which the provincial government promoted spatial development. This strategy has already started to attract foreign investments; in fact, a French diplomat considered it a prime opportunity for French investors in Quebec.[260]

Why was it so important for the Quebec Liberals to achieve success in the negotiation of CETA's investment chapter? On the one hand, as documented in the examination of the agenda-setting process, FDI was an instrument for economic development, a pillar of province-building. On the other hand, it was also an instrument for economic and political development, which rendered Quebec's investment policy less dependent on federal policy measures and which provided the provincial government with an additional instrument at their disposal without federal interference, and therefore also an element of their *political* development strengthening the position of Quebec in the Canadian federation. In this way, political development as a pillar of province-building intersected with the integration frame of the repertoire of federalism. At the same time, CETA also created an opportunity for reducing inter-provincial barriers to trade in Canada, another pillar of the repertoire of federalism. By enhancing investment opportunities in Canada across provincial borders and by giving the provinces a stronger voice in designing Canada's internal market, for instance through their ownership of natural resources or their jurisdiction on labour regulation, Quebec's Liberal government strengthened the integration frame as the prominent structure of the repertoire of federalism.

---

260 Interview with French diplomat, Montreal, 20 April 2015.

Building their discursive strategy on the attraction of foreign investment through increasing their international visibility, reducing their dependency vis-à-vis the Canadian federal government and creating new investment opportunities was not an entirely new strategy in Quebec. In the past, the provincial government had already deployed many instruments of provincial "paradiplomacy" to reach foreign investors' attention. For instance, the opening of economic missions abroad served the purpose of circumventing federal investment policy deemed disadvantageous for Quebec (Paquin, 2004). Already during CETA's agenda-setting stage, social movements criticized the argument that the reduction of barriers to investment would increase growth rates (Attac-Québec, 2008). However, this criticism was not politically influential at that time, but it would become important as negotiations unfolded.

Against the backdrop of these discursive developments, the PQ increasingly challenged the frames the Liberals tried to impose in their discursive strategy. When the details of CETA's investment provisions became known after negotiations started, the PQ contested the Liberals' assertion that CETA could contribute to province-building. In fact, establishing a coherent discourse was particularly challenging for the PQ. On the one hand, the party favoured free trade and investment as an instrument to achieve greater independence from the Canadian market, yet, on the other hand, its members also wanted to preserve a directive role for the provincial state in the economy. While they considered CETA as a way to enhance Quebec's anchoring in the international economy, the agreement also considerably reduced the state's capacity to steer economic development in their eyes, thereby jeopardising state dirigisme.

Overall, provincial representatives' interest in facilitating foreign investment was not purely based on the influence of the business community, but also on its utility for the Liberals' larger economic and political projects. The fact that CETA was instrumental to these projects had an impact on the Liberals' representation of provincial interests. During the agenda-setting stage, members of the PQ did not yet participate much in debates on CETA and investment in the National Assembly. However, they would become more involved after CETA negotiations had started officially. When they did, they contested the instruments the Liberals suggested for province-building and the development of Canadian federalism in their discourse. In fact, they put forward a different discursive strategy according to which they developed Quebec's interests regarding the investment chapter. Since the PQ members had a different understanding of how province-building could best be achieved, they identified Quebec's interests in CE-

TA's investment chapter differently and brought an alternative discursive strategy to the forefront.

b) A Controversy over the Need for State Dirigisme (2009-2012)

After the CETA negotiation had officially started in May 2009, Quebec's representatives considerably altered their discourse. In this new discourse, opponents to the Liberal government's discursive strategy used elements from the state dirigisme frame to challenge the Liberals' assumption that Quebec needed FDI at all costs to develop its economy. They did so for cultural industries,[261] which represented 13 percent of the discourse in the first negotiation stage. Deputies also shifted their focus from investment incentive measures towards a discussion about measures used by the host country to influence the investor's behaviour, mostly when extracting Quebec's natural resources: deputies mostly discussed performance requirements and natural resource attraction, which took 26 and 21 percent respectively of the discourse from 2009 to 2012, that is during the first negotiation phase, as table 23 reveals. As table 24 shows, these topics became less important as negotiations proceeded.

Even though the PQ supported the government's ambition to facilitate investment in Quebec, they challenged some of the Liberals' assumptions regarding foreign direct investment. Together with deputies form the CAQ, PQ deputies critically discussed the conditions in which foreign direct investment should be carried out. They highlighted that the state should be able to direct these investments according to their province-building projects. Thus, the beginning of the negotiations was a critical discursive moment: some deputies tried to restructure the repertoire of province-building by the dirigisme frame, leading to a reinterpretation of provincial interests on FDI. However, the Liberals stayed firm and reminded Quebeckers that investment settlement was essential in a situation where Quebec was a small economy with a large territory. This negotiation stage was thus characterised mainly by discursive confrontation: each group of representa-

---

261 Cultural industries are treated as a cross-sectoral issue in the CETA agreement. Provisions concerning culture are included in chapters on cross-border trade in services, domestic regulation, government procurement, investment and subsidies. I include them in the discussion of investment provisions, because deputies considered investment protection clauses as the major threat to safeguard independent cultural industries in Quebec.

tives tried to impose their respective discursive strategy, so that discursive conciliation seemed difficult.

Table 23 – Most Important Topics during First Negotiation Stage (Percentages of Total Discourse on FDI, 2009-2012)

Performance Requirements	Natural Resources Extraction	Investment Protection and Dispute Resolution	Negotiation Process	Cultural Industries	Others	Total (%)
26	21	13	15	13	12	100

Source: Analysis of parliamentary debates (N=10,813 words)[262]

Table 24 – Evolution of the Relative Importance of 'Performance Requirements', 'Natural Resource Extraction' and 'Cultural Industries' (Percentage at Different Negotiation Stages)

	2006-2009	2009-2012	2012-2014	2014	Total percentage (number of words)
Performance Requirements	0	88	12	0	100 (N=3,198)
Natural Resource Extraction	9	91	0	0	100 (N=2,458)
Cultural Industries	0	93	7	0	100 (N=1,556)

Source: Analysis of parliamentary debates[263]

When negotiations started in May 2009, the Liberal government evaluated Quebec's interests against the background of the small open economy frame they had established during the agenda-setting stage and represented foreign direct investment as a tool to increase Quebec's provincial economic and political development. They also added a new dimension to their

---

262 See appendix for full table.
263 See appendix for full table.

discursive strategy: the existence of global value chains. Chief negotiator Pierre-Marc Johnson reiterated the logic of this frame in the 2010 and 2011 hearings in the National Assembly's Committee on Institutional Affairs.[264] Establishing an equation between the low ratio of population to land and the high potential for European investment in Quebec, he asserted that attracting foreign direct investment was not an ideological choice, but an objective necessity:

> En matière d'investissement, je dirais que la problématique est relativement simple. Nous avons un immense territoire. Pour le développer, ça prend du capital. Nous avons peu de population. L'équation est simple : ça prend du capital qui vient de l'extérieur. Ce n'est même pas un choix idéologique, c'est un choix de gros bon sens. Et il faut remarquer que la quantité de capitaux investis qui sont d'origine canadienne en Europe est presque aussi importante que la quantité de capitaux investis par les Européens au Canada, alors qu'ils sont 12,5 fois plus nombreux que nous, au Canada.[265]

For the government and Quebec's negotiation team, provincial economic development could best be achieved through a strong integration of Quebec in global value chains. Representatives also stressed the relation between global value chains, investment and trade. According to them, investments generated the most positive outcome if they were fruitfully related to the negotiation of tariffs and rules of origin in CETA. In fact, Quebec would only be able to attract foreign investments, for instance in the natural resources sector, if the future investor would be able to export the intermediate good at an acceptable tariff rate. Therefore, investment and tariff provisions went hand in hand.[266]

In October 2011, European and Canadian offers on investment were tabled in the official negotiation process.[267] Consequently, heated debates on the conditions accompanying foreign direct investments took place in Quebec during the first negotiation period (2009-2012). Deputies mainly debated whether foreign control over assets in Quebec should be accompa-

---

264 Pierre-Marc Johnson, Assemblée nationale du Québec, 6 October 2010 (=1st hearing); Pierre-Marc Johnson, Assemblée nationale du Québec, 8 December 2011 (=2nd hearing).

265 Pierre-Marc Johnson, Assemblée nationale du Québec, 6 October 2010 (=1st hearing).

266 Maryse Gaudreault, Assemblée nationale du Québec, 5 October 2011.

267 Pierre-Marc Johnson, Assemblée nationale du Québec, 8 December 2011 (=2nd hearing).

nied by performance requirements regarding the related production processes, such as the obligation to hire local work force, transfer technology or transform extracted minerals on site. Such measures could also require local equipment, local work force, or local transformation.[268] Performance requirements were among the most contentious topics, often related to the extraction of natural resources.[269] Around 30 percent of discourse between 2009 and 2012 was on these two topics respectively.[270]

Guided by the frames they had established, members of political parties constructed their respective position on performance requirements. In their reaction to the negotiation offer, the Liberals strictly followed their previous discourse, arguing that banning performance requirements could contribute to establishing a more investment-friendly environment, thereby advancing provincial development.

In their discursive strategy, the Liberal Party could not rely on genuine support from the PQ for the investment chapter. They rather needed to acquire the PQ's support and find a common ground by deploying a coalitional strategy. In fact, some members of the PQ constructed their discourse according to the state dirigisme frame. Even though the PQ supported the attraction of foreign direct investment to foster provincial development, some of its members argued that the state could and should play a directive role to steer foreign investments made in the province. Among PQ members and those of other opposition parties, anxieties about preserving the state's regulatory capacity in steering foreign investments to the benefit of local and rural communities, and social and environmental standards induced a certain degree of caution about the benefits of investment provisions banning performance requirements.

Against the backdrop of contestation of investment provisions included in NAFTA and some recent high-profile investment protection cases brought against Canada for infringements by the provinces, some PQ members openly defied CETA investment provisions and argued that Quebec could negotiate a better deal, as Louise Beaudoin asserted with regard to NAFTA's chapter 11:[271] "Mais, moi, c'est : la mondialisation, oui, mais.

---

268 Pierre-Marc Johnson, Assemblée nationale du Québec, 6 October 2010 (=1st hearing); Pierre-Marc Johnson, Assemblée nationale du Québec, 8 December 2011 (=2nd hearing).

269 Performance requirements link investments to compulsory actions to be taken by the investor for the approval of the investment project, see section 1.3 for examples and their relation to international trade relations.

270 See appendix for full tables.

271 Louise Beaudoin, Assemblée nationale du Québec, 27 April 2010.

Tu sais, franchement, là, pas n'importe quoi." This revived, among PQ members, similar controversies as those which had accompanied the negotiation of the OECD's failed Multilateral Agreement on Investment. According to them, forbidding performance requirements confers the right on investors to exploit Quebec's abundant natural resources without necessarily engendering any local benefits. Therefore, a ban on performance requirements would inhibit development strategies such as the Plan Nord from realising their full potential in contributing to provincial development.[272]

According to the position promoted by the PQ, growth was not primarily generated by embedding production in global value chains, but by assuring that the province's population participates in the benefits of investment.[273] For the PQ, province-building could only be achieved if investment provisions allowed for measures encouraging direct local impacts, such as job creation, through performance requirements. With its discourse, the PQ was not alone in this assessment of performance requirements: most bilateral investment treaties concluded after the failure of multilateral negotiations on investment allowed the host state to impose performance requirements as a condition for establishment within the limits allowed by multilateral agreements to which states subscribed. According to Vandevelde (1998), the prohibition of performance requirements in BITs stemmed mostly from the US tradition.

Some civil society movements followed the PQ's discursive strategy and opposed the extraction of Quebec's resources and the establishment of foreign investors if local benefits were not guaranteed. An influential study in this regard was published by Alexandre Maltais for the *Institut de recherche en économie contemporaine*. In this study, Maltais highlighted several points of criticism, among them investment protection, the prohibition of performance requirements, the lack of clarity in defining indirect expropriations and the scope of liberalisation as well as the absence of a general exclusion of cultural industries (Maltais, 2011, p. 15-16). According to Maltais, the CETA provisions inhibit the achievement of the full potential of future investments for rural development: the prohibition of performance requirements annihilates positive effects for rural communities and could lead to

---

272 Alexandre Cloutier, Assemblée nationale du Québec, 8 December 2011; Pierre Curzi, Assemblée nationale du Québec, 16 February 2012.
273 Alexandre Cloutier, Assemblée nationale du Québec, 8 December 2011 (=2nd hearing).

a mere extraction of Quebec's natural resources to the advantage of multinational companies (Maltais, 2011, p. 20-23).

Facing opposition to its discursive strategy, the Liberal government reminded its opponents of the importance of international trade for Quebec province-building. First, the government highlighted that many performance requirements were forbidden by agreements concluded in the context of the WTO and NAFTA. Since Quebec aspired to remain an export-oriented economy and credible international partner, it needed to comply with these international obligations and secure European investors' trust.[274] Second, it also reworked its discursive strategy to engage with the claim that performance requirements allow the provincial state to steer Quebec's economy. However, refuting the PQ's framing was not an easy task in Quebec, where the provincial state occupied a key role in province-building, as described previously. In his discourse, Pierre-Marc Johnson remodelled the role of the state in the economy. According to him, the state's contribution to provincial development should be limited to the establishment of a level playing field for private economic actors. This rationale departed from the state dirigisme tradition in Quebec. In fact, Johnson suggested that the state foster local development by creating an investment-friendly environment where market forces spur economic development:

> La tendance, c'est de réduire la capacité d'imposer de telles conditions [obligations de résultats], qui ne sont pas compatibles avec le fonctionnement normal de l'économie de marché. Pourquoi? Bien, parce que ça part d'un raisonnement de base qui est le suivant : Qui est responsable du développement économique? Alors, est-ce que c'est l'État ou est-ce que c'est les personnes et le capital? Le monde dans lequel on fonctionne est un monde, maintenant, où on considère que l'initiative du développement est d'abord et avant tout celle du monde du capital, et des personnes, et des sociétés, et que le rôle de l'État est de protéger les citoyens, d'empêcher les abus et de voir au développement d'un certain nombre d'activités qu'il juge adéquat pour les collectivités.[275]

---

274 Pierre-Marc Johnson, Assemblée nationale du Québec, 8 December 2011 (=2nd hearing); Christyne Tremblay, Assemblée nationale du Québec, 6 May 2010; Pierre Arcand, Assemblée nationale du Québec, 24 October 2013.
275 Pierre-Marc Johnson, Assemblée nationale du Québec, 8 December 2011 (=2nd hearing).

Eventually, the PQ was not able to restructure the discourse on investment during the first negotiation stage, although it had engaged in a promising discursive strategy by employing the dirigisme frame. However, in the end, its deputies' objections to prohibiting performance requirements partially influenced Quebec's negotiation position. To some extent, this result can be explained by the fact that the most influential PQ members did not engage in criticism on these provisions. It was also related to the fact that performance requirements had not been included as a priority on the PQ's list of sensitive topics related to investment, as the future Minister of International Relations, the Francophonie and External Trade, Jean-François Lisée, later reported in the Assembly. According to Lisée, key issues for the PQ were regulatory capacity, privatisations, water, health and culture.[276] Another reason for the resilience of the Liberal government's discourse was the strength of the Liberals' discursive strategy: by convincingly establishing a link between Quebec's credibility as a host for international investment, on the one hand, and its economic, spatial, and even political development, on the other hand, they were able to legitimately refute these objections and establish a coalitional strategy which was compatible with some PQ deputies' discourse.

However, even though the PLQ had successfully established a coalitional strategy, this strategy stood on shaky grounds. In fact, the 2012 elections brought the PQ to office; therefore, one could expect the PQ to highlight contentious issues looming as a potential stumbling block again. The new governing party would have been in a strong position to sideline the existing discursive strategy and establish a new one. Furthermore, the PQ was elected at a time which could have induced it to change its discourse on performance requirements.

c) Protecting Provincial State Sovereignty (10.2012-04.2014; 05.-12.2014)

When the PQ was elected to government in September 2012, its members found an environment that encouraged their own unease with CETA's investment provisions. In the EU, opposition to CETA's investment provisions was broadening quickly. On the one hand, this was related to a spillover effect from opposition to the negotiations of a new trade and investment agreement between the US and the EU. On the other hand, recent international investment protection cases had attracted public attention.

---

276 Jean-François Lisée, Assemblée nationale du Québec, 15 February 2013.

Trade therefore became increasingly politicised in the EU and its member states, thereby leaving the realm of executive policy-making it had been confined to before.[277] Alliances between social movements on both sides of the Atlantic (Attac-Québec, 2013; Trade Justice Network/ Réseau pour un commerce juste, 2010) as well as media coverage of mounting European resistance to investment provisions allowed these emerging discourses to travel to Quebec and Canada. Before the CETA negotiations, trade had mostly stayed under the radar in European states.[278] Apart from civil society movements, some influential political parties in the European member states and the European parliament started to investigate the benefits and drawbacks of CETA investment provisions. As a Canadian diplomat pointed out, this growing criticism took CETA negotiators by surprise:

> Some of the discussions, some of the criticisms, I think, have grown quicker, become more prevalent than people thought initially would happen. This whole debate about investment, investor-state disputes settlement: all people weren't ready for that or didn't foresee that.[279]

In Quebec, these emerging discourses fell on fruitful ground with the PQ in government. Existing opposition could use them to legitimise their own position. In this situation, the PQ was torn between two conflicting interests. On the one hand, it wanted to attract foreign investments to foster economic development. Yet, on the other hand, it feared that the attraction of investment under the conditions offered by CETA interfered negatively with provincial economic and social development. In this situation, it could either develop a discursive conciliation or pursue one interest to the detriment of the other. More specifically, the topic that clearly prevailed between 2012 and 2014 was the intended dispute resolution mechanism with 40 percent of the total discourse on foreign direct investment. Performance requirements remained an important topic with 18 percent, although there was by far more speaking time accorded to discussions on investment.[280] Cultural industries took less speaking time in the Assembly than other topics, as table 25 highlights, yet it was a key issue for the PQ

---

277 Interview with European Commission official, Brussels, 23 July 2014.
278 With some exceptions, such as French societal opposition to the Uruguay negotiations and the potential inclusion of culture into multilateral trade agreements.
279 Interview with high-ranking Canadian diplomat, Brussels, 8 July 2014.
280 See the analysis of the previous negotiation stage (2009-2012), when performance requirements were the most important topic overall.

government. Cultural industries had already been a highly contentious topic during the first negotiation stage (2009-2012), as the preceding tables 23 and 24 depicted. The PQ government and deputies needed to devise a coalitional strategy to maintain their position on excluding cultural industries from CETA's investment chapter. In the following, I will focus on cultural industries, and investment protection and dispute resolution. I will trace where parties disagreed on these issues and how they managed to maintain Quebec's historical support for hosting foreign direct investment by engaging in a discursive strategy that allowed discursive conciliation between these two conflicting interests.

Table 25 – Most Important Topics during Second Negotiation Stage (Percentages of Total Discourse on FDI, 2012-2014)

Cultural Industries	Investment Protection & Dispute Resolution	Negotiation Process	Performance Requirements	Others	Total (%)
5	40	18	18	19	100

Source: Analysis of parliamentary debates (N=2,095 words)[281]

Table 26 – Evolution of the Relative Importance of 'Investment Protection and Dispute Resolution' at Different Negotiation Stages

	2006-2009	2009-2012	2012-2014	2014	Total percentage (words)
Investment Protection & Dispute Resolution	0	57	34	9	100

Source: Analysis of parliamentary debates (N=2,491 words)[282]

Cultural industries figured prominently on Quebec's negotiation agenda during the first and second negotiation stages. Quebec's representatives promoted the complete exclusion of cultural industries from the investment chapter. While the PQ advocated this interest more vocally, the PLQ also supported it. Among Canadian provinces, Quebec had already championed the protection of cultural industries in the context of international

---

281 See appendix for full table.
282 See appendix for full table.

trade and investment agreements. In the context of their province-building project, representatives wanted to protect their domestic cultural industries: as a consequence of its isolation as a Francophone community in North America, French Canadians and later Quebeckers have become highly sensitive to the protection of their cultural identity, including their language. Through various instruments ranging from subsidies to the conclusion of international agreements, the Quebec provincial state has actively promoted Quebec's cultural expressions and productions. Cutting across party lines, the public support given to and the protection of Quebec's cultural industries has figured high on the provincial political agenda and has contributed to its assertion as a nation in its own right, an important pillar of province-building. In addition, the external expression of Quebec's cultural identity also contributed to its development as an internationally active polity, another pillar of province-building. Recently, the experience of successfully playing a leading role in the negotiation of the UNESCO's Convention on the Protection and Promotion of the Diversity of Cultural Expressions (2005) concurred with the province's conviction of Quebec as a province-state with a distinct society and culture which can play a leading role, in its areas of jurisdiction, on the international scene (Gagnon, 2014).[283] Thus, established discourses made cultural industries a challenging issue for representatives' discursive strategy. In fact, how could they cherish their past international influence in promoting the UNESCO Convention and still promote CETA's investment chapter, which threatened the existence of their cultural industries?

Against the backdrop of the role local cultural industries have played in Quebec's social and political development, the exclusion of cultural industries from the investment chapter represented a fundamental condition for Quebec's representatives' overall support for CETA.[284] Across party lines—even though this position was advocated more openly by the PQ—representatives shared the interpretation that public policies ought to protect the province's distinctiveness by encouraging cultural industries. According to Minister of International Relations, the Francophonie, and External Trade Jean-François Lisée, public policies shielding cultural industries from the drawbacks of competition were part and parcel of Quebec's provincial development. In this strategy, the provincial state took a

283 Interview with senior Quebec official, Montreal, 15 October 2014; Interview with member of the National Assembly (PLQ), Québec, 8 October 2014.
284 Interview with Quebec diplomat, Montreal, 15 October 2014.

directive role in protecting and promoting Quebec's cultural industries. In the National Assembly, he asserted:

> Sur la question culturelle, nous voulions nous assurer absolument que la protection de la capacité de l'État québécois à faire la promotion et d'appuyer ses industries culturelles soit parfaitement protégée dans ce nouvel accord, [...]. Donc, là-dessus, oui, on est très politiques. Nous voulons absolument que ce ne soit pas le marché et les investisseurs qui décident des orientations politiques du peuple québécois, ça, c'est certain.[285]

The Liberals supported the PQ's demands,[286] and also the Canadian federal government backed the exclusion of cultural industries from CETA provisions, even though it was not a federal priority. In the past, the federal government successfully defended the exclusion of these industries from CUSFTA and NAFTA agreements, as well as from GATT and GATS provisions.[287] In a similar vein, the federal government also supported the exclusion of cultural industries from the failed OECD's Multilateral Investment Agreement (Lemieux and Jackson, 1999).

Apart from they played in Quebec's social development project, cultural industries also acquired discursive importance in Quebec's discourse on provincial international activities. Through their influence on the CETA negotiation process, provincial representatives hoped to shape future trade and investment agreements by setting a precedent. Against the background of the role of provincial international activity and their success during the UNESCO Convention negotiation, they were convinced that they could do so.[288] Furthermore, Quebec and Canada were aware that NAFTA's most-favoured nation clauses in Article 1103 would confer similar rights of establishment and protection in the cultural sector on US investors as those spelled out in CETA for European investors. Given the proximity of their economies and languages and the overall global predominance of US cultural industries, they feared to lose public policy instruments to protect and promote their own production, an important pillar of province-building.

---

285 Jean-François Lisée, Assemblée nationale du Québec, 15 February 2013.

286 Interview with Quebec diplomat, Montreal, 15 October 2014.

287 Canada was not successful, however, in shielding its periodicals industry, see *United States v. Canada* (1997 [Appellate Body Report].)

288 In the National Assembly, Lisée highlighted that the EU used CETA as a precedent for its trade and investment negotiations with the US, Assemblée nationale du Québec, 6 November 2013.

Unexpectedly, Quebec did not find close allies for this cause in the EU or its member states. Pierre-Marc Johnson asserted in the National Assembly that Quebec was surprised that the European Commission did not support the exclusion of cultural industries from CETA's investment chapter. He suspected that the European member states had not yet found a common position:

> Je dois dire que [...] j'ai accueilli avec une certaine surprise certains des propos européens qui désiraient pénétrer dans certains domaines de la culture et les voir soumis à l'accord. Je pense que tout ça fait l'objet d'un débat important à l'intérieur de l'Europe, cependant.[289]

Quebec thus faced hesitation and reluctance in Europe. In fact, according to Quebec diplomats, the European Commission did not have the same conception of the protection of cultural industries as Quebec.[290] Furthermore, the coalition Quebec had hoped to forge with France—basically the country of the "exception culturelle"—proved to be more fragile than expected.[291] Unexpectedly, France did not promote the exclusion of cultural industries from the investment chapter altogether. They were merely interested in excluding the audio-visual sector, the only sector where they feared competition from Canada.[292] Quebec's representatives thus needed to devise another coalitional strategy. In order to propagate their conviction that cultural industries ought to be excluded from the investment chapter, Quebec's government entered an unusual coalition with a non-governmental organisation, the *Coalition de la diversité culturelle*, based in Montreal but encompassing non-governmental organisations from several countries. This coalition's goal was to develop the rationale underlying the exclusion of cultural industries from international investment agreements[293] and explain it to federal Canadian, EU and member states' officials.[294] Through this coalitional strategy, the government could showcase to other negotiators that Quebec's political representatives and societal groups

---

289 Pierre-Marc Johnson, Assemblée nationale du Québec, 6 October 2010 (=1st hearing.)
290 Interview with Quebec diplomat, Montreal, 15 October 2014.
291 In the National Assembly, Jean Charest asserted that he met with French political leaders to discuss the topic of cultural industries, Assemblée nationale du Québec, 10 November 2011.
292 Interview with Quebec diplomat, Montreal, 15 October 2014.
293 Jean-François Lisée, Assemblée nationale du Québec, 15 February 2013.
294 Interview with Quebec diplomat, Brussels, 1 July 2014; Interview with Quebec diplomat, Montreal, 15 October 2014.

stood together on this issue. Furthermore, the coalition also helped the government to acquire access to these societal groups and convince them of the compromise on cultural industries they reached.

During the second negotiation stage (2012-2014), negotiators reached an agreement on cultural industries. First, they agreed that industries excluded from CETA's scope were specifically listed. Hence, there was no general exception of cultural industries. At first, actors representing the cultural industries opposed this approach. However, with the argument that an explicit list creates more legal security than a general exception, the Quebec negotiation team convinced them to support this compromise.[295] For Quebec's representatives, this provision safeguarded the role of the state in *existing* cultural industries. Second, cultural industries were excluded explicitly from some investment provisions, but not all of them. While they were not subjected to the establishment and non-discrimination provisions, they fell under the investment protection clauses, which means that rightfully established investments are protected through the new provisions. At the same time, the cultural exception was included in the agreement's preamble. Although some celebrated this as a big advance[296]—CETA was the first trade and investment agreement where the UNESCO's Convention (2005) was included in a trade and investment agreement—the legal status of preambles in international agreements remains uncertain.

Towards the end of CETA negotiations, representatives also focused on investment protection and dispute settlement, two highly contentious issues because they impact the directive role the provincial state can—or cannot—play in hosting foreign investments in Quebec. Between 2012 and 2014, around half of deputies' overall discourse on CETA in the National Assembly was on these two topics.[297] Although the issue did not attract as much attention among social movements as it did in the EU, Canadian think tanks and civil society movements nevertheless expressed strong concern about provisions on investment protection and about conflict resolution. In Quebec, the groups *Attac-Québec* and *Réseau Québécois pour l'Intégration Continentale* (RQIC), together with the pan-Canadian *Canadian Trade Justice Network*, were the most active cross-cutting civil society groups mobilising against CETA in this regard.[298] They found open ears

---

295 Interview with representative of *Coalition de la diversité culturelle*, Montreal, 24 October 2014.
296 Interview with Liberal member of Quebec's government, 23 October 2014.
297 See appendix for full tables.
298 Interview with representative of Attac-Québec, Montreal, 13 June 2016.

with some of the PQ members, although not all of them, as the following account will document.

For the PLQ, criticism about investment protection and dispute resoluti-on provisions represented a challenge for their discursive strategy groun-ded in Quebec's situation as a small and open economy. As mentioned above, accepting these investment provisions conferred an additional layer of international credibility on Quebec for the PLQ. According to the Libe-ral government, dispute resolution mechanisms display a polity's commit-ment to protecting foreign investments on their territory, and protect their investors abroad. When facing these societal demands, the PLQ had to up-date their discursive strategy, even though they continuously upheld that Quebec needed to appear a credible host for investment settlement, an ins-trument for economic development and a key pillar of their province-buil-ding strategy. For the Liberal government, dispute resolution was key in promoting further economic integration. Similar to the process during the CETA negotiation, the Quebec Liberal government also pushed the issue with regard to internal Canadian trade. Before the CETA negotiation was launched in 2009, the Council of the Federation discussed dispute resoluti-on among Canadian provinces on several occasions (Council of the Federa-tion, 2004a, p. 3-4; 2007, 2008a, b, 2009a, b).

The PQ representatives, to the contrary, increasingly started to challenge the benefits of investment protection and dispute resolution as foreseen by CETA. While most PQ deputies and members of the government agreed that dispute protection was a necessary part of CETA, they disagreed about the forms of dispute resolution foreseen in the case of an infringement. They interpreted the dispute resolution clauses against the background of the state dirigisme frame. At the core of their criticism was the dispersal of the state's regulatory capacity. Some members of the PQ asserted that the protection of investments and the constraint to compensatory payments might curtail governments' capacity to regulate in the environmental, soci-al or security realms.[299] In fact, CETA provided that a government needs to compensate investors if they encounter losses engendered by an expropria-tion. According to opponents to this provision, private investors' right to challenge regulatory activities and their entitlement to compensatory pay-ments may compel the state to reverse its legislation or refrain from taking future action. Martine Ouellet (PQ) asserted, for instance, that investment

---

299 Criticism with regard to environmental legislation was strongest, interview with Quebec diplomat, Montreal, 15 October 2014.

protection clauses curtail the state's capacity to steer economic development:

> Dans un contexte de mondialisation accrue et de perte d'autonomie graduelle des États souverains, il importe de préserver les leviers d'intervention encore disponibles. Le volet Investissement de l'accord Canada-Europe vise à protéger l'investisseur étranger contre l'État d'accueil.[300]

To underpin their argument, deputies of the PQ and civil society movements referred to case law on investment protection under NAFTA's chapter 11 and its bearing on provincial development (Attac-Québec, 2009a, b, 2010; Réseau québécois sur l'intégration continentale, 2013).[301] They cited the *Dow Agro Sciences vs. Canada* case to illustrate how private actors can use trade agreements to challenge regulatory decisions (2009 [Notice of Arbitration, settled]). In 2009, the company Dow Agro Sciences, operating in the pest control products, seed and agricultural biotechnology sectors and incorporated in Delaware in the United States, filed a notice of arbitration against Canada under NAFTA's chapter 11, claiming that the government of Quebec breached NAFTA provisions on minimum standard of treatment and expropriation when the province banned the sale and use of certain pesticides. Although the case was closed before trial and without settlements on any compensatory payments, it has evolved into a landmark case in Quebec political discourse, one to which opponents refer to illustrate the threats investment provisions pose to states' regulatory capacity. In the National Assembly, deputies more specifically discussed the provincial states' capacity to regulate environmental and health issues, as well as the federal level's ability to override provincial legislation potentially impeding Canada's international engagements.[302] A second case which informed the discourse on dispute settlement was *Lone Pine Resources vs. Canada* (2013 [Notice of Arbitration]). In 2013, Lone Pine Resources filed a notice of arbitration against Canada under NAFTA's chapter 11. According to the Delaware-incorporated company, the government of Quebec violated minimum standard of treatment and expropriation provisions when it revoked one out of five exploration licenses for petroleum, natural gas and underground reservoirs of the St. Laurent river basin, after the publication of several environmental and socio-economic impact studies highlighting the

---

300 Martine Ouellet, Assemblée nationale du Québec, 5 October 2011.
301 Françoise David, Assemblée nationale du Québec, 2 October 2014 (motion).
302 Scott McKay, Assemblée nationale du Québec, 5 October 2011.

risks of the extraction of natural resources in this area. According to Lone Pine Resources, this revocation was based on political rather than environmental grounds and caused the company damages assessed at USD 118.9 million.[303] These two cases represented recent instances where a private company challenged executive acts passed by the provincial government to protect the environment, which many members of the PQ interpreted as a violation of provincial sovereignty. For them, there was a conflict between two important pillars of province-building the PQ upheld, namely economic development through FDI and state capacity to steer economic development, as Quebec did in the past.

Apart from issues related to regulatory capacity, these two legal cases also illustrated the notion of indirect expropriation, which opponents most forcefully criticized. While they generally agreed that investors should be compensated for losses engendered by *direct* expropriation of their assets, those challenging investment provisions strongly objected to compensatory payments arising from *indirect* expropriations. They argued that there was no clear and generally accepted definition of an indirect expropriation. Therefore, the decision whether a regulatory action taken by the state constituted an indirect expropriation or a legitimate policy action was in the hands of a private arbitrator.[304] Thus, the interpretation of public actions was transferred into private hands. As a consequence, executives or legislatures cannot foresee if their regulatory action infringes their international commitments, as Maltais argued in a study published by the *Institut de recherche en économie contemporaine*:

> Cette indétermination entraîne une problématique majeure : l'impossibilité de prévoir la conformité d'une nouvelle réglementation aux dispositions interdisant les expropriations indirectes (Maltais, 2011).

As a consequence of legal insecurity, opponents suggested a second argument: CETA would freeze social, environmental and health regulation at existing levels. In doing so, they followed a discursive strategy that highlighted the role of the state in province-building. There were two reasons why CETA might lead to the preservation of the regulatory status quo. First, states might refrain from establishing new legislation in order to avoid being challenged in a dispute settlement procedure, given that there is no legal certainty about the notion of indirect expropriation. In this way,

---

303 A decision on this case was still pending in October 2019.

304 In comparison to European opposition to these clauses, criticism in Quebec did not focus as strongly on procedural aspects of private arbitration.

the prospect of unforeseeable compensatory payments may suffice to discourage the state from introducing new regulations. Second, opponents argued that CETA might initiate a regulatory drift towards lower degrees of regulation. In fact, the combination of high levels of investment protection and low tariffs might encourage investors to establish their business in jurisdictions with lower regulatory standards.[305] Simultaneously, CETA did not foresee a provision to discourage lowering regulation. Opponents considered this a harmful asymmetry. As a consequence, the provincial state would not only be deprived of instruments to steer future investments, but it would also potentially reduce the effects of existing instruments. In a situation where the provincial state played a directive role in Quebec's province-building strategy, these provisions were deemed unacceptable.

As a consequence of their interpretation of investment provisions' impact on provincial regulatory capacity, some PQ members, joined in their claims by *Québec Solidaire*, strongly criticized the veil of secrecy shrouding CETA negotiations.[306] They claimed that the process of surrendering parts of their sovereignty required an increased involvement of the National Assembly in the negotiation process to legitimise these decisions.[307] In other words, the provincial representatives at least wanted to be included in the decision to reduce their future capacity to steer economic development. Louise Beaudoin commented on this link between negotiation process, social opposition and loss of certain aspects of Quebec's sovereignty. According to her:

> Ces négociations-là, on le constate depuis plusieurs mois, entre le Canada et l'Union européenne, se déroulent dans la plus grande opacité et derrière des portes closes. [...] Mais il me semble qu'en amont on devrait justement faire en sorte que les députés comprennent bien les enjeux, et vous savez très bien qu'il y a déjà une coalition qui se prépare, pancanadienne d'ailleurs, mais avec des ramifications au Québec, qui se dit contre déjà cette entente pour toutes sortes de raisons, justement de perte de souveraineté.[308]

---

305 This argument also surfaced in an interview with a representative of Attac-Québec, Montreal, 13 June 2016.

306 Louise Beaudoin, Assemblée nationale du Québec, 27 April 2010 ; Martine Ouellet, Assemblée nationale du Québec, 5 October 2011 ; Amir Khadir, Assemblée nationale du Québec, 12 February 2014.

307 Louise Beaudoin, Assemblée nationale du Québec, 27 April 2010 ; Scott McKay, Assemblée nationale du Québec, 5 October 2011 (=2nd hearing).

308 Louise Beaudoin, Assemblée nationale du Québec, 27 April 2010.

Similar to fears in the 1970s that the federal investment legislation might consolidate economic structures to the detriment of Quebec, as mentioned above, some representatives in Quebec feared that CETA might consolidate the Canadian interest to the detriment of the Quebec interest. In a situation where Canadian heterogeneity did not permit finding a pan-Canadian position, representatives from the PQ drew upon one dimension of the repertoire of federalism—structured in the PQ's discourse according to an opposition between Quebec and the Rest of Canada—to claim that CETA might consolidate existing structures to the detriment of Quebec, where social and environmental standards tended to be higher than in other provinces. Underlying this argument was the concern that the Canadian federal government would defend the Canadian rather than the Quebec interest in the CETA negotiations. This claim was framed in terms of the independence frame structuring the repertoire of federalism. PQ Deputy Martine Ouellet argued that Quebec could negotiate a better deal as an independent state:

> Le gouvernement canadien est en train de négocier en cachette notre avenir économique. Les accords internationaux sont affaire de pays. Il nous faut donc être un pays pour avoir voix au chapitre. Un jour, quand nous nous ferons suffisamment confiance, nous aussi, au Québec, nous aurons voix au chapitre, nous aurons notre mot à dire dans nos accords internationaux.[309]

The PQ representatives faced the following dilemma: on the one hand, they supported the promotion of foreign direct investment in order to foster economic development, one pillar of province-building bringing Quebec closer to economic autonomy and future political independence. Yet, on the other hand, several of their members highlighted that investment protection and dispute settlement provisions curtailed the provincial state's regulatory capacity. In this situation, the PQ representatives had basically three options to devise their discursive strategy. They could reject investment protection provisions, but support CETA's FDI provisions in general, at the price of seeming incoherent. They could also shift the repertoire of reference—as they did for the agricultural chapter.[310] As a third option, they could restructure the repertoire of province-building and shift their discourse towards the small open economy frame.

---

309 Martine Ouellet, Assemblée nationale du Québec, 5 October 2011.
310 See chapter 5 on agriculture.

Eventually, the PQ representatives did not follow any of these three options. After lengthy consultations with legal experts as well as social movements,[311] they came to the conclusion that CETA did not represent a threat to provincial regulatory capacity. Indeed, the PQ government did not fundamentally restructure its discourse: it did not restructure the repertoire of province-building, nor did it anchor its discourse in the repertoire of federalism. To the contrary, the government's discourse remained anchored in previous repertoires and frames of reference, mainly the state dirigisme frame, but also the independence frame. Their discursive strategy consisted in showing that provisions foreseen by CETA's investment chapter did not represent a threat to state capacity. Thus, they established a coalitional strategy in which they could secure the Liberals' support and remain a credible international partner. A member of the PQ government asserted: [312]

> Nous au gouvernement du Parti Québécois, j'ai toujours été convaincu que c'était essentiellement des mesures qui étaient à l'avantage du Québec. Autrement dit, je ne les vois pas comme une atteinte à la souveraineté de l'Etat québécois. Mais il y a quand même des groupes dans la société civile québécoise qui contestent cette interprétation puis qui sont en désaccord avec ces clauses. Alors cela a été un sujet de discussion, je dirais. Même si, de notre côté, cela ne posait pas problème.

In this new coalitional strategy, members of the PQ government highlighted the contribution of new investments to the creation of jobs and growth, even though the effects of investment are not reflected in statistics about commercial exchanges.[313] By deploying this discourse, the PQ government not only joined the Liberals' discourse, but also stayed in line with the discourse established by the important PQ leaders Lévesque and Landry during the 1980s and early 2000s.

For the PQ, reversing their discursive and coalitional strategies was tricky: in fact, how could they legitimise, for societal groups and their electorate, their discursive shift to a position that they previously denounced? In their updated discursive strategy, they suggested three arguments in support of their reworked interpretation. First, they highlighted the continui-

---

311 Interview with a member of Quebec's PQ government (2012-2014), Skype, 24 April 2015.
312 Interview with member of Quebec's PQ government (2012-2014), Skype, 24 April 2015.
313 Jean-François Lisée (PQ), Assemblée nationale du Québec, 18 February 2013.

ty of CETA in comparison to other trade and investment agreements, as one senior member of the PQ did:[314]

> Par ailleurs, je veux tout simplement aussi mettre en lumière que ces clauses – le Québec a accepté cette situation – se sont répandues beaucoup, en fait, dans tous les accords commerciaux, dans toutes les ententes d'investissement du Canada avec d'autres pays dans le monde.

Furthermore, in their discursive strategy, the government argued that investment protection and dispute settlement provisions have considerably evolved since they were included in NAFTA. Through this discursive process, it reached the conclusion that CETA did not curtail the provincial state's regulatory capacity. According to CETA provisions, a company cannot force a government to change its legislation, governments cannot be subjected to punitive damages and the dispute settlement is limited to cases in which an investor considers a measure discriminatory or oppressive to an *individual* investment. A member of the PQ government explained this reasoning as follows: [315]

> Je pense que le point ultime c'est de se demander : " Est-ce qu'une nouvelle règlementation ou une nouvelle législation québécoise pourrait devoir être modifiée à la suite de l'exercice d'un tel recours? ". Et la réponse [...] c'est non. [...] Pour moi, l'élément fondamental c'est qu'on ne perdra pas la capacité, d'aucune manière, d'imposer une nouvelle règlementation ou une nouvelle législation.

According to senior PQ member and Minister for International Relations and Foreign Trade Jean-François Lisée, valid criticism by the PQ and social movements has led to a substantial evolution in dispute settlement. As a consequence, CETA's investment provisions curtail the dispute settlement mechanism so that it respects the limits of provincial sovereignty.[316] In suggesting this argument, the PQ'S discursive strategy rendered previous criticism legitimate: *of course*, the PQ government had to evaluate CETA's provisions to establish if they curtailed the role of the state in the economy, an essential driver of economic development. However, they came to the conclusion that they did not.

---

314 Interview with member of Quebec's PQ government (2012-2014), Skype, 24 April 2015.
315 Interview with member of Quebec's PQ government (2012-2014), Skype, 24 April 2015.
316 Jean-François Lisée, Assemblée nationale du Québec, 15 February 2013.

This dimension of their discursive strategy fed into their coalitional strategy. In fact, it allowed the PQ to include those party members opposed to CETA's provisions into their strategy, depicting their criticism as legitimate.

During the PQ's term in office, the way the party represented Quebec's interests did not change, as it did during the negotiations on public procurement or agriculture. Rather, the leaders of the PQ reached the conclusion—even if it remained contested within the party—that the provisions in CETA did not represent a threat to state capacity. Within the limits of the structure of the repertoire of province-building, the PQ government reached the conclusion that the attraction of foreign investment contributed to province-building. Their discursive and coalitional strategies remained thus within the established discursive parameters.

Conclusion

Both the Liberals and the PQ supported reducing barriers to cross-Atlantic direct investment flows through CETA, as they had already done during the NAFTA negotiations. They did so for partially different reasons, which were related to their respective interpretation of the structure of the repertoire of province-building. As a consequence, they devised the role attributed to the state or market forces differently. In essence, political representatives faced the dilemma of choosing between the contributions foreign direct investment could make to economic, political, spatial and social development, on the one hand, and the threat posed to provincial regulatory capacity, on the other hand. Overall, business on both sides of the Atlantic strongly supported these new provisions, while Quebec-based, pan-Canadian and cross-Atlantic civil society movements opposed them vigorously, which put representatives in the situation where they had to choose among a wide range of different and sometimes unstable interests. Two frames dominated the discourse: the small open economy frame and the state dirigisme frame. At some points, the integration and independence frame reinforced the positions representatives developed, particularly with regard to Canadian internal market integration.

Consistently framing Quebec's interest in terms of a small economy in need of foreign capital, the Liberal representatives integrated CETA's investment chapter in their province-building project. They continued to deploy their long-standing discourse that foreign investments create growth and employment, while also giving the opportunity to further integrate

Quebec in global value chains. Furthermore, they argued that Quebec could add to its credibility as an investment-friendly environment by limiting the state's role to assuring legal and political certainty for investors and by reducing states' influence on steering investment. In opposition, the PQ representatives' position was more volatile. It varied among party members and across negotiation stages. On the one hand, the PQ has traditionally been in favour of attracting foreign investment to reduce Quebec's dependence on the Canadian market and the policy-decisions of the federal government, as the NAFTA negotiations showed. In this logic, it supported reducing barriers to investment as a way to further Quebec's independence, a pillar of its interpretation of Canadian federalism. On the other hand, the drafted chapter on investments threatened the provincial state's regulatory capacity, notably through a ban on performance requirements, the potential coverage of cultural industries, and the intended investor-to-state dispute settlement mechanism. Reflecting a more prominent role of the state in controlling inward and outward investment flows, the PQ representatives claimed that the investment provisions could reduce provincial autonomy and expose Quebec to the Canadian federal government's vision of investment and development.

Bringing these two different appreciations of Quebec's interest on foreign direct investment together was the result of a coalitional strategy. Notwithstanding diverging representations of Quebec's interests, the leaders of the major political parties adhered to the repertoire of province-building. As a consequence, they could form a coalition on supporting the investment chapter in CETA, albeit for different reasons. This coalitional strategy unfolded exclusively as an internal Quebec process, despite the federal level's constitutional jurisdiction over foreign direct investment in Canada. Quebec representatives' strategy ultimately consisted in welcoming the investment provisions in CETA rather than rejecting them as contrary to provincial interests. In this way, both leading parties committed to the attraction of foreign capital for spatial development and province-building, as they did during the NAFTA negotiations. This coalition came to life only towards the end of negotiations.

The analysis of the discourse regarding the investment chapter has shown that the new bilateral agreement did not only concern trade, but economic integration. It touched upon the role of state influence on the economy and more specifically on production processes. Furthermore, investment negotiations allowed to investigate the role played by repertoires in guiding actors' interpretation of the economic interest. Sometimes, as the PQ representatives' position on investment showed, interests were not very clear to representatives themselves. In a discursive process, they needed to figure out what their interests were. This chapter showed how repertoires guided the way political actors conceived of their interests: the PQ's history related to sovereignty issues made it inevitable to reflect issues of investment and state capacity, while the Liberals interpreted CETA as increasing provincial economic autonomy by spurring growth, thereby isolating provincial development goals from federal policies while also firmly anchoring Quebec in the Canadian market. Contrary to public procurement and agriculture, where the restructuring of repertoires entailed a new interpretation of Quebec's interests, the case of investment was not so much an instance of a new representation of those interests. In fact, interests remained stable in comparison to the NAFTA negotiations. Rather, the existing structures of the repertoire were used as guidelines to evaluate to what extent CETA contributed to fulfilling these interests. Also, the investment chapter allowed to show how similar elements of the repertoire of province-building—the state, regulatory capacity, growth and autonomy—could be structured differently, leading to a re-evaluation of interests.

Chapter 5: Agricultural Trade – Abolishing the 'Loi du Camembert'?

Encumbered with a long history of unsuccessful international negotiations, agriculture was one of the most complex and sensitive sectors during the CETA negotiations on both sides of the Atlantic. All the key negotiation topics were under federal jurisdiction in Canada, although the provinces were highly active in pursuing their demands regarding CETA's agricultural chapter. Although tariffs and quota were at the centre of negotiations, non-tariff issues also played a role. One key non-tariff issue was the reciprocity of norms. In fact, lower tariffs or increased tariff-rate quotas were only attractive for producers if norms applicable in the target market were compatible with domestic productions. Another central concern were different agricultural support systems on both sides of the Atlantic. Canada has almost completely liberalised its agricultural production system except for milk, eggs and poultry. These three commodities are managed according to a well-calibrated system of supply management ("gestion de l'offre") based on output control, fixed prices, and tariffs and tariff-rate quotas. Canada strictly limited the import of these commodities and related secondary products to maintain control over domestic prices and support producers. The EU, on the other side, backed its agricultural producers through direct subsidies. These different agricultural support policies made it challenging to establish fair competition between producers on both sides of the Atlantic. Overall, Canada asked for better access to the European grain and red meat market, while the EU required better export opportunities for its dairy and fish products.

During the negotiations, Quebec was in a particularly challenging situation: it strongly promoted the conclusion of an overall agreement with the EU, yet it also opposed some, but not all, demands made by the EU. Quebec's representatives across party lines promoted the protection of Quebec's supply management production since the very beginning of the negotiation: during the agenda-setting and first negotiation stages, the Quebec Liberals made it very clear that they would not alter their traditional position on agricultural trade, which included opposing altering the Canadian system of supply management. The PQ government also supported this position. Against the backdrop of the relevance of these sub-sectors for province-building in Quebec, Quebec's representatives announced they would not make any concession on existing tariff barriers for milk, egg and poultry products. Furthermore, the highly concentrated and politically influential agricultural lobby opposed new imports. In the past, Canada's federal government successfully retained control over imports in international negotiations, even excluding these sub-sectors from the North American Free Trade Agreement (NAFTA, 1994) and to a large extent also from its multilateral commitments. Quebec's representatives were therefore confident that Canada's historic stance, Quebec's influence on Canada's negotiation position and provincial jurisdiction over crucial provisions in CETA would allow them to shield import-competing industries from international competition. Even critics,who referred to this system as "la Loi du Camembert", were quite sure that CETA would not jeopardise it (Dubuc, 2013).

Nevertheless, the EU included agricultural trade in its demands during CETA negotiations. The comprehensive nature of the economic agreement made their negotiators confident that an agreement on this sensitive sector could be reached, even though the Canadian federal and Quebec provincial governments were opposed to doing so. With European demands becoming more pressing as negotiations advanced, the cross-sectoral deal Quebec had hoped for —between provincial public procurement and access to European markets, excluding increased import quota for dairy products— did not materialise. Surprisingly, the federal government announced towards the end of the negotiations that it accepted European demand for better access to the Canadian cheese market, a concession lobby groups and many political leaders in Quebec depicted as a hard blow to Quebec's milk producers and cheese processors. Indeed, Quebec's Premier Pauline Marois leading the PQ government even threatened not to ratify CETA, thereby jeopardising implementation in provincial legislation.

But, shortly before the negotiations were officially closed in 2014, the newly elected Liberal government led by Philippe Couillard unexpectedly announced that his government would not jeopardise the overall trade and investment agreement in the name of a single issue, as reported by *Le Devoir* (2014):

> Je veux être très clair que le gouvernement du Québec ne mettra pas en péril la ratification de l'accord de libre-échange Canada-Europe sur un enjeu spécifique.

Against the background of Quebec's ability to refuse ratifying and implementing CETA, and the federal level's ability to protect its supply management system against US producers' export ambitions during the NAFTA negotiations, Quebec's reaction was not what many had anticipated. Not only was its reaction to the federal government's new position unexpected, but Quebec's representatives also participated, to some extent, in legitimising increased dairy imports. In the course of two years, Quebec's interest in protecting this sector at all costs changed considerably. Why and how this shift occurred will be documented in the following.This chapter is a case of fundamental discursive restructuring. Representatives' new discursive strategy underpinned the alteration of agricultural practices and reconfigured the internal dynamics of the Canadian market. .

Section 1: Agricultural Production and Trade in Quebec and Canada

Agriculture was and still is a crucial economic sector in Canada. It significantly contributes to the countries' positive trade balance. At the international level, Canada was and still is a strong supporter of liberalising trade in agricultural products. At the same time, as noted in the introductory remarks, Canada has also preserved sub-sectoral pockets which are highly protected from international competition and mainly geared towards domestic consumption. Underpinned by incommensurate discourses, they were the result of varying geographies, histories and political choices across Canadian provinces, which rendered provincial agricultural production systems—including the processing, distribution and consumption of agri-food products—heterogeneous. These differences among agricultural sub-sectors as well as the concentration of some productions in specific provinces made it difficult for the federal government to develop a coherent internal agricultural development plan as well as an international position on agricultural trade. Similar to foreign direct investment, commercial exchanges are regulated at the federal level, yet the provinces hold important adjacent competencies that make them key partners in Canada's agricultural policies. Therefore, agricultural trade was not only a source of economic development, but also of federal-provincial and inter-provincial conflict.

1. Agricultural Policies in Quebec and Canada before CETA: The Co-Existence of Dirigisme and Small Open Economy Frames

Agricultural production was part and parcel of Canada's economic development as well as nation- and state-building projects in the late 19th century (Skogstad, 2007, 2008). State dirigisme played a key role in the federal government practices: the federal government assisted and steered agricultural development by issuing regulations on the production and transport of agricultural commodities. Agricultural exports, mostly grains, oilseeds, livestock and meat, significantly contributed to Canada's GDP and positive trade balance until the Second World War. Considered to further broader national goals, agriculture also received important political attention not only in Canadian nation-building, but also in province-building projects, which sometimes fed into each other. Two federal initiatives stood out in particular: established by the Canadian Parliament in 1935, the Canadian Wheat Board was endowed with a monopoly to market wheat from the Prairies; and financial assistance programs were created to stabilise prices for eleven producer commodities, including grains, dairy and meat products. In the thirty years following the Second World War, the federal government tried to enhance agricultural productivity and make Canada's production internationally more competitive, again by intervening in the agricultural system. As a consequence, the industrialisation of Canada's agricultural production, transformation and distribution systems expanded, but the arrival of machinery at farms also created a gap between small and large producers, as Skogstad showed (Skogstad, 2007, p. 28-29). Therefore, the federal government created government programmes to assist those losing from expanded industrialisation. The federal government installed financial transfers to implement price stability, tried to stabilise wheat prices to allow for higher exports, and, by the mid-1970, together with provincial governments, had developed a system of supply management for dairy, poultry and eggs, sub-sectors concentrated in Quebec and Ontario. Until then, agricultural practices were underpinned by the state dirigisme frame structuring repertoires of province-building and nation-building at the federal level.

However, Canada's international commitments gradually inhibited its federal government from deploying dirigiste instruments in the agricultural sector while pursuing high export volumes at the same time. Mostly since the 1980s, the federal government has therefore gradually shifted towards less interventionist policies (Montpetit and Coleman, 1999). At the same time, the discourses underpinning agricultural production partially evolved. Underpinned by the frame of Canada as a small and open economy that benefits from its embeddedness in the international trade networks, the Canadian government developed an internationally competitive and export-oriented agricultural system in the majority of its agricultural sub-sectors. The state withdrew its support to a large extent, animated by the potential benefits of free competition. Since 2007, the contribution agriculture and the agri-food sector have made to Canadian GDP has grown gradually, except for 2009. In 2012, this sector generated CAD 103 billion, representing 6.7 percent of Canada's GDP. Canada is the world's fifth largest agriculture and agri-food exporter, accounting for 3.5 percent of the total global value in agricultural and agri-food trade. Leading export commodities are wheat, canola seed, lentils, soybeans and durum wheat. In the last years, the Canadian agricultural trade balance has been positive, with surpluses of around CAD 10 billion annually (Government of Canada – Agriculture and Agri-Food Canada, 2014a). At the level of international cooperation, Canada has been a founding member of the Cairns group, a group of agricultural exporting countries which advocate the further liberalisation of agricultural trade at the international level. In 2012, the Canadian Wheat Board's Single Desk as the sole marketing organisation of Canadian wheat was abolished after long-standing criticism and international disputes involving the US (Jeffrey, Laaksonen-Craig et al., 2006). Since the 1980s, the small open economy frame firmly established itself in Canadian discourses on agricultural production in the sub-sectors that are export-oriented.

Yet, five primary commodities (dairy, hatching eggs, table eggs, turkey, poultry) survived this process of "state retrenchment, regionalisation and globalisation in the 1980s and 1990s" (Skogstad, 2007, p. 29). In these sub-sectors, the small open economy frame did not supplant state dirigisme, and state policies still played a predominant role in structuring these sub-sectors. After recurrent experiences of overproduction and revenue fluctuations after the Second World War, the provincial and federal governments decided to increase their intervention in the organisation of the supply of these five commodities (see for an account of the historical development of supply management Skogstad, 2008, p. 144-152). Subsequently, the production of dairy, eggs, poultry and turkey was organised as a function of domestic demand, hence the denomination 'supply management' for this agricultural management scheme. Through directing primary agricultural output, the system aimed to guarantee producers stable and predictable revenues regardless of climate and market fluctuations without relying on subsidies. In this way, the power asymmetry opposing (a large number of) primary producers and (a small number) of processors and distributors was reduced. In order to retain control over production processes, these sub-sectors needed to be closed from international competition when many other sub-sectors were liberalised in the 1980s and 1990s, because the arrival of foreign competitors on the Canadian market would have jeopardised the well-calibrated match between demand, supply and prices for primary products. Overall, supply management depended thus upon three pillars: production control, administered pricing,[317] and restrictions on imports. Supply management was in place for milk, eggs, turkey and chicken by the mid-1970s, followed by broiler hatching eggs in 1986.

Today, agricultural production under supply management is a fine-tuned system of entangled federal and provincial public policies which shield the sector from international competition (Skogstad, 2012a). Federal and provincial marketing boards jointly determine the production output in order to match supply with the prospective demand of Canadian consumers. At the federal level, Canada sets tariff and tariff-rate import quotas to control the supply of these five commodities. The Canadian federal marketing agencies (i.e. the Canadian Dairy Commission, and the Farm Products Council of Canada for poultry and eggs) allocate fixed production quotas to the provinces. At the provincial level, provincial marketing boards allocate production quotas to farms and establish prices for fluid milk (table milk and cream), taking into account the recommendations issued by the Canadian Dairy Commission for industrial milk. Industrial milk, which is further processed into secondary products such as cheese, butter, ice cream or yoghurt, is regulated at the federal level.

Quebec and Ontario, where the system was developed, obtained the highest production quotas for milk, egg and poultry. The following table shows allocation quotas for milk. On several occasions, and mostly during international trade negotiations, prairie provinces' representatives' claimed that production quotas were unfairly allocated among provinces (Montpetit, 2006, p. 103). They suggested a reallocation on the basis of economic and demographic growth. In the poultry and egg sector, opposition to current allocation schemes was most vocal (Friesen, 2014). In 2001, a federal-provincial agreement on chicken was reached. Yet, conflict erupted again in the following years, with Alberta quitting, in 2013, Chicken Farmers of Canada, which has the two-fold mandate to regulate chicken supply and to represent farmers. In the context of a WTO trade dispute in the late 1990s, Western provinces also challenged the distribution of dairy quotas among provinces (Wilson, 1999). In the context of the Doha Round of the WTO, dairy quota again became a contentious topic among Canadian provinces. Opponents pinpointed high prices and inefficient production systems (Petkantchin, 2005).

---

317 For a detailed discussion of how milk prices are determined, see Goldfarb (2009, pp. 7-16).

Table 27 – Industrial and Fluid Milk Quota per Province (million kg of butter-fat, rounded), as of 1 August, for indicated year

Provin-ces	2006	2007	2008	2009	2010	2011	2012	2013	2014	2015
BC	23.3	24.5	24.8	24.8	25.2	26.1	25.75	25.8	26.0	26.7
AB	23.2	24.4	24.7	24.7	25.1	25.95	25.6	25.7	26.8	27.7
SK	8.1	8.5	8.6	8.6	8.8	9.04	8.9	9.0	9.8	9.9
MB	11.3	11.9	12.0	12.0	12.2	12.62	12.5	12.5	13.5	13.8
ON	94.8	97.1	97.5	96.9	97.8	100.00	99.3	99.9	98.5	100.8
QC	110.6	113.3	113.9	113.2	114.2	116.77	115.9	116.2	124.1	126.5
NB	5.0	5.1	5.2	5.1	5.2	5.29	5.3	5.3	4.4	4.3
NS	6.4	6.6	6.6	6.56	6.62	6.77	6.73	6.75	5.39	5.41
PE	3.8	3.9	3.9	3.9	4.0	4.0	4.0	4.0	4.5	4.6
NL	1.9	2.0	2.0	1.8	1.9	2.0	1.9	1.9	2.0	2.0
Canada	288.4	297.2	299.3	297.5	300.9	308.5	305.8	307.0	314.9	321.7

Source: Canadian Dairy Commission (Government of Canada, 2015a), adapted.

Quebec's representatives reworked their discourse and agricultural practices in a similar way as Canadian federal representatives had done. Today, export-oriented production, underpinned by the small open economy frame, and a production geared towards domestic consumption, underpinned by the dirigisme frame, co-exist as structuring elements of the repertoire of province-building in Quebec. Since 1997, the Quebec balance of foreign agricultural trade has tended to be slightly positive—a testimony to the co-existence and equal importance to agricultural production of agricultural industries promoting open trade and those favouring protection by the state. Therefore, Quebec's representatives found themselves in the complex situation to legitimise incommensurate practices with regard to Quebec's position on international agricultural trade (Schram, 2016). I will describe these two frames and the related practices in turn, starting by Quebec's export-oriented industries and then turning to supply management which dominates political discourse.

Despite the concentration of supply management in the Central provinces, Quebec is also home to vast export-oriented industries promoting more openness in agricultural trade. Agricultural exports have indeed grown fast: between 1992 and 2011, the average annual growth rate of agricultural exports to the world and the other Canadian provinces has been 8.5 percent. The pork industry has been leading this development and accounts for almost 25 percent of total exports followed by oleaginous and cacao products (Gouvernement du Québec, 2012a). Export-oriented agricultural production contributes to province-building by generating economic growth, but also by promoting a specific mode of agricultural production. A member of the PQ government highlighted, for instance, the high quality of Quebec pork exports as well as its pioneering role in establishing a sustainable yet competitive agriculture.[318]

Dominated by the dirigisme frame, the other part of Quebec's agricultural production is mainly geared towards domestic consumption. It is also anchored in the province-building repertoire, although the relation between stakeholders, the state, and spaces is different than in discourses underpinning agricultural practices in export-oriented industries. *First*, political leaders across party lines and the representatives of many agricultural producer groups upheld that agriculture was an instrument for economic development especially in provincial rural areas. The vastness of Quebec's territory, and its geological and climate situation, required public policies to direct agricultural production and assure a fair return to producers. Indeed, in many rural areas, agriculture is the most important economic sector (Dupont, 2009). Despite similar management practices at first glance, Quebec and Ontario representatives deployed different discourses on the role of the state in the economy and therefore developed diverging practices in agricultural policy-making. Quebec favoured more intrusive policies in agriculture than Ontario, while its neighbour relied more on self-regulation of the market (Montpetit and Coleman, 1999). Furthermore, Quebec favoured a producer network of small and often family-led farms rather than large farms, encouraged by the *Loi sur la protection du territoire et des activités agricoles* (1978). In addition, agriculture also played a role in attaining a higher degree of independence from the federal government's agricultural and agri-food policies, an important pillar of a conception of federalism in which Quebec reduces its reliance on federal action. During the Quiet Revolution and after, agricultural self-sufficiency was an important policy goal, as René Lévesque underscored during a speech on Quebec's agricultural policy (Lévesque, 1978):

> On découvre au fond l'impératif du maximum d'autosuffisance. [...] Et c'est non seulement essentiel pour l'équilibre économique d'une société, mais aussi essentiel pour sa dignité, son minimum de dignité dans un monde où la faim n'a pas encore été vaincue.

---

318 Interview with member of Quebec's government (2012-2014), Québec, 1 October 2014.

While the goal of agricultural self-sufficiency (Dagenais, 1978) has been abandoned, Quebec's governments continued to play a directive role in Quebec's agri-food system. For example, they encourage, across party lines, provincial consumers to value products originating from Quebec and legally recognise and protect specific modes of production anchored in defined spaces, a system known as geographical indications. In the 1990s, the PQ government introduced a system of geographical indications through the *Loi sur les appellations réservées* (1996), which is unique in Canada and North America. By doing so, the government underscored its commitment to valuing the various provincial regions, traditional modes of production and local knowledge. In 2006, the PLQ government updated and strengthened the system of geographical indications by the *Loi sur les appellations réservées et les termes valorisants* (Chazoule, Jouve et al., 2009). Furthermore, dirigiste state practices in agriculture also provide an opportunity for environmental policy-making, for example by assuring low transportation emissions through local production and consumption (Montpetit and Coleman, 1999).[319]

Second, agriculture was part of discourses on province-building and federalism. Agricultural management and more specifically supply management played an important role in building the provincial state and provincial societal networks, important pillars of province-building. Since the mid-1970s, when supply management systems had been installed to a large extent, the federal government has become increasingly disengaged from Quebec farming and reduced its expenditure, a gap where the Quebec provincial state readily stepped in, developed an expansionist agricultural policy and thereby expanded its area of policy-making. This led to Quebec farmers being increasingly involved in Quebec-based state and societal corporate structures and less engaged in Canadian ones. Subsequently, the loyalty of the farming community shifted towards the provincial state, which was perceived as the prime locus of agricultural policy-making, as Skogstad showed (Skogstad, 1998). During the 1990s' sovereignty debates, however, supply management became again an issue of Canadian federalism: During the referendum debate in the early 1990s, the fate of supply management in the event of Quebec sovereignty was one of the dominant elements in the discourse, even though the proportion of farmers active in the supply management system had declined since the 1980 referendum. "Canada's federal system and developments in the international trading

---

319 Interview with representatives of the Union des producteurs agricoles, Longueuil, 14 October 2014.

systems have contributed to [...] significant numbers of negative percepti-ons [of Quebec's farmers] of the Canadian federal system in the 1990s", ar-gued Skogstad (Skogstad, 1998, p. 28). In fact, while the federal govern-ment had reduced its activities in Quebec's agricultural system in the mid-1970s, its sole jurisdiction over tariffs became increasingly relevant for Quebec's farming community when international processes of opening tra-de in agri-food products challenged Quebec's supply management system, which depended directly upon Canadian tariffs. Quebec federalists argued that supply management relations in Canada were an excellent example of the benefits of federal union, because a pan-Canadian policy, in this case tariffs, protected Quebec from international pressures to open its milk, egg, and poultry productions to international competition. To the contra-ry, sovereignists highlighted that Quebec depended upon the federal go-vernment to preserve this system and made an argument for sovereignty and the ensuing control over tariffs, hence raising doubts about the bene-fits of membership in the Canadian federation.

The corporatist decision-making structure developed in the late 1960s and early 1970s gives the Quebecois agricultural lobby a particularly strong voice and political influence in sectoral practices and public policies (Montpetit, 2003, p. 202; Skogstad, 2008, p. 145-147). In Quebec, the *Union des producteurs agricoles* (UPA) is the exclusive marketing organisation for milk, poultry, and eggs. Furthermore, the UPA represents the interests of the Quebec farming community. Every Quebec-based agricultural pro-ducer is compelled to contribute to the UPA's financing, and more than 90 percent of the province's agricultural producers are represented by it. Counting among its members 12 regions and 26 production sub-sectors, the UPA often needs to develop a compromise if interests between regions or sub-sectors within Quebec diverge.

Overall, the disengagement of the federal government and the variety of agricultural policies in the Canadian provinces contributed to the esta-blishment of very different agricultural systems in the Canadian provinces, thereby contributing to the heterogeneity of Canadian provinces. Depen-ding on their respective province-building projects, provincial govern-ments pursued different agricultural policies both in terms of spatial and product configurations. In Canada as in Quebec, state dirigisme and small open economy frames co-exist. This discursive co-existence was disrupted on several occasions by Canada's international trade negotiations, as the following account will show.

2. International Trade and Agriculture in Canada (1986-2009)

In 1986, the free trade agenda of the GATT Uruguay Round considerably challenged the co-existence of the dirigisme and small open economy frames in Quebec. International negotiations and the institutions of Canadian federalism put considerable pressure on supply management (Montpetit, 2003, p. 204-207), by manoeuvring Canada into a difficult external position but also by creating tensions among provinces, and between producer and consumer groups (Baylis and Furtan, 2003). Yet, the Central provinces Quebec and Ontario successfully defended their system at the federal level, so that the federal government could not capitalise on the requirements of international trade liberalisations to abolish supply management, as many had hoped (Hall Findlay, 2012). Yet, the initial system underwent considerable changes subsequent to trade liberalisation processes.

While the issue of agriculture had been largely excluded from previous multilateral trade rounds, the Uruguay Round of the GATT (1986-1994) saw it being taken to the forefront of international trade negotiations. This put Canada in the delicate situation of representing an export-dependent economy arguing for agricultural liberalisation for some commodities, but not others. Therefore, Canada's federal representatives upheld import-restrictions on commodities under supply management, while they also advocated increased trade liberalisation for commodities for which Canada held a competitive advantage, such as grain and oilseeds (Skogstad, 1998; 2008, p. 5-6). These diverging interests were geographically concentrated in specific provinces. Therefore, during the Uruguay negotiations, a cleavage formed between the Prairie provinces—which favoured the liberalisation of grain and oilseeds trade in the multilateral arena because they depended on international markets and had suffered from depreciation wars between the US and the EU—and the Central provinces—which had produced mainly for domestic consumption and depended on the existence of Canadian tariffs (Montpetit, 2006, p. 102-103).

Within Quebec, a cleavage of a similar nature formed between producers favouring dirigisme in agricultural production because it generated stable and predictable revenues, and producers depending on exports and therefore calling for more openness in agricultural trade. According to the opponents of supply management in Quebec and other provinces, the system jeopardized Canada's free trade deals (Skogstad, 2008). They argued that Canada should follow the Australian model and liberalise their dairy, egg, and poultry sub-sectors. Furthermore, the advocates of increased market access also highlighted that supply management forced other Canadian provinces to be overcharged for dairy, egg, and poultry products in comparison with international market prices (Whalley, 1983, p. 170-171). In 1985, the Royal Commission on the Economic Union and Development Prospects for Canada, also known as the MacDonald Commission after its chairman Donald S. Macdonald, presented its recommendations on economic development to the Canadian federal government (Royal Commission on the Economic Union and Development Prospects for Canada (=Macdonald Commission), 1985). In its recommendations, the Macdonald Commission made a strong case that Canada ought to reject "protectionism and [a] dirigiste industrial strategy behind tariff and other barriers" (Shearer, 1986, p. 62). In particular, the Commission suggested that agricultural support policies be abolished. It did so in the name of Canadian nation-building: abolishing the cleavage on agriculture between the Prairie and Central provinces, the Commission argued, would contribute to restoring a "national sense of Canada" and, furthermore, reduce federal-provincial conflicts. Free trade with the US should play a key role in this process (1985, p. 357):

> Canadians elsewhere in the country still believe strongly that the manufacturing and industrial economy of central Canada is being maintained at their expense. To conclude a free-trade agreement with the United States would remove this long-standing cause of dissatisfaction at a single stroke. It is difficult to think of any other act of Canadian public policy that would have so comparably healing an effect.

As a consequence of the Uruguay Round, conflicting internal demands and a series of intergovernmental meetings between federal and provincial heads of government, and state officials, federal and provincial governments introduced a reform agenda into their agricultural policies that was clearly a compromise: subsidies were to be cut back both in the Prairie and Central provinces in exchange for market access during the Uruguay Round. However, as Montpetit (2006, p. 104-106) pointed out, these practices of executive federalism—the successful cooperation between federal and provincial governments in areas of joint or shared jurisdiction—did not last long: during the preparations for the WTO ministerial meeting in Seattle in 1999, provincial and federal governments consulted directly with societal and producer lobby groups before they entered intergovernmental meetings (Montpetit, 2003, p. 206-207). This increasingly territorialised agricultural politics rendered a pan-Canadian compromise more difficult. Thereby, governments inhibited the potential for reconciling the logics of dirigisme and small open economy in future intergovernmental meetings.

As a consequence of its GATT commitments resulting from the conclusion of the Uruguay Round in 1994, Canada needed to adjust its existing system of tariffs and import restrictions (Nguyen, Perroni et al., 1996). First, tariffs on butter, cheese, chicken, eggs, milk and yoghurt were to be reduced by 15 percent by 2000, a measure which did not, however, pose a threat to supply management. Second, members agreed on a ban on quantitative import restrictions on the grounds that they inhibited market access. However, as outlined in the special safeguard provisions in article 5 and Annex 5 of the Agreement on Agriculture (GATT, 1995), members were allowed to introduce or uphold tariff-rate quotas, which have the same prohibitive effect as quantitative restrictions. Tariff-rate quotas specify a certain volume of goods which enter a market at low or zero tariffs. Volumes exceeding in-quota imports are charged at higher tariffs, which might in practice inhibit imports, as the following figure illustrates. For each product, specific tariff-rate quotas apply. For example, the tariff-rate quota for turkey in 1995 was 4467 tonnes for WTO members or 3.5% of anticipated 1995 production for NAFTA members (Government of Canada – Global Affairs, 2014b). These quotas are allocated annually to distributors.

Figure 5 – Graphical Explanation of a Tariff-Rate Quota

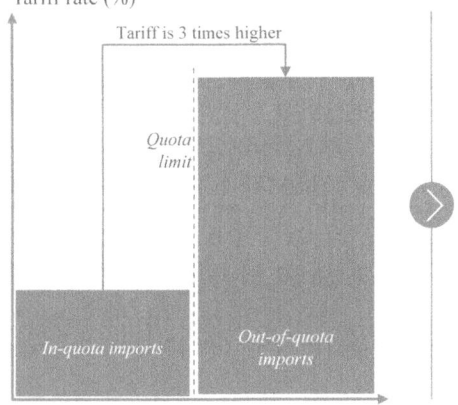

Tariff rate (%)

Tariff is 3 times higher

Quota limit

In-quota imports

Out-of-quota imports

Imported volume or value

- Imported goods are charged at **in-quota tariffs**, which are generally low, until a previously defined limit (volume or value) is reached

- Once the quota limit reached, imported goods will be charged at the **out-of-quota tariff rate**, which is generally higher

As a consequence of these special provisions of multilateral trade, Canada introduced tariff-rate quotas for dairy, eggs and poultry products, a system that is still operable today. In accordance with this system, Canada imports a certain volume of dairy, eggs and poultry products charged with low or no tariffs ("in-quota tariff-rate"), while the volume exceeding the specified quota is charged under higher most favoured nation tariffs,[320] averaging around 250 percent on dairy products and peaking at 314 percent, as documented by the Joint Study commissioned by the European Commission and the Canadian federal government in preparation for their trade and investment negotiation (European Commission and Government of Canada, 2008). In this system, the share of foreign products is thus static and to a large extent uncoupled from market mechanisms.

During the CUSFTA and NAFTA negotiations, Quebec also successfully defended its supply management system. The federal government continued to simultaneously pursue the goal of decreasing international barriers to entry on the grain and oilseed markets and protect its supply management system (Skogstad, 1998). The CUSFTA and NAFTA negotiations were cast very much against the backdrop of the ongoing Uruguay Round of the GATT, and heated discussion between the US and the EU (Cameron and Tomlin, 2000, pp. 37-39, 84, 96-97, 128; Morici, 1985, 1997). Furthermore, agriculture had been recognised as disruptive in overall North American trade relations, both between Canada and the US and in their relations with third countries (Marchildon, 1998). When Canada, Mexico and the US got to the negotiation table, Canada aimed at fully protecting supply management, which considerably limited its negotiation options. During the NAFTA negotiation, the US and Mexico decided to follow a bilateral avenue on agriculture, while Canada agreed to two separate agreements on agriculture. Under NAFTA, Canada could continue to impose tariff-rate quotas to restrict the quantities of the volume of commodities under supply management (dairy, poultry and eggs) permitted to be marketed or produced, as stipulated in Annex 702.2 Market Access Section B – Canada and Mexico, art. 7 (a), (b), referring to the rights and obligations of the Parties under Article XI:2(c)(i) of the GATT.

Canada's agricultural policies also led to international trade disputes. In most disputes, provincial measures were involved, forcing the federal and provincial governments to cooperate. Two cases were brought against Canada on measures concerning dairy exports by New Zealand and the US

---

320 According to the WTO, Most Favourite Nation Tariffs "refer to normal non-discriminatory tariff charged on imports (excludes preferential tariffs under free trade agreements and other schemes or tariffs charged inside quotas)", see World Trade Organization (2016b.)

respectively in the WTO framework.[321] The plaintiffs argued that Canada had violated its obligations on export subsidies by introducing a special "Milk Classes Scheme" which allowed exporters to have access to milk at considerably lower prices than otherwise available on domestic markets. A long dispute before several different panels followed, until the WTO's Appellate Body found that the replacement scheme was contrary to Canada's obligations in the multilateral framework.[322] In parallel, the US also challenged Canada under NAFTA, arguing that it applied tariffs on commodities under supply management that were in excess of those agreed by NAFTA. The Arbitral Panel determined, however, that Canada's tariffs conformed with NAFTA provisions (1996 [Arbitral Panel Report]). In these legal processes, Skogstad argued, executives of both levels were often able to devise a generally acceptable solution, thereby avoiding a situation in which the most recalcitrant party prevailed (Skogstad, 2012b, p. 213-214). During the Doha Development Round, supply management systems figured high on the agenda in agricultural negotiations. Adversaries of the system required that Canada increase its tariff-rate import quotas on sensitive products, yet Quebec was confident that Canada could, once again, protect the farming community in supply management (Barichello, Cranfield et al., 2009).

Through a slow process, as documented in this section, Canada's highly protected and regulated agricultural production was gradually opened, in most sub-sectors, to international competition, and state intervention in these sectors was reduced. From agricultural practices anchored in the state dirigisme frame with the goal to contribute to spatial development and nation-building, Canadian representatives gradually shifted towards a conception of Canada as an export-dependent economy. In this way, Canada developed one of the least protected agricultural sectors in the world and became the world's fifth largest agricultural exporter by 2012 (Government of Canada – Agriculture and Agri-Food Canada, 2014a, p. 22). Especially Alberta, Saskatchewan and Manitoba export the majority of their production, mainly oilseed, wheat, barley and other crops as well as beef

---

321 Case 1: Complainant: USA, WTO Dispute DS103 (Canada — Measures Affecting the Importation of Milk and the Exportation of Dairy Products), request for consultation received on 8 October 1997, panel report circulated 17 May 1999, mutually agreed solution notified on 9 May 2003. Case 2: Complainant: New Zealand, WTO Dispute DS113 (Canada — Measures Affecting Dairy Exports), request for consultation received on 29 December 1997, panel report circulated 17 May 1999, mutually agreed solution notified on 15 May 2003.

322 Article 3.3 and Article 8 of the Agreement on Agriculture.

(Skogstad, 2008, p. 24-26). However, supply management remained the dominant mode of production for milk, hatching and table eggs, chicken and turkey. Despite internal and external pressure, Canadian representatives did not abolish it (Skogstad, 2008, p. 141-178). State dirigisme as a mode of agricultural production dominates the discourse in Quebec, even though Quebec also has a large export-oriented agri-food business, as documented above. This is because production under supply management is concentrated in Quebec and because the province has chosen a more interventionist mode of agricultural management than its neighbour Ontario.

Section 2: From Province-Building to Federalism—Reconfiguring the Boundaries of Agricultural Production

As during past trade negotiations, Quebec's representatives were aware that CETA would pose a considerable threat to supply management and a challenge to their agricultural policies: representatives would not only need to defend the mode of production dominated by the state dirigisme frame both to export-oriented Canadian provinces and European negotiators, but also develop an internally coherent position on agricultural trade taking into account potentially incommensurate discourses underpinning the production practices in Quebec's different agricultural sub-sectors.

1. Agriculture throughout the CETA Negotiation Process (2006-2014)

As a consequence of multilateral economic integration, the average across-sector tariff level between Canada and the EU was already very low at the incipit of the CETA negotiation. However, tariff barriers remained considerably high in three sectors: agriculture and food, textiles and clothing, and automotive industries. Among these, agriculture exhibited the highest levels of tariffs with an average rate of 21.9 percent, as documented in the *Joint Study* commissioned by the European Commission and the Canadian federal government in preparation of the CETA negotiation (European Commission and Government of Canada, 2008, p. 34). Furthermore, the Joint Study pinpointed Canada's remaining tariffs and tariff peaks specifically for dairy products (out-of-quota tariff averages 251.3 percent and peaks at 313.6 percent) including cheese (out-of-quota tariff is 245.6 percent) and butter, cereals and products of the milling industry (9.5 percent, peak at 95.2 percent). These products mentioned in the Joint Study were agricultural goods for which the EU might ask for lower tariffs.

The EU, for its part, maintained high tariffs on beef (out-of-quota tariff reaches 400 percent), pork (on average 37.5 percent), wheat and oats (European Commission and Government of Canada, 2008, p. 35). Subsequently, the Joint Study projected considerable welfare gains in the abolition or reduction of tariffs in agricultural trade, and mainly so for Canada (European Commission and Government of Canada, 2008, p. 168). While the Joint Study focused on tariff barriers, the report of the Joint Scoping Group preparing the negotiation addressed the question of export subsidies, thereby highlighting the asymmetry between Canada's agricultural support policies and those of the EU (Canada and EU, 2009). In fact, while Canada only upheld supply management for five specific commodities and abolished direct subsidies, the EU still highly subsidises agricultural products across sub-sectors. By highlighting this difference, albeit indirectly, the Scoping Exercise recognised the importance of domestic policies in agricultural trade negotiations.

Negotiation demands and offers on both sides of the Atlantic mirrored the expectations of the Joint Study (European Commission and Government of Canada, 2008). On the European side, demands mostly concerned the dairy sub-sectors. In particular, France hoped to increase cheese exports.[323] On the Canadian side, representatives hoped to gain better access to European beef, pork, grain and oilseed markets. Crucially, Canada did not exclude sub-sectors related to supply management from its bilateral negotiations from the outset.

Perceptions of sectoral and cross-sectoral deals varied across the Atlantic. Canadian diplomats did not expect agricultural sub-sectors to be traded off against each other. As a Canadian diplomat asserted, sub-sectoral losses might not be outweighed by gains in other sub-sectors. Rather, negotiators hoped that the overall gains realised through CETA would mitigate the drawbacks of agricultural tariff reductions.[324] In Quebec, representatives hoped that their offer to allow European companies privileged access to procurement markets, including procurement by Hydro-Québec, would allow them to continue to protect their sub-sectors managed under the system of supply management.[325] At the incipit of agricultural negotiations,

---

323 Interview with French diplomat, Montreal, 20 April 2015; Interview with member of the European Commission, DG Trade, Brussels, 23 July 2014.

324 Interview with Canadian diplomat in July 2014.

325 Interview with Quebec diplomat, Montreal, 15 October 2014.

proponents of the new agreement, including liberal think tanks and the liberal press, also highlighted the importance of global value chains in the agri-food sector (Charlebois, 2013): for example, Canadian production of grains sold as livestock feeds to the EU would improve if European exports of red meat to Canada increased or dairy farmers could export their (male) calves as veal to the EU. Therefore, they argued, gains and losses resulting from increased trade could not directly be computed (McGregor, 2012). Yet, on the European side, complementary European and Canadian demands in agriculture made it easy to represent the agricultural outcome in terms of sub-sectoral trade-offs. A French diplomat asserted, for example, that the negotiations were made on a traditional mercantilist basis, meaning that Canadian red meat and wheat export interests could be traded against European dairy export interests.[326]

Agricultural negotiations were among the most difficult issues in the overall CETA negotiation and therefore left for the second half of the negotiation.[327] In October and November 2012, negotiators reached a stalemate which negatively impacted on the overall negotiations.[328] Quebec and Ontario in particular were increasingly prone to domestic Canadian pressure to make concessions regarding European demands on dairy products, given that supply management production is concentrated in Ontario and Quebec. Furthermore, supply management producers were increasingly challenged by Canadian manufacturers and service providers hoping to increase their exports to the European market, as well as by liberal think tanks and commentators who felt that Canada's supply management pricing and tariff system generated high prices for consumers and jeopardised Canada's most important trade project since NAFTA (Dawson, 2013). Since the beginning of the negotiations, Quebec's representatives across party lines left no doubt about their intention not to alter supply management policies in the course of CETA negotiations.[329] Quickly and unexpectedly, however, European and Canadian negotiators achieved consensus in mid-2013, shortly before Commission President José Manuel Barroso and Canadian Prime Minister Stephen Harper reached a political agreement on the key elements of CETA in October 2013. CETA provisions on agricultural trade foresee increased bilateral market access for several agricultu-

---

326 Interview with French diplomat, January 2015.
327 Interview with Quebec diplomat, 15 October 2014.
328 Interview with Quebec diplomat, 15 October 2014.
329 Jean Charest (PLQ), Assemblée nationale du Québec, 15 November 2011; Interview with Quebec diplomat, Montreal, 9 October 2014.

ral products. Many provisions in the agreement closely relate to agriculture although they do not concern agricultural tariffs, including sanitary and phyto-sanitary measures, intellectual property and rules of origin. Tariff-rate quotas was the most contentious issue with the most significant effect not only on specific sub-sectors, but on Quebec's agricultural system, which is why the following account focusses on tariff-rate quotas.

The negotiation outcome mirrors the trade potential already identified by the Joint Study (European Commission and Government of Canada, 2008). Annex X.5 specifies customs duties elimination.[330] European negotiators granted substantive market access rights to Canadian agricultural producers through increased duty-free tariff-rate import quotas for processed shrimps (23,000 tonnes, provisional rate), frozen cod (1,000 tonnes, provisional rate), low and medium quality common wheat (100,000, provisional rate), sweetcorn (8,000 tonnes), bison (3,000), fresh/chilled beef and veal (30,840 tonnes), frozen/other beef and veal (15,000 tonnes), and pork (75,000 tonnes). Furthermore, existing WTO tariff-rate quotas for high quality fresh, chilled and frozen meat of bovine animals will be duty-free once CETA enters into force. These increases were substantial and will probably allow Canadian red meat and wheat industries to compete on the EU market if they respect European regulatory standards.[331]

Concerning the Canadian tariff schedule, negotiators agreed to increasing tariff-rate quotas only with regard to (retail) cheese and industrial

---

330 The following figures refer to the 2014-version of the CETA text. They are per annum figures and refer to duty-free tariff-rate quotas after a transitional period, which reaches from none to seven years. Some tariff-rate quota lines were provisional.

331 Canada and the EU have a long-standing dispute on the use of substances having a hormonal effect on growth promotion on farm animals, mostly in beef (1998 [Arbitration Panel Report]). Currently, the EU prohibits the use of most substances having a hormonal action for growth promotion in farm animals (Directive 2003/74/EC amending Council Directive 96/22/EC concerning the prohibition on the use in stock farming of certain substances having a hormonal or thyrostatic action and of beta-agonists). Similarly, the EU also restricts the use of genetically modified crops (see Regulation (EC) 1829/2003 on GM food & feed; Directive 2001/18/EC on deliberate release into the environment; Commission Implementing Regulation (EU) 503/2013 on applications for authorisation of genetically modified food and feed in accordance with Regulation (EC) 1829/2003; Directive (EU) 2015/412 amending Directive 2001/18/EC as regards the possibility for the Member States to restrict or prohibit the cultivation of GMOs in their territory). If Canadian farmers want to export meat and grain to the EU, they need to conform with this and other regulatory standards.

cheese.[332] After a six-year transition period with a steady rise of the annual tariff-rate quota, Canada will allow the import of additional 17,700 tonnes of cheese duty-free from the EU. This new tariff-rate quota almost doubles the existing WTO tariff-rate quota of 20,412 tonnes for cheese imports to Canada, out of which 13,472 tonnes, or 66 percent, were already attributed to the EU.[333] This new tariff rate quota is split up in three different groups of customs duties applying to different tariff lines. According to article 2.4 (1), referring to Annex 2-A on tariff elimination, Canada needs to eliminate import duties on retail cheese for an additional 16,000 tonnes over a period of six years. Similarly, an additional tariff-rate quota of 1,700 tonnes of industrial cheese will be imported duty free after a period of six years. As a third requirement in relation to import quota for cheese, Canada will reallocate 800 tonnes of Canada's overall 20,412 tonnes WTO tariff-rate quota for cheese to the EU as soon as the agreement enters into force.

Even though this new quota for cheese may seem minor in terms of volume compared to the additional market access the EU granted Canadian farmers, it is quite substantive. First, the European consumer market is considerably larger, which reduces the effect of new imports in terms of market share. Furthermore, the differences between Canada and the EU in terms of agricultural support and regulatory policies shape the access exporters have to the host market. On the one hand, Canadian products will have to compete with EU products for market shares. They will also have to comply with EU regulations, which means that the meat and partially also the oilseed and grain producers will have to alter their mode of production if they want to export; that they would do so was not clear when CETA negotiations closed.[334] The situation for European exporters on the Canadian cheese market is markedly different: although there are differences in regulations concerning cheese, many European products can enter the Canadian market without alterations in the production mode. Most importantly, however, the Canadian cheese production and distribution

---

332 Industrial cheese is defined in CETA provisions as "cheese used as ingredients for further food processing (secondary manufacturing) imported in bulk (not for retail sale)" (Annex 2-A, 17d). Tariff-rate quota provisions specify the types of cheese concerned by referring to the Harmonized Commodity Description and Coding System developed by the World Customs Organisation.

333 The WTO Agricultural Agreement (1995) resulting of the 1986-1994 Uruguay Round of trade negotiations inhibits non-tariff measures inhibiting import, and replaced them with tariffs and tariff-rate quotas. These tariff-rate quotas are allocated to exporting economies.

334 Interview with representative of UPA, Longueuil, 22 October 2014.

systems will allow European exporters to transform the new quota directly into market shares on the Canadian market. This can be surmised because Canadian cheese import quota are already fully exploited, European products are considerably cheaper (because farms are directly subsidised), and the introduction of geographical indications gives European products an additional competitive advantage. On the Canadian retail cheese market, imports (before CETA) represent between 5 and 6 percent of the total domestic consumption, considering that Canada imports about 24 000 tonnes per year (Government of Canada – Canadian Dairy Information Centre, 2016a).[335] Additional imports will therefore lead to a reduction in Canadian production if domestic consumption remains stable, as Canadian producers will be priced out by their European competitors.

However, the final negotiation outcome cannot only be understood in terms of sub-sectoral deals. In fact, as documented above, market access through tariff reductions was substantively larger for Canada than for the EU in the agricultural sector. Therefore, it is likely that the provisions in the agricultural chapter represented trade-offs between different sectors rather than agricultural sub-sectors, reflecting the overall aim of comprehensive rather than sectoral negotiations. In essence, diplomats asserted that the overall welfare gains could be used to make advancements in agricultural trade which would not be possible in sectoral negotiations.[336]

2. Changing Interests on Agriculture? A Discursive Strategy for Legitimising Cracks in the Fabric of Supply Management

Despite the expectations raised by the role agriculture plays in Quebec's repertoire of province-building and the demands from the producer lobbies, Quebec's representatives did not refuse to accept this new quota, nor were they forced to do so. In their final position on agriculture, they crossed the red line of agricultural trade and allowed substantial competition to their cheese producers. The outcome of the agricultural negotiations is therefore one of the major empirical puzzles with regard to Quebec's negotiation position. Therefore, two questions require further explanation: why did Que-

---

335 Statistics Canada only publishes per capita consumption, which allows to calculate the total consumption market: each Canadian consumed 12.45 kg cheese in 2009 (all types), which represented 419,000 tonnes in 2009 in Canada. The tariff-rate import quota represented 5.7 percent of total consumption.

336 Interview with Canadian diplomat, Brussels, 8 July 2014.

bec representatives' position, at the beginning of the negotiation, to protect supply management at all cost change into making major concessions with regard to their agricultural sector, and how did representatives discursively legitimise this shift to political opposition and producer lobbies?

Quebec's representatives' discourse in the National Assembly mirrors the development of the official negotiation process. The relative importance of the agricultural chapter changed dramatically in the course of the negotiation process. From a topic completely absent from deputies' discourse, it developed into the most salient topic at the end of the negotiation. The following table gives an overview on the percentage of discourse on agriculture in Quebec's National Assembly for each negotiation period. As table 28 highlights, agriculture was not a prominent topic—proportionally speaking— during the agenda-setting and early negotiation stages. It was not even discussed during the agenda-setting phase in parliament, because deputies were convinced that it would be excluded from the negotiations. Agriculture was mentioned in a parliamentary debate for the first time in late April 2010, in an economy and labour committee session,[337] a year after the official launch of the negotiation. Until 2012, ministers for agriculture did not speak one single time on the issue in Quebec's National Assembly. The more the negotiations advanced, the more prominent the topic became, finally evolving into the most discussed topic in Quebec's National Assembly.

Table 28 – Coding on Agriculture per Negotiation Period (Percentage of Total Discourse on CETA, 2006-2014)

Period	Policy Cycle	Government in Office	Percentage
2006-2009	Agenda-Setting	PLQ	0
2009-2012	1st Negotiation Stage	PLQ	7
2012-2014	2nd Negotiation Stage	PQ	27
2014	Decision-Making	PLQ	81

Source: Analysis of parliamentary debates (plenary and committees, N= 159,527 words)

Throughout the negotiation process, deputies' discourse also became more focused on specific topics, as table 29 shows. In the first negotiation phase (2009-2012), although supply management took more than half of the to-

---

337 Assemblée nationale du Québec, 29 April 2010.

tal speaking time, other topics figured prominently on the agenda as well. Deputies regularly discussed other issues related to agricultural trade, including non-tariff barriers such as health and safety regulations, new export opportunities for Quebec's agri-food producers, and geographical indications. According to them, the European system of geographical indications represented a threat to Quebec producers, since they confer a marketing advantage on European producers. In fact, certain producers in Quebec would be forced to abandon their long-standing denomination for their food products, and consumers might not recognise the type or quality of the product any more. In the second negotiation stage (2012-2014), when regulatory issues related to agri-food products began to mobilise opposition in Europe, these topics rapidly declined in importance in Quebec's National Assembly. In fact, between 2012 and 2014, discussions focused almost exclusively on the topic of supply management. In the last negotiation stage (2014), supply management was the only topic discussed in the National Assembly.

Table 29 – Relative Importance of Specific Topics at Different Negotiation Stages (percentage of Total Discourse on Agriculture)

	Regulation	Export	Geogr. indications	Supply Mgmt.	Other	Total (Number of words)
2006-2014	2	5	1	53	39	100% (30,194)
2006-2009	0	0	0	0	0	100% (0)
2009-2012	14	18	8	60	2	100% (7,666)
2012-2014	0	11	0	89	100	100% (10,085)
2014	0	0	0	100	100	100% (12,443)

Source: Analysis of parliamentary debates (plenary and committees, N=30194 words)

This overview of the salience of agriculture in the overall discourse on CETA in the National Assembly and the development of the relevance of various topics allows to draw two preliminary conclusions regarding representatives' discursive strategy. First, deputies did not perceive agriculture as a problematic issue at the beginning of the negotiations, even though they knew that agriculture was included in the negotiation agenda. Second, the salience of agriculture increased dramatically in the overall discourse. Eventually, however, representatives agreed to accept CETA's agricultural chapter and increased tariff-free import quotas for cheese. This represented a major shift in Quebec's position from an overt rejection to accepting a significant increase in tariff-free import quotas. This discursive process will be traced in the following.

a) Firm Positions on Protecting Supply Management in Quebec (2009-2012)

During the first stage of the CETA negotiation (2009-2012), Quebec's representatives' discourse stayed firmly anchored in the structure of the dirigisme frame. Despite the Liberals' overall support for negotiating a new economic and trade agreement with the EU, they upheld that agriculture was a sector which would not benefit from increased competition. Similar to past trade negotiations, Quebec's representatives highlighted the contribution of supply management to rural development in Quebec's rural areas, an important pillar of province-building. In their discursive strategy, Quebec's representatives subordinated the interests of export-oriented industries in Quebec's agricultural sector to the needs of the dairy, eggs, and poultry sub-sectors. Deputies in the National Assembly across party lines agreed that the status quo in agriculture was non-negotiable. Similar to the deputies, the government was also strongly opposed to allowing alterations to supply management through CETA provisions. In a plenary question and answers period, Premier Charest explicitly supported the protection of supply management:[338]

> Maintenant, je veux réitérer que, du côté du Québec, [...] le gouvernement fédéral a réitéré la même position, qu'il ne s'agit pas pour nous, dans ces négociations, de remettre en question la gestion de l'offre. Et on a été très clairs là-dessus dans les négos avec l'Europe, on a été très clairs là-dessus aussi dans toute autre négociation.

---

338 Jean Charest, Assemblée nationale du Québec, 15 November 2011.

Similarly, a Quebec diplomat stressed that supply management represented a "red flag" ("drapeau rouge") for Quebec,[339] and Quebec's chief negotiator Pierre-Marc Johnson stressed the commitment of Quebec's government to protect supply management by all means:

> La position du gouvernement du Québec est claire là-dessus : elle défend le système de gestion de l'offre, et le monde agricole québécois n'a pas à s'inquiéter de, je dirais, de la force avec laquelle nous exprimons cette préoccupation auprès du gouvernement fédéral, qui est celui qui a la juridiction de négocier la clé de la gestion de l'offre que sont les tarifs.[340]

This position was in line with the demands of the agricultural producers' lobby not to alter the existing system of supply management in the dairy, eggs and poultry sub-sectors. Producers underlined that in order to do so, each pillar of supply management ought to be preserved. The agricultural lobby was represented by the socially and politically very influential *Union des producteurs agricoles* (UPA). Although the UPA also represented export-oriented agricultural sub-sectors, it had a firm position on supply management throughout the CETA negotiation, even though this position might jeopardise agricultural export opportunities. As documented, Quebec is home to a large export-oriented agricultural production, including pork, soy beans and maple syrup productions. However, these producer groups did not become more influential (Schram, 2016). In fact, throughout the CETA negotiation, the UPA insisted on fully protecting supply management and the producers and transformers active in related sub-sectors.[341]. In this corporatist network (Montpetit, 1999), representatives of export-oriented businesses were silenced to a large extent. Hence, producer interests were not at the origin of Quebec's representatives' acceptance of an increased import quota for cheese.

The UPA represented the interests of dairy, eggs and poultry producers together with the non-profit organisation *Solidarité Rurale du Québec (SRQ)*, channelling public and private demands of agricultural groups, and the *CoalitionGO5*, supported by high-ranking politicians and large companies. GO5 was formed in 2003 when supply management was increasingly

---

339 Interview with Quebec diplomat, Montreal, 9 October 2014.
340 Pierre-Marc Johnson, Assemblée nationale du Québec, 6 October 2010 (=1st hearing).
341 Interview with representative of the Union des producteurs agricoles, Longueuil, 14 October 2014.

challenged during WTO negotiations. Key in producers' argument was that increasing tariff-rate import quotas would equal handing over exactly this market share to foreign producers. In fact, the existence of production quota and fixed milk prices at the farm forbid domestic producers to benefit from international competition—which is usually a key argument made by advocates of free trade. Therefore, even if producers wanted to become more productive and lower their prices, they would not be allowed to.[342]

For Quebec's representatives, such a position was not easy to uphold in Ottawa and Brussels during the CETA negotiation. In fact, it contradicted their overall support for further economic integration between Canada and the EU. Remaining firmly opposed to European demands to reduce barriers to access the dairy, egg and poultry markets put Quebec's representatives in the delicate position of advocating trade liberalisation in most sectors—including some agricultural sub-sectors such as maple syrup—except for supply managed commodities, at the expense of the coherency of their overall negotiation position and their export-oriented agricultural producers. Contrary to members of government, Quebec's diplomats noted the contradiction between Quebec's position on agricultural trade and some of its export-oriented agricultural producers:

> Alors qu'on exporte pour un milliard de biens agricoles, il y toute une partie de l'UPA, les producteurs laitiers, qui défendent le concept de souveraineté alimentaire.[343]

Being in such a delicate position required Quebec's representatives to devise a coalitional strategy supporting their position. This coalitional strategy mirrored the Quebec Liberals' conception of Canadian federalism as a cooperation between Canadian provinces. Therefore, they mainly approached the other Canadian provinces instead of the federal government. First, they tried to find an ally in Ontario, home to a large part of supply management productions. However, this coalition was fragile because Ontario's primary production is more concentrated than Quebec's, making Ontario more likely to make concessions than Quebec whose small farms would be hit most severely.[344] Quebec's representatives also tried to forge

---

342 Interview with representative of milk producers, UPA, Longueuil, 17 October 2014.
343 Interview with Quebec diplomat, Montreal, 15 October 2014.
344 Interview with representative of the Union des producteurs agricoles, Longueuil, 14 October 2014.

alliances with other provinces in an attempt to showcase inter-provincial agreement on the topic.

Quebec was also able to secure support from the other Canadian provinces through the Council of the Federation. During the agenda-setting stage of CETA, Premiers highlighted their full support for supply management and agreed to protect these sectors in inter-provincial trade (Council of the Federation, 2008b):

> Premiers welcomed the recent agreement by Agriculture Ministers to finalize a new Agriculture chapter by October 31, 2008. Premiers noted that the new Chapter will ensure all technical measures that improperly limit the interprovincial trade of agricultural and food goods will be prohibited, and that federally and provincially regulated supply management systems and marketing boards be preserved.

This can be observed in the Premiers' support for the protection of supply management in the internal Canadian market integration process. In parallel to the CETA negotiation, the provinces took measures to ease agricultural trade among Canadian provinces by reducing interprovincial technical barriers. These barriers include laws, regulations and technical standards pertaining to agricultural and food products, for instance the federal Agricultural Products Marketing Act, different meat inspection programmes, certain sanitary and phytosanitary measures, and packaging standards (Coulibaly, 2010). However, in this market integration process, Premiers also underlined their full commitment to supply management and therefore extended the coverage of provisions excluding the institutions of supply management from the Agreement on Internal Trade. Hence, CETA fed into a process of Canadian internal market integration by promoting homogeneous technical standards in Canada. By doing so, it contributed to strengthening the integration of Quebec's agricultural production into the Canadian market, an important pillar of strengthening the Canadian federation in the Quebec Liberals' discourse. However, the Quebec Liberals also promoted the exclusion of supply management from this process because the repertoire of province-building and the state dirigisme frame still dominated their discourse in the sub-sectors concerned.

Although negotiators represented CETA as a comprehensive agreement in which everything, including agriculture, would be on the table, Quebec's representatives under the Liberals' lead were confident that no products under supply management would be included in CETA provisions. In 2009, Premiers agreed on a new chapter on inter-provincial agricultural trade excluding measures related to supply management (Council of the

Federation, 2009a). Recently, the successful conclusion of Free Trade Agreements with Colombia (signed 2008, in force 2011) and Peru (signed 2008, in force 2009), in which the system of supply management was not altered, also made Quebec's representatives confident that the agricultural negotiation with the EU would yield similar results. Furthermore, they did not expect to make far-reaching advancements in terms of international trade outside the multilateral rounds.[345]

Not everyone was as confident as the Liberals, though. On the producer side, the UPA distrusted the government and claimed that the government would not compromise the chances of concluding an agreement with the EU by insisting on excluding commodities under supply management.[346] Similar to farmers, the PQ mistrusted the Liberal government's ability to defend supply management at the negotiation table. On the one hand, they questioned the government's ability to convince the federal government to exclude supply management from CETA as well as the Liberals' candidness on defending each pillar of supply management, including restricted tariff-rate import quotas. On the other hand, they were aware of the demands from European negotiators to access the Canadian dairy market and the pressures this created on Quebec, as the following contribution in the National Assembly by Alexandre Cloutier (PQ) showed:

> La gestion de l'offre a traditionnellement toujours été exclue des éléments de négociation de tout accord de commerce international. Or, dans la présente négociation, le Canada est incapable d'affirmer clairement que la gestion de l'offre, dont son pilier, le système de quotas, ne sera pas affectée par cet accord. Une des principales demandes de l'Union européenne est d'avoir accès à nos marchés dans le domaine agricole, et particulièrement dans le secteur laitier. Ce matin, le premier ministre a affirmé que le régime de gestion de l'offre est non négociable. Est-ce qu'il peut nous dire maintenant qu'il ne joue pas sur les mots, que non seulement la gestion de l'offre sera protégée, mais son cœur, le système de quotas, ne sera pas altéré, modifié ou affecté de quelque manière que ce soit?[347]

Furthermore, the PQ members dreaded that the current power relation among Canadian provinces and the federal government might compromi-

---

345 Interview with Quebec diplomat, Montreal, 15 October 2014.

346 Interview with representative of milk producers, UPA, Longueuil, 17 October 2014.

347 Alexandre Cloutier, Assemblée nationale du Québec, 15 November 2011.

se Quebec's stance on supply management. According to the influential PQ member Nicolas Marceau, an economist and later Finance Minister, two factors could lead to the marginalisation of supply management supporters. A first factor was the high degree of influence of Western provinces on the current federal government led by the Conservative Party. Second, the shared jurisdiction on agriculture and the different agricultural management practices in the Central provinces—Quebec and Ontario—and the Western provinces—British Columbia, Alberta, Saskatchewan and Manitoba—created a situation in which the federal government faced incommensurate claims with regard to CETA's agricultural chapter. Since the current federal government led by the Conservative Party considered Canada a small and open economy, and since the Conservative Party had won the elections in the Western provinces, the federal government might have an open ear for the claims made by the Western provinces and tend to defend a trade and investment agreement with the EU to the detriment of supply management. In the National Assembly, Marceau summarised his conception of agricultural negotiations in the following way, highlighting the heterogeneity of agricultural production structures in the provinces:

> Et il y a des tensions, il y a des divergences à l'intérieur du Canada. Je prends un exemple, celui de l'agriculture. Il est bien connu [...] que, par exemple dans l'Ouest, la gestion de l'offre, ça ne passe pas très bien. Il est bien connu que, dans certaines provinces, on s'en passerait volontiers, alors qu'au Québec, en Ontario, dans les Provinces maritimes, la gestion de l'offre, c'est quelque chose avec lequel on est d'accord. Mais, M. le Président, nous pouvons légitimement nous inquiéter de ce que les provinces de l'Ouest, qui ont un poids énorme dans le gouvernement Harper actuellement, on peut légitimement s'inquiéter de ce que, à la table de négociation avec l'Europe, on pourrait lâcher le morceau[348]

Accordingly, the Western Canadian provinces would benefit from concessions made on supply management by gaining better market access to the EU. This stance mirrored the way the PQ representatives structured the repertoire of federalism. According to the independence frame, Quebec could defend its interest in trade better if it did not depend on the federal government to do so. Based on this observation, representatives reached the conclusion that agricultural production structures among the different

---

348 Nicolas Marceau, Assemblée nationale du Québec, 5 October 2011.

Canadian provinces are too heterogeneous to allow a common agreement for Canada on the agricultural chapter in CETA. PQ deputies developed a story of Quebec province-building within the Canadian federation. Subsequently, they feared that negotiations on CETA were conducted along opposition between provinces.

Contrary to the PLQ which considered Canada mainly to be a federation of provinces, the PQ more strongly emphasised the contrast between different Canadian regions and their specific development projects. Its members also attached more relevance to the influence of the federal government. Contrary to the Quebec Liberals who continued to support the Council of the Federation, where all provinces had re-affirmed their support for supply management, the PQ's doubt about the Liberals' conception of Canadian federalism made them doubt the commitment of export-oriented provinces for supply management when the chips are down. Thereby, they obscured the existence of strong export-oriented producers in Quebec and the existence of supply management productions in other provinces.[349]

Contrary to the PQ, Quebec's negotiation team conceived of Quebec's interests more in transatlantic terms at this stage of the negotiations, thereby paving the way for trade-offs between European and Canadian demands. During two hearings in the committee on institutions, chief negotiator Johnson stressed that Canadian supply management and European agricultural subsidies presented equally sensitive topics which would not be discussed during CETA negotiations:

> Les gens de la Commission européenne, au début de cette négociation, ont parlé de l'agriculture, sachant que c'est le gorille de 800 livres dans le milieu de la pièce. Et, à l'occasion d'une rencontre tout à fait informelle chez le délégué du Québec [à Bruxelles], où il y avait un ensemble de négociateurs invités, j'ai eu l'occasion de m'entretenir avec le délégué européen et lui demander s'ils avaient l'intention d'abolir l'ensemble des subventions à l'agriculture en Europe. Il a souri, et j'ai l'impression que ça a clos le débat pour un certain temps. Je demeure convaincu à ce stade, compte tenu des engagements du gouvernement fédéral, qu'il ne modifiera pas les tarifs d'une façon qui mettrait en péril le régime de gestion de l'offre [350]

---

349 Interview with member of Manitoba's government (2007-2009), by phone, 11 July 2017.

350 Pierre-Marc Johnson, Assemblée nationale du Québec, 8 December 2011 (=2nd hearing).

Against this background, we would have expected a preservation of the status quo, including no change in import quota, or the imposition of the international-market frame upon the province Quebec by the federal level during the CETA negotiations. Yet, none of these two scenarios materialised, as the following account will document.

b) Mounting Tensions between State Dirigisme and Small Open Economy: Challenges for the Co-Existence of two Incommensurate Frames (10.2012-04.2014)

When the Parti Québécois was elected in 2012, the new government did not alter the negotiation mandate under which chief negotiator Pierre-Marc Johnson operated.[351] Hence, similar to the Liberal government, the PQ government expressed its continuous support for protecting supply management. Even though the negotiation mandate on agriculture did not change, the PQ represented itself as an advocate of rural Quebec during the CETA negotiations even more than the Liberals.[352] The historical cross-party consensus of opinion on the benefits of Quebec's singular agricultural system (Montpetit, 2003) remained thus intact when the PQ was elected to government. Hence, changes in the governing party were not at the origin of Quebec's altered position on supply management.

Coordinating the government's position on CETA, Finance Minister Nicolas Marceau reiterated his government's full support for supply management in the National Assembly, mirrored in the negotiation mandate:

> Il y a des enjeux sur lesquels nous défendrons nos intérêts avec acharnement, M. le Président. [...] Et le mandat que nous avons donné à notre négociateur [...] Pierre Marc Johnson, il est très clair : nous voulons maintenir l'intégrité de la gestion de l'offre.[353]

Similarly, Minister for Agriculture François Gendron highlighted his support for supply management as well as his endeavour to convince the Canadian Minister for Agriculture of the need to support the system:

> J'ai répété à satiété que la position du gouvernement, c'est qu'on ne touche pas à la gestion de l'offre. J'ai eu, la semaine dernière, des dis-

---

351 Interview with Quebec diplomat, Montreal, 15 October 2014; Interview with member of Quebec government (2008-2012), Montreal, 23 October 2014.
352 Interview with Quebec diplomat, Montreal, 15 October 2014.
353 Nicolas Marceau, Assemblée nationale du Québec, 14 February 2013.

cussions avec le ministre, M. Gerry Ritz, qui est le ministre responsable à Ottawa : M. Ritz, on ne touche pas à la gestion de l'offre.[354]

In the deputies' discourse in the National Assembly, the issue of supply management became more specific and more pressing during the PQ's term of office, although its importance was already increasing during the last six months of the Liberal government. As table 29 above already showed, almost all discourse on agriculture during the PQ government in the National Assembly was on supply management.

In the second half of the CETA negotiation, European demands became more focussed on the Canadian dairy market. A potential increase in Canada's dairy import quotas was mentioned for the first time in the Assembly in December 2011 by PQ member Alexandre Cloutier. Cloutier referred to the EU's demand to export more dairy products by increasing Canada's tariff-rate import quota. Cloutier highlighted the importance of maintaining the coherency of the three-pillar system of supply management:

> Notre compréhension à nous, c'est que, pour les Européens, l'enjeu, c'est les produits laitiers. Alors, ce qu'ils souhaitent, c'est de pouvoir exporter davantage de produits laitiers, et donc, par conséquent, augmenter les quotas. Il me semble que, si on joue dans les quotas, on joue nécessairement aussi dans la définition de la gestion de l'offre. Et, lorsqu'on nous garantit que la gestion de l'offre sera maintenue, il me semble qu'on devrait également nous garantir que les quotas seront maintenus tels qu'ils existent présentement. Est-ce que je comprends qu'on n'est pas à l'heure actuelle en mesure d'avoir cette confirmation-là?[355]

At the end of 2011, agriculture appeared on the official negotiation agendas and the EU tabled its demand to increase market access to Canada for European-manufactured cheese.[356] This demand caused upheaval in Quebec because it went to the heart of supply management: almost 40 percent of Canada's dairy cows were registered in Quebec in 2013 (Government of Canada – Canadian Dairy Information Centre, 2013), with almost half of Canadian total cheese production and 60 percent of retail cheese production based in the province (Government of Canada – Canadian Dairy Information Centre, 2015a), as the following graph highlights. To the contra-

---

354 François Gendron, Assemblée nationale du Québec, 14 February 2013.
355 Alexandre Cloutier, Assemblée nationale du Québec, 8 December 2011.
356 Interview with French diplomat, 23 January 2015.

ry, Canada's federal government and the EU argued that increasing consumption would absorb new import quota (Radio Canada avec Agence France Presse, 2013).

Table 30 – Cheese Production by Province (1000 tonnes, 2003-2015)

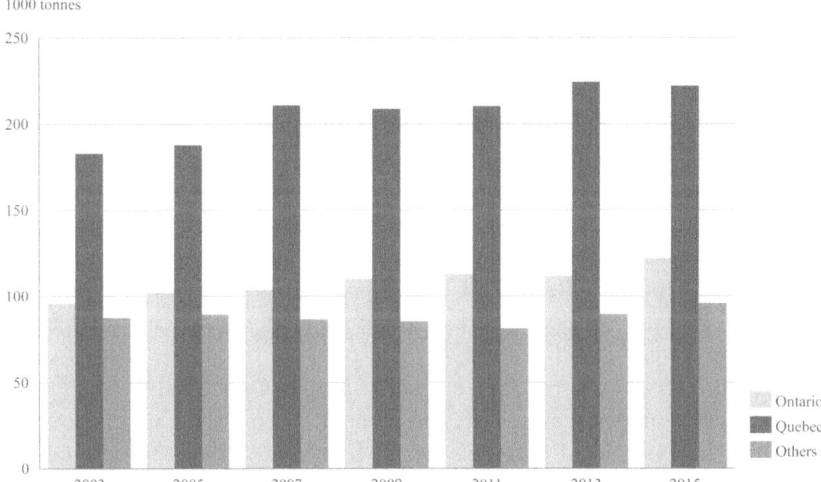

Source: Based on data by Government of Canada – Canadian Dairy Information Centre (2015a)

These demands made by the EU gave opponents to supply management an opportunity to voice their concerns with the system in general (an overview of the academic arguments against supply management can be found in Hall Findlay, 2012). Liberal think tanks played a leading role in delegitimising state dirigisme discourses. Several contributions highlighted the absence of market mechanisms in the supply management system. These authors referred both to a corporatist decision-making process dominated by a small group of producers and a system that confers a high social standing on agricultural producers and transformers, thereby counteracting Quebec's need to participate in global trade (Chassin and Geloso, 2013). According to the Fraser Institute, an influential liberal Canadian think tank based in Vancouver, increasing the Canadian participation in international cheese trade might also reduce consumer prices and hinder Canada from acquiring access to European agricultural markets, especially for beef and pork (Dawson, 2013). Another important criticism advanced against the system was that it was socially regressive in the sense that every consumer equally subsidised the system, leaving a higher burden on low-income households. Systems based on governmental subsidies, to the contrary, function according to a logic of contribution potential. This argument challenged the practices of state dirigisme because they engendered social injustice (Dubuc, 2013). In addition, critics also argued that supply management kept transforming industries from expanding to international markets, which is important for economic development, a pillar of province-building: since transforming industries cannot acquire their primary resources at international market prices, they are not competitive internationally. Hence, the system precludes Canadian companies from expanding into new markets and therefore blocks the development of Canada's trade activities. According to the liberal Institut économique de Montréal, a more demand-oriented production could increase the competitive advantage of the agri-food sector (Charlebois, 2013). Therefore, increasing quota did not only concern the market shares provided to European producers, but also legitimised opponents to supply management and gave their arguments more weight and visibility in the political discourse. In this way, their arguments based on the representation of Quebec as a small and open economy might replace state dirigisme in discourse on agriculture.

Others in Quebec's diplomatic circles highlighted that the new quota would only increase the European market share on the Canadian cheese market from 3 to 6 percent, which would not challenge Canada's entire supply management system.[357] By doing so, these diplomats introduced the repertoire of federalism into the discourse on agricultural trade: by enlarging the market of reference to the whole Canadian market, the effects of increasing tariff-rate quotas for cheese were represented as less important. These projections were based on the entire Canadian cheese market, thus also including fresh and industrial cheese, which opponents to the new quotas mostly excluded from their calculations. Similarly, a Liberal deputy also represented supply management as an issue of Canadian federalism. He highlighted that Quebec was the prime beneficiary of the federal supply management policy and that this policy posed a threat to the representation of Quebec as a small and open economy, the Liberals' representation of province-building:

> Le Québec est le bénéficiaire de la politique fédérale de quotas dans le lait. [...] Éventuellement cela risque d'être un problème, parce que cet-

---

357 Interview with Quebec diplomat, Montreal, 15 October 2014.

te politique de quotas est une politique de renfermement sur soi de l'organisation économique d'un produit qui s'appelle le lait.[358]

In this way, the repertoires of federalism and province-building interacted in the Quebec Liberals' discourse. At this point, the projected effect of the new import quota depended upon the way actors interpreted and defined the (spatial) boundaries of the relevant market. For some, Quebec's borders constituted the benchmark for evaluating the effects of CETA, while others reasoned in terms of the Canadian internal market.

Producer representatives opposed European demands. Opposing this new discourse, the UPA argued that increased quota represented a first step towards the abolition of supply management, because the system depended on shielding domestic markets from foreign competition:

> Ils nous ont dit jusqu'à la dernière minute qu'ils vont protéger la gestion de l'offre. Ils disent encore qu'ils vont protéger la gestion de l'offre. Mais, le pied est dans la porte maintenant.[359]

Furthermore, UPA representatives highlighted that the negotiation with the EU might incite Canada's other trade partners to require similar market access rights.[360] In addition, the UPA also highlighted that the reciprocity argument presented in support of agricultural trade liberalisation was invalid in its eyes. In fact, new tariff-rate quotas potentially benefitting Canadian exporters might not have the same effect as quota allocated to the EU. According to the UPA's analyses, the Quebec pork and beef sub-sectors, for instance, would not be able to benefit from new export quotas, in fact, existing unused quota already foreshadowed that development. One reason was that the adoption of European certification and packaging rules might render exports unprofitable.[361] Furthermore, the EU maintained its position on the prohibition of hormones and ractopamine.[362] The PQ government supported this analysis. A member of the PQ government argued for instance that

---

358 Interview with PLQ deputy, Quebec, 8 October 2014.
359 Interview with representative of the Union des producteurs agricoles, Longueuil, 14 October 2014.
360 Interview with representative of the Union des producteurs agricoles, Longueuil, 14 October 2014.
361 Interview with member of Quebec's government (2012-2014), Québec, 1 October 2014.
362 Interview with French diplomat, 23 January 2015.

> Il faut s'entendre sur la réciprocité des normes, parce que s'il n'y a pas de réciprocité dans les normes, par définition, l'espèce de capacité qui me laisse voir d'entrer du bœuf et du porc en Europe, en échange d'entrer du fromage ici pour équilibrer les pertes de l'un avec les gains de l'autre, ça ne passera pas si les normes ne sont pas pareilles.[363]

However, European demands also disclosed frictions among UPA members. In fact, the prospect of new tariff-rate quotas fed into a process of some producers contesting the existence and distribution of production quotas. Among producers, the *Union paysanne*, a producer lobby contesting the UPA's representative monopoly, launched a campaign supporting out-of-quota production in Canada. In this campaign, the lobby supported a reform of supply management against the background of international agreements challenging the system. According to them, state dirigisme in the allocation of production quota inhibited new farmers from entering the Canadian milk market. This system also harms, according to the Union paysanne, regional development because it encourages concentration of milk producers in proximity to transformers (such as cheese producers) (Union paysanne, 2014). Similarly, the *Conseil des entrepreneurs agricoles* challenged the status quo of the supply management system on the grounds of the UPA's representative monopoly and the rigidity of the system. More specifically, the lobby group called for a free choice of marketing mechanisms, thereby challenging the UPA's marketing monopoly. For example, chicken and egg producers claimed higher quotas to satisfy existing demands for locally farmed products which are currently inhibited by the distribution of production quota (Bérubé, 2016).

When the issue of quota allocation surfaced, the historical power asymmetry between (milk) producers, on the one hand, and distributors and processors, on the other hand, became salient again. Since cheese imported from the EU would be distributed by existing *Canadian* distributors, how new import quotas would be allocated and how this might even benefit distributors to the detriment of milk farmers was a major point of contention among producer groups, processors of different sizes and distributors. In fact, the final CETA text did not foresee a mechanism to manage the allocation of the new quota. According to the text published in 2014, Canada would administer the tariff-rate quota either through an import licensing system, e.g. allocate the new quota to distributors, or agree upon ano-

---

363 Interview with member of Quebec's government (2012-2014), Québec, 1 October 2014.

ther mechanism together with the EU (Annex 2-A, 17). In Canada, cheese is not imported according to the principle of first-come-first-served, but import quotas are allocated to Canadian distributors according to Canada's *Export and Import Permits Act* (1985, amended 2014). Only companies figuring on the quota holding lists issued by Canada's Ministry for International Affairs are allowed to import according to quotas allocated to them.

Large distributors lobbied for the allocation of new quotas to those groups already holding import quotas on the grounds that they were familiar with the system.[364] Contrary to primary agricultural producers, Canada's dairy processing and distributing industry is fairly consolidated and vertically integrated. Four groups dominated the production, marketing and distribution of the Canadian and Quebec dairy products when negotiations were launched: Saputo, Kraft Canada, Agropur Cooperative, and Parmalat. Together, they recorded a combined value share of 85 percent in the 2014 cheese market. Saputo, Agropur and Parmalat represented 83 percent of the drinking milk market (Government of Canada – Canadian Dairy Information Centre, 2014c). Saputo is the largest group:[365] it accounted for around 35 percent of Canada's milk transformation and 32 percent of Canada's cheese production in 2009. Apart from Canada, Saputo is also active in production and distribution in the US, the EU and Argentina (Saputo, 2009, p. 16-18). With total sales of CAN 5.8 billion, the Montreal-based group was ranked 12th company globally in terms of dairy turnover (Government of Canada – Canadian Dairy Information Centre, 2009; Saputo, 2009). Parmalat Group[366] generated € 4 billion of net revenues in 2009. In Canada, Parmalat generated CAN 2.2 billion revenues in 2009, representing 35 percent of Parmalat's overall revenues (Parmalat, 2009, pp. 36, 48). The dairy cooperative Agropur with headquarters in Saint-Hubert, Quebec, generated revenues of CAN 3.1 billion in 2009. With only 17 percent of revenues coming from the US and Argentina, Agropur is mainly present on the Canadian market, contrary to Saputo and Parmalat (Agro-

---

364 Interview with representative of the Fédération des producteurs de lait du Québec, Longueuil, 17 October 2014.

365 Saputo markets its products under various brand names. Brand names in 2009 included Saputo and Alexis de Portneuf, Armstrong, Baxter, Dairyland, Danscorella, De Lucia, Dragone, DuVillage 1860, Frigo Cheese Heads, Kingsey, La Paulina, Neilson, Nutrilait, Ricrem, Stella, Treasure Cave, HOP&GO!, Rondeau et Vachon (Saputo, 2009, p. 16).

366 Parmalat brand names in 2009 included Fibresse, Omega 3 Plus, Physical, vaalia, and zymil. local brand in Canada include Astro, Beatriceo, Lactania, and Black Diamond (Parmalat, 2009, p. 11).

pur Cooperative, 2009, p. 18-19). New cheese import quota created the possibility for large distributors to acquire more import quotas. Once new quotas acquired, distributors would set the price for imported products, and potentially realise a large margin of profit given the lower price of cheeses of European origin. They could also sell European cheeses at lower prices than Canadian products, thereby still realising a large margin of profit and potentially gaining new market shares. In this sense, CETA's new cheese quotas were increasing competition to milk producers, as well as small cheese producers which managed to have access to distributors, yet not large processors and distributors.[367]

Even though Agropur also held important volumes of import quotas for cheese, the company had a position which was closer to that of milk producers. In fact, Agropur is owned by more than 3000 milk producers based in Quebec, Ontario, Nova Scotia, New Brunswick and Newfoundland and Labrador. In 2013, the cooperative produced around 94,000 tonnes of cheese and feared that increasing import quotas by 10,000 tonnes would considerably decrease their market share (Riendeau, 2013). The company also responded to concessions made in the supply management production areas by commissioning a study from an external consultant (Agropur, 2015?). With this study, Agropur tried to influence the debate about the benefits and drawbacks of abolishing supply management. This study found that ending supply management would set 50 percent of Quebec milk producers at risk. Apart from losses engendered for producers and processors, the study also highlighted that lowered production and processing costs did not always translate, in other cases of deregulation, into lower consumer prices. Nor was there a direct link between price change and consumption (Agropur Cooperative, 2015?, p. 50).

Contrary to large distributors, Quebec diplomats argued that new quotas should be allocated to processors with small market shares which would probably register the highest losses from new import quotas. In this way, small cheese processors could be compensated for the losses engendered by increased European competition.[368]

These conflicting societal demands put the PQ government in a difficult position. On the one hand, it strongly supported free trade, as the party had done in the past, in the name of province-building and preparing for future political independence. On the other hand, and against the background of historical cross-party support for supply management in the na-

---

367 Interview with Quebec diplomat, Montreal, 15 October 2014.
368 Interview with Quebec diplomat, Montreal, 15 October 2014.

me of economic and regional development, the PQ did not want to appear as the government abolishing supply management. Faced with this conundrum, the PQ government not only needed to aggregate conflicting societal demands, including conflicting producer demands, but also to establish a hierarchy of interests regarding their conflicting goals of fostering free trade yet protecting agricultural dirigisme. In the government's discourse, the small open economy and state dirigisme frames, two ways to structure the repertoire of province-building, were at odds.

Hence, CETA triggered a reflection process in which the PQ government needed to re-evaluate Quebec's interests. At the beginning, despite a large group of actors favourable to increasing import quota, albeit for different reasons, Premier Marois threatened not to ratify CETA in Quebec's National Assembly if no solution was found on the cheese question (Larocque, 2013). Thus, the government discourse stayed firmly anchored in the state dirigisme frame. A member of the Marois government asserted that Quebec threatened the federal government not to ratify CETA if no agreement on supply management was found—despite Quebec's overall support for the agreement with the EU:

> On a menacé, même si on était des défenseurs de l'accord, qu'on ne le signerait pas, nous. On était au pouvoir quand on a dit ça. Puis on n'a pas juste menacé. [...] Madame Marois, Première Ministre du Québec avait des discussions avec monsieur Harper : c'est allé jusqu'au Premier Ministre canadien.[369]

Yet, unexpectedly and in spite of the government's previous announcements, in early 2013, the government hinted at the possibility that the tariff-rate cheese quota might be increased. In the official negotiation process between Canada and the EU, negotiators took the decision to increase Canada's tariff-rate import quota for cheese during the PQ's time in office,[370] most probably towards the end of 2013 (Bélair-Cirino, 2013). According to the Montreal-based weekly newspaper *Les Affaires*, Jean-François Lisée, Minster for External Relations and Trade, disclosed, at a press conference, that Quebec's government might accept increasing the tariff-rate import quota for cheese. The weekly cited Lisée stating that Quebec re-evaluated

---

369 Interview with member of Quebec's government (2012-2014), Quebec, 1 October 2014.
370 Interview with member of Quebec's PQ government (2012-2014), Skype, 24 April 2015.

the agricultural chapter in CETA in terms of overall gains deriving from a new trade agreement (Normand, 2013):

> On va juger au mérite, a déclaré Jean-François Lisée, en insistant sur le fait que la question des emplois était cruciale dans cet enjeu. On fait l'accord pour avoir plus d'emplois. Si on perd beaucoup d'emplois dans le milieu laitier à cause de ça… On décidera au mérite. On verra le libellé final, ce que les Canadiens auront réussi à obtenir, ce que l'UPA en pense.

Was Quebec forced by the federal government to accept this new quota?

Since the federal level legislates on tariffs and tariff-rate quotas, the federal government might have imposed this new quota on Quebec. However, this is an unlikely account. First, the Canadian government depended upon the provinces for the overall implementation of CETA provisions and for handling future trade disputes. Even though agricultural tariffs and quota did not fall under provincial jurisdiction and therefore did not require implementation at the provincial level, the key role provincial participation played in the overall CETA negotiation process de facto deprived the federal government of its ability to force agricultural provisions upon the provinces. Furthermore, the federal government might also require provincial cooperation in the future in the event of trade disputes, as "the two orders of government effectively share the policy-making authority in disputes involving agricultural trade" (Skogstad, 1998, p. 233). Thus, the federal government might depend on provincial willingness to share their knowledge about agriculture if Canada wants to defend its interests successfully at the international level. Second, the Central provinces were successful in defending the exclusion of these commodities during the NAFTA negotiation (Skogstad, 2012a, p. 147; 2008, p. 154-156). Since CETA gave the provinces, for the first time in Canadian trade negotiations, a platform to negotiate in their areas of jurisdiction, provincial influence even widened. This made it unlikely that the federal government forced agricultural provisions upon them this time. In addition, even though the provinces were not present in negotiations on tariffs, the Canadian chief negotiator Steve Verheul informed them about new developments.[371] It was therefore unlikely that provincial negotiators were not aware of Canada's acceptance of the new tariff-rate import quota for cheese. At the very least, Quebec tacitly acquiesced to Canada's position, a sign that its interest to protect its dairy industry at all cost had changed.

---

371 Interview with Quebec diplomat, Montreal, 15 October 2014.

Lisée's declaration during the above-mentioned press conference reflected a shift in the way the PQ perceived Quebec's interest. This position represented a major shift in Quebec's position on the agricultural chapter: contrary to their previous announcements, they did not fully protect all aspects of supply management during the negotiations. Throughout the negotiation process, provincial representatives had insisted on the fact that supply management was a non-negotiable issue. How was it possible, then, that Quebec's provincial representatives accepted higher import quotas for cheese without threatening, for example, to refrain from ratifying the agreement? How could they combine their position that existing public policies would remain unaffected by CETA with accepting quota that were almost doubled? Why did the hierarchy of provincial interests change, and how did representatives legitimise this shift?

Quebec's representatives deployed a discursive strategy to re-evaluate the provincial interest and to legitimise their new position in a situation where they faced conflicting demands. In this discursive process, the PQ government embedded the agricultural chapter in the PQ's long tradition of supporting free trade. In fact, it was no coincidence that Minister for International Relations Lisée made his declaration during a press conference following a speech at the Montreal Council on Foreign Relations[372] (Lisée, 2013). In this speech, Lisée underlined the crucial role Quebec played in many international agreements, most notably CUSFTA (1988) and NAFTA (1994), the UNESCO Convention on the Protection and Promotion of the Diversity of Cultural Expressions (2005) as well as CETA.

Quebec's government accepted the new tariff-rate cheese quota in furtherance of free trade for two complementary reasons. First, it did so in the name of province-building. It nested its new discourse on supply management in the small open economy frame of the repertoire of province-building, entailing different consequences for the evaluation of Quebec's interests than before. In fact, as the announcement by Minister Lisée highlighted, the PQ government hoped to create local jobs in Quebec, even though there might be job losses in the milk production sub-sector. For him, Quebec's interest to strengthen economic development through the participation in international trade and investment relations replaced the imperative to preserve the current position of Quebec's system of dairy production in the domestic and international economy.

Second, the government accepted this new quota because it aligned with the PQ's conception of Canadian federalism. Both repertoires fed into each

---

372 Conseil des Relations Internationales de Montréal (CORIM).

other to structure the government's discourse. However, contrary to the Liberals, the PQ structured the repertoire of federalism according to the independence frame: rather than pushing for the integration of the internal Canadian market, its representatives highlighted the difference between Quebec and other Canadian provinces in the management of their agricultural production. Hence, for the PQ government, the unfolding of the agricultural negotiations was a case in point to highlight that Quebec could have achieved a better deal if it negotiated as an independent state. For the PQ, the Quebec mode of agricultural production was part of its distinct "culture", an important pillar of province-building.[373] A member of the PQ government argued for instance:

> Il n'y a que le Québec qui a développé un modèle agricole avec un financement et des programmes. Est-ce que l'Ontario, le Manitoba, le Saskatchewan ont ce modèle de programmes agricoles, de programmes d'accompagnement pour les risques dans la production agricole aussi développés que le Québec? La réponse c'est non. Il n'y a que le Québec qui a tout un mécanisme de fonctionnement depuis des années où il y a une corrélation dans ces programmes très étroite entre.[374]

Was this therefore a case of issue-linkage in Quebec, where Quebec's representatives felt compelled to accept a new tariff-rate quota for cheese in exchange for wider access to the European market? Issue linkage involving agricultural trade is in fact often part of the dynamics of international negotiations (Davis, 2004). According to this argument, issue linkage alters the influence of interest groups and promotes liberalisation. An account focussing on the specific negotiation dynamics of international trade negotiations remains valid yet incomplete. With CETA, issue linkage provided a compelling argument, given the broad coverage of the agreement. To some extent, it was true that the comprehensive nature of the Canada-EU agreement allowed Quebec's representatives to highlight the benefits of the overall agreement for Quebec as a small and open economy, thereby legitimising losses in the agricultural sector. However, Quebec had in the past successfully advocated the exclusion of the Canadian dairy sector from Canada's commitments under NAFTA and to a large extent in the WTO framework. In addition, Quebec's negotiation team wanted to link provincial public procurement to provincial acquiescence to CETA, thereby shielding supply management. However, the EU did not consider access to pro-

---

373 Interview with member of the PQ government, Quebec, 1 October 2014.
374 Interview with member of the PQ government, Quebec, 1 October 2014.

vincial procurement markets a large enough benefit for their exporters, so they also required concessions in Canadian supply management, even though this was not the negotiation tactics intended by Quebec's representatives. [375] Furthermore, it was not only puzzling that Quebec accepted the new cheese quota, but also how its representatives *reacted* to these provisions: in fact, they argued that opening supply management would actually benefit Quebec, as Minister Lisée did for example at the CORIM press conference mentioned above.

In legitimising Quebec's new position, timing played an important role. Quebec's diplomats adhered to the negotiators' tactic on both sides of the Atlantic consisting in starting the CETA negotiation with topics where both sides would benefit from enhanced trade—a tactic which of course predestined agriculture for the final stages of the CETA negotiation. As explained above, agriculture was one of the most contentious issues in international trade, and one of the key reasons for the failure of the Doha Development Round (2003; Josling, Tangermann et al., 1996; Tyers and Anderson, 2011). Therefore, agriculture was not brought to the negotiation table at an early stage in the CETA negotiation process. The more negotiations advanced and heralded positive effects for Quebec, the less probable it would become that the entire agreement was rejected because of the agricultural sector. In a public hearing in Quebec's National Assembly, Johnson revealed that both parties implicitly agreed not to talk about agriculture too early in the process:

> La raison pour laquelle on n'a pas parlé beaucoup, on peut être francs et candides à ce moment-ci : on s'est tous promis qu'on discuterait ça vers la fin. C'est un peu comme des tabous, hein? Pensez-vous vraiment que l'Europe va abolir ses 56 milliards de subventions à la classe agricole? Et pensez-vous vraiment qu'ils s'attendent à ce qu'on renonce à maintenir les régimes de protection de la classe agricole? Et la réponse m'apparaît s'imposer, mais je ne peux pas la donner, parce qu'on s'est promis d'en parler seulement plus tard.

In legitimising Quebec's new position, the repertoire of federalism played an important role in complementing the repertoire of province-building. While there had been a disengagement, to a large extent, of Quebec's farm community from the federal government and an understanding of agriculture as an issue of provincial authority before the CETA negotiation (Skogstad, 1998), CETA brought the shared competency between the two levels

---

375 Interview with Quebec diplomat, Montreal, 15 October 2014.

of government to the forefront of political discourse again. As the following table exemplifies, province-building and federalism simultaneously structured deputies' discourse in the second negotiation stage (2012-2014). As a consequence, Quebec's representatives restructured their discourse on agricultural trade.

Table 31 – Repertoires Used by PQ and PLQ at Different Negotiation Stages

PQ	12.2006-05.2009	06.2009-09.2012	10.2012-04.2014	05.2014-12.2014
Province-Building	0	56	80	45
Federalism	0	44	20	55
	(100%)	100%	100%	100%
PLQ	2006-2009	2009-2012	2012-2014	2014
Province-Building	100	84	87	50
Federalism	0	16	13	50
	100%	100%	100%	100%

Source: Analysis of parliamentary debates (plenary and committees, N=43,811 words)

Two discursive options were available to Quebec's representatives. They could have claimed responsibility for agricultural negotiations, allowing them to reject the outcome of agricultural negotiations. In fact, the provinces shared jurisdiction over agriculture—albeit not over tariffs—and could have required participation in the definition of Canada's negotiation position. Yet, during the negotiation, the Quebec government consciously disengaged from decision-making on agriculture and explained that the federal government has sole authority over tariffs.

Through this disengagement process, the PQ government introduced a discursive shift from Quebec owning the issue of agriculture towards the federal government owning it. This shift did not alter, in a first step, the institutional relation between the two orders of government, nor the distribution of competencies. Yet, this shift was major in the sense that Quebec's government discursively assigned responsibility on agricultural trade to the federal government. Chief negotiator Johnson summarised this discursive strategy of shifting the blame to the federal government in the following terms:[376]

> C'est la position [du Québec] que j'ai transmise au gouvernement fédéral, à différents niveaux, et à ce stade c'est entre les mains du gouvernement canadien, qui a pris des engagements publics à cet effet. Je dirais cependant aux agriculteurs d'être vigilants jusqu'à la fin.

Quebec's representatives thus started a process leading to restructuring the relation between the actors in agricultural policy-making. This process changed the issue ownership of the agricultural negotiations. The responsibility to secure a good deal during the CETA negotiations did not belong any more to Quebec's government, but shifted towards the federal level on the grounds that the competency for tariff lines and import quotas belongs to the federal level. For example, PQ Finance Minister Marceau declared in the National Assembly that the decision to increase import quota for cheese depended upon the federal, not the provincial, government: [377]

> Ayant dit cela, effectivement, il y a une décision qui a été prise par le gouvernement fédéral de consentir à une augmentation du contingent de fromages hors tarifs, une augmentation de 17 000 tonnes. Cette décision n'est pas la nôtre.

As a consequence of the presence of the repertoires of province-building and federalism in Quebec's discourse, Quebec's representatives re-evaluated the province's interest in opposing altering tariff-rate quotas and attributed the blame to the federal level. Introducing the repertoire of federalism allowed them to legitimate the shift of interest made against the backdrop of introducing the small open economy frame in discourse on agriculture. In order to carry out this strategy, Quebec's government displayed a high degree of ambiguity on its position on trade in dairy products. As chief negotiator Johnson affirmed in Quebec's National Assembly, it gave the federal government considerable leeway to alter *existing* import quotas[378]. Through this strategy of ambiguity enabled through a disengagement of Quebec from the decision-making process, Quebec could legitimately shift the blame to the federal level, while also being able to argue that the changes introduced did not challenge the entire system of supply

---

376 Pierre-Marc Johnson, Assemblée nationale du Québec, 8 December 2011 (=2nd hearing).
377 Nicolas Marceau, Assemblée nationale du Québec, 22 October 2013.
378 Interview with Quebec diplomat, Montreal, 15 October 2014.

management. Subsequently, Quebec's representatives were apparently taken by surprise by the federal governments' decision to increase the tariff-rate cheese quota (Bélair-Cirino, 2013), although some lobby groups suspected the government was aware of the outcome,[379] which was consistent with the regular briefings between the federal and provincial negotiators.[380] According to representatives' discourse, the federal government confronted them with their decision to allow increased cheese quota for European companies.

While the European negotiators had been their main opponent, the other provinces and the federal government now played that role. This cleavage was not new in the Parti Québécois' structure of the repertoire of federalism; more than the Liberals, they contrasted Quebec with the Rest of Canada in their discourse on continental economic integration (Rocher, 2003, p. 464-468). In this way, the battle was not about winning against the EU any more, but about facing other provinces and the federal government.

Political opposition vigorously criticized Minister Lisée's declaration made at the CORIM press conference. Criticism came mainly from a newly formed party, the Coalition Avenir Québec (CAQ), and extended to the PLQ. Lisée's declaration also revealed existing cleavages within all three parties. Lines formed along the question whether Quebec should challenge CETA in the name of supply management. Within the CAQ, several members argued that the overall gains expected from CETA would outweigh the losses in the cheese retail market. In this sense, the government's role lay in securing privileged access to European markets, not in unduly blocking European access to Canada. This position stemmed from the CAQ's support of a strong provincial presence on the international scene and in the CETA negotiations. For instance, CAQ member Stéphane le Bouyonnec, spokesperson for economic affairs and later party President, argued that the agricultural chapter needed to be evaluated in terms of a balance of export-oriented and import-competing interests: [381]

> Entre autres, on sait très bien qu'il y a la gestion de l'offre, mais c'est en agriculture, mais aussi on sait très bien que la libéralisation des échanges permettrait entre autres au sirop d'érable d'être exporté davantage. Donc, tout n'est pas blanc, tout n'est pas noir.

---

379 Interview with UPA representative, Longueuil, 17 October 2014.
380 Interview with Quebec diplomat, Montreal, 15 October 2014.
381 Stéphane le Bouyonnec, Assemblée nationale du Québec, 14 February 2013.

However, the CAQ also expressed its support for the fine cheese industry developed in Quebec over the last 20 years. Both the UPA and the Quebec government invested important resources in creating a consumption market for fine cheese in Quebec. In order to remain profitable, this niche sector needed protection from international competition. Thus, policy makers needed to find a way to buffer the negative effects of CETA for fine cheese producers.[382] The PLQ was less vocal in its criticism of the current government's altered position on supply management. Stéphane Billette, the official Liberal spokesperson for agriculture and fisheries, briefly referred to Quebec's cheese producers by referring to rural employment and regional development opportunities, constitutive elements of the state dirigisme frame,[383] yet overall, the Liberals were not very vocal in opposing the government's stance.

In the overall process of negotiating agriculture, making agricultural negotiations an issue of federal cooperation or conflict enabled the provincial representatives' position to become generally acceptable and coherent with the governmental party's specific party-political discourse. This strategy allowed Quebec's representatives to remain in the negotiation circle and to allow the negotiations to move forward, while they could satisfy domestic demands for agricultural protection at the same time.

Partially shifting their discourse to the repertoire of federalism opened Quebec's representatives the way for new policy options. Indeed, altering the repertoires structuring the discourse on agricultural trade also changed conflict lines: while opposition had been structured along the conflict between actors within Quebec representing province-building in line with the state dirigisme or the small open economy frame, the repertoire of federalism realigned conflict along provincial borders. Quebec devised a discursive strategy which put it in a strong bargaining position vis-à-vis the federal government, as a member of the PQ government asserted:

> Mon collègue Nicolas Marceau a dit; " Hey, je ne ferai pas accroire à ça à la Première ministre du Québec ". Pour qu'elle ait du bargaining

---

382 Sylvie d'Amours (CAQ), Assemblée nationale du Québec, Commission de l'agriculture, des pêcheries, de l'énergie et des ressources naturelles, 13 February 2013.

383 Stéphane Billette (PLQ), Assemblée nationale du Québec, Commission de l'agriculture, des pêcheries, de l'énergie et des ressources naturelles, 13 February 2013.

power dans la discussion avec monsieur Harper, il fallait avoir une certaine couverture.[384]

Subsequently, the introduction of the repertoire of federalism allowed Finance Minister Marceau to require compensation payments for the losses faced by Quebec's cheese producers from the federal government: [385]

> Nous avons exigé du gouvernement fédéral qu'un mécanisme de compensation soit prévu pour compenser nos producteurs laitiers et nos producteurs de fromage. Ce mécanisme de compensation sera établi, dessiné, construit dans la prochaine année, et il n'est pas question, pour notre gouvernement [...] d'entériner et de déposer l'accord de libre-échange tant que nous n'aurons pas cette garantie.

Disengaging from responsibility on agricultural policy and constructing agriculture as an issue of provincial heterogeneity legitimised Quebec to ask for financial compensation for losses encountered by Quebec producers. The compensation mechanism the PQ government had required further legitimised accepting increased import quotas. In order to acquire this bargaining power, Quebec insisted on written assurances from the federal government. This letter was important to confer higher bargaining power vis-à-vis the federal government on the provincial government.[386] On 13 October 2013, federal Minister for Trade Ed Fast addressed a letter to Quebec's Minister for Finance Nicolas Marceau in which he made three points.[387] First, the federal government committed to compensating the cheese industry if a negative impact upon revenues materialised as a consequence of CETA's increase in European cheese quota. Second, the compensation mechanism would be determined before the formal ratification process in Quebec's National Assembly. Third, the federal government asked Quebec's government for assistance in determining how compensation procedures would be designed.

In the April 2014 general elections, the Liberal Party defeated the incumbent Parti Québécois. Although agriculture had become salient in political discourse and had triggered public debate about the benefits and

---

384 Interview with member of Quebec's government (2012-2014), Quebec, 1 October 2014.

385 Nicolas Marceau, Assemblée nationale du Québec, 22 October 2013.

386 Interview with member of Quebec's government (2012-2014), Québec, 1 October 2014.

387 The letter has been filed in Quebec's National Assembly by deputy Villeneuve (PQ) on 2 July 2014.

drawbacks of supply management, CETA played a minor role in the election campaigns. Political parties focused on identity debates, such as language (Projet de loi 14),[388] or social and national cohesion (Projet de loi 60).[389] At the end of the PQ's term in office, Quebec had accepted increased tariff-rate quotas for fine and industrial cheese through the deployment of a discursive strategy highlighting the overall benefits of CETA for province-building. At the same time, the PQ also highlighted that the federal government, not Quebec, was in charge of negotiating tariffs and quotas; through this use of the repertoire of federalism, the PQ government could shift the blame for this negotiation result to the federal level. Overall, the reaction the PQ exhibited showed that a shift of interests took place in Quebec against the backdrop of a replacement of the state dirigisme frame through the small open economy frame.

c) Anchoring Agriculture as a Federal Issue (05.2014-12.2014)

Under the Liberal government, the repertoires of federalism and of province-building both continued to structure political discourse on CETA's agricultural chapter.

The compensation of Quebec's cheese producers was a key topic between May and December 2014, when the official CETA negotiation was closed and deputies debated whether Quebec had represented its interests well during the negotiation. Quebec's representatives focused on the specific design of compensation from the federal government. Unexpectedly, Liberal Premier Philippe Couillard suggested that his government would not sacrifice the agreement for cheese, as reported by the Quebec daily newspaper *Le Devoir* in June 2014 (2014). Accordingly, Quebec would ratify the agreement even without a detailed plan to compensate the province and its producers.

After its defeat, the PQ became the official opposition party. Since the PQ representatives had introduced federal issue ownership and required compensation for their producers, its deputies could not criticize the PLQ on the ground that they did not oppose an increase in cheese quotas. Ra-

---

388 Loi modifiant la Charte de la langue française, la Charte des droits et libertés de la personne et d'autres dispositions législatives.

389 Charte affirmant les valeurs de laïcité et de neutralité religieuse de l'État ainsi que d'égalité entre les femmes et les hommes et encadrant les demandes d'accommodement.

ther, the PQ focused on the ratification process. PQ deputies questioned the Liberals' position to ratify CETA even if no prior agreement was found with the federal government on the exact design of the compensation mechanism. According to them, the Liberal government's position considerably weakened Quebec's bargaining position.

In fact, the exact design of the compensation had not been clarified yet. Several groups advocated different compensation systems. There were three different conceptions about how to design compensations for losses engendered by increased imports of European cheese. A first option consisted in organising direct financial compensation to those producers most affected by more competitive products. According to a representative of the UPA, middle-sized cheese producers would be most affected: they managed to become part of large distributing chains and therefore faced direct price competition. Smaller producers, to the contrary, usually benefitted from a local distribution chain and customer loyalty based on the quality of their product.[390] A second option was to grant the most affected producers the new import quota. In this way, losses engendered by increased competition would be balanced by income generated by the commercialisation of European cheese. This option would mean a shift from production to distribution.[391] At the federal level, Canadian milk producers supported the management of new tariff-rate quotas to the benefit of dairy producers (Office of the Commissioner of Lobbying of Canada, 2016). Third, compensation payments could be used to generate new demand in other Canadian provinces, and to increase Quebec demand, to absorb the increased volume of cheese on the Canadian market. The UPA favoured this option. In fact, according to its representatives, an analysis of the development of cheese production in Quebec reveals that marketing activities generated consumer demand for speciality cheese in Quebec. This process in Quebec made the UPA confident that a similar process could be launched in the other provinces. In this way, Quebec could continue to serve a niche market of fine cheese and acquire a competitive advantage over other provinces which have not invested in fine cheese production.[392]

The conflict between the Liberals and the PQ centred on the question whether Quebec's government should ratify CETA in the National Assembly if the federal government had not presented a fully-fledged plan to compensate cheese producers for potential losses. Discussions now revol-

---

390 Interview with UPA representative, Longueuil, 17 October 2014.
391 Interview with Quebec diplomat, Montreal, 15 October 2014.
392 Interview with UPA representative, Longueuil, 17 October 2014.

ved around the question how the compensation should be designed and if it should be tied to the ratification process. For instance, André Villeneuve (PQ), official opposition critic for agriculture and food, filed a motion—which failed—in the National Assembly, together with Amir Khadir (Québec solidaire) and Sylvie D'Amours (CAQ) to commit the deputies not to submit CETA for ratification *prior* to full knowledge of the compensation mechanism.[393]

Sylvie d'Amours (CAQ), second opposition critic for agriculture, vigorously opposed a flexible negotiation position according to which the government might ratify the agreement even without a fully-fledged plan on how to compensate cheese producers. In her opinion, such a flexible negotiation position jeopardised the power relations between Quebec and the federal government and weakened Quebec's position in the federation. According to her, Quebec should not accept to ratify the agreement if there was no detailed plan concerning the compensation of agricultural producers. The agricultural chapter also revealed, however, internal conflicts within the party, as it did for the PQ. On two occasions after D'Amours contribution, Stéphane Le Bouyonnec (CAQ), second opposition spokesperson for economic affairs and trade, highlighted in the Assembly that the government needed to retain a flexible position and focus on the overall gains CETA brought to Quebec. His reply underlined the cleavages within his party, a pattern that is repeated across various parties and which stems from different frames that structure the ways party members interpret province-building and Canadian federalism.

Meanwhile, because it did not take the federal government's commitment for compensatory measures for granted, Quebec's government tried to develop a coalitional strategy supporting compensatory measures. Building coalitions with other provinces was not an easy task, given that many of them had waited for an opportunity to challenge the existing distribution of production quota among provinces, as explained above. Liberal Minister for Agriculture Pierre Paradis tried to coalesce with Ontario, the second largest dairy producing province and with other provinces' Ministers for agriculture during the annual meeting of federal, provincial and territorial Ministers for Agriculture, usually held in July. He also re-included the UPA in Quebec's coalitional strategy to represent Quebec's producers, even though producer representatives' "capacity to prevail [through] the ability of farm groups to forge alliances with provincial governments"

---

393 André Villeneuve, Amir Khadir, Sylvie D'Amours, Assemblée nationale du Québec, 12 June 2014 (motion).

(Skogstad, 2007, p. 27) proved to be fragile during the official negotiation process. Paradis consulted with them on the design of the compensatory mechanisms: [394]

> [Les Ministres de l'Agriculture se rencontrent] à Winnipeg le 16, 17 juillet prochain. Moi, j'ai déjà contacté mon collègue de l'Ontario par-ce que les producteurs de l'est de l'Ontario vivent — les producteurs laitiers — le même problème que les producteurs québécois. On a be-soin d'une solidarité pancanadienne dans ce dossier-là, et j'ai l'intenti-on de travailler dans ce sens-là.

The Liberal government also evaluated Quebec's interest against the back-drop of the federalism repertoire, arguing that an increased in-tariff-rate cheese quota on Quebec. To the contrary, the Canadian internal market would provide Quebec producers with new export opportunities. Quebec's government supported producers in establishing themselves in Ontario, Alberta and other provinces. Furthermore, increased cheese volumes would allow Quebec producers to adapt to new markets and become more export-oriented. Embedding Quebec cheese production firmly in the Ca-nadian market would allow to absorb increased volumes of cheese. Minis-ter Paradis argued in this line:

> Moi, je fais confiance au gouvernement fédéral, je suis un fédéraliste — autant que vous, j'imagine — mais je veux être là pour les analyser, les dégâts, puis exiger les compensations. Puis on n'a pas arrêté là, là. Moi, la semaine dernière encore, quand on parlait de regarder l'avenir avec un peu d'optimisme, là, on a signé des conventions où on aide une fromagerie québécoise, puis on est prêts à en aider d'autres à s'en aller sur le marché de Toronto, sur le marché de Calgary puis sur le marché de Vancouver. Parce qu'on n'attendra pas que l'entente soit ra-tifiée, là, on va, tout de suite, aller à l'assaut des marchés. Je pense qu'on produit au Canada à peu près les meilleurs fromages. Je pense qu'on peut se dire ça, là, humblement sans se péter les bretelles puis sans passer pour des chauvins. Ça fait que, si on peut aller les vendre sur le marché de Toronto, puis sur le marché de Calgary, puis sur d'au-tres marchés, on va y aller, puis on va assister nos producteurs là-dedans.[395]

---

394 Pierre Paradis (PLQ), Assemblée nationale du Québec, 7 July 2014.
395 Pierre Paradis (PLQ), Assemblée nationale du Québec, Commission de l'agricul-ture, des pêcheries, de l'énergie et des ressources naturelles, 2 July 2014.

By doing so, Quebec's Liberal government re-interpreted Quebec's interests related to cheese production against the backdrop of the small open economy and the integration frames. As table 32 highlights, the integration frame became important in deputies' discourse during the decision-making stage. Hence, the repertoires of province-building and of federalism mutually reinforced each other.

Table 32 – *Frames at Different Negotiation Stages (Percentages of Total Discourse at Specified Negotiation Stage, 2006-2014)*

	12.2006-05.2009	06.2009-09.2012	10.2012-04.2014	05.2014-12.2014
Small Open Economy	24	15	11	18
State Dirigisme	76	70	76	50
Independence	0	7	4	12
Integration	0	8	8	20
	100 %	100 %	100 %	100%

Source: Analysis of parliamentary debates (plenary and committees, N=43,811words)

These policy changes also affected the existing management practices in the agri-food sector, including the production, transformation, distribution and consumption practices. In fact, the result of CETA negotiations empowered distributors to the detriment of producers. While supply management had initially been a policy that sought to improve the bargaining power producers had vis-à-vis processors by guaranteeing producers a fixed income, the new policies suggested with CETA modified this relation in favour of processors and distributors, because the latter control import quota. The three leading cheese distributors Saputo, Parmalat and Agropur, if they acquire new import quota, will have two options at hand. They can either push other Quebec producers out of the market by offering European cheese at lower prices, or realise high return margins by selling at or slightly below Canadian market prices.[396]

Apart from distributors, CETA also empowered producers who rejected the system of supply management and the way the UPA represents agricul-

---

396 Interview with Quebec diplomat, Montreal, 15 October 2014.

tural interests. First, the European demands empowered all those opposed to supply management. In fact, the agricultural market in Quebec cannot simply be considered to be closed and oriented towards domestic consumption. Even though the proponents of a protected agricultural sector downplayed the existence of an export-oriented agriculture production, a large part of the agricultural production in Quebec was export-oriented and internationally competitive, with over CAN 5bn generated in agro-alimentary exports (Gouvernement du Québec, 2012a). CETA also revealed that agricultural producers aggregated within the UPA had conflicting demands. Interestingly, many small local producers started to contest the system. In fact, many small cheese producers operated on local markets and had established a local reputation. They did not succumb to the competition on prices delivered by the large Canadian dairy groups, and consequently did not dread competition from large European companies. Furthermore, small producers started to complain about the production quotas that were allocated to producers. De facto, these production quotas generated a stable income, but also prevented successful (small) entrepreneurs from expansion. Reading off the interests of these producers from the market structure they operate in thus proves difficult. Consequently, international trade has an impact upon internal power structures in Quebec's agricultural sector.

In sum, during the CETA negotiation process (2009-2014), Quebec's position on agricultural trade altered considerably: from rejecting any change to supply management, Quebec came to accept a considerable increase of the tariff-rate import quota for cheese. Even though other negotiation chapters could herald a shift towards the small open economy frame dominating discourses on agriculture in Quebec, this did not happen. Rather, representatives introduced the repertoire of federalism in the discourse. Quebec's governments only accepted this position because dairy quotas were made an issue of federal responsibility, although the exact design of the compensation mechanism had not been specified yet at the end of the formal negotiation process. Under the Liberal government, Quebec furthermore advocated the position that a reconfiguration of the internal Canadian market could absorb increased volumes of cheese in the Canadian market. In this way, they reconfigured the boundaries of the consumer market for cheese.

Conclusion

Traditional theories in trade policy often look at producers' structural position in the international or domestic economy to account for countries' trade policy positions. Regarding the agricultural negotiation in CETA, such a perspective might still be true, given that agricultural negotiations remain dominated by tariffs and quota more than behind-the-border issues. However, looking at Quebec's policy position on CETA's agricultural chapter exclusively through the lens of structural factors cannot account for the province's change regarding its position on agriculture. In fact, export-oriented and import-competing producers based in Quebec confronted Quebec's representatives with the difficult choice between pursuing the interests of either one of these groups. Both claimed to contribute to province-building by fostering economic development, albeit in different ways. During the trade negotiations, the incompatibility of the dirigisme and small open economy frames materialised in diverging demands placed upon the provincial government. The agricultural chapter is therefore a key case to demonstrate that political interests do not solely depend on structural factors, but also on the interpretation political representatives make of these structures on the basis of prevailing frames.

At the beginning of the negotiation, provincial representatives wanted to defend supply management at all costs against European demands, in a situation where they conceived of supply management as an instrument for rural development and therefore province-building. At the end of the negotiation, however, provincial representatives made far-reaching concessions by allowing doubling the tariff-free import quota for cheese to Canada. Furthermore, they did not oppose this provision and even tried to legitimise it. How did Quebec's representatives reach the conclusion that doubled quota for cheese were acceptable for Quebec's interests, thereby allowing negotiations to move forward, even though they acted against the wishes of domestic interest groups? In a nutshell, I interpreted this process as a *discursive strategy* that allowed provincial representatives to remodel agriculture as an issue of Canadian federalism. Rather than remaining confined to internal Quebec development policies, political discourse on agriculture widened its scope to encompass a larger, pan-Canadian space. This allowed new stakeholders to enter the stage and altered the relation between stakeholders and spaces. In this strategy, actors shifted repertoires in order to enable collective action. In fact, by highlighting the benefits of inter-provincial trade in agricultural products, the Liberal government offered new development perspectives to its cheese producers and strengthened the internal Canadian market, an objective of the Quebec Liberal's perception of Canadian federalism.

A shift in issue-ownership enabled this policy-shift: the provincial government in Quebec openly refused to take responsibility for the agricultural chapter and the PQ and the Liberal governments repeatedly assured that the full responsibility in matters pertaining to tariffs lay with the federal government. The option to refuse ratification was not pursued, although briefly discussed in the National Assembly. Thereby, the issue cleavage, which had first opened between European and Canadian interests, shifted to become an internal Canadian cleavage. This shift enabled the representatives of Quebec to find an inner-Canadian solution to the requirements of international trade, which was based on the fact that Quebec did *not* claim issue leadership.

More than mere rhetoric, this shift in the way interests were developed guided actors' choices among a multitude of potential choices; it had consequences on the relation between the federal government and the provinces, and on the internal Canadian market. In fact, the representation of heterogeneous provincial interests allowed provincial representatives to legitimately ask for compensation payments for their producers, thereby establishing a new system of inter-provincial transfers in agriculture. At the same time, this discursive strategy also allowed the Liberal government to further its strategy of Canadian market integration. It also had consequences for domestic practices in agriculture: the negotiation result challenged the power relations between producers, on the one hand, and processors and distributors, on the other hand. It also affected spatial development, since it reconfigured the internal Canadian market and might lead to a reduction of very small farms in Quebec's Northern areas. Although the increased quota for cheese did not thwart the entire system of agricultural support in Quebec at first glance, they transformed agricultural practices and challenged existing power relations by questioning two fundamental principles on which the Quebec system of agricultural production relied, namely the collective control of agricultural output in poultry, egg and milk production, on the one hand, and privileged access of agricultural unions to provincial decision-makers, on the other hand.

The case of agriculture highlighted the added value of actor-centred constructivism in international trade policy negotiations. Since the structural position of agricultural actors in the international and domestic markets and the high political influence of organised agricultural interests would have led to another outcome than the one observed empirically, agriculture becomes an important case in support of a more constructivist reading of international trade policy. Agriculture is also a case that considerably increases the generalisability of the framework developed earlier. It is one of the very few sectors where tariffs and quotas still played a predominant role in the negotiations. Therefore, conventional trade policy explanations could have prevailed. Furthermore, the analysis of cheese quota, as a commodity under supply management, illustrates how a policy that has shown particular resilience to agricultural internationalization—other instruments such as the Canadian Wheat Board have already been abolished—were subject to a policy shift.

Furthermore, the way Quebec's representatives constructed their interest on agriculture during the CETA negotiations differed from their stance taken on the later Trans-Pacific Partnership (TPP), signed in 2016: during a 2015 negotiation round, Quebec's Minister for Agriculture staged a defence event on dairy production together with the Ministers for Agriculture from Ontario, Nova Scotia and New Brunswick, as the *Globe and Mail* reported on the 1st of October 2015 (Chase, 2015). With the CETA negotiations, we observed thus a one-time and unexpected change in the way Quebec's representatives developed the provincial interest on agricultural trade through a discursive strategy centred on Canadian market integration. This shows that the definition of provincial interests depended not only on the structural condition of the province's agricultural production in the global and domestic economy (because it did not change between CETA and the TPP), but also on the interpretation provincial representatives made of the contribution that international trade provisions could make to province-building and the reconfiguration of the Canadian federal setting. These long-term development projects embed the way representatives developed their interests. Hence, the dynamics between trade negotiations and these projects influence the way representatives develop and re-evaluate interests.

Conclusion: results and outlook

In the preceding chapters, I documented how Quebec's representatives constructed their policy position on trade. Focussing on four cases—agenda-setting, public procurement, foreign direct investment and agriculture—I demonstrated that discursive processes played a key role in trade policy-making and that a systematic empirical analysis of political discourse contributes to a better understanding of contemporary trade policy and complements conventional approaches by including provincial development projects in the analysis. The investigation of the repertoires and frames representatives utilised shed light on the discursive construction of trade policy through which collective action was made possible: as representatives moved along the negotiation process, they deployed discursive and coalitional strategies.

Throughout the negotiation process, provincial representatives followed three different discursive strategies, as the following table summarises. Representatives either shifted their repertoire to adjust their discourse, or they restructured a repertoire, or engaged in discursive reconciliation.

Table 33 – Summary of Repertoires, Frames and Discursive Strategies Deployed by Quebec's Representatives

	Repertoires	Dominant Frames	Discursive Strategy
Agenda-Setting	– Province-Building – Federalism	– Small Open Economy	– Discursive Conciliation
Public Procurement	– Province-Building – Federalism (lesser degree)	– State Dirigisme – Small Open Economy – Integration	– Restructuring Repertoire of Province-Building
Investment	– Province-Building – Federalism (lesser degree)	– State Dirigisme – Small Open Economy – Integration	– Discursive Conciliation
Agriculture	– Province-Building – Federalism	– State Dirigisme – Independence – Integration	– Changing Repertoire

Public procurement and agriculture most visibly demonstrated the utility of my theoretical and conceptual framework, because they represented instances where representatives re-evaluated provincial interests, without there being any structural change to the position of local producers in the domestic or international economy.

In the case of public procurement, representatives re-structured the repertoire of province-building. Before the CETA negotiations, representatives evaluated provincial procurement contracts as a tool for their dirigiste practices; during the negotiations, however, they re-evaluated their interests because they accorded high importance to the new export opportunities European procurement markets could offer to their companies. This process illustrated that interests change when actors change the discourse underpinning them. In reworking their strategy, representatives abandoned the frame of state dirigisme that had structured public procurement for decades, and adopted the small open economy frame while staying within the repertoire of province-building. In a situation where Quebec suffered from collusion and where its representatives wanted to acquire access to the European procurement markets for their companies, they re-evaluated provincial interests. They concluded that Quebec was too small not to open its procurement markets to foreign competition and reckoned that increased competition would benefit the provincial budget and their companies. Instead of clinging to closed procurement markets as an instrument of development, Quebec's representatives came to represent opening these markets as an asset for provincial economic development against the backdrop of a shift from the state dirigisme to the small open economy frame. They represented this shift in the province-building project in step with their previous positions on public procurement, even though actual behaviour changed considerably. In this discursive process, the repertoire of federalism and the two different frames structuring it in the Quebec Liberals' and the PQ's discourse respectively oriented how representatives perceived of Quebec's interests and fed into their respective strategies. In this way, the repertoires of province-building and federalism interacted on some occasions. In addition, representatives also promoted the integration frame and contributed, in this way, to Canadian internal market integration. Therefore, they offered European companies access to their procurement markets *because* of their province-building project, not in spite of it.

In the case of agriculture, representatives altered the repertoire in which they embedded their discourse when they became aware that restructuring the existing repertoire of province-building would not allow them to find a viable coalition on agriculture. In fact, they did not evaluate European demands regarding increased cheese imports as a threat to supply management, while other influential actors did. In a situation where agricultural production was strongly structured by the dirigisme frame, representatives could not simply restructure province-building according to the small open economy frame, as they had done for provincial public procurement. Consequently, they had to find another discursive strategy allowing them to continue pursuing the strategy of dirigisme established in the 1980s. In fact, in the middle of the negotiation process, they changed their repertoire: while the representation of their interests had been cast in terms of province-building before, they now remodelled provincial interests in agriculture in terms of the repertoire of federalism. By doing so, they re-evaluated their interests in terms of the configuration of the internal Canadian market and the political relations among the provinces and the federal government. By finding a compensation mechanism straightening out the differences among Canadian provinces, Quebec's representatives could legitimately keep to the dirigisme frame, both in the eyes of domestic party political and agricultural lobby opposition, representatives from the Canadian federal and other provincial governments, as well as European negotiators. At the same time, especially the Liberal government also promoted the export of cheese produced in Quebec to other Canadian provinces, thereby contributing to Canadian internal market integration and to rural economic development. In this way, they were able to accept some of the demands from the EU without threatening not to ratify CETA. Similar to public procurement, this shift highlights that interests change when actors re-evaluate them against the backdrop of a different discourse and a new repertoire.

Even though the agenda-setting and foreign direct investment cases did not represent instances where provincial representatives re-evaluated their interests, they nevertheless exemplify how representatives adjusted and reworked their discursive strategies to construct their interests and convince their opponents to follow them. In these instances, they devised strategies of discursive conciliation, which allowed their opponents to adhere to their strategy. In this process, the repertoire of province-building played a key role. It was sometimes complemented by the federalism repertoire. In fact, opponents joined representatives' strategies in the name of their common goal of provincial economic, political, spatial and social development, albeit for diverging reasons. Regarding agenda-setting, the Quebec Liberal Party drew upon the cross-party consensus established since NAFTA, namely that Quebec as a small economy needed to engage in international activities to promote provincial development and that they had the constitutional prerogative to do so. For the PQ, provincial economic development was a way to strengthen the province's economic independence from the Canadian market, a dimension of the PQ representatives' representation of Canadian federalism. At the same time, the Liberals also used the small open economy frame to convince European negotiators of the necessity to include Canadian provinces in the negotiation process, because many issues included in contemporary trade negotiations fall under their jurisdiction. Hence, Quebec's political and economic projects interlocked in this instance, and were brought together by its representatives' discursive strategy to launch trade and investment negotiations between Canada and the EU.

Foreign direct investment was a case where representatives' discourse at the beginning and the end of the CETA negotiation remained essentially the same. However, comparing these two moments in time obscures the discursive struggles that provincial representatives engaged in during the negotiations. In fact, some PQ deputies as well as societal groups strongly contested the course of action suggested by the Liberal government and tried to impose the dirigisme frame: they claimed that CETA investment provisions threatened provincial regulatory capacity. Therefore, the Liberals had to engage in a strategy of discursive reconciliation in which they reminded their opponents of the benefits of free trade for Quebec's overall province-building project.

This review of the various discursive strategies that provincial representatives deployed throughout the negotiation process allows me to make two remarks about my contributions to trade policy analysis and actor-centred constructivist literature.

First, and contrary to the expectations raised by conventional accounts of trade policy that highlight the importance of the position a state or sector occupies in the domestic or international economy, looking only at structural factors leaves several questions unanswered. On the one hand, although provincial interests can be traced back in most cases to specific sectoral interests, these accounts do not explain why provincial representatives favoured one set of sectoral interests over competing ones. In these complex situations, my framework documented that actors embedded the interests they had developed in larger societal, in Quebec's case: province-building, projects, thereby legitimising when they gave what to whom. This raises awareness for the constructed nature of trade policy interests. On the other hand, accounts based on the location in the domestic or international economy are not well suited to explain outcomes in contemporary non-tariff trade issues which cut across sectors, and reflect public policy choices that have historically grown and do not necessarily reflect sectoral interests. The growing relevance of non-tariff barriers, the increasing issue complexity and uneven economic integration across policy fields in trade negotiations requires these new analytical instruments.

Looking at trade policy through this lens acknowledges that actors do not simply *carry* interests with them, but need to identify them in complex situations while facing multiple and sometimes incommensurate demands. Thus, interests do not simply follow from the position actors occupy in the international economy. As documented, actors move through the different stages of the negotiation process, identify, discursively construct and constantly re-evaluate their interests, and appeal to potential coalition partners. By making choices, they stabilise a certain interpretation of material reality. While the clock is ticking, they make decisions and explain these decisions publicly in order to legitimise them and allow for collective action in the complex fields of international trade. They strategically link their decisions to past events and project them into the future. Thereby, they stabilise a certain interpretation of the material facts that they face and develop their interests. In this process of strategic *discursive* stabilisation, the discursive construction of interests and the strategies representatives developed were co-constitutive. Hence, trade interests are not stable, unequivocal or predictable. To the contrary, they are frequently context-dependent, multifaceted and unstable. For this reason, actors may develop an interest in supporting free trade while at the same time recognising issues where they challenge trade agendas. This ambivalence occurs frequently and stems from the simultaneous embeddedness of actors in a multitude of discourses.

Second, my contribution to actor-centred constructivism is of a conceptual nature. By developing concepts that capture unfolding discursive processes, I documented these processes empirically and through a systematic analysis. Furthermore, my concepts offer one answer among many to the question where and how the interests and ideas actors mobilise originate. Furthermore, I also demonstrated that, in order to be successful, actors need an institutional basis to make their claim (see for a similar argument Jegen and Mérand, 2013); actors grounded their claims either in constitutional prerogatives or existing practices. However, my analyses recorded that institutional variables do not have a linear effect. Rather, actors can, within certain limits, engage creatively with the structures in that they are embedded. Sometimes, these structures become relevant in discourse and sometimes they do not. Whether they matter for actors depends more on their discursive needs in a specific situation than on constitutional factors;

in fact, representatives engaged creatively with the institutions of federalism which could be seen in the case of public procurement: before CETA, they served provincial representatives to legitimise closing their public procurement markets to foreign competitors, while they now instrumentalised them to acquire a seat at the CETA negotiation table.

As highlighted already, the discourses actors deployed had consequences for their negotiation position and the subsequent CETA outcome. In addition to the impact of actors' discourses on the outcome of the CETA negotiations, it also impacted upon internal Canadian market integration. Chrystia Freeland, the Canadian Minister of International Trade, reported in a public interview that, "CETA has been a big driver of that agreement [...] between our provinces [Agreement on Internal Trade]" (Freeland, 2016, sequence 59:30-1:00:45). On the other hand, representatives' discourse also reconfigured lines of societal conflict and cleavage, by changing the power relations between various societal groups. These shifts will probably have impacts far beyond the direct effects of CETA.

These empirical results also opened avenues for further research. First, my framework of analysis could be developed further by carrying out a comparison across political systems to show, on the one hand, how repertoires and frames vary across places, and, on the other hand, in which situations they are most likely to influence policy makers' decision. In fact, the strong tradition of state dirigisme in Quebec, combined with a highly salient development project, might have rendered repertoires and frames more visible than in other political systems. Furthermore, it calls for a more detailed analysis of contemporary trade policy-making at the sub-federal, but also on the municipal or community levels. These levels will become increasingly relevant actors in trade policy, not only because they have the formal power to block implementation, but also because they might simply refrain from taking part in the processes of *positive* economic integration through a convergence of regulatory and administrative practices in areas which only recently came centre-stage on trade agendas.

Primary Empirical Sources[397]

I. Press Articles and Opinion Pieces

Anonymous/ Le Devoir. 2014. Philippe Couillard abandonne les producteurs de fromage, accuse le PQ. *Le Devoir*, 21 June.

Anonymous/ Radio Canada avec Agence France Presse. 2013. Québec ouvert à l'accord Canada-UE malgré les quotas de fromage. *Radio Canada avec Agence France Presse*, 11 February.

BÉLAIR-CIRINO, M. 2013. Libre-échange Canada-UE: un appui sans réserve du Québec. Ottawa s'est engagé à verser des indemnisations aux producteurs de lait et de fromage. *Le Devoir*, 19 October.

BERGERON, M. 2007. Charest propose un 'plan B' à Doha. Le premier ministre veut faire le libre-échange avec l'Union européenne. *La Presse*, 27 January.

BÉRUBÉ, S. 2016. Poulet et oeufs: de petits producteurs réclament le droit de grandir. *La Presse*, 11 April.

CHAREST, J. 2008. Un nouvel espace économique pour le Québec. *La Presse*, 26 March.

CHASE, S. 2015. Canada's provincial farm ministers unite against TPP. *The Globe and Mail*, 1 October 2015.

CHASSIN, Y. & GELOSO, V. 2013. *C'est le camembert qui fait et défait les gouvernements*. Montréal: Montreal Economic Institute.

CHAREST, J. 2008. Un nouvel espace économique pour le Québec. *La Presse*, 26 March.

CHARLEBOIS, S. 2013. System that keeps dairy prices high needs adjustment. *The Gazette*, B07.

CORRIVEAU, J. 2010. Voitures de métro – La loi spéciale adoptée à l'unanimité à Québec. *Le Devoir*, 8 Octobre.

COUSINEAU, S. 2012. PQ a wild card in Quebec's attitude to free trade. *The Globe and Mail*, 2 October.

DAWSON, L. 2013. *How soon will we get cheaper cheese? Managing expectations for the CETA*. Fraser Institute.

DUBUC, A. 2013. La loi du camembert. *La Presse*, 5 June.

LAROCQUE, S. 2013. Pauline Marois pourrait mettre des bâtons dans les roues du libre-échange avec l'Europe. *La Presse*, 28 January.

---

397 Excluding interviews conducted, see chapter 1, section 3 for a comprehensive overview.

MCGREGOR, J. 2012. 5 key issues in the Canada-EU trade deal. 2-day ministerial talks in Brussels attempt to nail down final details of agreement. *CBC News*.

NORMAND, F. 2013. Quotas de fromage: Québec pourrait faire un compromis. *Les Affaires*, 11 February.

RIENDEAU, S. 2013. Libre-échange – Le Canada ne doit pas sacrifier ses fermiers laitiers, dit Agropur. *Le Devoir*, 14 February.

ROBITAILLE, A. 2008. Charest mise sur le Nord. *Le Devoir*, 29 September.

SÉGUIN, R. 2012. PQ sees economic nationalism as key to a better future. *The Globe and Mail*, 9 August.

II. Policy Documents

1. Overview of Parliamentary Debates on Trade with Europe in Quebec's National Assembly (2008-2014)

Government led by Jean Charest (Parti Libéral du Québec)	
Assembly	13 March 2008
Assembly	19 March 2008
Assembly	13 June 2008
Assembly	29 October 2008
Committee – Finances publiques	3 April 2008
Committee – Institutions	16 April 2008
Assembly	10 March 2009
Assembly	19 March 2009
Committee – Économie et travail	30 April 2009
Committee – Institutions	1 May 2009
Committee – Institutions	27 April 2010
Assembly	28 April 2010
Committee – Économie et travail	29 April 2010
Committee – Agriculture, pêcheries, énergie et ressources naturelles	5 May 2010
Committee – Économie et travail	6 May 2010
Committee – Institutions (=1st hearing of Pierre-Marc Johnson)	6 October 2010
Assembly	5 October 2011

Assembly	6 October 2011
Assembly	19 October 2011
Assembly	2 November 2011
Assembly	10 November 2011
Assembly	15 November 2011
Assembly	1 December 2011
Assembly	2 December 2011
Assembly	6 December 2011
Committee – Institutions (=2nd hearing of Pierre-Marc Johnson)	8 December 2011
Assembly	16 February 2012
Assembly / Petition	16 February 2012
Government led by Pauline Marois (Parti Québécois)	
Committee – Aménagement du territoire	26 April 2012
Assembly	28 November 2012
Committee – Agriculture, pêcheries, énergie et ressources naturelles	13 February 2013
Committee – Culture et éducation	13 February 2013
Committee – Finances publiques	13 February 2013
Assembly	14 February 2013
Committee – Économie et travail	14 February 2013
Committee – Institutions	15 February 2013
Committee – Institutions	18 February 2013
Assembly	10 April 2013
Assembly	22 October 2013
Assembly	24 October 2013
Assembly	6 November 2013
Assembly	12 February 2014
Assembly / Petition	12 February 2014
Government led by Philippe Couillard (Parti Libéral du Québec)	
Assembly	21 May 2014
Assembly	12 June 2014
Committee – Finances publiques	12 June 2014

Assembly	13 June 2014
Committee – Transports et environnement	19 June 2014
Committee – Institutions	30 June 2014
Committee – Agriculture, pêcheries, énergie et ressources naturelles	2 July 2014
Committee – Institutions	2 July 2014
Assembly	3 July 2014
Assembly / Submission of letter by the Canadian Minister of International Trade, Ed Fast	3 July 2014
Assembly	2 October 2014

2. Overview of Press Releases on Commerce by the Council of the Federation (2004-2014)

Title	Author	Date
Conseil de la fédération : Plan de Travail	Council of the Federation	23 February 2004
Plan de travail sur le commerce intérieur	Council of the Federation	23 February 2004
Le Conseil de la Fédération prend des mesures pour faciliter le commerce au Canada	Council of the Federation	24 February 2004
Communiqué	Council of the Federation	12 August 2005
Lettre de Paul Martin au Conseil de la fédération	Paul Martin	23 December 2005
Plan de travail sur le commerce intérieur. État d'avancement des travaux	Council of the Federation	1 January 2006
Lettre de Stephen Harper au Conseil de la Fédération	Stephen Harper	12 January 2006
Communiqué	Council of the Federation	28 July 2006

Title	Author	Date
Les premiers ministres s'entendent pour renforcer le commerce	Council of the Fede-ration	10 August 2007
Communiqué	Council of the Fede-ration	28 January 2008
Commerce – Capitaliser sur nos forces, au Canada et à l'étranger	Council of the Fede-ration	18 July 2008
Le Conseil de la fédération réitère sa confiance dans l'économie	Council of the Fede-ration	20 October 2008
Déclaration du Conseil de la fédé-ration : Appui à la négociation d'un nouvel accord économique à portée large avec l'Union europé-enne	Council of the Fede-ration	20 February 2009
Le Conseil de la fédération fait appel aux pays pour annuler l'interdiction d'importer la viande de porc canadienne	Council of the Fede-ration	13 May 2009
Les premiers ministres font des avancées en matière de commerce intérieur	Council of the Fede-ration	7 August 2009
Le Canada dans l'économie mon-diale Une stratégie pour mobili-ser les forces des provinces et des territoires et aider le Canada à être plus concurrentiel dans l'éco-nomie mondiale	Council of the Fede-ration	2011
Government of Newfoundland and Labrador's position on CETA	Newfoundland and Labrador Govern-ment	2014

3. Other Policy Documents and Public Statements

3.1. Governmental/ International Organizational Sources

ADLUNG, R. & MAMDOUH, H. 2013. How to design trade agreements in services: top down or bottom up? *Staff Working Paper ERSD-2013-08*. World Trade Organization, Economic Research and Statistics Division.

BLACKHURST, R. & OTTEN, A. 1996. Trade and foreign direct investment. *New Report by the WTO*. World Trade Organisation.

CAMERON, R. A. & LOUKINE, K. 2001. *Canada – EU Trade and Investment Relations. The Impact of Tariff Elimination*. Department of foreign affairs and international trade. Trade and economic analysis division. Ottawa.

CHAREST, J. 2007. *Jean Charest et Raymond Bachand plaident en faveur d'un accord de libre-échange Canada-Union européenne* [Press conference]. Québec: Gouvernement du Québec (Premier Ministre).

CLARKE, S. F. 2015. *Government Procurement Law and Policy: Canada*. The Library of Congress.

CONSEIL MUNICIPAL DE MONTRÉAL 2012. *Déclaration concernant l'accord économique et commercial global (AECG)*. Montreal.

COUNCIL OF THE EU 2009. *Recommendation from the Commission to the Council in order to authorize the Commission to open negotiations for an Economic Integration Agreement with Canada*. Brussels: Coreper to Council.

COULIBALY, A. L. 2010. *Does the Agreement on Internal Trade Do Enough to Liberalize Canada's Domestic Trade in Agri-food Products?* Library of Parliament Research Publications. Ottawa: Library of Parliament.

DEARDORFF, A. V. & STERN, R. M. 1997. *Measurement of Non-Tariff Barriers*. OECD Economics Department Working Papers. Paris: Organisation for Economic Cooperation and Development.

DUPRAS, D. 1993. *NAFTA: Implementation and the Participation of the Provinces*. [Ottawa]: Library of Parliament/ Law and Government Division, Research Branch.

FREDRIKSSON, T. & ZIMNY, Z. 2004. Foreign Direct Investment and Transnational Corporations. In: KASAHARA, S. & GORE, C. (eds.) *Beyond Conventional Wisdom in Development Policy: An Intellectual History of UNCTAD 1964-2004*. New York, Geneva: United Nations.

EUROPEAN COMMISSION 2016a. *Services and investment in EU trade deals. Using 'positive' and 'negative' lists*. Brussels.

EUROPEAN COMMISSION, DIRECTORATE GENERAL FOR TRADE 2016b. *Canada – Trade Statistics*. Brussels.

EUROPEAN COMMISSION & GOVERNMENT OF CANADA. 2008. *Assessing the Costs and Benefits of a Closer EU-Canada Economic Partnership*. Available online: http://trade.ec.europa.eu/doclib/html/141032.htm [Accessed 1 August 2015].

EUROPEAN UNION & GOVERNMENT OF CANADA 2002. *EU-Canada Summit Declaration*. Joint Statement by the EU and Canada. Ottawa.

EUROPEAN UNION & GOVERNMENT OF CANADA 2008. *EU-Canada Summit Statement*. Quebec.

EUROPEAN UNION & GOVERNMENT OF CANADA 2009. *Joint Report on the EU-Canada Scoping Exercise*.

FAUCHER, P. 1989. Politique d'achat et developpement technologique: le cas d'Hydro-Québec. In: GOUVERNEMENT DU QUÉBEC, CONSEIL DE LA SCIENCE ET DE LA TECHNOLOGIE (ed.) *Le marché public et le développement technologique au Québec. Six rapports d'étude*. Sainte-Foy, Québec.

FEDERATION OF CANADIAN MUNICIPALITIES 2010. *Municipal Principles for Free and Fair International Trade*.

FEDERATION OF CANADIAN MUNICIPALITIES 2013. *Statement by FCM President Following the Signing of the Canada-Europe Trade Agreement*. Ottawa.

FREELAND, C. 2016. *Growing Trade the Progressive Way* [conference contribution]. Department of International Relations public lecture. London: The London School of Economics and Political Science.

GLOBAL AFFAIRS CANADA 2013a. *Canada-EU Trade and Investment Enhancement Agreement*. Ottawa: Government of Canada.

GLOBAL AFFAIRS CANADA. 2013b. *Canada – U.S. Agreement on Government Procurement* [Online]. Available: http://www.international.gc.ca/trade-agreements-a ccords-commerciaux/agr-acc/other-autre/us-eu.aspx?lang=eng [Accessed].

GORDON, W. C. 1957. *Royal Commission on Canada's Economic Prospects*.

GOUVERNEMENT DU QUÉBEC 2007. *Commerce international des marchandises du Québec*. Institut de la statistique. Québec.

GOUVERNEMENT DU QUÉBEC 2007-2013. *Consommation d'énergie par forme*. Ministère de l'énergie et des ressources naturelles.

GOUVERNEMENT DU QUÉBEC 2009. *Faire Affaire avec l'Etat. Introduction aux Accords de Libéralisation*. Secrétariat du Conseil du Trésor. Quebec.

GOUVERNEMENT DU QUÉBEC [2011]. *Dépenses en immobilisation du secteur privé non résidentiel selon le pays ayant le contrôle de l'entreprise, Québec, 2004-2011*. Institut de la statistique. Québec.

GOUVERNEMENT DU QUÉBEC 2012a. Les exportations bioalimentaires internationales du Québec. Evolution des vingt dernières années et perspectives de croissance. *BioClips+ Regards sur l'industrie agroalimentaire*, 15.

GOUVERNEMENT DU QUÉBEC 2012b. *Capital investment in machinery, equipment and non-residential construction by country of company ownership*. Québec.

GOUVERNEMENT DU QUÉBEC 2013. *Statistiques sur les contrats des organismes publics du réseau de l'Administration gouvernementale. 2012-2013*. Secrétariat du Conseil du Trésor. Québec.

GOUVERNEMENT DU QUÉBEC 2016a. *Annexe. Principaux éléments du nouvel accord de libre-échange Canadien (ALEC)*. Premier Ministre. Québec.

GOUVERNEMENT DU QUÉBEC 2016b. *Marchés publics*. Ministère de l'économie, de la science et de l'innovation. Québec.

GOUVERNEMENT DU QUÉBEC 2016c. *Partage des responsabilités et secteurs d'activité*. Ministère des transports, de la mobilité durable et de l'électrification des transports. Québec.

GOUVERNEMENT DU QUÉBEC 2016d. *Statistiques sur les contrats des organismes publics*. 2014-2015. Direction de l'évaluation de la conformité. Québec.

GOUVERNEMENT DU QUÉBEC 2016e. Ententes internationales [Online]. Available online: http://www.mrif.gouv.qc.ca/fr/ententes-et-engagements/ententes-int ernationales [Accessed 28 February 2017].

GOVERNMENT OF CANADA 1983. *Canadian trade policy for the 1980s : a discussion paper*. Department of External Affaires. Ottawa: Supply and Services Canada.

GOVERNMENT OF CANADA – STATISTICS CANADA 2003. Energy industry in Canada: impact on provincial economies. In: LAURENT, A. (ed.) *Trends in provincial and territorial economic statistics: 1981 – 2002*. Ottawa.

GOVERNMENT OF CANADA 2009. *Top 20 World Dairy Companies – 2009*. Canadian Dairy Information Centre. Ottawa.

GOVERNMENT OF CANADA 2013. *Number of Farms, Dairy Cows and Heifers*. Canadian Dairy Information Centre. [Online]. Available: http://www.dairyinfo. gc.ca/index_e.php?s1=dff-fcil&s2=farm-ferme&s3=nb [Accessed 9 September 2014].

GOVERNMENT OF CANADA 2014a. *An Overview of the Canadian Agriculture and Agri-Food System*. Agriculture and Agri-Food Canada. Ottawa.

GOVERNMENT OF CANADA 2014b. *Levels of Tariff Rate Quotas For Agricultural Products* [Online]. Global Affairs. Ottawa. Available: http://www.international.g c.ca/controls-controles/notices_avis/exp/list_liste/509-access-quant-acces.aspx?lan g=eng [Accessed 25 July 2017].

GOVERNMENT OF CANADA 2014c. *Key points about the dairy manufacturing industry*. Canadian Dairy Information Centre. [Online]. Available: http://www.dai ryinfo.gc.ca/index_e.php?s1=dff-fcil&s2=proc-trans&s3=kp-pc [Accessed 26 March 2015].

GOVERNMENT OF CANADA 2015a. *Manufacturing of Dairy Products – Cheese* Canadian Dairy Information Centre. [Online]. Available: http://dairyinfo.gc.ca/i ndex_e.php?s1=dff-fcil&s2=proc-trans&s3=psdp-pvpl&s4=cp-pf [Accessed 18/05/2016 2016].

GOVERNMENT OF CANADA – STATISTICS CANADA 2015b. Gross domestic product (GDP) at basic prices, by North American Industry Classification System (NAICS), provinces and territories. Cansim table 379-0028. Ottawa.

GOVERNMENT OF CANADA 2016a. *Canadian Dairy Imports – Cheese* Canadian Dairy Information Centre. [Online]. Available: http://www.dairyinfo.gc.ca/inde x_e.php?s1=dff-fcil&s2=imp-exp&s3=imp [Accessed 6 July 2016 2016].

GOVERNMENT OF CANADA 2016b. *10 Key Facts on Canada's Natural Resources*. Natural Resources Canada. Ottawa.

GOVERNMENT OF CANADA 2016c. *Canada-EU: Comprehensive Economic and Trade Agreement (CETA). Technical Summary of the Final Negotiated Outcomes* (October 2013). Global Affairs Canada. Ottawa.

HOEKMAN, B. M. & MAVROIDIS, P. C. 1995. *The World Trade Organization's Agreement on Government Procurement. Expanding Disciplines, Declining Membership?* The World Bank, Europe and Central Asia, and Middle East and North Africa Technical Department, Private Sector and Finance Team, March 1995.

LEMIEUX, R. & JACKSON, J. 1999. Cultural Exceptions in Canada's Major International Trade Agreements and Investment Relationships. *In Brief.* Ottawa: Parliamentary Research Branch, Library of Parliament.

LÉVESQUE, R. 1978. Allocution du Premier ministre Monsieur René Levesque. Secrétariat permanent des conférences socio-économiques. *L'Agro-alimentaire : rapport de la conférence sectorielle tenue à Québec les 10, 11 et 12 avril 1978,* Quebec.

LISÉE, J.-F. 2013. *Québec: des ambitions mondiales.* Discours prononcé devant le CORIM, 11 February 2013.

MARKETPLACE CANADA (MARCAN) 2017. *Statistics on Procurement, total by year/ by party.*

OFFICE OF THE COMMISSIONER OF LOBBYING OF CANADA. 2016. *Les Producteurs de lait du Québec* [Online]. Ottawa. Available: https://lobbycanada.gc.ca/app/secure/ocl/lrs/do/clntSmmry;jsessionid=wrPQ_EHrUnLk5ViCFpesyt3X.app-ocl-01?clientOrgCorpNumber=290805&sMdKy=1363782151119.

ORGANISATION FOR ECONOMIC COOPERATION AND DEVELOPMENT 2015. *General government procurement as percentage of GDP and as share of total government expenditures, 2013. Government at a Glance 2015.* Paris: OECD Publishing.

ROYAL COMMISSION ON THE ECONOMIC UNION AND DEVELOPMENT PROSPECTS FOR CANADA (=MACDONALD COMMISSION) 1985. *Report – Royal Commission on the Economic Union and Development Prospects for Canada.* Ottawa.

SARKOZY, N. 2008a. *Conférence de Presse conjointe de M. Nicolas SARKOZY, Président de la République française, de Monsieur Stephen HARPER, Premier Ministre du Canada, José Manuel BARROSO, Président de la Commission européenne.* Québec.

SARKOZY, N. 2008b. *Discours du Président de la République devant l'Assemblée nationale du Québec.* Québec.

SECRÉTARIAT GÉNÉRAL DES AFFAIRES EUROPÉENNES 2008. *Présidence française du Conseil de l'Union européenne. Bilan et perspectives. 1er juillet – 31 décembre 2008. Une Europe qui agit pour répondre aux defis d'aujourd'hui.*

TETLEY, WILLIAM (CHAIRMAN) 1973, revised 1974. *Le cadre et les moyens d'une politique quebecoise concernant les investissements étrangers : rapport (= Tetley Report).* Québec: Comité interministériel sur les investissements étrangers.

TETLEY, W. 1972. *Lettre à M. Herb Gray, Ministre du Revenu. Reproduced in "Le cadre et les moyens d'une politique québécoise concernant les investissements étrangers"* (*Teltey report, 1974*), 14 June.

TETLEY, W. 1973. *Lettre à M. Alastair Gillespie, Ministre de l'Industrie et du Commerce. Reproduced in "Le cadre et les moyens d'une politique québécoise concernant les investissements étrangers" (Tetley Report, 1974)*, 15 March.

THE STANDING SENATE COMMITTEE ON ENERGY, THE ENVIRONMENT AND NATURAL RESOURCES 2012. *Federal, Provincial and Territorial Energy Jurisdication. Now or Never: Canada Must Act Urgently to Seize its Place in the new Energy World Order.* Ottawa: The Parliament of Canada, Senate.

TORONTO CITY COUNCIL 2012. *City Council Decision. Request to protect City of Toronto interests and existing powers in any trade agreements signed between the Government of Canada and the EU – Motion MM14.14 referred by City Council on November 29, 2011.* Toronto.

WORLD TRADE ORGANIZATION 2015. *Trade Policy Review: Canada.*

WORLD TRADE ORGANIZATION 2016a. *Agreement on Trade Related Investment Measures.*

WORLD TRADE ORGANIZATION 2016b. *Agriculture: fairer markets for farmers* [Online]. Available: https://www.wto.org/english/thewto_e/whatis_e/tif_e/agrm 3_e.htm [Accessed 14 June 2016].

WORLD TRADE ORGANIZATION 2016c. *Glossary* [Online]. Available: https://w ww.wto.org/english/thewto_e/glossary_e/glossary_e.htm [Accessed 14 June 2016].

3.2. Company/ Interest Group Sources

AGROPUR COOPERATIVE 2009. *Annual Report.* Longueuil.

AGROPUR COOPERATIVE 2015. *Analysis of the potential impacts of the end of supply management in the Canadian dairy industry.* Longueil.

ATTAC-QUÉBEC 2008. *L'extension du libre-échange prôné par le Parti libéral du Québec n'est pas une solution pour contrer la crise financière.*

ATTAC-QUÉBEC 2009a. *ATTAC-Québec signe la pétition "Protégeons notre Code de gestion des pesticides! Résistons aux menaces de Dow Chemicals".*

ATTAC-QUÉBEC 2009b. *Consultation sur les négociations commerciales.*

ATTAC-QUÉBEC 2010. *Commentaire envoyé à la Commission des Institutions de l'Assemblée nationale du Québec le 4 octobre 2010.*

ATTAC-QUÉBEC 2013. *Déclaration transatlantique "Arrêtons les cadeaux aux multinationales!".*

CANADA EUROPE ROUND TABLE FOR BUSINESS 1999a. *Canada Europe Round Table Launched.* Brussels.

CANADA EUROPE ROUND TABLE FOR BUSINESS 1999b. *Canadian and EU Government meet with CERT Business Leaders.* Ottawa/Brussels.

CANADA EUROPE ROUND TABLE FOR BUSINESS 1999c. *Recommendations directed at Canadian Government and EU.* Brussels.

CANADA EUROPE ROUND TABLE FOR BUSINESS 2000. *Maclaren to co-chair Canada-Europe Round Table for Business*. Ottawa/Brussels.

CANADA EUROPE ROUND TABLE FOR BUSINESS 2004. *High-Level Energy Conference to Take Place in Brussels*. Brussels.

COUNCIL OF THE CANADIANS 2013. *A Fracktivist's Toolkit. How you can take action to protect water and stop fracking*. Ottawa.

FÉDÉRATION DES CHAMBRES DE COMMERCE DU QUÉBEC 2007. *Le rôle de la Caisse de dépôt et placement du Québec vu par la Fédération des Chambres de commerce du Québec*. Montréal.

FÉDÉRATION DES CHAMBRES DE COMMERCE DU QUÉBEC 2008. *L'indicateur FCCQ*. Édition 2008. Montréal.

FÉDÉRATION DES CHAMBRES DE COMMERCE DU QUÉBEC 2010. *Les indicateurs FCCQ*. Édition 2010. Montréal.

FÉDÉRATION DES CHAMBRES DE COMMERCE DU QUÉBEC 2013. *Pour une vision budgétaire pluriannuelle. Recommandations de la FCCQ au Gouvernement du Québec*.

FRIESEN, R. 2014. Chicken industry struggles with production quota allocation. *Manitoba Co-Operator*.

GOLDFARB, D. 2009. *Making Milk: The Practices, Players, and Pressures Behind Dairy Supply Management*. Ottawa: The Conference Board of Canada.

HYDRO-QUÉBEC 2010. *Rapport annuel 2009. Façonner l'avenir*. Montréal.

PARMALAT 2009. *Annual Report*. Collecchio.

RÉSEAU QUÉBÉCOIS SUR L'INTÉGRATION CONTINENTALE 2013. *Accord de libre-échange Canada–Union européenne (AÉCG) – Notre souveraineté est prise d'assaut*.

SAPUTO 2009. *Notice annuelle*.

SOCIÉTÉ DE TRANSPORT DE MONTRÉAL. *1997-2016. Histoire du métro* [Online]. Available: http://www.stm.info/fr/a-propos/decouvrez-la-STM-et-son-histoi re/histoire/histoire-du-metro [Accessed 30 August 2016].

SOCIÉTÉ DE TRANSPORT DE MONTRÉAL 2010. *Contract signing for the procurement of Montréal's métro cars. New cars introduced into service starting in 2014*. 22 October 2010.

SYNDICAT CANADIEN DE LA FONCTION PUBLIQUE & CONSEIL DES CANADIENS 2010. *Eau publique à vendre : comment le Canada va privatiser nos systèmes publics d'eau*. Rapport aux gouvernements provinciaux, territoriaux et municipaux concernant l'Accord économique et commercial global (AECG) entre le Canada et l'Union européenne.

TRADE JUSTICE NETWORK, TONY BIDDLE 2010. *Top Ten Reasons Why CETA is Bad for Canada*.

TRADE JUSTICE NETWORK/ RÉSEAU POUR UN COMMERCE JUSTE 2010. *Accord de libre-échange Canada-Union européenne : quels enjeux pour le Québec, face à quelle Europe? Conférence publique avec des représentants du mouvement social européen.* Conference organized in collaboration with Institut d'ètudes internationales de Montréal et Attac-Québec. 20 April, Montreal.

UNION PAYSANNE 2014. *Vers une gestion de l'offre 2.0 au Canada. + de fermes, de paysans, de relève agricole. Document de réflexion.* Lachute, QC.

WILSON, B. 1999. Quota dispute seen as threat to milk system. *The Western Producer.*

III. Legal Cases

Judicial Committee of the Privy Council, Labour Conventions, The Attorney General of Canada versus The Attorney General of Ontario and others 1937.

NAFTA Arbitral Panel, Tariffs Applied by Canada to Certain U.S.-Origin Agricultural Products, 1996.

NAFTA Arbitral Panel, Ethyl Corporation v. Government of Canada, 1997.

WTO Appellate Body, United States v. Canada, 1997.

WTO Appelate Body, Measures Concerning Meat and Meat Products (Hormones), 1998.

NAFTA Arbitral Panel, Dow AgroSciences LLC v. Government of Canada, 2009.

NAFTA Arbitral Panel, Lone Pine Resources Inc. v. Government of Canada, 2013.

Bibliography

ALONS, G. 2013. Farmers versus ideas: explaining the continuity in French agricultural trade policy during the GATT Uruguay Round. *Journal of European Public Policy*, 21, 286-302.

ANDERSON, L. M. 2014. Both Too Much and Too Little: Sources of Federal Instability in Canada. *American Review of Canadian Studies*, 44, 15-27.

ANDERSON, R. D. & ARROWSMITH, S. 2011. The WTO regime on government procurement: past, present and future. In: ARROWSMITH, S. & ANDERSON, R. D. (eds.) *The WTO Regime on Government Procurement: Challenge and Reform*. Cambridge: Cambridge University Press.

ANGERMÜLLER, J. & SCHWAB, V. 2014. Zu Qualitätskriterien und Gelingensbedingungen in der Diskursforschung. In: ANGERMÜLLER, J., NONHOFF, M., HERSCHINGER, E., MACGILCHRIST, F., REISIGL, M., WEDL, J., WRANA, D. & ZIEM, A. (eds.) *Diskursforschung. Ein interdisziplinäres Handbuch. Band 1: Theorien, Methodologien und Kontroversen*. Bielefeld: Transcript.

ARNDT, S. W. 2012. Free trade and its alternatives. In: KREININ, M. & PLUMMER, M. G. (eds.) *The Oxford handbook of international commercial policy*. Oxford, New York: Oxford University Press.

ATKEY, R. G. 1971. The Role of the Provinces in International Affairs. *International Journal: Canada's Journal of Global Policy Analysis*, 26, 249-273.

ATKINSON, M. M., BÉLAND, D., MARCHILDON, G. P., MCNUTT, K., PHILLIPS, P. W. B. & RASMUSSEN, K. 2013. *Governance and Public Policy in Canada: A View from the Provinces*, Toronto, University of Toronto Press.

AVERYT, W. F. 1989. Quebec's Economic Development Policies, 1960–1987: Between Étatisme and Privatisation. *American Review of Canadian Studies*, 19, 159-175.

BACCHI, C. 2010. Policy and Discourse: Challenging the Construction of Affirmative Action as Preferential Treatment. *Journal of European Public Policy*, 11, 128-146.

BALTHAZAR, L. 1988. Quebec's Triangular Situation in North America: A Prototype? In: DUCHACEK, I. D., LATOUCHE, D. & STEVENSON, G. (eds.) *Perforated sovereignties and international relations : trans-sovereign contacts of subnational governments*. New York: Greenwood Press.

BALTHAZAR, L. 2003. Les relations internationales du Québec. In: GAGNON, A.-G. (ed.) *Québec. Etat et Société*. Montréal: Éditions Québec/Amérique.

BANDELJ, N. 2011. Relevance of nationality in cross-border economic transactions. *The Journal of Nationalism and Ethnicity*, 39, 963-976.

BANTING, K. 2005. Canada: nation-building in a federal welfare state. In: OB-INGER, H., LEIBFRIED, S. & CASTLES, F. G. (eds.) *Federalism and the Welfare State. New World and European Experiences.* Cambridge, New York e.a.: Cambridge University Press.

BARA, J., WEALE, A. & BICQUELET, A. 2007. Analysing Parliamentary Debate with Computer Assistance. *Swiss Political Science Review*, 13, 577-605.

BARICHELLO, R., CRANFIELD, J. & MEILKE, K. 2009. Options for the Reform of Supply Management in Canada with Trade Liberalization. *Canadian Public Policy / Analyse de Politiques*, 35, 203-217.

BARROWS, D. & JANSEN, G. 1991. International Trade and the Management of Federal-Provincial Relations. In: BROWN, D. M. & SMITH, M. G. (eds.) *Canadian Federalism: Meeting Global Economic Challenges.* Kingston, ON: Institute of Intergovernmental Relations and Institute for Research on Public Policy.

BAUMGARTNER, F. R., DE BOEF, S. & BOYDSTUN, A. E. 2008. *The Decline of the Death Penalty and the Discovery of Innocence*, Cambridge: Cambridge University Press.

BAYLIS, K. & FURTAN, H. 2003. Free-Riding on Federalism: Trade Protection and the Canadian Dairy Industry. *Canadian Public Policy / Analyse de Politiques*, 29, 145-161.

BAZELEY, P. & JACKSON, K. 2013. *Qualitative Data Analysis with NVivo*, Thousand Oaks: Sage.

BÉLAND, D. 2009. Ideas, institutions, and policy change. *Journal of European Public Policy*, 16, 701-718.

BÉLAND, D. & COX, R. H. 2011. Introduction. Ideas and Politics. In: BÉLAND, D. & COX, R. H. (eds.) *Ideas and Politics in Social Science Research.* Oxford, New York: Oxford University Press.

BÉLANGER, L. 1995. L'espace international de l'État québécois dans l'après-guerre froide : vers une compression? In: GAGNON, A.-G. & NOEL, A. (eds.) *L'espace québécois.* Montréal: Éditions Québec/Amérique.

BÉLANGER, Y. 1994. Québec inc : la dérive d'un modèle? In: GAGNON, A. (ed.) *Québec : Etat et société.* Montréal: Les Editions Québec/Amérique.

BÉLANGER, Y., BRUNELLE, D. & DEBLOCK, C. 1999. L'intégration économique continentale et ses effets sur les gouvernements infra-étatiques : de l'ALE à l'ALÉNA et au-delà. *Cahiers de recherche sociographiques*, 32, 85-118.

BENFORD, R. D. & SNOW, D. A. 2000. Framing Processes and Social Movements: An Overview and Assessment. *Annual Review of Sociology*, 26, 611-639.

BERGER, P. L. & LUCKMANN, T. 1966. *The Social Construction of Reality. A Treatise in the Sociology of Knowledge*, Garden City, N.Y.: Doubleday.

BERNARD, J.-T. 1982. L'exportation d'électricité par le Québec. *Canadian Public Policy / Analyse de Politiques*, 8, 321-333.

BERNARD, J.-T. 2014. La rentabilité du développement hydro-électrique au Québec. In: BERNIER, R. (ed.) *Les défis québécois. Conjonctures et transitions.* Québec: Presses de l'Université du Québec.

BERNIER, R. 2014. *Les défis québécois. Conjonctures et transitions*. Québec: Presses de l'Université du Québec.

BERNARD, J.-T. & DOUCET, J. A. 1999. L'ouverture du marché d'exportation d'électricité québécoise: réalité ou mirage à l'horizon? *Canadian Public Policy / Analyse de Politiques*, 25, 247-258.

BERNIER, L. 1988. The Foreign Economic Policy of a Subnational State: The Case of Quebec. In: DUCHACEK, I. D., LATOUCHE, D. & STEVENSON, G. (eds.) *Perforated sovereignties and international relations : trans-sovereign contacts of subnational governments*. New York: Greenwood Press.

BERNIER, L. 2001. Mulroney's International 'Beau Risque': The Golden Age of Québec's Foreign Policy. In: MICHAUD, N. & RICHARD, K. (eds.) *Diplomatic Departures: The Conservative Era in Canadian Foreign Policy, 1984-1993*. Vancouver: UBC Press.

BERNIER, L. 2012. Les entreprises publiques. In: TREMBLAY, P. (ed.) *L'administration contemporaine de l'État : une perspective canadienne et québécoise*. Quebec: Presses de l'Université du Québec.

BERNIER, L. 2014. Hydro-Québec, la commercialisation d'une société d'État. In: BERNIER, R. (ed.) *Les défis québécois. Conjonctures et transitions*. Québec: Les Presses de l'Université du Québec.

BERNIER, L. & GARON, F. 2003. Les sociétés d'État québécoises : après les privatisations, l'adaptation à l'économie mondialisée. In: GAGNON, A.-G. (ed.) *Québec. Etat et Société*. Montréal: Les Éditions Québec/Amérique.

BICQUELET, A., WEALE, A. & BARA, J. 2012. In a Different Parliamentary Voice? *Politics & Gender*, 8, 83-121.

BLATTER, J., JANNING, F. & WAGEMANN, C. 2007. *Qualitative Politikanalyse. Eine Einführung in die Forschungsansätze und Methoden*, Wiesbaden, Verlag für Sozialwissenschaften.

BLYTH, M. 2002. *Great transformations : economic ideas and institutional change in the twentieth century*, Cambridge, Cambridge University Press.

BLYTH, M. 2011. Ideas, Uncertainty, and Evolution. In: BÉLAND, D. & COX, R. H. (eds.) *Ideas and Politics in Social Science Research*. Oxford, New York e.a.: Oxford University Press.

BODEUR, S. & VAN ASSCHE, A. 2014. Nike versus New Balance: Trade Policy in a World of Global Value Chains. *Revue internationale de cas en gestion*, 12.

BOGNAR, J. M. 2011. Explaining the Diverging Regulatory Approaches to Risk Regulation between Canada and the EU: the Case of Genetically Modified Food Labelling. In: HÜBNER, K. (ed.) *Europe, Canada and the Comprehensive Economic and Trade Agreement*. London e.a.: Routledge.

BOVIS, C. H. 2012. *EU Public Procurement Law*. 2 ed. Chaltenham: Edward Elgar.

BREWER, G. D. & DELEON, P. 1983. *The foundation of policy analysis*, Chicago: Dorsey Press.

BROWN, D. M. 1993. The Evolving Role of the Provinces in Canada-US Trade Relations. In: BROWN, D. M. & FRY, E. H. (eds.) *States and Provinces in the Interrnational Economy*. Berkeley: Institute of Governmental Studies Press.

BROWN, D. M. 2003. *Getting Things Done in the Federation: Do We Need New Rules for an Old Game? A Series of Commentaries on the Council of the Federation.* Queens, Montréal: Institute of Intergovernmental Relations, Institute for Research on Public Policy.

BRÜHL-MOSER, D. 2012. Der Föderalismus Kanadas: interstaatlich, exekutiv und asymmetrisch. In: HÄRTEL, I. (ed.) *Handbuch Föderalismus – Föderalismus als demokratische Rechtsordnung und Rechtskultur in Deutschland, Europa und der Welt.* Berlin, Heidelberg: Springer.

BRUNELLE, D. & DEBLOCK, C. 1995. Review: New Issues on the NAFTA Front. *International Journal*, 50, 619-629.

BRUNELLE, D. & DEBLOCK, C. 1997. Free Trade and Trade-Related Issues in Quebec: The Challenges of Continental Integration. *American Review of Canadian Studies*, 27, 63-85.

BUSHNELL, S. I. 1980. The Control of Natural Resources through the Trade and Commerce Power and Proprietary Rights. *Canadian Public Policy / Analyse de Politiques*, 6, 313-324.

CAIRNS, A. C. 1971. The Judicial Committee and Its Critics. *Canadian Journal of Political Science / Revue canadienne de science politique*, 4, 301-345.

CAIRNS, A. C. 1977. The Governments and Societies of Canadian Federalism. *Canadian Journal of Political Science / Revue canadienne de science politique*, 10, 695-725.

CAMERON, M. & TOMLIN, B. W. 2000. *The making of NAFTA : how the deal was done*, Ithaca, NY: Cornell University Press.

CAMPBELL, R. M. 1995. Federalism and Economic Policy. In: ROCHER, F. & SMITH, M. (eds.) *New Trends in Canadian Federalism*. Peterborough: Broadview Press.

CHAZOULE, C., JOUVE, F. & LAMBERT, R. 2009. L'émergence des Indications Géographiques au Québec : construction, liens au lieu, protection et valorisation. *Revue canadienne des sciences régionales*, 32, 297-308.

CHECKEL, J. T. 1998. The Constructive Turn in International Relations Theory. *World Politics*, 50, 324-348.

CHESTERS, G. & WELSH, I. 2005. Complexity and Social Movement: Process and Emergence in Planetary Action Systems. *Theory, Culture and Society*, 22, 187-211.

CHONG, D. & DRUCKMAN, J. N. 2007. Framing Theory. *Annual Review of Political Science*, 10, 103-126.

COLLINS, D. A. 2008. Canada's Sub-Central Coverage Under the WTO Agreement on Government Procurement. *Public Procurement Law Review*, 17.

COLLINS, D. A. 2011a. Canada's sub-central government entities and the Agreement on Government Procurement: past and present. In: ARROWSMITH, S. & ANDERSON, R. D. (eds.) *The WTO Regime on Government Procurement: Challenge and Reform*. Cambridge: Cambridge University Press.

COLLINS, S. 2011b. Recent Decisions under the Investment Canada Act: Is Canada Changing its Stance on Foreign Direct Investment? *Northwestern Journal of International Law and Business*, 32, 141-164.

CONCEIÇÃO-HELDT, E. 2011a. *Negotiating Trade Liberalization at the WTO: Domestic Politics and Bargaining Dynamics*, Basingstoke, Palgrave Macmillan.

CONCEIÇÃO-HELDT, E. 2011b. Variation in EU member states' preferences and the Commission's discretion in the Doha Round. *Journal of European Public Policy*, 18, 403-419.

CONCEIÇÃO-HELDT, E. 2013. Two-Level Games and Trade Cooperation: What Do We Know? *International Politics*, 50, 579-599.

CONVERSE, P. E. 1964. *The Nature of Belief Systems in Mass Publics*. In: APTER, D. E. (ed.) *Ideology and Discontent*. London, New York: The Free Press, Collier-MacMillan Limited.

CORNUT, J. 2016. The Special Relationship Transformed. The Canada–Quebec–France Triangle after de Gaulle. *American Review of Canadian Studies*, 46, 162-175.

COX, R. H. 2001. The social construction of an imperative: why welfare reform happened in Denmark and the Netherlands but not in Germany. *World Politics*, 53, 463–498.

DAGENAIS, F. 1978. The Development of a Food and Agriculture Policy in Quebec. *American Journal of Agricultural Economics*, 60, 1045.

DAVIS, C. L. 2004. International Institutions and Issue Linkage: Building Support for Agricultural Trade Liberalization. *American Political Science Review*, 98, 153-169.

DE BIÈVRE, D. & DÜR, A. 2005. Constituency Interests and Delegation in European and American Trade Policy. *Comparative Political Studies*, 38, 1271-1296.

DE BIÈVRE, D. & POLETTI, A. 2014. The political science of European trade policy: A literature review with a research outlook. *Comparative European Politics*, 12, 101-119.

DE BOER, S. 2002. Canadian Provinces, US States and North American Integration: Bench Warmers or Key Players? *Choices. Canada's Options in North America* [Online]. Available: http://irpp.org/wp-content/uploads/assets/research/new-research-program/new-research-article-7/vol8no4.pdf.

DEBLOCK, C. 1988. Tendances récentes de l'investissement au Canada. In: BEAUD, M. & DOSTALER, G. (eds.) *Investissement, emploi et échanges internationaux*. [Montréal]: ACFAS.

DELAGRAN, L. 1992. Conflict in Trade Policy: The Role of the Congress and the Provinces in Negotiating and Implementing the Canada-U.S. Free Trade Agreement. *Publius: The Journal of Federalism*, 22, 15-29.

DELLA PORTA, D. 2016. The Global Justice Movement. An Introduction. In: DELLA PORTA, D. (ed.) *The global justice movement: cross-national and transnational perspectives*. Abingdon, New York: Routledge.

DIEKHOFF, A. 2014. Le nationalisme Québécois dans une perspective comparée. In: GAGNON, A.-G. (ed.) *La politque Québécoise et canadienne. Une approche pluraliste*. Québec: Presses de l'Université du Québec.

DONGES, J. B., FREYTAG, A. & ZIMMERMANN, R. 1997. TAFTA: Assuring its Compatibility with Global Free Trade. *World Economy*, 20, 567-583.

DORNBUSCH, R. & FRANKEL, J. 1987. Macroeconomics and protection. In: STERN, R. M. (ed.) *US Trade Policies in a Changing World Economy*. Cambridge, MA: MIT Press.

DUFOUR, P. 2006. Projet national et espace de protestation mondiale: des articulations distinctes au Québec et au Canada. *Canadian Journal of Political Science / Revue canadienne de science politique*, 39, 315-342.

DUPONT, D. 2009. *Une brève histoire de l'agriculture au Québec : de la conquête du sol à la mondialisation*, Montréal: Fides.

DYSON, K. H. F. 1980. *The State Tradition in Western Europe. The Study of an Idea and Institution*, New York: Oxford University Press.

EDWARDS, R. H. J. & LESTER, S. N. 1997. Towards a more Comprehensive World Trade Organization Agreement on Trade Related Investment Measures. *Stanford International Law Journal*, 33, 169-214.

EHRLICH, S. D. 2007. Access to Protection: Domestic Institutions and Trade Policy in Democracies. *International Organization*, 61, 571-605.

ELGSTRÖM, O. & FRENNHOFF LARSÉN, M. 2010. Free to trade? Commission autonomy in the Economic Partnership Agreement negotiations. *Journal of European Public Policy*, 17, 205-223.

FAFARD, P. & LEBLOND, P. 2012. *Twenty-First Century Trade Agreements: Challenges for Canadian Federalism*. Montreal: The Federal Idea.

FAFARD, P. & LEBLOND, P. 2013. Closing the deal: What role for the provinces in the final stages of the CETA negotiations? *International Journal: Canada's Journal of Global Policy Analysis*, 68, 553-559.

FAUCHER, P. & BERGERON, J. 1986. *Hydro-Quebec: la societe de l'heure de pointe*, Montréal: Presses de I'Universite de Montreal.

FEARON, J. D. 1998. Domestic Politics, Foreign Policy, and Theories of International Relations. *Annual Review of Political Science*, 1, 289-313.

FEREDAY, J. & MUIR-COCHRANE, E. 2006. Demonstrating Rigor Using Thematic Analysis: A Hybrid Approach of Inductive and Deductive Coding and Theme Development. *International Journal of Qualitative Methods*, 5, 1-11.

FINBOW, R. 2013. CETA and Multi-Level Governance: Implications for Provincial and Municipal Governments. *CETA Policy Briefs Series* [Online]. Available: http://labs.carleton.ca/canadaeurope/wp-content/uploads/sites/9/ FINBOW_CETD_CETA-and-Multi-Level-governance.pdf [Accessed 26 March 2015].

FINLAYSON, J. A. & BERTASI, S. 1992. Evolution of Canadian Postwar International Trade Policy. In: CUTLER, C. & ZACHER, M. W. (eds.) *Canadian Foreign Policy and International Economic Regimes*. Vancouver: University of British Columbia.

FINNEMORE, M. & SIKKINK, K. 2001. Taking Stock: The Constructivist Research Program in International Relations and Comparative Politics. *Annual Review of Political Science*, 4, 391-416.

FRANK, A. G. 1966. The development of underdevelopment. *Monthly Review*, 28, 17-31.

FRASER INSTITUTE 2008. Survey of Mining Companies 2007/2008. In: MC-MAHON, F. & VIDLER, C. (eds.) *Annual Survey of Mining Companies*.

FRIEDEN, J. A. 1988. Sectoral Conflict and Foreign Economic Policy, 1914-1940. *International Organization*, 42, 59-90.

FRIEDEN, J. A. 1999. Actors and Preferences in International Relations. In: LAKE, D. A. & POWELL, R. (eds.) *Strategic Choice and International Relations*. Princeton, NJ: Princeton University Press.

FROST, E. L. 1997. *Transatlantic Trade: A Strategic Agenda*, Washington, DC, Institute for International Economics.

GAGNON, A.-G. 1995. The Political Uses of Federalism. In: ROCHER, F. & SMITH, M. (eds.) *New Trends in Canadian Federalism*. Orchard Park, NY: Broadview Press.

GAGNON, A.-G. 2003. Le dossier constitutionnel Québec-Canada. In: GAGNON, A.-G. (ed.) *Québec : État et société*. Montréal: Les Éditions Québec/Amérique.

GAGNON, A.-G. 2014. Five Faces of Quebec: Shifting Small Worlds and Evolving Political Dynamics. In: BICKERTON, J. & GAGNON, A.-G. (eds.) *Canadian Politics*. 6 ed. Toronto: University of Toronto Press.

GAGNON, A.-G. & MONTCALM, M. B. 1992. *Québec : au-delà de la Révolution tranquille*, Montréal: VLB Editeur.

GAGNON, A.-G. & NOEL, A. (eds.) 1995. *L'espace québécois*, Montréal: Les Editions Québec/Amérique.

GAMSON, W. A. & MODIGLIANI, A. 1989. Media Discourse and Public Opinion on Nuclear Power: A Constructionist Approach. *American Journal of Sociology*, 95, 1-37.

GANDOLFO, G. 2014. *International Trade Theory and Policy*. 2nd ed. Berlin, Heidelberg: Springer-Verlag.

GARRETT, G. 1992. International cooperation and institutional choice: the European Community's internal market. *International Organization*, 46, 533-560.

GATTINGER, M. & SAINT-PIERRE, D. 2010. The "Neo-Liberal Turn in Provincial Cultural Policy and Administration in Québec and Ontario: The Emergence of "Quasi-Neoliberal" Approaches. *Canadian Journal of Communication*, 35, 279-302.

GENDRON, P.-P. 2005. Un problème imposant: améliorer l'attrait du Québec pour l'investissement. *Bulletin de recherche*. Institut C.D. Howe.

GESTRIN, M. & RUGMAN, A. 2005. Rules for Foreign Direct Investment at the WTO: Building on Regional Trade Agreements. In: MACRORY, P. F. J., APPLETON, A. E. & PLUMMER, M. G. (eds.) *The World Trade Organization: Legal, Economic and Political Analysis*. New York: Springer.

GILPIN, R. 1975. *U.S. power and the multinational corporation: The political economy of foreign direct investment*, New York: Basic Books.

GLOBERMAN, S. 1984. The Consistency of Canada's Foreign Investment Review Process-A Temporal Analysis. *Journal of International Business Studies*, 15, 119-129.

GOFAS, A. & HAY, C. 2010. The Ideational Turn and the Persistence of Perennial Dualisms. In: GOFAS, A. & HAY, C. (eds.) *The Role of Ideas in Political Analysis. A Portrait of Contemporary Debates.* London: Routledge.

GOFF, P. M. 2000. Invisible Borders: Economic Liberalization and National Identity. *International Studies Quarterly*, 44, 533-562.

GOLDSTEIN, J. 1988. Ideas, institutions, and American trade policy. *International Organization*, 42, 179-217.

GOLDSTEIN, J. & KEOHANE, R. O. (eds.) 1993. *Ideas and foreign policy : beliefs, institutions, and political change*, Ithaca : Cornell University Press.

GOLDSTEIN, K. 2002. Getting in the Door: Sampling and Completing Elite Interviews. *PS: Political Science and Politics*, 35, 669-672.

GORDON, P. H. & MEUNIER, S. 2001. *The French Challenge: Adapting to Globalization.* Washington DC: Brookings Institution Press.

GOUREVITCH, P. 1978. The second image reversed: the international sources of domestic politics. *International Organization*, 32, 881-912.

GOUREVITCH, P. 1987. *Politics in hard times : comparative responses to international economic crises*, Ithaca, Cornell University Press, London.

GOWA, J. S. 1994. *Allies, adversaries, and international trade*, Princeton, N.J.: Princeton University Press.

GRADY, P. & MACMILLAN, K. 1999. *Seattle and Beyond. The WTO Millennium Round.* Ottawa: Global Economics.

GRAHAM, W. C. 1983. Government procurement policies: GATT, the EEC, and the United States. In: TREBILCOCK, M. J., PRICHARD, J. R. S., COURCHENE, T. J. & WHALLEY, J. (eds.) *Federalism and the Canadian Economic Union.* Toronto: University of Toronto Press.

GREENWOLD, S. 1994. NAFTA's procurement provisions and their likely market consequences. *European Journal of Purchasing & Supply Management*, 1, 98-106.

HAINMUELLER, J. & HISCOX, M. J. 2006. Learning to Love Globalization: Education and Individual Attitudes Toward International Trade. *International Organization*, 60, 469-498.

HAJER, M. & LAWS, D. 2008. Ordering Through Discourse. In: GOODIN, R. E., MORAN, M. & REIN, M. (eds.) *The Oxford Handbook of Public Policy.* Oxford, New York: Oxford University Press.

HALE, G. 2008. The Dog That Hasn't Barked: The Political Economy of Contemporary Debates on Canadian Foreign Investment Policies. *Canadian Journal of Political Science / Revue canadienne de science politique*, 41, 719-747.

HALL FINDLAY, M. 2012. Supply Management: Problems, Politics and Possibilities. *SPP Research Papers.* University of Calgary/ The School of Public Policy.

HALL, P. 1986. *Governing the Economy : The Politics of State Intervention in Britain and France.* New York: Oxford University Press.

HALL, P. A. 1989. Introduction. In: HALL, P. A. (ed.) *The Political Power of Economic Ideas: Keynesianism across Nations.* Princeton: Princeton University Press.

HALL, P. A. 1993. Policy Paradigms, Social Learning, and the State: The Case of Economic Policymaking in Britain. *Comparative Politics*, 25, 275-296.

HARLEN, C. M. 1999. A Reappraisal of Classical Economic Nationalism and Economic Liberalism. *International Studies Quarterly*, 43, 733-744.

HARNISCH, S. & STAHL, B. (eds.) 2009. *Vergleichende Außenpolitikforschung und nationale Identitäten. Die Europäische Union im Kosovo-Konflikt 1996-2008*, Baden-Baden: Nomos.

HARRISON, K. 2003. Passing the Environmental Buck. In: ROCHER, F. & SMITH, M. (eds.) *New Trends in Canadian Federalism*. Peterborough, Ont./ Orchard Park, NY: Broadview Press.

HART, M. 2004. Canada—U.S. Relations after Free Trade: Lessons Learned and Unmet Challenges. *American Review of Canadian Studies*, 34, 603-619.

HART, M. 2010. Trade, Globalization, and Canadian Prosperity. In: COURTNEY, J. C. & SMITH, D. E. (eds.) *The Oxford Handbook of Canadian Politics*. Oxford, Toronto: Oxford University Press.

HAY, C. 1999. Crisis and the structural transformation of the state: interrogating the process of change. *The British Journal of Politics & International Relations*, 1, 317-344.

HAY, C. 2011. Ideas and the Construction of Interests. In: BÉLAND, D. & COX, R. H. (eds.) *Ideas and Politics in Social Science Research*. Oxford, New York e.a.: Oxford University Press.

HECHT, G. 2009. *The Radiance of France. Nuclear Power and National Identity after World War II*, Cambridge, Mass.: MIT Press.

HINAREJOS, A. 2012. Free Movement, Federalism, and Institutional Choice: a Canada-EU Comparison. *Cambridge Law Journal*, 71, 537-566.

HOCKING, B. 2004. Changing the terms of trade policy making: from the club to the multistakeholder model. *World Trade Review*, 3, 3-26.

HOWLETT, M., RAMESH, M. & PERL, A. 2009. *Studying public policy : policy cycles and policy subsystems*, New York, Toronto: Oxford University Press.

HÜBNER, K. 2010. CETA: Stumbling Blocks in Ongoing Negotiations. Interview with Christopher Kukucha. *Policy Brief*. Carleton: Canada-Europe Transatlantic Dialogue: Seeking Transnational Solutions to 21st Century Problems.

HÜBNER, K. 2011. Canada and the EU. Shaping transatlantic relations in the twenty-first century. In: HÜBNER, K. (ed.) *Europe, Canada and the Comprehensive Economic and Trade Agreement*. London, New York: Routledge.

INSTITUT ÉCONOMIQUE DE MONTRÉAL 2005. Les coûts économiques de la taxe sur le capital. *Les Notes Économiques, Collection " Fiscalité "*. Montréal.

JABKO, N. 2006. *Playing the market: a political strategy for uniting Europe*, Ithaca: Cornell University Press.

JACKSON, R. J. & JACKSON, D. 1990. *Politics in Canada. Culture, Institutions, Behaviour and Public Policy*, Scarborough, ON: Prentice-Hall Canada.

JEFFREY, B., LAAKSONEN-CRAIG, S., NIQUIDET, K. & VAN KOOTEN, G. C. 2006. Resolving Canada-US Trade Disputes in Agriculture and Forestry: Lessons from Lumber. *Canadian Public Policy / Analyse de Politiques*, 32, 143-155.

JEGEN, M. & MÉRAND, F. 2013. Constructive Ambiguity: Comparing the EU's Energy and Defence Policies. *West European Politics*, 37, 182-203.

JENSON, J. 1989. Paradigms and Political Discourse: Protective Legislation in France and the United States before 1914. *Canadian Journal of Political Science / Revue canadienne de science politique*, 22, 235-258.

JENSON, J. 1991. All the World's a Stage: Ideas, Spaces and Times in Canadian Political Economy. *Studies in Political Economy*, 36, 43-72.

JENSON, J. 1995. Mapping, naming and remembering: Globalization at the end of the twentieth century. *Review of International Political Economy*, 2, 96-116.

JOBERT, B. & MULLER, P. 1987. L'État en action. *Politiques publiques et corporatismes*, Paris: Presses universitaires de France.

JOCKEL, J. T. & DAVID, C.-P. 1997. Introduction: A Sovereign Quebec and the United States. *American Review of Canadian Studies*, 27, 9-10.

JOHANNSON, P. R. 1978. Provincial International Activities. *International Journal: Canada's Journal of Global Policy Analysis*, 33, 357-378.

JOHNSON, P. M., MUZZI, P. & BASTIEN, V. 2013. The voice of Quebec in the CETA negotiations. *International Journal: Canada's Journal of Global Policy Analysis*, 68, 560-567.

JOSLING, T. 2003. Key Issues in the World Trade Organization Negotiations on Agriculture. *American Journal of Agricultural Economics*, 85, 663-667.

JOSLING, T., TANGERMANN, S. & WARLEY, T. K. 1996. *Agriculture in the GATT*, New York: St. Martin's Press.

KAROL, D. 2000. Divided Government and U.S. Trade Policy: Much Ado About Nothing? *International Organization*, 54, 825-844.

KATZENSTEIN, P. J. 1985. *Small States in World Markets. Industrial Policy in Europe*, Ithaca: Cornell University Press.

KATZENSTEIN, P. J. 2003. Small States and Small States Revisited. *New Political Economy*, 8, 9-30.

KEATING, M. 1997. Stateless Nation-Building: Quebec, Catalonia and Scotland in the Changing State System. *Nations and Nationalism*, 3, 689-717.

KEATING, M. 2003. Nations sans État ou États régionaux? Le débat sur la territorialité et le pouvoir à l'heure de la mondialisation. In: GAGNON, A. G. (ed.) *Québec : État et société*. Montréal: Québec Amérique.

KEATING, T. 1999. Thinking Globally, Acting Regionally: Assessing Canada's Response to Regionalism. In: BARRY, D. & KEITH, R. C. (eds.) *Regionalism, Multilateralism, and the Politics of Global Trade*. Vancouver, Toronto: Vancouver University Press.

KEOHANE, R. O. & NYE, J. 2012 [1977]. *Power and Interdependence*, Boston: Longman.

KINDLEBERGER, C. P. 1951. Group Behavior and International Trade. *Journal of Political Economy*, 59, 30-46.

KINDLEBERGER, C. P. 1973. *The world in depression, 1929-1939*, Berkeley, CA: University of California Press.

KINGDON, J. W. 1995. *Agendas, Alternatives, and Public Policies*, New York: Longman.

KIRKEY, C., PAQUIN, S. & ROUSSEL, S. 2016. Charting Quebec's Engagement with the International Community. *American Review of Canadian Studies*, 46, 135-148.

KRASNER, S. D. 1976. State Power and the Structure of International Trade. *World Politics*, 28, 317-347.

KRASNER, S. D. 1978. *Defending the National Interest. Raw Materials Investments and U.S. Foreign Policy*, Princeton, NJ: Princeton University Press.

KRESL, P. K. 1997. Quebec Independence and the Likelihood of Trade Conflict with the United States. *American Review of Canadian Studies*, 27, 87-103.

KRIESI, H., GRANDE, E., LACHAT, R., DOLEZAL, M., BORNSCHIER, S. & FREY, T. 2006. Globalization and the transformation of the national political space: Six European countries compared. *European Journal of Political Research*, 45, 921-956.

KRIESI, H., GRANDE, E., LACHAT, R., DOLEZAL, M., BORNSCHIER, S. & FREY, T. 2008. Globalization and its impact on national spaces of competition. In: KRIESI, H., GRANDE, E., LACHAT, R., DOLEZAL, M., BORNSCHIER, S. & FREY, T. (eds.) *West European Politics in the Age of Globalization*. Cambridge, New York: Cambridge University Press.

KUKUCHA, C. J. 2003. Domestic politics and Canadian foreign trade policy: Intrusive interdependence, the WTO and the NAFTA. *Canadian Foreign Policy Journal*, 10, 59-85.

KUKUCHA, C. J. 2004. The Role of the Provinces in Canadian Foreign Trade Policy: Multi-Level Governance and Sub-National Interests in the Twenty-First Century. *Policy and Society*, 23, 113-134.

KUKUCHA, C. J. 2008. *The Provinces and Canadian Foreign Trade Policy*, Vancouver, Toronto: UBC Press.

KUKUCHA, C. J. & HÜBNER, K. 2010. CETA: Stumbling Blocks in Ongoing Negotiations. Interview with Christoph Kukucha. *Canada-Europe Policy Brief, May 2010*, Carleton.

KUKUCHA, C. J. 2011a. Dismembering Canada? Stephen Harper and the Foreign Relations of Canadian Provinces. In: BRATT, D. & KUKUCHA, C. J. (eds.) *Readings in Canadian Foreign Policy. Classic Debates and New Ideas*. Donn Mills, ON: Oxford University Press.

KUKUCHA, C. J. 2011b. Provincial pitfalls: Canadian provinces and the Canada-EU trade negotiations. In: HÜBNER, K. (ed.) *Europe, Canada and the Comprehensive Economic and Trade Agreement*. New York: Routledge.

KUKUCHA, C. J. 2013. Canadian sub-federal governments and CETA: Overarching themes and future trends. *International Journal: Canada's Journal of Global Policy Analysis*, 68, 528-535.

KUKUCHA, C. J. 2016. Provincial/Territorial Governments and the Negotiation of International Trade Agreements. *IRPP Insight*.

LAKE, D. A. 1988. *Power, Protection, and Free Trade*, Ithaca, London: Cornell University Press.

LAKE, D. A. 2009. Open Economy Politics: A Critical Review. *The Review of International Organizations*, 4, 219-244.

LAKE, D. A. & POWELL, R. 1999. International Relations: A Strategic-Choice Approach. In: LAKE, D. A. & POWELL, R. (eds.) *Strategic Choice and International Relations*. Princeton, NJ: Princeton University Press.

LAMONT, M. & THÉVENOT, L. (eds.) 2000. *Rethinking Comparative Cultural Sociology: Repertoires of Evaluation in France and the United States*, Cambridge: Cambridge University Press.

LANOUE, R. & HAFSI, T. 2010. *Société d'Etat? Pourquoi pas? Concilier politique et performance. Les secrets de la réussite d'Hydro-Québec*, Québec: Presses de l'Université du Québec.

LATOUCHE, D. 1988. State-buildig and Foreign Policy at the Subnational Level. In: DUCHACEK, I. D., LATOUCHE, D. & STEVENSON, G. (eds.) *Perforated sovereignties and international relations : trans-sovereign contacts of subnational governments*. New York: Greenwood Press.

LATOUCHE, D. 1995. Le Canada et le Québec à l'heure de la globalisation et de l'incertitude. In: GAGNON, A.-G. & NOEL, A. (eds.) *L'Espace québécois*. Montréal: Éditions Québec/Amérique.

LATOUCHE, D. 2011. Quebec in the Emerging North American Configuration. In: BEHIELS, M. D. & HAYDAY, M. (eds.) *Contemporary Quebec. Selected Readings and Commentaries*. Montreal & Kingston e.a.: McGill-Queen's University Press.

LEBLOND, P. 2010. CETA and Multi-Level Governance: Implications for Provincial and Municipal Governments. *Policy Options*. Institute for Research on Public Policy.

LEBLOND, P. & STRACHINESCU-OLTEANU, M. A. 2009. Le libre-échange avec l'europe : Quel est l'intérêt pour le canada? *Canadian Foreign Policy Journal*, 15, 60-76.

LEMIRE, M. 2003. Les mouvements sociaux face à la globalisation des marchés. In: GAGNON, A.-G. (ed.) *Québec : État et société*. Montréal: Les Éditions Québec/Amérique.

LOHMANN, S. & O'HALLORAN, S. 1994. Divided government and U.S. trade policy: theory and evidence. *International Organization*, 48, 595-632.

LOWENFELD, A. F. 2003. Investment Agreements and International Law. *Columbia Journal of Transnational Law*, 42, 123-130.

LUZ, M. A. 2000-2001. Nafta, Investment and the Constitution of Canada: Will the Watertight Compartments Spring a Leak? *Ottawa Law Review/ Revue de Droit d'Ottawa*, 32, 35-84.

LUZ, M. A. & MILLER, C. M. 2002. Globalization and Canadian Federalism: Implications of the NAFTA's Investment Rules. *McGill Law Journal*, 47, 951-997.

MAJONE, G. 2008. Agenda-Setting. In: MORAN, M., REIN, M. & GOODIN, R. E. (eds.) The *Oxford Handbook of Public Policy*. Oxford, Toronto: Oxford University Press.

MALTAIS, A. L. 2011. L'investissement dans l'Accord économique et commercial global Canada-Europe et ses conséquences pour le Québec. *Rapport de recherche de l'Iréc*.

MANSFIELD, E. D., MILNER, H. V. & PEVEHOUSE, J. C. 2007. Vetoing Co-operation: The Impact of Veto Players on Preferential Trading Arrangements. *British Journal of Political Science*, 37, 403-432.

MANSFIELD, E. D., MILNER, H. V. & ROSENDORFF, B. P. 2002. Why Democracies Cooperate More: Electoral Control and International Trade Agreements. *International Organization*, 56, 477-513.

MARCHILDON, G. P. 1998. Canadian-American Agricultural Trade Relations: A Brief History. *American Review of Canadian Studies*, 28, 233-252.

MARCANKOWSKI, F. 2014. Framing als politischer Prozess. Eine Einleitung. In: MARCANKOWSKI, F. (ed.) *Framing als politischer Prozess. Beiträge zum Deutungskampf in der politischen Kommunikation*. Baden-Baden: Nomos.

MARTIN, P. 1995a. Le nationalisme québécois et le choix du libre-échange continental. In: GAGNON, A.-G. & NOEL, A. (eds.) *L'espace québécoise*. Montréal: Éditions Québec/Amérique.

MARTIN, P. 1995b. When nationalism meets continentalism: The politics of free trade in Quebec. *Regional & Federal Studies*, 5, 1-27.

MARTIN, T. 2008. Hydro Development in Quebec and Manitoba: Old Relationships or New Social Contract? In: MARTIN, T. & HOFFMAN, S. M. (eds.) *Power Struggles: Hydro Development and First Nations in Manitoba and Quebec*. Winnipeg: University of Manitoba Press.

MARTIN, T. 2010. Vers la fin du "contrat colonial moderne"? Le cas des ententes hydroélectriques au Québec et au Manitoba. *Globe : Revue internationale d'études québécoise*, 10, 125-150.

MATTHES, J. 2012. Framing Politics: An Integrative Approach. *American Behavioral Scientist*, 56, 247-259.

MCADAM, D. 1996. The Framing Function of Movement Tactics: Strategic Dramaturgy in the American Civil Rights Movement. In: MCADAM, D., MCCARTHY, J. & ZALD, M. (eds.) *Comparative Perspectives on Social Movements*. New York: Cambridge University Press.

MCBRIDE, S. 2006. Reconfiguring Sovereignty: NAFTA Chapter 11 Dispute Settlement Procedures and the Issue of Public-Private Authority. *Canadian Journal of Political Science*, 39, 755-775.

MCCULLOCH, T. 2016. A Quiet Revolution in Diplomacy: Quebec–UK Relations since 1960. *American Review of Canadian Studies*, 46, 176-195.

MCILLROY, J. 1997. NAFTA and the Canadian Provinces: Two Ships Passing in the Night. *Canada-United States Law Journal*, 23, 431-440.

MCKIBBEN, H. E. & TAYLOR, T. W. 2014. Let's Talk About Trade: The Politicization and Framing of International Trade Policy. *American Political Science Association Conference*. Washington DC.

MCMURTRY, J.-J. 2014. The Political Economy of Procurement. *Canadian Public Policy / Analyse de Politiques*, 40, 26-38.

MCNAMARA, K. R. 1998. *The currency of ideas : monetary politics in the EU*, Ithaca N.Y.: Cornell University Press.

MCROBERTS, K. H. 1993. *Quebec: Social Change and Political Crisis*, Toronto: McClelland & Stewart.

MCROBERTS, K. H. 2003. Conceiving Diversity: Dualism, Multiculturalism, and Multinationalism. In: ROCHER, F. & SMITH, M. (eds.) *New Trends in Canadian Federalism*. Peterborough, Ont./Orchard Park, NY: Broadview Press.

MEHTA, J. 2011. The Varied Roles of Ideas in Politics. From "Whether" to "How". In: BELAND, D. & COX, R. H. (eds.) *Ideas and Politics in Social Science Research*. Oxford, New York: Oxford University Press.MEUNIER, S. 2005. *Trading Voices: The EU in International Commercial Negotiations*, Princeton, NJ: Princeton University Press.

MEUNIER, S. 2007. Managing Globalization? The EU in International Trade Negotiations. *Journal of Common Market Studies*, 45, 905–926.

MEUNIER, S. 2013. France and the Global Economic Order. In: COLE, A., MEUNIER, S. & TIBERJ, V. (eds.) *Developments in French Politics 5*. Basingstoke: Palgrave.

MEUNIER, S. & NICOLAIDIS, K. 1999. Who speaks for Europe? The delegation of trade authority in the EU. *Journal of Common Market Studies*, 37, 477-501.

MILES, M. B. & HUBERMAN, A. M. 1994. *Qualitative Data Analysis: An Expanded Sourcebook*. 2nd ed. Thousands Oaks: Sage.

MILKE, M. 2014. *Government Subsidies in Canada: A $684 Billion Price Tag. Taxpayer Subsidies to Corporations, Government Businesses, and Consumers*. Vancouver: Fraser Institute.

MILLER, D. 1995. *On nationality*, Oxford: Oxford University Press.

MILNER, H. V. 1999. *Interests, Institutions, and Information: Domestic Politics and International Relations*. Princeton: Princeton University Press.

MILNER, H. V. & KUBOTA, K. 2005. Why the Move to Free Trade? Democracy and Trade Policy in the Developing Countries. *International Organization*, 59, 107-143.

MILNER, H. V. & ROSENDORFF, B. P. 1996. Trade Negotiations, Information and Domestic Politics: The Role of Domestic Groups. *Economics and Politics*, 8, 145–189.

MONTPETIT, É. 1999. Corporatisme québécois et performance des gouvernants : analyse comparative des politiques environnementales en agriculture. *Politique et Sociétés*, 18, 79-98.

MONTPETIT, É. 2003. Les réseaux néocorporatistes québécois à l'épreuve du fédéralisme canadien et de l'internationalisation. In: GAGNON, A. (ed.) *Québec : État et société*. Montréal: Les Editions Québec/Amériques.

MONTPETIT, É. 2006. Declining Legitimacy and Canadian Federalism: An Examination of Policy-Making in Agriculture and Biomedicine. In: HANS, M. & DE CLERCY, C. (eds.) *Continuity and Change in Canadian Politics*. Toronto: University of Toronto Press.

MONTPETIT, É. & COLEMAN, W. D. 1999. Policy Communities and Policy Divergence in Canada: Agro-Environmental Policy Development in Quebec and Ontario. *Canadian Journal of Political Science / Revue canadienne de science politique*, 32, 691-714.

MORGENSTERN, S., TAMAYO, A. B., FAUCHER, P. & NIELSON, D. 2007. Scope and Trade Agreements. *Canadian Journal of Political Science / Revue canadienne de science politique*, 40, 157-183.

MORICI, P. 1985. U.S.-Canada Free Trade Discussion: What are the Issues? *American Review of Canadian Studies*, 15, 311-323.

MORICI, P. 1997. Assessing the Canada-U.S. Free Trade Agreement. *The American Review of Canadian Studies*, 26, 491-497.

MOU, H., ATKINSON, M. M. & UL-MUNIM, A. 2014. The Cost of Government: Decomposing Provincial Expenditures, 1981–2007. *Canadian Public Policy / Analyse de Politiques,* 40, 84-97.

MURRAY, J. A. & GERACE, M. C. 1972. Canadian Attitudes Toward the U.S. Presence. *The Public Opinion Quarterly*, 36, 388-397.

MURRAY, J. A. & LEDUC, L. 1976. Public Opinion and Foreign Policy Options in Canada. *The Public Opinion Quarterly*, 40, 488-496.

NAKANO, T. 2004. Theorising economic nationalism. *Nations and Nationalism*, 10, 211-229.

NGUYEN, T. T., PERRONI, C. & WIGLE, R. M. 1996. Uruguay Round Impacts on Canada. *Canadian Public Policy / Analyse de Politiques*, 22, 342-355.

NOEL, A. 2006. Il suffisait de presque rien: Promises and Pitfalls of Open Federalism. In: BANTING, K. G., GIBBINS, R., LESLIE, P. M., NOEL, A., SIMEON, R. & YUONG, R. (eds.) *Open Federalism. Interpretations, Significance*. Kingston, Ont.: Institute of Intergovernmental Relations.

NOEL, A. 2010. Quebec. In: COURTNEY, J. C. & SMITH, D. E. (eds.) *The Oxford Handbook of Canadian Politics*. Oxford, Toronto: Oxford University Press.

NOSSAL, K. R., ROUSSEL, S. & PAQUIN, S. 2015. *The Politics of Canadian Foreign Policy, Montreal*, Kingston, McGill Queen's University Press.

OREFICE, G. 2016. Non-Tariff Measures, Specific Trade Concerns and Tariff Reduction. *The World Economy*, 40, 1807-1835.

PAGE, E. C. 2008. The Origins of Policy. In: MORAN, M., REIN, M. & GOODIN, R. E. (eds.) *The Oxford Handbook of Public Policy*. Oxford, Toronto: Oxford University Press.

PAHRE, R. 2001. Most-Favored-Nation Clauses and Clustered Negotiations. *International Organization*, 55, 859-890.

PANKE, D. & RISSE, T. 2007. Liberalism. In: DUNNE, T., KURKI, M. & SMITH, S. (eds.) *International Relations Theories: Diversity and Discipline*. Oxford, New York: Oxford University Press.

PAQUET, M. 2014. The Federalization of Immigration and Integration in Canada. *Canadian Journal of Political Science / Revue canadienne de science politique*, 47, 519-548.

PAQUIN, S. 2001. *La revanche des petites nations. Le Québec, la Catalogne et l'Écosse face à la mondialisation*, Montréal: VLB.

PAQUIN, S. 2004. La paradiplomatie identitaire : Le Québec, la Catalogne et la Flandre en relations internationales. *Politique et Sociétés*, 23, 203-237.

PAQUIN, S. (ed.) 2006. *Les relations internationales du Québec depuis la Doctrine Gérin-Lajoie (1965-2005)*, Québec: Presses de l'Université Laval.

PAQUIN, S. 2010. Federalism and Compliance with International Agreements: Belgium and Canada Compared. *The Hague Journal of Diplomacy*, 5, 173-197.

PAQUIN, S. 2013. Federalism and the governance of international trade negotiations in Canada: Comparing CUSFTA with CETA. *International Journal: Canada's Journal of Global Policy Analysis*, 68, 545-552.

PAQUIN, S. 2016. Quebec–US Relations: The Big Picture. *American Review of Canadian Studies*, 46, 149-161.

PAQUIN, S. 2017. *Fédéralisme et négociations commerciales au Canada : l'ALE, l'AECG et le PTP comparés*, 48, 347-369.

PARIZEAU, J. 1997. *Pour un Québec Souverain*, Montréal: VLB Éditeur.

PARIZEAU, J. 1998. *Une bouteille à la mer? Le Québec et la mondialisation*, Montréal: VLB Éditeur.

PARIZEAU, J. 1999. L'AMI menace-t-il la souveraineté des Etats? *L'Action Nationale*, 89, 37-54.

PARSONS, C. 2002. Showing Ideas as Causes: The Origins of the EU. *International Organization*, 56, 47-84.

PARSONS, C. 2003. *A Certain Idea of Europe*, Ithaca: Cornell University Press.

PATTON, M. Q. 2002. *Qualitative research and evaluation methods*, Thousand Oaks: Sage.

PETKANTCHIN, V. 2005. *Sour milk system*. Montreal Economic Institute.

POLLETTA, F. & HO, M. K. 2006. Frames and their Consequences. In: GOODIN, R. E. & TILLY, C. (eds.) *The Oxford Handbook of Contextual Political Analysis*. Oxford, New York e.a.: Oxford University Press.

POTTER, E. H. 1999. *Trans-Atlantic Partners: Canadian Approaches to the EU*, Montreal: McGill-Queen's University Press, published for Carleton University Press.

PRATT, L. 1977. The State and Province-Building: Alberta's Development Strategy. In: PRANITCH, L. (ed.) *The Canadian State: Political Economy and Political Power*. Toronto: Toronto University Press.

PRÉMONT, M.-C. 2014. Hydro-Québec et le délestage des grandes régions productrices d'hydroélectricité. In: BERNIER, R. (ed.) *Les défis québécois. Conjonctures et transitions*. Québec: Presses de l'Université du Québec.

PRINCE AGBODJAN, H. & ROUSSEAU, S. 2016. La Loi sur investissement à l'épreuve de l'attractivité: contribution à la modernisation du cadre juridique canadien de l'investissement étranger. *Revue du Barreau canadien*, 94, 111-147.

PUTNAM, R. D. 1988. Diplomacy and domestic politics: the logic of two-level games. *International Organization*, 42, 427-460.

RABY, J. 1990. The Investment Provisions of the Canada-United States Free Trade Agreement: A Canadian Perspective. *The American Journal of International Law*, 84, 394-443.

RANKIN, D. M. 2004. Borderline interest or identity? American and Canadian opinion on the North American Free Trade Agreement. *Comparative Politics*, 36, 331-351.

ROBINSON, I. 1995. Trade Policy, Globalization, and the Future of Canadian Federalism. In: ROCHER, F. & SMITH, M. (eds.) *New trends in Canadian Federalism*. Peterborough, Ont. [e.a.]: Broadview Press.

ROBINSON, I. 2003. Neo-Liberal Trade Policy and Canadian Federalism. In: ROCHER, F. & SMITH, M. (eds.) *New Trends in Canadian Federalism*. Peterborough, ON, Orchard Park, NY: Broadview Press.

ROCHEFORT, D. A. & COBB, R. W. 1993. Problem Definition, Agenda Access, and Policy Choice. *Policy Studies Journal*, 21, 56-71.

ROCHER, F. 1994. Le Québec en Amérique du Nord : la stratégie continentale. In: GAGNON, A.-G. (ed.) *Québec : État et société*. Montréal: Les Éditions Québec/Amérique.

ROCHER, F. 2003. Le Québec dans les Amériques : de l'ALE à la ZLEA. In: GAGNON, A.-G. (ed.) *Québec : État et société*. Montréal: Les Éditions Québec/Amérique.

ROCHER, F. & SMITH, M. 2003. The Four Dimensions of Canadian Federalism. In: ROCHER, F. & SMITH, M. (eds.) *New Trends in Canadian Federalism*. Peterborough, Ont./Orchard Park, NY: Broadview Press.

ROGOWSKI, R. 1987. Trade and the variety of democratic institutions. *International Organization*, 41, 203-223.

ROGOWSKI, R. 1989. *Commerce and Coalitions. How Trade Affects Domestic Political Alignments*, Princeton, NJ: Princeton University Press.

ROSCHLAU, M. W. 2008. Public transport policy in Canada and the United States: Developing political commitment from the federal government. *Research in Transportation Economics*, 22, 91-97.

SABATIER, P. A. 1988. An advocacy coalition framework of policy change and the role of policy-oriented learning therein. *Policy Sciences*, 21, 129-168.

SABATIER, P. A. & JENKINS-SMITH, H. C. 1993. Preface. In: SABATIER, P. A. & JENKINS-SMITH, H. C. (eds.) *Policy Change and Learning. An Advocacy Coalition Approach.* Boulder, San Francisco, Oxford: Westview Press.

SAINT-MARTIN, D. 2016. Systemic corruption in an advanced welfare state: lessons from the Quebec Charbonneau inquiry. *Osgoode Hall Law Journal*, 53, 66-106.

SAKSENA, J. & ANDERSON, L. 2008. Explaining Variation in the Use of NTBs in Developed Countries: The Role of Political Institutions. *International Politics*, 45, 475–496.

SALACUSE, J. W. 2010. The Emerging Global Regime for Investment. *Harvard International Law Journal*, 51, 427-473.

SARCINELLI, U. 1998. Politikvermittlung und Demokratie: Zum Wandel der politischen Kommunikationskultur. In: SARCINELLI, U. (ed.) *Politikvermittlung und Demokratie in der Mediengesellschaft. Beiträge zur politischen Kommunikationskultur.* Opladen: Westdeutscher Verlag.

SAURUGGER, S. 2013. Constructivism and public policy approaches in the EU: from ideas to power games. *Journal of European Public Policy*, 20, 888-906.

SAVOIE, D. J. 2010. *Power: where is it?*, Montreal: McGill-Queen's University Press.

SCHARPF, F. 1999. *Governing in Europe: Effective and Democratic?* Oxford, New York: Oxford University Press.

SCHMIDT, V. A. 1996. The Decline of Traditional State Dirigisme in France: The Transformation of Political Economic Policies and Policymaking Processes. *Governance: An International Journal of Policy and Administration*, 9, 375-405.

SCHMIDT, V. A. 1997. *From State to Market? The Transformation of French Business and Government*, Cambridge: Cambridge University Press.

SCHRAM, S. 2020 (forthcoming). Reconceptualising Provincial Development: Evolving Public Procurement Practices in Quebec. IN: BROSCHEK, J., GOFF, P. (eds.) The Multilevel Politics of Trade. Toronto: University of Toronto Press.

SCHRAM, S. 2016. "La loi du camembert" as an Issue of Federalism. Reconciling Liberalism and Protectionism in Quebec. In: LEHMKUHL, U., LÜSEBRINK, H.-J. & MCFALLS, L. (eds.) *Spaces of Difference. Conflicts and Cohabitation.* Münster, New York: Waxmann, 155-180.

SCHWARTZ, M. A. 1998. NAFTA and the Fragmentation of Canada. *American Review of Canadian Studies*, 28, 11-28.

SHEARER, R. A. 1986. The New Face of Canadian Mercantilism: The Macdonald Commission and the Case for Free Trade. *Canadian Public Policy / Analyse de Politiques*, 12, 51-58.

SHENKIN, T. S. 1994. *Trade-Related Investment Measures in Bilateral Investment Treaties and the GATT: Moving toward a Multilateral Investment Treaty.* University of Pittsburgh Law Review, 55, 541-606.

SHONFIELD, A. 1965. *Modern Capitalism: The Changing Balance of Public and Private Power.* London: Oxford University Press.

SILES-BRÜGGE, G. 2011. Resisting Protectionism after the Crisis: Strategic Economic Discourse and the EU-Korea Free Trade Agreement. *New Political Economy*, 16, 627-653.

SKOGSTAD, G. 1998. Canadian Federalism, Internationalization and Quebec Agriculture: Dis-Engagement, Re-Integration? *Canadian Public Policy / Analyse de Politiques*, 24, 27-48.

SKOGSTAD, G. 2000. Globalization and Public Policy: Situating Canadian Analyses. *Canadian Journal of Political Science / Revue canadienne de science politique*, 33, 805-828.

SKOGSTAD, G. 2007. The Two Faces of Canadian Agriculture in a Post-Staples Economy. *Canadian Political Science Review*, 1, 26-41.

SKOGSTAD, G. 2008. *Internationalization and Canadian Agriculture: Policy and Governing* Paradigms, Toronto: Toronto University Press.

SKOGSTAD, G. 2012a. Canadian Federalism, International Trade, and Regional Market Integration in an Era of Complex Sovereignty. In: BAKVIS, H. & SKOGSTAD, G. (eds.) *Canadian Federalism. Performance, Effectiveness, and Legitimacy*. Oxford: Oxford University Press.

SKOGSTAD, G. 2012b. International Trade Policy and the Evolution of Canadian Federalism. In: BAKVIS, H. & SKOGSTAD, G. (eds.) *Canadian Federalism. Performance, Effectiveness, and Legitimacy*. Oxford: Oxford University Press.

SKOGSTAD, G. 2013. Global Governance and Canadian Federalism: Reconcilig External Accountability Obligations through Internal Accountability Practices. In: GRAEFFE, P., SIMMONS, J. M. & WHITE, L. A. (eds.) *Overpromising or Underperforming? Understanding and Evaluating New Intergovernmental Accountability Regimes*. Toronto: University of Toronto Press.

SLOWEY, G. A. 2008. The State, the Marketplace, and First Nations: Theorizing First Nation Self-Determination in an Era of Globalization. In: MARTIN, T. & HOFFMAN, S. M. (eds.) *Power Struggles: Hydro Development and First Nations in Manitoba and Quebec*. Winnipeg: University of Manitoba Press.

SMITH, A. D. 2010a. *Nationalism. Theory, Ideology, History*, Cambridge: Polity Press.

SMITH, D. E. 2010b. Canada: A Double Federation. In: COURTNEY, J. C. & SMITH, D. E. (eds.) *The Oxford Handbook of Canadian Politics*. Oxford, New York, e.a.: Oxford University Press.

SMITH, M. R. 1994. L'impact de Québec inc., répartition des revenus et efficacité économique. *Sociologie et sociétés*, 26, 91-110.

SMYTHE, E. 2003. Just Say No!: The Negotiation of Investment Rules at the WTO. *International Journal of Political Economy*, 33, 60-83.

SMYTHE, E. 2011. Frustrated Multilateralism: Canada and the Negotiation of Multilateral Investment Rules. In: BRATT, D. & KUKUCHA, C. J. (eds.) *Readings in Canadian Foreign Policy. Classic Debates and New Ideas*. Donn Mills, ON: Oxford University Press.

SNOW, D. A. 2004. Framing Processes, Ideology, and Discursive Fields. In: SNOW, D. A., SOULE, S. A. & KRIESI, H. (eds.) *The Blackwell Companion to Social Movements*. Malden, Mass. e.a.: Wiley-Blackwell.

SNOW, D. A. & BENFORD, R. D. 1992. Master frames and cycles of protest. In: MORRIS, A. D. & MCCLURG MUELLER, C. (eds.) *Frontiers in Social Movement Theory*. New Haven, Connecticut: Yale University Press.

SNOW, D. A., ROCHFORD, E. B., JR., WORDEN, S. K. & BENFORD, R. D. 1986. Frame Alignment Processes, Micromobilization, and Movement Participation. *American Sociological Review*, 51, 464-481.

STAHL, B. 2006. *Frankreichs Identität und außenpolitische Krisen. Verhalten und Diskurse im Kosovo-Krieg und der Uruguay-Runde des GATT*, Baden-Baden, Nomos.

STAIRS, D. 1999. The Pursuits of Economic Architecture by Diplomatic Means: The Case of Canada in Europe. In: BARRY, D. & KEITH, R. C. (eds.) *Regionalism, multilateralism, and the politics of global trade*. Vancouver, Toronto: UBC Press.

STEINBERG, M. W. 1998. Tilting the frame: Considerations on collective action framing from a discursive turn. *Theory and Society*, 27, 845-872.

STEVENSON, G. 1977. Federalism and the Political Economy of the Canadian State. In: PANITCH, L. (ed.) *The Canadian State: Political Economy and Political Power*. Toronto: Toronto University Press.

STEVENSON, G. 2009 [1979]. *Unfulfilled Union. Canadian Federalism and National Unity*, Montréal, McGill-Queen's University Press.

SUREL, Y. 2000. The role of cognitive and normative frames in policy-making. *Journal of European Public Policy*, 7, 495-512.

TANGUAY, B. 2003. Sclérose ou parfait état de santé? Examen du système de partis au Québec au XXIe siècle. In: GAGNON, A.-G. (ed.) *Québec. Etat et société*. Montréal: Les Éditions Québec/Amérique.

TANSEY, O. 2009. Process-Tracing and Elite Interviewing: A Case for Non-probability Sampling. In: PICKEL, S., PICKEL, G., LAUTH, H.-J. & JAHN, D. (eds.) *Methoden der vergleichenden Politik- und Sozialwissenschaften. Neue Entwicklungen und Anwendungen*. Wiesbaden: Verlag für Sozialwissenschaften.

THAKUR, R. 2012. Chapter 11 of NAFTA and the Provinces – Will the Constitutional Question Be Asked? *Canada-United States Law Journal*, 37, 251-272.

THOMAS, K. P. 2011. Regulating Investment Attraction: Canada's Code of Conduct on Incentives in a Comparative Context. *Canadian Public Policy / Analyse de Politiques*, 37, 343-357.

TILLY, C. 1977. Getting It Together in Burgundy, 1675-1975. *Theory and Society*, 4, 479-504.

TILLY, C. 2006. *Regimes and Repertoires*, Chicago: University of Chicago Press.

TINBERGEN, J. 1965. *International economic integration*, Amsterdam e.a.: Elsevir.

TREW, S. 2013. Correcting the democratic deficit in the CETA negotiations: Civil society engagement in the provinces, municipalities, and Europe. *International Journal: Canada's Journal of Global Policy Analysis*, 68, 568-575.

TREW, S. 2014. Public Procurement. In: SINCLAIR, S., TREW, S. & MERTINS-KIRKWODD, H. (eds.) *Making Sense of the CETA. An Analysis of the Final Text of the Canada-EU Comprehensive Economic and Trade Agreement.* Ottawa: Canadian Centre for Policy Alternatives.

TSEBELIS, G. 1995. Decision Making in Political Systems: Veto Players in Presidentialism, Parliamentarism, Multicameralism and Multipartyism. *British Journal of Political Science*, 25, 289-325.

TSEBELIS, G. 2002. *Veto Players: How Political Institutions Work*, Princeton, NJ: Princeton University Press.

TYERS, R. & ANDERSON, K. 2011. *Disarray in World Food Markets. A Quantitative Assessment*, Cambridge e.a.: Cambridge University Press.

VAN ASSCHE, A. 2012. Global Value Chains and Canada's Trade Policy. Business as Usual or Paradigm Shift? *IRPP Study*.

VAN ASSCHE, A. 2016. Ceta: A New Type of Free Trade Agreement in Line wth a New Global Trade Reality. In: VAN OVERMEIRE, X. & NYCHAY, N. (eds.) *The Comprehensive Econonic and Trade Agreement between Canada and the E.U.: An Overview.* Toronto: Lexis Nexis.

VAN BIESEBROECK, J. 2010. Bidding for Investment Projects: Smart Public Policy or Corporate Welfare? *Canadian Public Policy / Analyse de Politiques*, 36, 31-47.

VAN OVERMEIRE, X. & NYCHAY, N. 2016. *The Comprehensive Economic and Trade Agreement between Canada and the E.U.: An Overview*, Toronto: Lexis Nexis.

VANDEVELDE, K. J. 1998. The Political Economy of a Bilateral Investment Treaty. *The American Journal of International Law*, 92, 621-41.

VANDUZER, J. A. 2013. Could an intergovernmental agreement increase the credibility of Canadian treaty commitments in areas within provincial jurisdiction? *International Journal: Canada's Journal of Global Policy Analysis*, 68, 536-544.

VORMANN, B. & LAMMERT, C. 2014. A Paradoxical Relationship? Regionalization and Canadian National Identity. *American Review of Canadian Studies*, 44, 385-399.

WALTZ, K. N. 1959. *Man, the State, and War: A Theoretical Analysis*, New York: Columbia University Press.

WHALLEY, J. 1983. Induced distorsions of interprovincial activity: an overview of issues. In: TREBILCOCK, M. J., PRICHARD, J. R. S., COURCHENE, T. J. & WHALLEY, J. (eds.) *Federalism and the Canadian Economic Union.* Toronto: University of Toronto Press (for the Ontario Economic Council).

WHALLEY, J. 2009. Disciplining Canada's Interprovincial Barriers: The Subnational WTO Approach as Another Option with or beyond an Extended TILMA. *Canadian Public Policy / Analyse de Politiques*, 35, 315-323.

WILDER, M. & HOWLETT, M. 2016. Province-building and Canadian Political Science. In: DUNN, C. (ed.) *Provinces: Canadian Provincial Politics.* Toronto: University of Toronto Press.

WOLL, C. 2006. Lobbying in the EU: From sui generis to a comparative perspective. *Journal of European Public Policy*, 13, 456-469.

WOLL, C. 2011. Who scripts European trade policies? Business-government relations in the EU-Canada partnership negotiations. In: HÜBNER, K. (ed.) *Europe, Canada and the Comprehensive Economic and Trade Agreement.* London and New York: Routledge.

WOOLCOCK, S. B. 2010. Trade Policy. A Further Shift Towards Brussels. In: WALLACE, H., POLLACK, M. A. & YOUNG, A. R. (eds.) *Policy-Making in the EU.* 6 ed. Oxford, New York: Oxford University Press.

WOOLCOCK, S. B. 2011. EU trade policy: the Canada-EU Comprehensive Economic and Trade Agreement (CETA) towards a new generation of FTAs? In: HÜBNER, K. (ed.) *Europe, Canada and the Comprehensive Economic and Trade Agreement.* London, New York: Routledge.

WOOLCOCK, S. B. 2012. *EU economic diplomacy: the role of the EU in external economic relations,* Farnham, UK: Ashgate.

YOUNG, A. R. 2007. Trade Politics Ain't What It Used to Be: The EU in the Doha Round. *Journal of Common Market Studies,* 45, 789–811.

YOUNG, A. R. 2016. Not your parents' trade politics: the Transatlantic Trade and Investment Partnership negotiations. *Review of International Political Economy,* 23, 345-378.

YOUNG, R. A., FAUCHER, P. & BLAIS, A. 1984. The Concept of Province-Building: A Critique. *Canadian Journal of Political Science / Revue canadienne de science politique,* 17, 783-818.

ZAHARIADIS, N. 2003. *Ambiguity and Choice in Public Policy. Political Decision Making in Modern Democracies.* Washington: Georgetown University Press.

ZAHARIADIS, N. 2013. Building better theoretical frameworks of the EU's policy process. *Journal of European Public Policy,* 20, 807-816.

Index